THE
BUSINESS STUDENT'S HANDBOOK

Visit *The Business Student's Handbook*, *third edition* Companion Website at **www.pearsoned.co.uk/cameron** for useful weblinks and for forms to complete and record the book's practical exercises and activities, including:

- Questionnaires such as 'How effective is your time management?' and 'Assess your own confidence' are available to print off
- Checklists on essay planning, project planning, job application and interviews
- Advice on topics such as 'How to deconstruct essay and exam questions' and 'How to check your written communication'

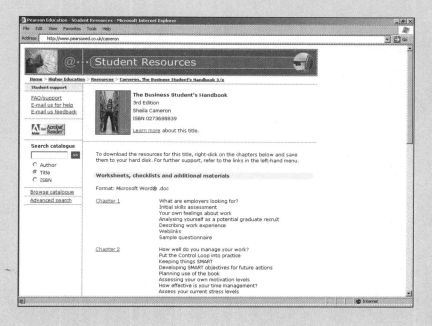

PEARSON
Education

We work with leading authors to develop the strongest
educational materials in business, finance and marketing,
bringing cutting-edge thinking and best learning practice
to a global market.

Under a range of well-known imprints, including
Financial Times Prentice Hall, we craft high-quality print
and electronic publications which help readers to
understand and apply their content, whether studying or
at work.

To find out more about the complete range of our
publishing please visit us on the World Wide Web at:
www.pearsoned.co.uk

THE
BUSINESS STUDENT'S
HANDBOOK

Learning skills for study and employment

Third Edition

SHEILA CAMERON
The Open University Business School

FT Prentice Hall
FINANCIAL TIMES

An imprint of **Pearson Education**
Harlow, England • London • New York • Boston • San Francisco • Toronto
Sydney • Tokyo • Singapore • Hong Kong • Seoul • Taipei • New Delhi
Cape Town • Madrid • Mexico City • Amsterdam • Munich • Paris • Milan

Pearson Education Limited

Edinburgh Gate
Harlow
Essex CM20 2JE
England

and Associated Companies throughout the world

Visit us on the World Wide Web at:
www.pearsoned.co.uk

First published 1999
Second edition published 2002
Third edition published 2005

ISBN 0 273 68883 9

British Library Cataloguing-in-Publication Data
A catalogue record for this book is available from the British Library

Library of Congress Cataloging-in-Publication Data
A catalog record for this book is available from the Library of Congress

10 9 8 7 6 5 4 3 2 1
09 08 07 06 05

Typeset in 9.5pt Stone Sans by 3
Printed by Ashford Colour Press Ltd, Gosport

The publisher's policy is to use paper manufactured from sustainable forests.

Contents

Part 1 LEARNING AND ITS CONTEXT

Part 4   CONCEPTUAL SKILLS

Supporting resources

Visit **www.pearsoned.co.uk/cameron** to find valuable online resources

Companion Website for students

Useful weblinks and forms to complete and record the book's practical exercises and activities, including:

- Questionnaires such as 'How effective is your time management?' and 'Assess your own confidence' are available to print off
- Checklists on essay planning, project planning, job application and interviews
- Advice on topics such as 'How to deconstruct essay and exam questions' and 'How to check your written communication'

For instructors

- Complete, downloadable Instructor's Manual
- PowerPoint slides that can be downloaded and used as OHTs

For more information please contact your local Pearson Education sales representative or visit **www.pearsoned.co.uk/cameron**

List of figures

Preface

This book was written because many students get so much less out of their degree studies than they could. Some of these do little work, some work very hard. Yet in each case they fail to enjoy the work, learn very little, get a poor degree, and fail to get a good job on graduation. This is a tragic waste of their efforts, and the efforts of their lecturers, and a waste of a lot of money. At the same time, graduate recruiters repeatedly complain that it is difficult to find good recruits because graduates lack key skills.

Note that this is true of graduates in most subjects. Although the book was written primarily for business students, it is relevant to any graduates seeking to maximise both their learning and their employment opportunities.

This book is intended to prevent such waste of resources, and help you to enjoy your studies, while getting a good degree, and developing the skills that employers seek. Fortunately these skills are precisely those needed to gain *academic* benefit from a course. By developing them, you can get a better degree for less effort. To do this you need an active approach towards *managing* your learning and a clear idea of what you need to learn (above and beyond the academic content of your course). This book applies basic management concepts to the process of learning in order to help you do this.

These concepts will be – or become – familiar to you if you are on a business studies programme. If you are not, you will still find the book useful. The principles apply to any undergraduate programme, and all necessary concepts are clearly described. The basic skills of reading and note-taking, using numbers, finding information – whether from libraries, the Internet or your own research – working in groups, and writing essays and reports are essential for almost any study, as are the skills of managing yourself, your time, your stress levels and your learning.

Cartoon by Neill Cameron, www.planetdumbass.co.uk

You need, too, to be able to *demonstrate* your skills, first to your examiners, then to potential employers. Thus you need to prepare a good CV and job application, and perform well in interviews and other selection tests. Once you are in employment you will still need to exercise your self-management and other skills, and continue to learn, if you are to have a successful career.

The book is not a textbook. It offers few 'facts' and fewer theories. Instead it is an invitation to address the challenge of *developing yourself* as a project. It offers a programme of activities designed to achieve this. Although the book is easy to *read*, the thinking and practice that it demands will be hard work, and reading is not enough. You do need to do the activities! The potential rewards for this effort are substantial – more effective and enjoyable learning, better grades, a richer student experience and a more successful and stimulating working life.

ACKNOWLEDGEMENTS

Among the many people I should like to thank are Penelope Woolf for persuading me to write this book in the first place, The Open University as an institution, and close colleagues in particular for giving me the space to write, and my students for being an endless source of challenge, stimulus and ideas. Last but definitely not least, I should particularly like to thank Hester, Neill and James for their research, comments, suggestions and general support throughout, and in particular Neill for the superb artwork in this edition.

Guided tour of the book

A **website icon** in the margin highlights where checklists, additional exercises, and other useful resources are available on the book's companion website (**www.pearsoned.co.uk/cameron**) to further help you with your studies.

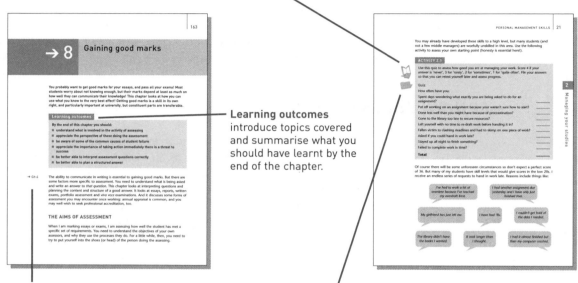

Learning outcomes introduce topics covered and summarise what you should have learnt by the end of the chapter.

Chapter linking arrows highlight the connections between chapters and indicate where you can find further details about a topic or concept.

A **file icon** in the margin highlights important activities that you should add to your file or portfolio.

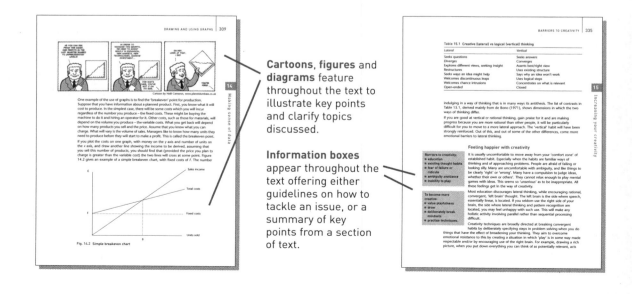

Cartoons, figures and **diagrams** feature throughout the text to illustrate key points and clarify topics discussed.

Information boxes appear throughout the text offering either guidelines on how to tackle an issue, or a summary of key points from a section of text.

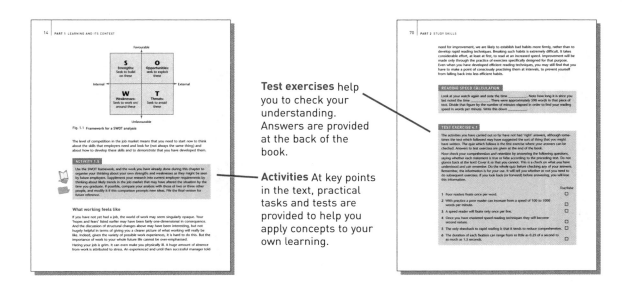

Test exercises help you to check your understanding. Answers are provided at the back of the book.

Activities At key points in the text, practical tasks and tests are provided to help you apply concepts to your own learning.

Helpfiles offer 'back to basics' guidance to mastering key skills such as maths, grammar, and examination terms.

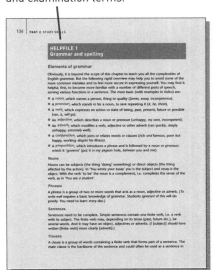

Summaries pull together the key points addressed in the chapter to provide a useful reminder of topics covered.

Further information offers sources of additional information for those who wish to explore a topic further.

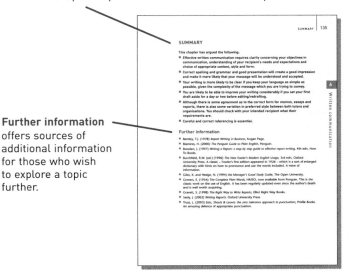

Guided tour of the website

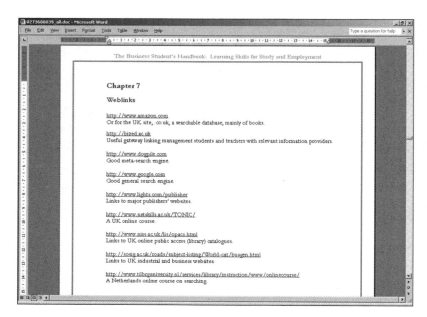

Useful weblinks take you directly to sources of information on topics such as effective web-search practice, services for management students, government and business sites.

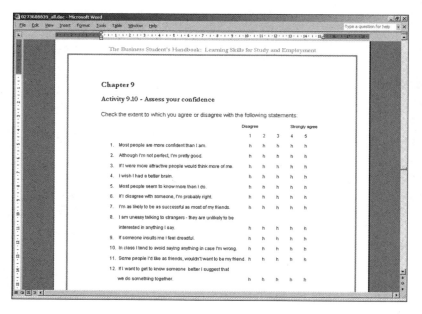

Questionnaires such as 'How effective is your time management?' and 'Assess your current stress levels' enable you to assess your own personal skills development.

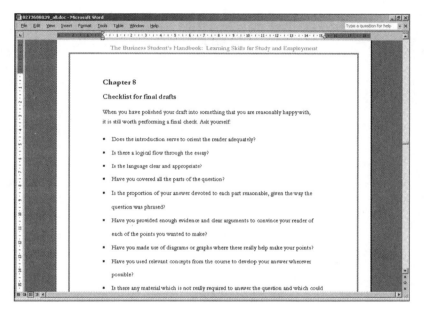

Practical checklists on essay planning, project planning, job application and interviews help you to prevent mistakes and improve critical awareness of your skills and work.

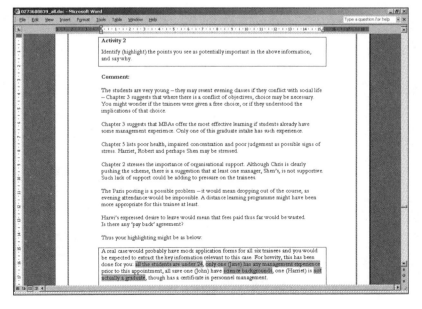

Activities and advice on topics such as 'How to deconstruct essay and exam questions' and 'How to check your written communication' help you to get your head around more difficult topics.

Password protected lecturer's resources include an Instructor's Manual (with teaching comments, activity support notes, handouts and additional ideas for activities), PowerPoint slides and weblinks.

→ **Part 1** **LEARNING AND ITS CONTEXT**

1 Learning, skills and employment
2 Managing your studies
3 The learning process

Introduction to Part 1

Studying for a degree represents a major investment in your future – an investment by taxpayers, by educational institutions, perhaps by your parents, but most of all by you yourself. You are spending three or more years studying when you could be travelling, or making your first million!

This book addresses the issue of *managing* your learning so that you maximise the return on that investment, for yourself and for the other stakeholders in the process. It is designed to help you to develop the skills that you need for learning, both as a student and in your working life. The good news is that many of the skills addressed are common to all these areas.

The first part of the book addresses the context in which you are likely to be employed. The world of employment has changed radically in recent years, with particular impact on the kind of managerial roles to which graduates have traditionally been recruited. The first chapter looks at how jobs, and the skills needed to succeed in them, have changed as a result of organisational restructuring.

The second chapter looks at the ability to manage yourself, and to plan effectively. There is a huge overlap here: the skills that employers claim to be seeking are crucial to success as a student. Time management, stress management and project management are all vital.

The third chapter looks at how students – and managers – learn. It introduces ideas drawn from the psychology of learning. Your immediate task is to manage your own learning, and these ideas will help you to understand how to develop the skills you need. This will make student life more rewarding and enjoyable. But equally importantly, the ability to learn is something that employers particularly seek in graduates. Organisations are in a state of constant change, and lifelong learning is important for both individual and organisational success.

As you work through the book you will find that topics are often interrelated. As a result, they may be dealt with in more than one place. An idea or technique may be introduced in one context, and developed in a later chapter. In such cases a marginal symbol is used to point you to the chapter where you can find more on the subject.

An important part of skill development is the use of activities which will enable you to practise skills and gain feedback on your performance – from yourself, fellow students and teaching staff. This part of the book aims to establish a habit of active and reflective learning through frequent exercises, pauses for reflection and filing of the results of activities within a file, or portfolio. You can draw on this during your study, and it will be an invaluable resource when you want to demonstrate your skills to potential employers or assessors for professional qualifications.

Most of the activities which form an important component of the book will contribute to this file, but when they are particularly important, there will be a file icon in the margin (see the example here). To help with this there will often be proformas available as web resources. As with other web resources, these will be indicated by another icon, as shown.

Some activities will serve more than one purpose. It is important that you *do* the activities as suggested, rather than merely reading them. If at all possible, work through the exercises with one or two other people. Confucius said, over 2000 years ago:

> When three of us are walking together I am sure to have a teacher. Having noted his competencies, I imitate them: his incompetencies I avoid.

A rather more interactive way of working as a group, giving each other feedback on perceived competence and incompetence, can be even more effective. Working in this way will require more time and effort than merely reading the book passively. But this effort is essential if you want to develop the skills covered and to reap the many potential benefits for study or for employment.

→ 1 Learning, skills and employment

In deciding to study, you have taken a major investment decision – to invest in yourself! This chapter looks at the market in which you will be operating as a graduate, and at what you can do to maximise the return on your investment. Developing 'transferable skills', those skills that will help you do well both as a student and as a manager, is a large part of this.

Learning outcomes

By the end of this chapter you should:

- understand what is meant by 'transferable skills'
- be starting to plan how you can develop these skills during your studies
- appreciate the ways in which organisations have changed in recent years
- understand the implications of these changes for graduate employment
- appreciate what 'graduate recruitment' means to employers and what they seek when recruiting
- be beginning to consider what you might want from a job.

If you are at the start of your university studies, you are making a major investment in yourself – in the time you are committing, the income you are foregoing, and the fees you are paying. Presumably you are hoping that this will lead to an enjoyable and well paid career. The bad news is that this is by no means certain – I know many graduates currently facing their 30th birthdays in jobs that frustrate and bore them, and pay very little. The good news is that if you start *now* to manage your learning, to think about the sort of job you want, and to develop the skills you need to be attractive as an employee, you can greatly increase your chances of a profitable and fulfilling career. The even better news is that most of the skills that employers value will help you get a better class of degree!

So, although looking at employment skills may seem slightly bizarre at this stage, when your career may seem impossibly far in the future, it makes a lot of sense. This chapter looks at the employment context to clarify *what* you need to learn, suggests ways of starting to develop your learning skills, starts you on the process of thinking about the sort of career you would like, and shows you how you can start to *use* this book to become a successful learner.

As you may already be discovering, learning at university (like learning at work) is likely to be very different from learning at school: the main responsibility will be yours, and you will be learning a much wider range of skills. You need to be able to *manage* your own learning: planning and time management skills are essential for this. You will need to learn with others: team working and communication skills will be important. You will need to locate and use a wide range of information sources: this will require knowledge management skills. But above all you need to understand what learning *means* at this level, why it is so important and how to do it well!

WHAT EMPLOYERS LOOK FOR IN GRADUATES

It is never too soon to consider what you want from your working life, and what employers think they want when recruiting graduates. The job market is highly competitive, and you can greatly increase your chances of a successful career if you start thinking *now*. If this sounds impossible, don't worry. This chapter will give you a clearer idea of what is important to you, and help you clarify your employment goals. The final part of the book will complete the process.

The introduction to Part 1 alerted you to the fact that you will need to *respond* at intervals, rather than merely sit back and read. The process starts *now*: you need to capture your starting position. Then you can return to it at intervals, develop your thoughts further, note how they are changing and check that you have not inadvertently ignored something important.

ACTIVITY 1.1

If you have access to anyone who employs graduates, ask them what they seek in recruits. Look in the recruitments sections of a few papers, or visit the web sites for companies you might like to work for, and build a list of the qualities mentioned as essential or desirable in interesting graduate vacancies.

_____

_____

_____

Were you more impressed by the similarities between employers, or the differences? Employers are far from agreed on what being a graduate can bring to a job. Since they will be recruiting to widely disparate jobs, it is not surprising that there are as many different views of what constitutes the 'ideal graduate recruit' as of the 'ideal husband/wife'. They may be looking for people to interact with customers, to solve technical problems, to work with pre-existing teams of various kinds, to 'fit in' and be effective as quickly as possible, or to act as a force for change.

Organisations may be huge or tiny, bureaucratic or flexible and innovative. What they seek from recruits depends on where they sit on these different dimensions. As a graduate this variability may be an asset. Someone, somewhere, is going to see your set of skills as just what they want. Your task while a student is to ensure that the skill set you develop is attractive to the sort of employer for whom you really want to work! This means deciding on the sort of job you want, the sort of organisation you want to work for, identifying those skills, and then making sure that you develop them.

You may also have been struck by similarities in requirements. My own recent and somewhat random trawl of the papers yielded adverts for:

- 'graduates who are ambitious, motivated, good communicators and able to work to deadlines'
- 'a rigorous approach to work matched by highly developed communication and interpersonal skills'
- 'a strategic thinker . . . an excellent communicator with strong networking and negotiating skills'
- 'strong leadership skills, excellent communication and organisation skills, an ability to resolve complex problems and personal resilience and stamina'
- 'competency in a range of business planning issues, excellent writing skills and experience of giving effective presentations'.

Note the similarities. Every advert I found sought good communication skills, and many mentioned other interpersonal skills, planning skills and motivation. You will probably find similar overlaps in requirements in your own investigations. It is these widely relevant, transferable skills that you need to develop.

KEY SKILLS AND APPLICATIONS FOR LEARNING AND EMPLOYMENT

Higher Education's Quality Assurance Authority (QAA) has specified a set of core skills which they feel all graduates should have. They have developed a set of benchmark standards for these. You can obtain the full set of benchmarking standards from the QAA website at **www.qaa.ac.uk**. They include:

- **Cognitive skills** – critical thinking, analysis and synthesis. You need, for example, to be able to identify assumptions, evaluate statements in terms of evidence and check the logic of an argument.
- **Problem-solving and decision-making skills** – quantitative and qualitative. You need to be able to identify, formulate and solve business problems, and generate and evaluate options.
- **Research and investigative skills** – individual and team. You need to be able to identify relevant information sources and research methodologies, and use them to resolve problem situations at work.

- **Information and communications technology skills** – you need to be able to use a range of business applications in any job.
- **Numeracy and quantitative skills** – data analysis, interpretation and extrapolation. You need to be able to use models and to draw conclusions from the information you obtain.
- **Communication skills** – oral and written, using a range of media. You need, for example, to be able to write business reports.
- **Interpersonal skills** – talking and listening, negotiation. You need to be able to interact effectively with a range of people, including colleagues and customers.
- **Team-working skills** – leadership, team-building, influencing. You need to be able to manage or contribute to group projects.
- **Personal management skills** – time planning, motivation, initiative – the need for these skills is obvious.
- **Learning skills** – reflective, adaptive and collaborative. You need to be motivated to learn and able to do so effectively in a range of contexts.
- **Self-awareness** – sensitivity and openness to others who are different from you. You need to be alert to how others will react to situations – the significance of 'emotional intelligence' is now becoming recognised.

ACTIVITY 1.2

For each of the above categories, think about your current skill level (use any available evidence, including feedback from friends, teachers, past employers, and your own feelings. Give yourself a rating on a scale 1–10 where 1 is very low, 10 as high as you can imagine needing. File your responses for future reference, as you will need them for subsequent work. (An electronic proforma is available to make this easy.)

The relevance of these sets of skills to work is fairly obvious (though whenever the skills are addressed in the book, their relevance to work will be explored in some detail). What may be less immediately apparent is the extent to which these 'employment skills' will help you to learn more effectively at university, and to get better marks. Communication is obviously crucial to working with others, for example in group projects. Good communication skills will help you to present information face to face, and to write better assignments. Self-management skills are valuable for improving your own learning and performance and performing your own part of a group's task. Addressing problems involves using information. You can see not only that the skills are relevant in both contexts – they are highly *transferable* – but that they are closely inter-related. Finding a simple classification of something as complex as higher-level human skills is difficult!

There have been many other attempts at providing lists of sets of skills. For example, Harvey *et al.* (1997), drawing on information from a wide range of graduate employers, suggested the importance of looking at skills involved in:

- **fitting in** – blending into a team and becoming effective quickly
- **persuading** – whether within the team or in relation to the wider organisation or customers beyond it
- **developing ideas** – analysing situations rather than merely responding to them, often best done in a team
- **transforming** – which adds to all the above the ability to apply intellectual skills and leadership skills in order to steer change.

You may find this shorter list helps you think slightly differently about the skills you have and need to develop. Although it covers much of the same ground, the emphasis is slightly different. Finally, you might like to look at the results of a study carried out in the USA (Luthans et al., 1988) into what a wide range of managers actually did. They found that managerial activities could be categorised into the following four sets:

- **communication** – paperwork and exchanging information
→ Ch 2
- **'traditional management'** – planning, decision making and controlling (more on this in the next chapter)
- **networking** – interacting with outsiders, socialising and politicking
- **human resource management** – motivating, disciplining, managing conflict, staffing and training.

ACTIVITY 1.3

Look back at your assessment of your own strengths and weaknesses in the light of what you have subsequently read. Amend your earlier list if improvements suggest themselves at this point. Add in any areas where you now feel that your study, as well as your employability, might benefit from development.

As you will now realise, the many activities scattered throughout the book will often be cumulative, and you need a file (paper or electronic) in which to store your responses to these for easy subsequent reference. You will probably find it useful to file your answers and notes by chapter to start with. Once you have accumulated enough material, there will be suggestions as to how you can organise your notes into a more
→ Ch 3
structured *Personal Development File.*

CAREERS WITHIN TODAY'S ORGANISATIONS

Earlier I suggested that careers are becoming far more fluid: this means that at regular intervals you will need to think about what you want from work. This will allow you to decide which jobs are most likely to meet your needs, and then to concentrate on the most relevant skills for development.

Learning, skills and employment

ACTIVITY 1.4

Log your initial thoughts about working life, both good and bad. Don't agonise about your answer. Just write down the first thing that comes into your head. Aim to write down between 10 and 20 words in response to the following prompts:

The things I am afraid a job might be:

_____

_____

Characteristics of my ideal job would be:

_____

_____

If possible, discuss your answers with four or five other people, to see where their views differ from yours and where they are similar. How many of you are afraid a job will be boring? How many of you want it to offer variety or the chance to meet interesting people? Do you want the chance to learn more, or to travel, or to help other people? Is status important? Were the responses from those who had already had jobs different from those who had not? If the discussion made you aware of things that are important to you but which you had omitted from your list, then construct a revised version and file this as well.

Career – a series of jobs seen in retrospect?

If your 'fears' included boredom, predictability, lack of freedom (the sort of thing that I was worried about most as a student), you were possibly thinking of the traditional 'graduate career' within a large, many-layered organisation, where good behaviour and following the rules would lead to steady progression. Large employers do still recruit graduates, but massive organisational restructuring in recent years has reduced the volume – though at the same time many of these jobs are if anything more interesting.

The 'career' as an organised succession of increasingly senior jobs has probably always been less common in reality than people believed. I can still remember being struck in 1971 by the 'definition' of career as 'a series of jobs seen in retrospect' by Ruth Lancashire, then one of the main researchers in the area, speaking at a conference on careers. Charles Handy (1989) describes how, when starting his first job in the 1950s, he was given an outline of his future career. This was to culminate in a job as chief executive of a particular company in a particular country. He left long before he was expected to reach this pinnacle, but already both the projected company, and the country, had ceased to exist!

Certainly my own subsequent 'career' could not have been 'planned' and seemed at the time to have been driven primarily by external forces. Yet the different jobs I have done have prepared me remarkably well for my present role, one which is more rewarding

Cartoon by Neill Cameron, www.planetdumbass.co.uk

1

than any job I could have dreamed of as a student. And careers are becoming ever more 'unplanned' because of the ways in which organisations are changing.

Competitive pressures have driven major restructuring. Organisations have sought to cut costs and increase the speed with which they can respond to competitors and to changes in markets. Developments in information and communications technology have meant that many of the things which managers traditionally did – to do with filtering and funnelling and transmitting information – no longer need so much human intervention.

Organisations are changing

Most large organisations responded to competitive pressures by taking a hard look at their hierarchies and 'delayering', cutting out whole layers of middle management, just the sort of jobs which many graduates have filled in the past. While this decimation of management in itself cut employment costs, many organisations 'downsized' or 'rightsized' (euphemisms in this area abound!) more generally, reducing the number of employees at other levels too. They also identified their 'core' business and concentrated on this, looking at ways of contracting out more peripheral activities such as cleaning, catering, warehousing, IT and even graduate recruitment.

The aim was to avoid using full-time permanent staff for non-core work. Such staff are expensive, and it may be slow and expensive to reduce staffing when business is poor. Increasingly, organisations have 'outsourced' non-core activities to specialist suppliers. Flexibility in staffing was also increased by using part-time employees or those on short-term contracts. Also, many large, specialist departments at 'head office' have been reduced by devolving a lot of their responsibilities to line managers.

Organisations may have gone too far in their rush to cut employment costs; terms like 'corporate anorexia' and 'corporate amnesia' have been used to describe the loss of experience and expertise in the wholesale redundancies that have occurred. Knowledge is increasingly seen to be a key resource in organisations. There are now some signs of a reaction, with increased graduate recruitment by larger organisations as part of a drive to rebuild both expertise and future potential.

The 'spinning out' of non-core business has encouraged growth in smaller enterprises; working with these has added to the variety and challenges already a feature of managing the cross-functional and more autonomous teams often created during organisational restructuring. Also important, of course, is information technology, a feature of almost all jobs in these 'new' organisations and one where use of contract staff is extremely common.

IMPLICATIONS FOR GRADUATE EMPLOYMENT

These organisational changes were reducing traditional graduate openings at the same time as major expansion in universities was *increasing* the numbers graduating. Inevitably many graduates were forced to work in what were traditionally 'non-graduate jobs'. A 1997 Department for Education and Employment (DfEE) survey of those graduating in the last six years found only half were in 'graduate jobs'.

At the time of writing, prospects for graduates are more favourable. The AGR Graduate Recruitment Survey (July 2004) of some of the UK's leading employers showed that following three (more) years of reduced vacancies for graduates, the number of positions for graduates leaving university this summer had risen by 15.5%. Carl Gillead, chief executive of the AGR, commented that:

> The findings are good news for the graduate recruitment industry and great news for graduates themselves. Vacancy levels have risen and we expect both salaries and vacancies to continue to remain stable in 2005.

(www.agr.org.uk)

Of course given the fluctuations prior to this, it is impossible to predict what the situation will be by the time you graduate. (You can find information each year from the Prospects web site – their 2004 report showed that only 6% of those graduating in 2002 were by then believed to be unemployed.)

Note, however, that even the 'improved' 2004 situation was highly competitive. The employers in the survey received an *average* of 37.6 applications for every vacancy during the 2003–4 recruitment year (this compared with 42.1 applications per vacancy in 2002–3). The most attractive vacancies will receive many more applications than this. So use this book to develop your skills, and make yourself highly attractive to potential employers!

It is worth noting that any reduction in traditional career opportunities for graduates has been accompanied by the development of a host of other avenues for interesting employment. Some are in smaller enterprises, others at levels which previously would not have attracted graduates, but which now offer precisely the challenges and satisfactions that would have been deemed lacking in the past. Indeed the DfEE survey mentioned above found that those in 'non-graduate jobs' in smaller organisations were less likely to feel that their graduate skills were under-utilised than those in larger ones.

If present trends continue, you can expect to work for a wider range of organisations than did your parents' generation and to change organisations, whether by free choice or necessity, every few years. If you want a higher-level job you may *need* to move:

flatter organisations inevitably offer far fewer promotion opportunities than their multi-layered predecessors. So developing a 'career' will require positive action on your part and moves through several organisations.

Alternatively, you may change because you are seeking to develop additional skills or to broaden your experience. This is an important consideration: the wider your skills and experience, the greater your chances of obtaining a higher-level job, or of finding another role or job if your own falls victim to restructuring. It is vital in the current situation to take responsibility for your own development, always considering yourself through the eyes of other potential employers. This will maximise your chances of continued satisfying employment, come what may.

Seeing yourself as a product

You will thus need to regard yourself as, in one sense, a *product*, one which you are continually developing with an eye to the *market* for this product, now and in the future. Those responsible for marketing a product find that SWOT analysis is a useful framework for thinking about their strategy. If you have not yet come across this, it is very easy to understand and use. SWOT is shorthand for thinking in terms of:

- **Strengths** – which you already have, and might build on.
- **Weaknesses** – which you have but could possibly reduce or otherwise work around.
- **Opportunities** – which the market offers and you might be able to exploit better than other people.
- **Threats** – again from outside, which you need to be aware of and take action against.

Figure 1.1 shows this framework diagrammatically. To carry out a SWOT analysis in this context you need to be continually alert to likely developments in the employment market, aware of the types of skill and experience that are assuming importance and have a sound assessment of your own skills and experience. You also need to think about how you can *continually* develop these in ways that will open up future employment opportunities. Otherwise you may find you face an ever more restricted range of possible jobs.

Being highly employable means:
- seeing yourself as a product
- watching the market
- developing yourself continuously
- being prepared for change.

Such an approach means taking a much more active, and proactive, approach to your own 'career', seeing it as *your* responsibility rather than that of your employers. Seeking continuous learning and development will be a part of this. You will probably need to make absolutely sure you take advantage of all the training and job moves available in your company. If your employer does not encourage training, you may need to pursue a further qualification in your own time and at your own expense while working. The prospect of taking responsibility for your own development can be somewhat frightening. However, if 'boredom' and 'security' were listed as fears rather than as desiderata in the exercise above, the excitement and risk associated with owning your own future should appeal to you.

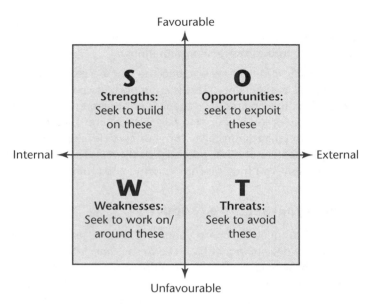

Fig. 1.1 Framework for a SWOT analysis

The level of competition in the job market means that you need to start *now* to think about the skills that employers need and look for (not always the same thing) and about how to develop these skills and to *demonstrate* that you have developed them.

ACTIVITY 1.5

Use the SWOT framework, and the work you have already done during this chapter to organise your thinking about your own strengths and weaknesses as they might be seen by future employers. Supplement your research into current employer requirements by thinking about likely trends in the job market that may have altered the situation by the time you graduate. If possible, compare your analysis with those of two or three other people, and modify it if this comparison prompts new ideas. File the final version for future reference.

What working feels like

If you have not yet had a job, the world of work may seem singularly opaque. Your 'hopes and fears' listed earlier may have been fairly one-dimensional in consequence. And the discussion of structural changes above may have been interesting, but not hugely helpful in terms of giving you a clearer picture of what working will really be like. Indeed, given the variety of possible work experiences, it is hard to do this. But the importance of work to your whole future life cannot be over-emphasised.

Hating your job is grim. It can even make you physically ill. A huge amount of absence from work is attributed to stress. An experienced and until then successful manager told me the other day that he had been to see his doctor because he could no longer eat, sleep or think straight. Whenever he heard his manager's voice he felt physically sick. Indeed, when telling his doctor about all this he burst into tears. A stressful job with an over-controlling boss had reduced him to total misery and an inability to function.

In contrast, a challenging and worthwhile job can leave you exhilarated and longing to get back to work next day. The difference between these two extremes is so important that it is worth making every effort to take the challenge posed by this book seriously and do everything you can *now* to ensure that your working experience is positive. This starts with exploring your own views about work, a process that you will need to repeat at intervals throughout the book, and indeed throughout your working life.

ACTIVITY 1.6

List as many words as you can that might be used to describe any of your own experience of work. Ask as many other people as you can to provide up to 10 words which describe their own experience of current, or previous work.

_____

_____

_____

You may have been surprised at the emotional level of some of the responses you get. Work forms a major part of most people's lives. For some, it is boring, so routine and dehumanising that it is highly stressful and each day becomes something to be endured with difficulty. For others, work is so exciting that they would far rather be working than doing anything else. For some, it is a source of self-esteem; for others, the treatment they receive totally destroys any self-esteem they may have had. Many marriage breakdowns are blamed on the stresses and demands of one partner's job (or both jobs). Some jobs have specific health or physical risks associated with them. More generally, sickness rates correlate to different sorts of work. Studies show that to be without a job at all is highly stressful, destructive of self-esteem and associated with ill health and relationship difficulties.

In evolutionary terms, the centrality of work is perhaps not surprising. Survival has almost always been dependent on wresting food and physical safety from a competitive, if not hostile, environment, normally as part of a social group. And reproductive success, as with other primates, will have depended on status within that group. Without work (whether hunting and gathering or farming or manufacture of some kind), the life expectancy of a person and of any dependants would have been short indeed. Indeed family members would have been involved in work from a very early age. Survival without work is, in evolutionary terms, very recent.

If you feel it would be helpful to know more about what different types of work offer, there are a number of steps that you can usefully take. The first is to pursue any opportunities for work placements during your course (more of this later – the learning opportunities offered by such placements are important in a number of different ways). The second is to extend the previous activity, and ask as many people as possible to describe their work experience to you in more detail. Try asking relatives, friends already in employment, fellow students who worked before the course started or who have already been on work placements. The third is to read about the experience of others, and suggested reading is given at the end of this chapter.

If you are asking people about their work experience, which may after all be extensive, it can help to have a framework of questions. If you are working in a group, discuss possible questions, and agree a common list. The following are merely suggestions to get you started:

- What most surprised you on starting work with your present employer?
- What are the most common difficulties you encounter at work?
- What are the most common frustrations?
- What has given you most satisfaction in the last week (or month or year)?
- If you could choose a new job, how would it be different from your present one?
- How would it resemble your present job?
- How much freedom do you have at work?
- How much impact do you feel you have on the way the organisation operates?
- What advice would you give to someone starting out in your organisation?
- What characteristics would the ideal employee have in your organisation?

The answers to such questions will reflect the person answering as much as the job they are doing. The same job could be very satisfactory to one person and hardly bearable to another. Nevertheless, if you can question a number of different people of graduate or equivalent ability about their experience, you should be better informed than before about the characteristics of jobs and possible reactions to them. This should help you become more aware of the nature of the type of job you would like yourself.

ACTIVITY 1.7

Devise a set of questions for asking about work experience, preferably with a group of others, and use this to question a range of people. If working in a group, discuss the results, comparing what those you asked seem to want from work with what *you* think you might want, and using what they say about their work experience to extend your own expectations and awareness. Add any additional 'wants' to your 'ideal job' file entry. You can find a starter questionnaire, based on the questions above, on the website.

STRUCTURE OF THE BOOK

To help you see how to make best use of the rest of the book, a brief overview of the remaining chapters follows. This will help you to get a feel for how you can use it to develop those skills which you will need, both to succeed as a student, and to be highly desirable to potential employers when you start to apply for jobs.

The first part of the book maps out 'the territory' of employment, management skills and learning. Once you are more familiar with this context, you will be better able to use the second part of the book, which addresses the specific skills that you will need in order to do well academically: reading and note taking; writing clearly; working with numbers; using computers and the Internet; and doing well in assessment (including exams). You may already be more than expert in some of these areas. If so, it will be good time management to identify and concentrate on those where you are weaker. Although the main aim of this part is to help you do well in your course, most of the skills covered will be also be useful long after you have graduated.

The third part reverses this emphasis. It addresses communication and other aspects of working with other people, either one-to-one or as a member of a team. Although you will need these skills while a student and will have many opportunities to develop them, you have already seen that they are absolutely crucial to success at work.

The fourth part addresses skills of equal relevance to study and work: the 'trained mind' that graduates were traditionally deemed to possess. More specifically, it looks at the skills needed to react creatively and appropriately to complicated situations, to investigate them, gather and make sense of relevant information and decide on a way forward. Your course will be addressing problem solving skills within a specific academic area, but much of the teaching may be implicit. This part of the book aims to make aspects of these skills more explicit, and to increase your awareness of them. This should shift your approach to study slightly, so that you are better prepared to tackle problem situations at work.

In the last part, the different areas are brought together in looking at project management, both in general and in the context of any project that is part of your course. Finally, the 'project' of finding a good job is addressed. In this way the circle is completed and you will come back to the issues raised in this chapter, refining your work objectives and developing the skills needed for making a successful job application and doing well in interviews.

The structure of the book in terms of the skills covered can be diagrammed as shown in Figure 1.2. Inevitably, there are many interconnections between the skills covered in different chapters. In particular, the end of the book is designed to draw on almost all that has gone before. You can see that when you are ready to organise your file you will face a considerable challenge. But by then you should have a clearer idea of the skills that are important to you for more effective study, as well as those which are likely to be important to your chosen prospective employers. This will make it easier to design a system well suited to your particular situation.

This chapter has looked mainly at the world of work, arguing that there is a major overlap in the skills needed for study and for employment, and that given the competitive nature of employment you need to start *now* to think about what you want

1

Learning, skills and employment

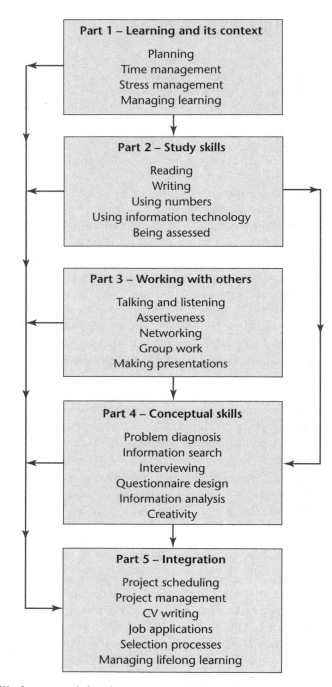

Fig. 1.2 A skills framework for the purpose of this book

from a job, and what skills you will need to develop it. You will find as you work through the book that each skill addressed will have the added benefit of helping you gain higher grades. This will help you further in your search for a better job. The transferability of most of the skills covered has its roots in two factors. One, obviously, is that if you are studying a course designed to prepare you for employment, then you are likely to be asked to develop those skills that employers value. The second, and less obvious, factor is that the most successful managers are those who continually develop themselves. The ability to learn is vital in an organisational context that is fluid, and constantly presenting new challenges. Becoming an effective learner is thus crucial to both contexts. And it is effective learning, and the equally important ability to display your learning ability, that this book primarily addresses, as the next two chapters make clear.

SUMMARY

This chapter has argued that:

- Studying for a degree represents a major investment in terms of opportunity costs and direct financial costs.
- You need to take responsibility for your learning if you are to get good grades, and become an attractive employee.
- Organisational restructuring has reduced traditional graduate opportunities. The situation is improving, but is still highly competitive.
- Expectations of a career within a single organisation, with regular promotions, are unrealistic.
- Challenging jobs now exist at levels previously unattractive to graduates: restructured jobs often offer increased variety, team working and autonomy.
- You need to understand what is important to prospective employers if you are to develop and demonstrate the skills they seek.
- A core set of transferable skills, both interpersonal and intellectual, are relevant to both study and employment.
- These transferable skills include the skill to learn, the ability to manage yourself and basic skills in numeracy, literacy and IT, interpersonal, group-working and communication skills, and conceptual/analytical/problem-solving skills.

Further information

- Fineman, S. and Gabriel, Y. (1996) *Experiencing Organisations*, Sage. An easy-to-read set of stories told by students after their six-month work placements.
- Frost, P.J., Mitchell, V.F. and Nord, W.R. (eds) (1997) *Organisational Reality: Reports from the Firing Line*, 4th edn, Addison Wesley Longman.

- **www.agr.org.uk** – the Association of Graduate Recruiters – for information from the perspective of the employer.
- **www.prospects.ac.uk** – 'the UK's official graduate careers website' for a range of information on graduate employment.
- **www.qaa.ac.uk** for more information on benchmarking and academic standards.

1

Learning, skills and employment

→ 2 Managing your studies

According to Drucker (1999), history's great achievers have all been good self-managers. If you develop your skills in planning, managing your time, managing your stress levels and motivating yourself, you will be far more successful in your studies and your career.

Learning outcomes

By the end of this chapter you should:

- understand what is involved in management
- see why you need to manage your study
- understand the basic concepts of planning and control
- appreciate the importance of motivation and how to motivate yourself
- be starting to improve your time management
- understand how stress can arise and how to reduce it.

The last chapter identified personal management, including time planning and motivation, as a key skill area. By the end of this chapter you should have assessed your own development needs in this area, and be planning to meet them. The main focus is on clarifying your objectives, and planning, and acting, to achieve these (adjusting plans where necessary). To do this, you need to understand the idea of 'control'.

Managing time, managing stress, and sustaining motivation are critical to student and career success. This chapter will introduce models to help you do this: the ability to use a range of conceptual frameworks to make sense of situations is a further key transferable skill.

→ Ch 8, 12

PERSONAL MANAGEMENT SKILLS

Actively managing yourself and your learning will enable you to achieve considerably more with the same or less effort. 'Management', both as taught at university and as practised in organisations, is all about making effective use of resources in order to achieve objectives and satisfy a market. A widely accepted definition of management is 'a process of achieving objectives through the effective use of resources'. As a student, your resources include time, brain power, books and university facilities. These resources are finite, and need to be actively *managed*. You also need to manage the processes, including the learning process, in which these resources are deployed.

You may already have developed these skills to a high level, but many students (and not a few middle managers) are woefully unskilled in this area. Use the following activity to assess your own starting point (honesty is essential here!).

ACTIVITY 2.1

Use this quiz to assess how good you are at managing your work. Score 4 if your answer is 'never', 3 for 'rarely', 2 for 'sometimes', 1 for 'quite often'. File your answers so that you can retest yourself later and assess progress.

Quiz

How often have you:

Spent days wondering what exactly you are being asked to do for an assignment? _____

Put off working on an assignment because your weren't sure how to start? _____

Done less well than you might have because of procrastination? _____

Gone to the library too late to secure resources? _____

Left yourself with no time to re-draft work before handing it in? _____

Fallen victim to clashing deadlines and had to skimp on one piece of work? _____

Asked if you could hand in work late? _____

Stayed up all night to finish something? _____

Failed to complete work in time? _____

Total _____

Of course there will be some unforeseen circumstances so don't expect a perfect score of 36. But many of my students have skill levels that would give scores in the low 20s. I receive an endless series of requests to hand in work late. Reasons include things like:

> I've had to work a lot of overtime because I've reached my overdraft limit.

> I had another assignment due yesterday and I have only just finished that.

> My girlfriend has just left me.

> I have had 'flu.

> I couldn't get hold of the data I needed.

> The library didn't have the books I wanted.

> It took longer than I thought.

> I had it almost finished but then my computer crashed.

Cartoon by Neill Cameron, www.planetdumbass.co.uk

Other problems concern work submitted more or less on time, but with concerns about quality: 'I couldn't get into it, so I haven't done as much as I should', or 'I'm not sure if this is quite what was wanted.' Or regarding a forthcoming exam: 'I had my marketing exam today, so I've been revising for that. And I've got quantitative analysis tomorrow so I've only got half a day to revise it *all*.'

I said that students were not the only ones finding personal management difficult. Sadly, major problems are often caused at work by faulty planning for totally predictable events or failure to build in slack for the unpredictable. Deadlines are missed because of conflicts between different tasks which could have been foreseen, or poor prioritisation. Projects are held up because key materials were not ordered in advance and cannot be delivered for weeks, or because information is not available at the time when it is wanted. A new recruit to my own team had to work her full three months' notice, yet when she left her employers had still taken no steps to start recruiting her (very necessary) successor! Even I sometimes spend whole days on small tasks, because I cannot face starting a difficult but far more important job.

There are many other sorts of inefficiency. One organisation placed an (expensive) advertisement in the national press. It generated a gratifyingly large number of replies, too many to fit on the desk of the person dealing with them. So she carefully piled them on top of her wastepaper basket, leaving them there when she went home for the weekend. Understandably, the cleaners failed to grasp that her bin was now her 'pending' tray! This was an extreme example of poor filing, but it is amazing how often other filing lapses, whether paper or electronic, mean that something important is lost. Poor self-management can cause chaos, and the financial (and emotional) costs can be enormous.

It is not surprising, then, that employers in the Harvey *et al.* survey already referred to saw personal attributes relating to self-regulation and self-motivation as important. Indeed, personal competences such as 'planning to achieve results' and 'managing oneself' feature in many vocational competence frameworks (more on these in the next chapter). Improving your self-management skills will make you much more attractive to potential employers, and far more effective in whichever job you accept.

→ Ch 3

Learning skills are another key area. Organisations need to adapt to a continually changing environment, so they need employees who can also adapt, through learning.

Hence the key skill of 'improving own learning and performance' introduced earlier and the 'willingness to learn' identified as important in the survey by Harvey *et al.*

Skills in managing yourself and your learning and development are thus crucial for your eventual success in employment. But even more important, improving these skills will have an immediate impact upon your studies. You will find that you learn far more effectively, enjoy the process more and get much better grades once you start to use these skills and actively *manage* your studies. And you will probably find that they will enable you to do more outside your course and enjoy that more too. All this can result from understanding and applying some of the most basic ideas about management, ideas which have been around for almost a century.

THE CLASSIC VIEW OF MANAGEMENT

It is hard to think of management without thinking at least in part of control. Luthans *et al.* (1988), quoted in the last chapter, found planning, decision making and controlling to be a major part of the job of 'real' managers. (Human resource management, including motivation, was another.) Indeed, the first management guru in the modern sense, and still the most quoted writer on management, Henri Fayol, suggested in 1916 that management had five main elements:

- *forecasting*, then *planning* for the anticipated future
- *organising* physical and human resources
- *commanding*, or setting in action and continuing, the activities needed to implement plans
- *coordinating* activities to meet goals
- *controlling* this activity to ensure that it is done properly.

Forecasting and planning

Planning is essential. It is no good thinking that you can spend the run-up to a week of wall-to-wall exams revising only for the first one. Nor should you spend the next fortnight working on an essay due on the Tuesday, totally ignoring the one due on Wednesday. It is poor 'planning' to try to borrow the single library copy of a necessary book the night before the assignment for which everyone needs it is due. You need to work out ahead of time (that is the forecasting element) what is likely to be needed, and then plan to achieve it.

As well as planning for the predictable, you need to make contingency plans for the unpredictable. For winter exams it makes sense to allow some slack in your revision timetable: then if you catch flu you can spend a few days in bed. (Even in summer it is possible to get ill!) Most people are incorrigible optimists assuming that everything that can go wrong will go right.

The surprising thing about forecasting and planning is how often they are neglected, whether at work or in other contexts. Indeed, the more pressure you are under, the stronger the temptation to act like an ostrich and refuse to look ahead! But the act of looking ahead and planning to be in a position to meet future requirements and situations is as important for your present success as it will be if you become a director of a multinational company. The sections on planning techniques and time management in this chapter should help you to start improving your forecasting and planning *now*.

Organising

Fayol was talking more at the level of putting together factories and work teams, but you too need to assemble the resources needed to implement your plan. If you are going home during a study break and have an assignment due on your return, you need to ensure that you take with you *all* the materials that you will need to complete the necessary work. If you are applying for a work placement, you need to check that your named referees will be willing to vouch for you and will be in the country at the time the request for a reference is likely to be sent. If you are working on a group assignment, you need to make sure that the group has the right mix of skills and that the tasks are distributed to make use of people's strengths where possible.

Commanding

The term is somewhat archaic in this context, but the idea of 'setting action in motion' should be a familiar problem area! My grandmother's (irritatingly) favourite comment was 'Procrastination is the thief of time' – perhaps you can relate to this cliché. It is no good having the plans and organising the resources if things don't then start to happen. And this can be just as much a problem in managing yourself as in trying to get a group of uncommitted employees to deliver on what is planned. Whether you are trying to motivate a whole factory, ensure that everyone in a group does their bit or just stop procrastinating and write that essay, getting things moving can be a real challenge. An understanding of motivation is equally important in either case.

Coordinating

The idea of coordinating yourself may have seemed strange at first. But if you have already experienced group working, problems of coordination will be familiar. You may already have developed ways of tackling them, such as frequent progress checks and rebalancing of workloads where necessary. If you are working alone, the distinction between organising and coordinating may be too fine to be worth trying to make at this stage, though it *will* become significant if you are doing a project.

→ Ch 16

Control

Control has authoritarian overtones these days, but is absolutely essential to any form of management. There are few situations where you can set things in motion and then sit back and wait for them to work out as planned. Instead, you need to make adjustments as you go along. The world seldom sits quietly and lets you carry out your original plans according to schedule. Even if it does, you may have forecast badly, or have drawn up a faulty schedule.

Perhaps you discover a few days into your revision schedule that at your present rate of progress you are going to cover less than half the syllabus. Clearly you need to 'adjust' and either spend more hours a day on revision or change the way in which you are revising. Another such 'control' action might be telling a friend that you cannot go to the cinema as planned because you have fallen behind schedule on an essay. Plans often need such adjustments to ensure that you achieve your objectives. In making these adjustments, you are exercising control.

The idea of a control loop, drawn from engineering, is a very simple framework which can be of great use in analysing management situations. The ability to use such frameworks constructively will be an important part of the problem-solving skills addressed in Part 4 and the frameworks or models themselves are likely to form the substance of much that you learn at university. The next section, which explores the basic control loop idea in more detail, is therefore important on a number of levels. The part of your file based on exercises related to control is one to which you may need to refer on a number of subsequent occasions.

BASIC IDEAS OF CONTROL

If you have a physics or engineering background, or are even fond of DIY around the house, you may already be familiar with a version of the very basic control loop diagram shown in Figure 2.1. In engineering contexts the way such a loop operates is fairly obvious. You have something like a central heating system, made up of physical parts. Gas and air (say) and water will go into the boiler and the water will emerge at a different temperature to warm the radiators. Other outputs are waste gases. There is a target, which from your perspective is likely to be the air temperature of the house

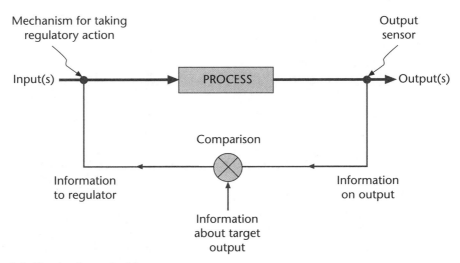

Fig. 2.1 The basic control loop

rather than the water temperature. You decide on the setting for this, adjusting the thermostat on the wall of (say) your living room. The thermostat will continuously sense the air temperature and when it falls sufficiently below the setting will send a message to the boiler to switch on and start heating the water for the radiators again.

The same basic control loop can also be used as a framework for thinking about control in more complex management situations. The key feature of the model is that it shows control as a process of checking what is happening against what should be happening and making adjustments to bring things nearer to what is desired. This happens whenever you are trying to do something – examples range from throwing the spaghetti at the wall to see if it is done (or, less dramatically, tasting a bit), to weighing yourself once a week if you are trying to lose weight, or checking your pulse rate if exercising. Exams can be regarded as the 'measuring output' part of a control loop by which a university seeks to maintain academic standards.

So how do you 'use' the model to improve your personal management? The value of the model is that it makes explicit the different parts of the loop that need to exist for control to operate. Thus you can use it as a prompt as you think about what is actually happening, asking yourself how these parts map on to reality. This can help you to realise why something is 'out of control', in that objectives are not being achieved, and to see what might be changed to improve the situation.

Looking at the model, you can see that the essential parts of the loop are:

- a goal or target – 'What am I *trying* to do?' – without this the whole idea of control makes no sense
- a way of sensing or measuring what is happening – 'What am I *actually* doing?'
- some means of comparing this with the target – '*How* am I doing?'
- some way of taking action if a discrepancy is found – 'What *should* I be doing to improve?'

The loop needs to be complete, or closed, for ongoing control to be exercised. Absence of any of these components will mean that there is no control: shortcomings in any one of them will mean that control is seriously weakened.

ACTIVITY 2.2

Think of at least one recent occasion when you, or someone you know, failed to do something as intended. Try to show what was going on by drawing a control loop, identifying each of the elements in the situation.

What were the inputs? What were the goals or targets? How explicit were they? How did you check on progress? What measures were you using and how did you compare these with the target? What did you do when a discrepancy was found? Could you modify the inputs, or did you need to change the process? Or did you decide that the target was unrealistic, and modify it?

If possible, compare your diagram with those drawn by several other people and try to see which parts of the loop seem most susceptible to failure. If you can, repeat the exercise with situations involving different objectives – longer or shorter term, more or less complex than the one you first chose.

> - 'Easy to apply' models can provide useful checklists.
> - 'Difficult' ones can change the way you think.

This exercise should have shown you a number of things. First, it can be surprisingly difficult to apply a simple framework to a complex situation. Second, it may be far from straightforward to express goals in a way that progress towards them can be measured. This will be discussed in more detail shortly. Third, it may be surprisingly difficult to *do* anything, even though you are fairly sure that something needs to be done. The reasons are many, but motivation is a crucial component and again there will be more on this later.

The fact that it is difficult to use models in this way does not mean that they are useless. On the contrary, it is the *effort* of bending a complicated situation to a simple model that produces the benefit. The exercise forces you to think differently about things, to 'try on' different ways of looking at a situation and to come up with new insights. And this is where genuine progress lies. 'Easy' models can be useful checklists, but not much more. If you can instantly say 'this is this, that is that' and map reality on to model without effort, the model is unlikely to help you advance your thinking. This is a theme that will be revisited later. It is an important part of coping with complexity and of becoming more creative. You may curse the difficulty, because mental effort is something we tend to avoid. But 'no pain' usually means 'no gain', in thinking as much as in physical training.

OBJECTIVE SETTING

Specifying goals in such a way that progress towards them can be *measured* may be difficult. Most organisations appraise employees at least annually, discussing performance over the last year, evaluating it and setting new targets. There is a saying that 'What gets measured gets done', and this is why targets and measures are crucial. Set the wrong ones – perhaps because they are easier to measure than other, more appropriate ones – and it can have a *negative* effect on the goals you really want to achieve. Yet frequently this is what happens.

A major bank once set new, very high, lending goals to its branches, hoping to increase business thereby. Only one branch in the region met the targets. Because all other branches found it impossible, they asked the secret of success. It turned out that what got measured was the paperwork on loan applications. Normally if a loan was clearly out of the question, the branch would simply tell the applicant so and that would be that: no paperwork was necessary. What the 'successful' branch had realised was that it could prepare the initial paperwork for *all* applications, even those which had no hope of being accepted. Of course, this took a lot of (wasted) time and the number of ultimately successful applications that could be dealt with was therefore reduced. The 'successful' branch was actually lending *less* money. But it was meeting the targets it had been set in terms of what was measured!

'SMART' Objectives

Because setting appropriate targets is difficult, various guidelines have been developed. The most memorable is that objectives should be SMART (some say CSMART), that is:

- **C**hallenging
- **S**pecific
- **M**easurable
- **A**chievable
- **R**elevant
- **T**ime defined.

This is a common expansion of the acronym. There are others, but the message is the same. It is fairly obvious. Vague objectives make it difficult to plan and even more difficult to monitor progress, and therefore to know when control action is needed. There is little point in setting out to fail, so setting unachievable objectives is not sensible, despite the frequency of such objectives within organisations! (It is surprisingly common to set oneself impossible goals, too – optimism is rife.)

The discussion of motivation which follows gives further reasons why unachievable objectives are a bad idea and suggests why objectives also need to be challenging. The bank example makes the point about relevance – the measure used meant that effectively the objective became to increase paperwork! Time will always be important, so the point by which a goal should be achieved needs to be specified. It is no good saying only that 'my goal is to revise these three topics'. They need to be revised by a certain point.

ACTIVITY 2.3

Revisit your examples of non-achievement in the last exercise and think about whether the objectives in question were 'SMART'. If not, rewrite them more clearly below, using these criteria. (For the purpose of control, they need only be SMART; if you want to find out why you were not *motivated* to achieve them you may need to look at the C as well.)

C _____

S _____

M _____

A _____

R _____

T _____

The time dimension is so important that it is worth a little more thought. The aim of control is to ensure that you *meet* objectives, rather than find out afterwards that you have failed to do so. It is therefore essential that you know there is a problem in time to do something about it. The more frequently you measure progress, the more likely you are to detect the need for action while there is still time for such action to be effective. For a fairly major and long-term goal – for example to submit a 10 000 word project in six months' time or to sign up 40 new major customers over a similar period – you need to be able to check your progress at regular intervals. It is no good realising four months into the period that you have done about one-tenth of the required work. The following steps are useful here:

- break down objectives into hierarchies of sub-objectives
- identify critical paths through these hierarchies
- identify 'milestones', i.e. points on these paths at which you will check your progress
- check as per this schedule.

Hierarchies of objectives

In order to achieve one thing you may need to do several others. To travel by bus to another city, you need to find out where the bus goes from and when it leaves. You may need to buy a ticket in advance. You need to get yourself to the bus station in time. You can only succeed in your overall objective by succeeding in these lesser ones. Figure 2.2 shows how sub-objectives might be organised in a hierarchy.

In an objectives tree each 'rootlet' is something that needs to be achieved if the objective above it is to be achieved.

To construct such a hierarchy you start with the top goal and ask: 'For this to happen, what must I achieve?' And then for each of the sub-objectives identified you ask the same question. Move down the tree until your objectives are simple actions which cannot sensibly be broken down further. Constructing such a tree can be extremely useful, highlighting sub-objectives for which you might otherwise neglect to

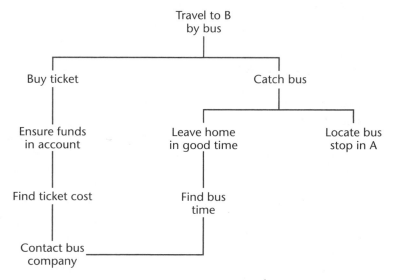

Fig. 2.2 Hierarchy of objectives for getting from A to B (assuming prior purchase of ticket needed)

2

Managing your studies

plan. It also gives you a series of much more specific objectives than the overall goal. You can start to think about scheduling the achievement of these objectives, with specific deadlines against which you can measure progress.

Note that you do not start with the first thing you need to do at the top, as might feel natural. You start with the ultimate objective, and then identify things that need to be done before this as you move down the page. This is the logic of an objectives tree, or hierarchy of objectives. Once you get the hang of this slightly counter-intuitive way of proceeding it becomes easy.

ACTIVITY 2.4

Think about something you would really like to achieve in the medium term. Examples might include finding a vacation job, writing an article for a periodical, learning a new skill, making an expedition or gaining a qualification in something outside your course. Try to draw a hierarchy of sub-objectives by asking of each objective 'To achieve this, what do I first need to achieve . . .?' in order to tease out the objectives beneath it. When writing each objective try to make it 'SMART'.

When you have done this, if possible get someone to check the logic of the tree. It is all too easy for parts of it to come out upside down, with the objectives served being under the sub-objectives rather than on top. Try to arrange your various sub-objectives into a sensible schedule, with time targets attached to each. File this schedule and check progress against it at intervals.

Again, a seemingly simple exercise can turn out to be surprisingly difficult, but if anything this enhances rather than detracts from its value. Try to get into the habit of drawing an objectives tree for each of your goals. You will be surprised at the way it helps you to increase your success in achieving them.

ACTION PLANNING

What you were doing in the activity above was to start to produce an *action plan*. Action planning is invaluable when you want to make sure that something actually happens, rather than staying at the level of good intentions. There are several possible formats for such a plan, but any format should include a list of actions with target dates, and leave room to show completion. More complex plans may list resources needed, specify standards to be achieved, and allow room for ongoing commentary on progress. An example of an extract from a very simple plan is shown in Table 2.1.

The action plans you draw up while working through the book will combine to help you plan and carry out activities that will help your personal development. Many organisations require staff to draw up formal 'Personal development plans', often as part of the perfomance appraisal system. Professional institutes may do the same, as one feature of professionalism is to take responsibility for ensuring that your professional skills are continuously updated. Personal development plans normally

Table 2.1 Example of a simple action plan

Goal: Organise next meeting

Actions	Target date	Completed
Book room	27/3	26/3
Notify members	31/3	30/3
Arrange catering	4/4	4/4
Inform security staff	7/4	7/4

specify development needs, learning objectives/outcomes, responsibility for development (individual, manager or HR department), timing and results – what was done, when, and how effective was it? Complexity is not always desirable. The Chartered Institute for Personnel and Development (CIPD) guidelines suggest a format with five columns: What do I want/need to learn?; What will I do to achieve this?; What resources or support will I need?; What will my success criteria be?; Target dates for review and completion.

While organisations often like plans to be in a concise format for easy reference, you may find it helpful to use a more narrative approach. You could devote a page to each objective. You might want additional headings for reasons for objective, and room to report on progress as you go along. A place to note future actions needed might also be helpful. (An expanded version, building on the CIPD suggestion, is available as a web resource, for you to use as a starting point if your institution does not specify a format.)

For quick overall progress monitoring you could provide a simple summary sheet listing each main objective and key target dates, allowing you to check on those dates if you are on track. The key thing is to work out a format that suits *you* and use it at appropriate points during the book. Many of the plans thus generated will be potential portfolio exhibits should you be required to assemble materials to demonstrate your skills.

Remember when action planning to check that each objective is 'CSMART'. You will find this technique can be amazingly powerful in helping you to achieve your objectives. This is because it forces you to think logically about what you need to do, and when, and provides you with a set of targets against which you can monitor progress. This will show you when you need to take corrective action. It will also provide visible signs of progress, thus sustaining your motivation.

Planning charts and critical paths

For complex projects you may need a more refined way of thinking about scheduling of sub-objectives and the tasks needed to achieve them. A common approach uses the idea of critical paths. Some tasks will have to be completed before others can be started. For example in planning a recent walk starting on Lindisfarne, we needed to know when we were going to do the walk before we could plan the route, as we needed to find out the tide times that day and therefore when the causeway would be open.

Activity	Week	5	6	7	8	9	10	11	12	13	14	15	16	17	18	19	20	21	22	23	24	25	26	27	28	29	30
Recruit authors		▓	▓	▓																							
Allocate roles					▓																						
Draft workbooks							▓	▓	▓	▓																	
Critical reading												▓															
Redraft workbooks													▓	▓													
Send materials for client approval															▓												
Edit materials																		▓	▓	▓	▓						
Pack materials																									▓	▓	▓
Recruit video producer		▓	▓																								
Develop video plans					▓	▓																					
Arrange filming								▓	▓	▓	▓																
Film														▓	▓												
Edit																	▓										
Write video notes																						▓					
Edit video notes																								▓			

Fig. 2.3 Planning chart for course preparation

→ Ch 17

Figure 2.3 shows part of a planning chart for a course development project. (Charts of this form are called Gantt charts. You can use computer software to help you generate them. Chapter 17 discusses how to draw more complex charts, based on networks, for managing complex projects.)

Note that some of the activities cannot start until something else is completed. Workbook drafting cannot start before authors are appointed! For others there is a definite time by which they are needed. The solid part of the bar shows how much time they will take, defining the latest point at which they could be started. But they could be started much earlier if you wanted – the time period between the earliest and latest points at which they could be started is called 'slack'. This may be denoted by a broken bar or lighter shading (see Figure 2.3). You will often need to plan to use this slack in order to make full use of available time and to help you avoid scheduling more into a period than you can possibly achieve. For example, the first book I wrote had a publisher's deadline that coincided with a deadline for completing 100 pages of course material. Clearly, the last stages of each project were going to be heavily time-consuming. Trying to do both at once would have been a recipe for disaster – and probably a nervous breakdown with it. Because I was writing the book alone, whereas others were producing some of the course material for me, I brought forward the work on the book, completing it a month ahead of schedule. It would have been difficult to persuade colleagues to bring their deadlines forward for my convenience, but there was nothing to stop me rescheduling my own work. You may need to make similar 'personal schedules' with earlier deadlines than the official ones if you have several pieces of work with coinciding handover dates.

ACTIVITY 2.5

Scan the chapter headings for this book. Think about how they relate to your particular course needs. When will you need to be able to work effectively in groups? When will you use numbers or information technology? When will you need to be able to manage a project? When do you want to get a job?

Once you have worked out your own needs in relation to the topics covered, try to draw a planning chart for your work on the remainder of the book. Show any slack time as well as latest possible start dates. From this, work out a schedule for your study. File it and check your progress (or revise the plan if necessary) at intervals.

MOTIVATION

It is one thing to decide what needs to be done, but another to *do* it. You may know that it is only a month until your exam and that you really ought to start revising, but somehow it is impossible to get down to it. Or that you are becoming unfit, and need to take up a sport or start going regularly to the gym. But somehow you continue to spend your spare time in the pub drinking beer!

When I was writing this book I did not find it easy to sit at the keyboard day after day in order meet my deadline. Nor was it easy to rewrite those parts of a first draft which, on re-reading, prove far less clear than I intended. A friend finds it hard, when taking the hundredth abusive complaint, to remember that 'the customer is always right'. Yet if he does not remain courteous, there will be serious consequences for the organisation, and for his job.

Success as a manager depends on ensuring that staff for whom you are responsible are motivated to put effort into achieving whatever it is that you require them to do. Organisations can succeed or fail depending on the motivation levels of their employees. Ensuring you sustain your own motivation is, equally, an important feature of self-management.

If you are motivated you will enjoy what you are doing and will find considerable satisfaction in succeeding. And your success will motivate you to further effort. This 'virtuous circle' is significantly different from the control loop. There, the emphasis was on achieving a steady output in line with target values. Where these deviated from target, action was taken to bring them back on line. With *self*-control you can set higher targets in response to success. This increases both achievement and satisfaction. There is a 'higher-order' loop within which the basic loop is nested.

The expectancy model of motivation

Again, conceptual models can help you think about conditions which are likely to increase or decrease motivation. One such model is called the expectancy theory of motivation (Vroom, 1964; Lawler and Porter, 1967). It can be viewed as a development of a 'control of effort' loop. And, as with the more general control loop, this model

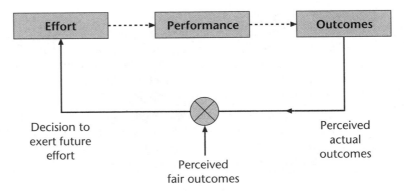

Fig. 2.4 The expectancy model of motivation

helps you to think of the components which must be included if motivation, and therefore effort, is to be present. Figure 2.4 shows a version of this model in diagrammatic form.

Reading this diagram, you immediately notice differences from the basic control loop. There is not one 'black box' – a mysterious 'process' – but two named boxes, *effort* and *performance*. The *outcomes*, to be sensed (and evaluated against what is deemed fair or appropriate), are rewards and punishments or costs and benefits. Because what is important here is the link between performance and outcomes, they are shown as a third box, rather than as a line as in the standard diagram. All three boxes constitute important elements in motivation. The decision to exert effort is the manifestation of motivation – the unmotivated will not bother, the motivated will exert considerable effort. It is the remainder of the loop that determines which is the case.

The next important thing to notice is that the arrows joining effort to performance and performance to outcomes are dotted rather than solid. This is to make the point that it is the *subjective* link, the connection that a person believes to exist rather than any objective reality, which affects motivation. The decision to exert effort depends on a belief that the effort will result in performance and that performance will be rewarded.

If you believe that you will fail no matter how hard you try, you will not make the effort to succeed. (Remember the 'A' in SMART; this is the same point. Objectives which are not achievable will not be motivating. Effort will not be 'wasted' in trying to achieve them.) How many times have you not even tried something because you didn't think you'd be able to do it? Similarly, if you feel that no matter how well you perform there will be no reward for performing – or worse, that performance will be punished – then you will again regard effort directed towards that performance as wasted.

This may all seem fairly obvious, but it is a far more complex view of motivation than is held by many managers. And the expectancy framework provides a good basis for exploring why people are, or are not, motivated and just what they are motivated to do. Is motivation low because people do not believe that they can achieve the required performance. If so, why? Do they feel that 'rewards' are not dependent on performance? If not, are the intended 'rewards' of little or no value to the person rewarded? Indeed, 'rewards' can be disincentives on occasion.

For example, when my son was nine the local authority decided to discourage absence by 'rewarding' all children who had not missed a day of school in the year. They were invited to a special ceremony in the town hall, received a certificate and their names were read out in assembly. Ever after, my son (and I suspect many others in the '100% club') was 'ill' for a day fairly soon after the school year started so that he could be sure to avoid this 'reward' in future. Adults may similarly differ in what they perceive as rewarding and what as punishing. Being singled out for managerial praise may be something to be avoided in a coherent and 'negative' workgroup.

Maslow's hierarchy of needs

Another model helps with understanding what is likely be rewarding, and hence motivating. The first principle here is that something is satisfying if it meets a need, and therefore motivation stems from needs. A clinical psychologist called Abraham Maslow (1943) suggested a categorisation of needs that is still widely quoted today. There are many other such lists of motives, but Maslow's has the virtues of simplicity and a fair degree of logic, apart from being familiar to almost anyone who has studied management. He suggested that human needs could be classified into:

- self-actualisation needs
- esteem needs
- love needs
- safety needs
- physiological needs.

Furthermore, Maslow suggested that the list above is a hierarchy. Needs lower on the list are stronger than those higher up. Until they are met, any higher needs will not operate. This makes excellent evolutionary sense. If you are starving, your first priority is to find food, and you will take risks you would not take if better fed. Reproductive success is linked to status

It is probably not worth paying too much attention to this idea of hierarchy – for most people, physiological and safety needs are likely to be met. But if you run out of money you may find your motivation to put in overtime on a part-time job is higher than your motivation to polish an essay (esteem/self-actualisation?).

Intrinsic and extrinsic motivation

Expectancy theory suggests two categories of outcome, *intrinsic* and *extrinsic*. Extrinsic outcomes are those separate from the performance itself. They might be pay, praise, promotion or whatever. If you reward yourself with a Mars bar when you finish writing an essay, this is an extrinsic reward. Intrinsic outcomes are those which stem from the performance itself and the sense of achievement which it gives. Simply knowing that what you have written 'hangs together' and contains some telling arguments can in itself be powerfully rewarding.

How then can you arrange for work – whether paid employment or study – to offer possibilities of intrinsic motivation? The first point is to ensure that you have a strong perceived effort–performance link. Not only must objectives be clear, and believed to be achievable, but other conditions must be met. The resources you need (time, tools, information) must be available and you must have the necessary skills. (This is where some of the other chapters in this book may help – they will address areas where you may feel your skills need to be improved to increase your chances of successful performance.)

The second step is to ensure that the necessary conditions exist for performance to lead to intrinsic outcomes. One set of conditions suggested (Hackman and Lawler, 1971) is that jobs should feature four core dimensions if they are to have scope for satisfying those motivated by higher-order needs. These dimensions are:

- variety
- autonomy
- task identity – this is the extent to which tasks have a clear beginning, middle and end
- feedback on performance.

It has subsequently been suggested that it is important that the job also has some sort of social value and significance.

ACTIVITY 2.6

Stop and think for a minute about what you are likely to be working on during the next week. How strongly motivated do you feel about the various tasks facing you? How can you explain this in terms of the conditions necessary for motivation, as described above? What can you do to strengthen your motivation in the light of your analysis?

You may have realised that by breaking things down into sub-tasks with their own targets, as you did in the exercise on hierarchies of objectives, you can greatly increase task identity. Thinking of sub-tasks in the context of the wider enterprise can increase significance. Writing this book is a clearly defined task, but the timescale is so long that there would be few satisfactions along the road if I did not set myself shorter-term tasks such as completing single chapters. As each is completed and printed and filed (paper is far more visible and satisfying than a computer file), I feel a sense of achievement and am motivated to keep working. But I also check each off against a list of chapters for the whole book, thus retaining the wider sense of significance.

I vary the work by mixing writing fairly straightforward chapters with reading material relevant to other chapters which are harder to plan and write, or talking to other people to check their views on a topic. I also alternate between writing the first draft of some chapters and redrafting others written earlier. In the work context, if you are designing jobs for others, variety is an important factor to consider. If possible, the variety should come from doing different parts of a whole task. This increases task identity as well. If it is variety for variety's sake – lots of different, unrelated things – it can be of limited usefulness in increasing the motivating potential of a job. Did your suggestions for improvements include any increase in variety? If not, think now whether this might be possible.

→ Ch 9 Reading my own work also gives me feedback. Provided I can leave a decent interval between writing and re-reading, I can be fairly critical of my work – but also sometimes pleasantly surprised at how something has worked. Try this with your own writing, but remember to build the 'decent interval' into your schedule. Of course, feedback from others is even better, as long as it is constructive (*see* Chapter 9 on how to receive – and give – feedback constructively). What other ways of increasing feedback did you think of in planning your week's work? They might have included making a checklist of sub-objectives and ticking them off when completed (visual feedback on progress), reporting to a supervisor on how you were progressing with something and getting their response, or setting yourself tests to check how well you have learned something that you are revising. Placing completed exercises from this book in a growing portfolio, and revisiting them at intervals, will give you further feedback.

Autonomy is not a problem in the case of writing this book: I have been given a fairly free hand by the publisher!

→ Ch 10 Social value is a harder dimension to exploit. In the work context, employees often do not see where their particular task fits into the bigger picture. If so, finding some way of making this clear to them can increase motivation considerably. (In your case it may help to think about your wider life objectives from time to time and relate your particular activities to these.) Feeling as if the task demands that you use skills that not everyone possesses also contributes to the sense of value. And if you are working with a group on a shared project, you can help everyone's motivation by making sure that they each clearly understand the overall purpose and relate every task completed to progress towards this. Praising and celebrating achievements (a drink when the first stage is completed?) can also be highly motivating.

In fact, your work as a student, provided that you *do* regard it as part of a wider learning enterprise, has the potential to be far more rewarding than the jobs in which many people spend their entire lives. It is more under your control, you do get feedback and there is a degree of task identity. Furthermore, you should be 'self-actualising' and developing your potential more intensively than is possible in many jobs.

ACTIVITY 2.7

If you are still not finding your study motivating, think very carefully about why this is. It may be that the reasons go beyond the issues covered so far. If you do have a persistent problem in this area, seek your tutor's help in addressing it as soon as possible.

TIME MANAGEMENT

Do you often feel that you have wasted time? Have you ever run out of time when working on something, or wished you had more time to do something properly? Organisations pay large sums for two- or three-day courses designed to teach time management. And yet the principles involved are amazingly simple and really only a specific case of the general principles of management discussed above. Working through them should reinforce much of what has already been said in this chapter, as well as developing an eminently transferable skill.

The difficulty lies in the discipline needed to put these principles into action. Changing habits is difficult, particularly to begin with. Once established, good time-management habits will become second nature, and life will become much better. A course can help by making you more motivated. Alternatively you can work on your time management with a group of others, so that you can support each other through the first stages.

Basic time-management principles

The basic principles are simple:

- You should direct your effort *appropriately*, that is, towards the things that are most important.
- You should direct your effort *efficiently*, that is, maximise what is achieved by the expenditure of time and energy.
- You should reduce *time wastage*.

To do this you need to *manage* your time, along the basic principles identified by Fayol: plan your use of time and be clear about your objectives, organise other resources needed, motivate yourself to exert the necessary energy and control the process, monitoring your progress to ensure that you are not slipping back into old and bad habits.

ACTIVITY 2.8

Reflect on your last week and your achievements during this period. This exercise can be applied equally to a week of paid employment, or a week working on your course. Jot down the answers to the following questions:

- How clear were you about your various objectives?
- To what extent did you achieve them?
- How many hours did you work?
- How many of these hours were spent directly on work aimed at achieving your objectives?
- If you would have liked to work more hours, what prevented you?
- For how many of these hours do you think your work was fully effective?
- What prevented you from being more effective during the hours you did work?
- Did you spend time working on something less important, leaving a more important task undone?

Save your answers in your working file. You can repeat the exercise at intervals (say every two months) to see how well you are progressing. A version is available on the website.

If this exercise suggested that you could indeed be using your time to achieve more, you need to think carefully about each of the principles and how you can put it into practice in your particular context.

Directing your effort appropriately

The main hazards in this area if you are studying tend to be:

- *Poor prioritisation,* working on something interesting and neglecting something more boring or more difficult. The neglected work may be a particular assignment, or even a whole course which you find tedious. It may be displaced by reading something fascinating, but not really necessary.

- *Aiming for unnecessary perfection.* This may apply to essays or projects, for example, and lead you to endlessly polish a piece of work, rather than handing it in and getting on with the next task.

- *Failing to clarify requirements* for an assignment and putting effort into something that is not what your lecturer or tutor wanted.

- *Failing to apportion time fairly* between different assignments set within the same time frame, working exclusively on the first one tackled for much of the time available for all of them – this is very close to the first problem.

All of these hazards arise in employment too. Additionally, managers may misdirect their effort by supervising subordinates too closely, failing to delegate or over-committing themselves by agreeing to take on more assignments than they can realistically handle. While you may encounter some of these hazards in group projects, you are even more likely to meet them at work.

Achieving better direction

The secret of avoiding misdirection is planning. Review your progress towards objectives *daily*, and think about how to make further progress. Some find this review is best done at the start of the working day, others prefer to do it just before they finish work for the day. Whichever you choose, aim to make it a regular habit. Habits save energy!

If you are over-committed, and with the best plan in the world cannot achieve what you want, think about why the situation has arisen. Talk to a tutor or supervisor and work out an emergency remedial plan as soon as you possibly can. Until the problem is resolved, most of your time and energy will go into worrying about the situation and you will feel unmotivated to do *anything* since you know you cannot do everything. Think too about how to avoid a repeat of the situation in future – this may require you

→ Ch 9 to practise assertiveness skills (*see* Chapter 9) in order to be firm in avoiding agreeing to more than is realistic.

If your review showed that you are too much of a perfectionist, do something about this. Modern definitions of quality refer to fitness for purpose, not to absolute perfection. If you bear this in mind you may find it easier to persuade yourself to settle for quality rather than perfection! When thinking about objectives, and planning how to achieve them, think very hard about how good/detailed you need something to be in order to meet learning or assessment requirements. Unless you have spare time, do not devote more time to the task than necessary.

If your review shows that you are spending time on things that are not really necessary, then think hard about whether you can afford this time. One of the joys of being a student should be the freedom to read things and pursue ideas out of pure interest and it would be a huge shame if you could not continue to do this. But your priority has to be meeting course requirements.

Most jobs have considerable scope for doing unnecessary things in the guise of work. Many people fill in unnecessary forms, file unnecessary papers and attend unnecessary meetings. If you get into the habit of questioning the necessity of work now, you may find it easier to avoid such misdirected efforts when you are in employment.

Sources of ineffectiveness

Once you are directing your effort appropriately, you need to think about how to make it more effective in terms of what you achieve. Procrastination causes many to waste effort on worrying about what they should be doing rather than getting on and doing it. Another source of ineffectiveness is lack of organisation. This might cause you to waste time hunting for mis-filed notes, or to forget to prepare an important meeting with a project supervisor. In employment the scope for being ineffective through disorganisation will be even greater!

It is ineffective to waste your 'best' times of day on unimportant or undemanding work. Most of us have daily rhythms and will be far clearer headed and more energetic at some times of day than at others. These times are precious. Try to reserve them for your most difficult work. Similarly, it is a waste of time to struggle on when you are so tired that you are getting nowhere. It may be far better to stop work for an hour, or even a day, using the time to make yourself feel better. Indeed, you may be able to increase your 'good' times significantly by simple changes such as going to the pub less often, resisting late nights during busy periods and getting more exercise. If you are seriously worried that you are achieving less than you need to, such drastic measures may have to be considered.

The other common problem is 'flitting'. Instead of working on a task long enough to make substantial progress, you switch between tasks or between task and non-task. If you allow other people to interrupt you at will, this is likely to be a problem. Getting into a task takes energy and if you are switching repeatedly, then you are wasting this 'start-up' energy. Some variety is needed for motivation, but try to not switch tasks too often.

Making effort more effective

The first requirement is obviously to be better organised. Aim to keep your desk (and floor) fairly clear – you will find that you can concentrate far better if you are not surrounded with clutter. Work out a system for keeping things needed for particular tasks together in one place. This is important whether you work with paper or keep your notes, drafts and any data electronically. If you do work primarily electronically, you must also be very disciplined about keeping backup copies of everything. The worst ineffectiveness of all is to have months of work totally lost because your computer is stolen or crashes completely. Once you *are* organised, you may be surprised at how much easier it is to work, and therefore how much more you enjoy it, as well as how much more time you have.

For more effective use of
time avoid:
■ procrastination
■ 'flitting'
■ displacement activity
■ perfection
■ poor prioritisation.

Stop devoting energy to *not* doing things. That is, find a cure for procrastination! This is easier said than done, but well worth the effort. Procrastination is the thief not just of time, but of huge amounts of energy. This is expended on thinking of excuses for not starting, all the displacement activities (making coffee, going to the library to look for something you don't really need, moaning to people about how impossible it is to get started) which you will indulge in to put off the evil day, and coping with the feeling of impending doom that comes from having a large and unstarted piece of work hanging over you.

There may be a good reason why you cannot start something. Or you may have deliberately chosen to postpone an activity. In either case, don't waste energy worrying about the task. This may be easier if you 'book the work' for some time in the future. Deciding in advance to do it at a specific time will make it much easier when that time comes simply to get started. And until that time comes, you are less likely to worry about it.

You can extend this technique to making sure that you get full value from the time when you are genuinely not working. No one can work all the time. Remember Maslow. We need exercise, sleep, food, time with our friends, time pursuing non-work interests. Scheduling your non-working time as well as your work time will help you convince yourself that it is a valid part of your time-management strategy. Time off is essential for you to maintain full effectiveness. So schedule such time and enjoy it. Don't spoil it by thinking, 'I should really be working.' Enjoying *some* time off will help you achieve your objectives.

Some tasks are so large that fear of their magnitude causes procrastination. If this is the case, try to 'divide and conquer'. This is a variant of the 'hierarchy of objectives' approach suggested earlier. If the task can be broken down into sub-tasks, each with their own objectives, then it will be much more manageable and less likely to be postponed. Completion of each sub-task will be rewarding, motivating you to continue. Even if you cannot break a job down into discrete tasks, it is still worth setting yourself the target of doing some work on the job each day. This is because during the time you are not working on something, resistance to starting actually increases, making it more and more difficult. Even a small amount of work each day or two will prevent the build-up of this negative anticipation.

Make sure that your planning includes sensible deadlines for each task, arranged so that all deadlines can be met. Remember the need for objectives to be 'T' – time defined. And remember too that often you will need to set your own deadlines ahead of official ones and stick to these. Use planning charts to help keep these in mind and to aid your motivation – colour in the relevant bar each time you complete a task!

2

Managing your studies

STRESS MANAGEMENT

You will almost certainly be subjected to stress at various points in your life. You may feel that now is one of them! Many stressors arise from life circumstances, key among these being relationship problems, shortage of money, house moves and illness of those close to you. Some physiological factors – tiredness, illness or fluctuating hormones – may reduce your ability to handle stress.

But work is another and major source of stress. This may be because you have more to do than you know how to handle, or indeed because you have far too little to do and are bored out of your mind. It may be because you lack the resources or skills or information to do what is required of you. You may even be unsure what *is* required – think back to expectancy theory and the E→P link. Or it may be because people are not supportive, snipe at you in little ways, make you feel uncomfortable, or in the worst case actually bully you. Stress in a job is a significant cause of sickness absence, because there are so many potential stressors at work. (A European Foundation for the Improvement of Living and Working Conditions survey in 2000 found that 28% of employees surveyed reported work-related stress as a health problem, and many more will say they are stressed, though not yet at a level where it impacts upon their health.)

Learn techniques for coping with stress now, and the pressures of your course will become challenges rather than something negative. You will *feel* better and *do* better. You will also be better equipped to face the pressures of employment when you graduate. (Stress levels at work are typically highest during the early stages of a new job, whether in a new organisation or after a promotion.)

→ Ch 9

Many of the techniques already described in this chapter will serve to reduce stress. Being clear about your objectives and exercising time-management skills will go a long way to making any work situation less stressful. Interpersonal skills, particularly assertiveness (covered in Chapter 9), will help too. If work is less stressful, you will be better able to handle pressures arising outside work. If you manage stress outside work better, you will be better able to handle the job. There are some things, however, which are specific to managing stress and which you need to know.

Recognising stress

Stress tends to creep up on us gradually. As it increases we become less capable of rational thought about our situation. Others may therefore be far more aware of the fact that you are stressed than you are yourself. However, there are a number of signs to watch out for. Almost all of these could have other causes, but if you show many of them, you may need to reduce your stress levels. Symptoms include:

- difficulty sleeping, lying awake worrying about things
- frequent minor ailments such as headaches or digestive problems
- asthma and/or eczema
- drinking more than is good for you
- eating problems, either eating too much or not enough

- irritability and poor judgement
- forgetting things (particularly things you should have done)
- general feeling of tenseness.

ACTIVITY 2.9

Think about how stressed you are at present. (Note: you should repeat this exercise at intervals, particularly shortly after any change in circumstances such as starting a new job.)

How did you feel this morning about the day to come? Full of eager anticipation, or with a dull sense of dread and of things to be endured?

_____

How many of the symptoms listed above do you have?

_____

As a result of thinking about these questions, rate your stress level on the following scale:

1	2	3	4	5
(low)		(medium)		(very high)

Without telling them your score, ask friends how stressed they would say you were, using the same scale. How do the scores compare? Think about what the two sets of scores suggest (a questionnaire is available on the website).

If you feel splendidly stress-free at present, and your friends agree, leave this chapter until later. But repeat the exercise above roughly every two months and resume work on the chapter if you become aware of stress levels rising. If you already feel somewhat stressed, work on.

Reducing stress

There are two strands to any approach to managing stress: reducing those stressors which you can do something about and learning how to cope better with those that are inevitable. The first step, of course, is to know which is which.

ACTIVITY 2.10

List all the pressures or other factors in your life which are contributing to your feelings of stress. Remember to consider things to do with your life in general, with your work in particular and physical factors such as ill health. Divide them into those things which might be capable of being changed and those which you can do nothing whatsoever about. (This may not always be easy. For example, you may be able to do nothing about having insufficient money – unless there is the possibility of earning some more – but may be able to do something about what you are spending it on and therefore how much is available for essentials!)

Things you can do something about

Once you have identified stressors which might be reduced, think about possible ways of doing something about them. You might find it helpful to work with one or two friends on this, to come up with a wider range of ideas and increase your motivation to take some action. The creativity ideas in Chapter 15 will be useful.

→ Ch 15

> **ACTIVITY 2.11**
>
> Work out an action plan, with deadlines, for reducing your stress levels. You may find it beneficial to use a hierarchy of objectives as a step in this. File this, and monitor progress towards your objective(s). Revise plans where necessary to achieve your overall objective of stress reduction. A description of this 'campaign', if not too personal, would be an excellent item to include in a portfolio of evidence of transferable skills. It would show planning and control skills and might also, depending on your chosen actions, show effective time-management and interpersonal skills, as well as an understanding of, and ability to practise, one important aspect of stress management.

Coping with the inevitable

Many features on your list may be things you can do nothing whatsoever about. But this does not mean that you can't become better at dealing with them. The three main approaches to coping with the inevitable are:

- changing your attitudes
- learning to relax
- becoming physically better able to cope.

Attitude change is not easy to achieve but is important. The old prayer asks for the strength to change what can be changed, the patience to endure what must be endured and the wit to know the difference. I hope you are now more aware of the difference, and no longer wasting energy on trying to change what cannot be changed. Wishing things were different or trying to achieve the impossible can also waste energy. Are you setting yourself unrealistic targets? If so, realise that you don't have to be superman/woman. Being yourself, with your own ability levels, is actually worthwhile: the world needs very few 'superhumans'.

Cope with unavoidable stress by:
- acceptance
- relaxation
- exercise
- good food
- sleep.

Similarly, don't rail against fate or regret past decisions: accept where you are and do the best with that. If a decision *can* be retaken, consider the cost of doing so and whether you are prepared to pay. Perhaps you chose a wrong programme of study. Can you change that choice, perhaps by repeating a year? If so, do you want this enough actually to do it? If not, what can you do to maximise the benefits of your original choice? Above all, do not expend precious energy on what might have been but cannot be. A close friend of mine lost a daughter in a road accident. She said that the hardest thing was to stop thinking 'if only'. If only she had said something to prevent her going out, if only her own car had been repaired and she had not needed to accept a lift. I hope your regrets will be about lesser things. But if you stop thinking 'if only' you will still reduce your stress levels.

Relaxation techniques can be enormously helpful, but need to be learned. You cannot relax on demand if you have not developed the skill. There are good self-help tapes available. You may be able to find a short course which teaches relaxation. Meditation and yoga also help. If you feel stressed by things which you cannot change, it would be well worth learning some form of relaxation technique.

Finding a relaxation course is best, but if no suitable course is on offer, the following extremely basic approach may help. Find a quiet room with low levels of lighting where you can be alone, or with others wishing to practise relaxation. Sit comfortably or lie down. Think about your breathing, trying to keep it fairly slow and regular. You may wish to focus your thoughts on your diaphragm. Gently discard any thoughts that float into your mind. Return your thoughts to your breathing each time. If you prefer a visual image, instead of your breathing (though keep this slow and regular) focus on a picture in your mind. A lily, rippling water, a cliff top, anything which you can 'see' clearly in your mind and which means peace to you. If you are not a visual person, then repeating a short 'peaceful' phrase over and over in time with your breathing may help more. Again, whether using an image or phrase, gently put aside other thoughts which surface, returning each time to the focus of your concentration.

When you have finished your relaxation, 'surface' gently. Get up slowly, move around slowly, let your thoughts gently come back, rather than instantly rushing around. Practise this concentration for five minutes at first. Eventually, build up to 15 to 20 minutes per day.

Simpler forms of relaxation include a long hot bath, perhaps with a few drops of pure lavender or other relaxing essential oil added. Listen to music, or read poetry or a novel for pleasure. It is an excellent idea to programme some 'unwinding' time when you finish work, before going to bed. This is not wasting a study opportunity. You will be using time in which you would probably have been too tired to achieve much. And it will ensure a far better night's sleep than you would otherwise have had. This will leave you in a position to achieve more the next day. If despite your relaxation time you still feel under too much pressure to find sleep coming easily, a few drops of lavender oil (if you buy only one oil this is the one to get) on a tissue by your pillow can help a lot.

Keeping in good physical shape is essential if you are to cope with pressure without feeling stressed. Eating a healthy diet (as fresh as possible and with the emphasis on fruit and vegetables, with animal proteins and fats as accompaniments rather than the focus of a meal) is important. All too often we eat unsuitably (chocolate bars, crisps, biscuits) or drink unsuitably (more than the recommended alcohol unit intake per week) *because* we feel stressed and yet this makes us less able to cope with stress. Indeed, worry about food or alcohol may itself become a source of stress, another example of a vicious circle.

Physical exercise is excellent for reducing stress, counteracting depression and making you better able to use your brain effectively. It is not important what exercise you choose, as long as it raises a sweat for half an hour or so. What is important is that you do something you like doing, as you really need to exercise two or three times a week as a minimum. If you spend this long walking briskly or cycling to lectures, then any further exercise will be a bonus. If you take no exercise as part of your routine, then you need to experiment with swimming, jogging, a ball game or longer walks at weekends – or of course a mixture of these things. Exercising with friends is not only more fun, but means that on the evenings when you feel too tired (most evenings?) to go and do it, you will have to go anyway, or let them down. Once you get there, you will almost certainly enjoy it, so the initial pressure will have been worthwhile.

If you have not exercised recently, start gently. If you overdo it, you will build up a subconscious resistance to further exercise that will be almost impossible to overcome. So deliberately start by doing less than you feel you could manage. And avoid being competitive while you are building up to full fitness. There is always a temptation to 'prove' something, by running further or faster than is comfortable, or trying to beat someone at squash who is far fitter than you are. This will not only cause the psychological resistance just mentioned, but will also put you at serious risk of injury, which will set back your plans considerably.

Sleep is important for good health too. You will find that if you exercise more you will probably sleep better. But if exercising in the evening allow time afterwards for relaxation before bed.

ACTIVITY 2.12

If you did not use stress management as the basis of an 'exhibit' for your file, and are not taking enough exercise, then consider using this as an example of target setting and self-management. Work out an exercise plan, set yourself interim targets and monitor progress towards them. Adjust targets if experience shows them to have been too hard or too easy, and comment on these adjustments. (Do this with one or two friends if at all possible, to increase your chance of success.) Keep your original plans, revised plans and achievements, together with comments, in your portfolio.

If you are exercising, but are aware of not eating or drinking for optimal health, then set targets for this and document progress towards your targets. (If this is more of a threat to your well-being than low exercise levels, you might like to start with this exercise anyway.)

SUMMARY

This chapter has argued the following:

■ Management is about effective use of resources to achieve objectives.
■ You need to manage your own time, energy and other resources to be successful as a student and in employment.
■ The principles of self-management in either case are broadly similar to those of management as more generally understood – the management of other people.
■ Applying basic conceptual models (the control loop, the expectancy model and the

idea of a hierarchy of needs) can help you understand how to improve your personal management, and show, more generally, how models can aid analysis.

- The first essential is to be clear about objectives. Ideally, targets will be specific, will be measurable and will have a time specified for their attainment.

- There also needs to be a way of measuring ongoing progress. This will enable you to monitor the extent to which you are on track and to take corrective action if you find things are not going to plan.

- This ongoing monitoring will help you keep your motivation high, as will objectives that are achievable but challenging, and which will bring rewards if achieved.

- Time is a finite and usually scarce resource. Successful self-management will therefore involve good time management: you need to check that objectives are clear and appropriate, make sure that your efforts are directed efficiently, so that you gain the maximum result for your effort, and check that you are not indulging in activities which waste time.

- It can be surprisingly difficult to change habits, and developing good time management usually requires sustained and conscious effort until new habits are established.

- Stress is a common feature of both university and working life. Causes include relationship difficulties, health problems, money worries and time pressures. Symptoms may be physical (e.g. sleep or health problems), behavioural (e.g. drinking or eating problems), mental (e.g. difficulty concentrating) or emotional (e.g. irritability).

- Remedies for stress involve reducing sources of stress where possible and increasing your ability to cope with unavoidable stress through, for example, exercise, relaxation and attitude change.

Further information

- Adair, J. and Allen, M. (2003) *The Concise Time Management and Personal Development*, Thorogood.
- Bird, P. (1998) *Teach Yourself Time Management*, Hodder Arnold Teach Yourself.
- Caunt, J. (2000) *Organise Yourself*, Kogan Page.
- Clegg, B. (1999) *Instant Time Management*, Kogan Page.
- Lifeskills International (1999) *Staying Healthy at Work*, Gower. This addresses stress, physical health, interpersonal relations and lifestyle planning.

2

Managing your studies

→ 3   The learning process

Good grades come from knowing what and how to learn. This chapter will help you to understand the learning process, recognise your own preferred learning style and develop your learning skills. You will then gain better grades, and be able to maximise the learning potential of any situation you meet at work.

Learning outcomes

By the end of this chapter you should:

- have a better idea of what 'learning' means
- appreciate the difference between knowledge, concepts, skills and competence
- understand what is meant by learning style and recognise your own preferred style
- have started to develop less preferred styles
- understand the role of feedback in the development of both practical and conceptual skills
- have explored the learning opportunities offered by your degree programme, identified any gaps and be starting to plan to fill these
- be developing a systematic approach to evidencing skills relevant to employment.

You have been learning since you were born, but most of the time you will not have been aware of the process. As you work through this chapter you will become more aware of how you learn, and will start to apply your developing self-management skills to improve your learning both on your course and outside it. Managers who know how they learn, and who go on learning, are far more effective than colleagues who lack this awareness.

LEARNING THEORY

Children are voracious learners, eager to master walking and talking and a host of other skills. They learn which people are important to them, how not to upset them (and how to infuriate them too). They learn to play games, to read and to manage their pocket money. As a child, you were probably seldom aware that you were learning, despite the rate at which you were doing so. You know that the official objective of higher education is to foster learning. You will hear the phrase 'lifelong learning' on the lips of politicians and many others. But how often do people look in detail at what helps and hinders the process? Indeed, what exactly *is* learning?

ACTIVITY 3.1

Write a brief definition of learning as you understand it. Discuss this with some other people if possible. Unless you have all just done a course on 'learning' which included an approved definition, you may be surprised at the range of possible ways of understanding the term.

_____

_____

_____

Traditionally, learning was seen as acquiring knowledge. There are still countries where 'education' even at university level consists of telling students things and then testing that they can repeat them. The underlying metaphor is of 'jug and mug', with the 'knowledge' being poured from the jug (lecturer) to the mug (you). Yet in many situations, academic knowledge is not enough. You may *know* that to ride a bicycle you sit on the saddle and use your feet to turn the pedals and your hands to steer via the handlebars. But this knowledge would not stop you falling off the first time you tried to ride. Being able to *do* things is also important. Beyond both, there is the ability to *understand* and interpret situations and respond effectively, even if the situation is different from any you have yet encountered.

It is this learning of *conceptual* skills that is most exciting. And for this, the passive mug metaphor is singularly inappropriate. Learning conceptual skills is necessarily an *active* and continuous process, not a one-off operation performed on a passive recipient. Some 50 years ago, Krishnamurti approached the idea of learning from a very different background and for a different purpose, but came to a similar conclusion. He wrote of a psychological learning which goes beyond the accumulation of knowledge or the acquisition of skills. For example, he says:

> *Learning is one thing and acquiring knowledge is another. Learning is a continuous process, not a process of addition. Most of us gather knowledge as memory, as idea, store it up as experience . . . we act from knowledge, technological knowledge, knowledge as experience, knowledge as tradition, knowledge that one has derived through one's particular idiosyncratic tendencies. . . . In that process there is no learning. Learning is never accumulative, it is a constant movement. . . . You learn as you are going along.*
> (Krishnamurti, 1995, meditation for 12 January)

Refer to your definition of learning above. Did it include *skills* as well as *knowledge*? Was there any reference to understanding, or to a conceptual dimension? One workable definition of the sort of learning that this book addresses, though it has an accumulative dimension that could be seen to conflict with the view quoted above, is:

> *learning is purposeful activity aimed at acquisition of skills, knowledge and ways of thinking that improve effectiveness in future situations.*

This begs many questions about what constitutes effectiveness and which situations are relevant, but it teases out a number of dimensions that it will be useful to explore. It covers the three aspects of knowledge, skills and thinking. It also highlights the need to *use* what is learned and implies that others will only know that you *have* learned by observing your more effective behaviour. (You might, subjectively, know that you have learned something because you are aware of increased understanding, but others will need you to translate this into something – words or action – that they can observe.)

ACTIVITY 3.2

Rewrite your definition, taking these ideas into account. There is no need to use exactly the words above. Try to find a way of defining learning that feels right to you, as a reflection of what you now think learning is. Then think of three recent instances when you have felt you learned something of significance and check that each would be learning according to your definition. Note your thoughts below:

_____

_____

_____

Competence and vocational qualifications

In the UK, and some other countries, it was increasingly realised from the early 1980s that the important issue at work is what you can *do*, rather than merely what you *know*. This led to a profound change in the approach to vocational and professional training and qualifications, and the construction of a set of National Vocational Qualifications (NVQs, or SVQs in Scotland). Each of these qualifications is based on a set of occupational standards deemed to constitute competent performance at various levels within the occupation or profession. Organisations frequently construct their own set of standards, or competence frameworks, and use them as the basis for their recruitment and employee development. Professional institutes may also base their assessment of candidates for membership on a set of standards.

Although there is still not a single agreed definition of 'competence' in the abstract, a working one is:

> *competence is an underlying characteristic of a person, a mix of motives, traits and skills, leading to effective or superior job performance.*

→ Ch 2

The British competence movement has tended to emphasise 'effective' performance, the USA preferring 'superior'. This definition begs even more questions than the definition of learning, but note the emphasis on skills and performance rather than merely knowledge. This links back to the 'improved effectiveness' that is part of the earlier definition of learning. The reference to motives also links with the previous chapter. Although in many situations competence will depend on underlying knowledge and understanding, it is the resulting performance that is critical.

Assessment for competence-based qualifications is therefore based on evidence of performance relating to the different elements of competence deemed important for that qualification. Candidates are asked to assemble a portfolio demonstrating their competence against each element of the standards. Throughout the book, you will be asked to file the results of activities directed towards developing (and demonstrating) your skills. This will result in a portfolio you can draw upon if you decide to seek a competence-based qualification, or for evidence to impress potential employers. It will give you a greater understanding of how to assemble such a portfolio, and practice in assembling evidence. This is in addition to the main purpose of the activities, which is to help you to *develop* the competences involved and appreciate their potential for use in job applications.

There are many different sets of standards, each complex and detailed, and all will be updated at intervals. There is therefore little point in trying to spell out all the elements of any one. Most sets of standards will reflect a wide range of employer views and can therefore be a useful guide to the skills that you will need in a job. This is particularly true of the GNVQ (General National Vocational Qualifications) key skills, which were designed to be 'portable' and relate to many different occupations. Because this shift towards 'competence' has been one of the most significant changes in approach to education, training, assessment and recruitment in recent years, it is worth understanding the basic principles

The approach provides a useful complement to more traditional teaching methods. An appreciation of the way in which complex skills can be broken down into elements, and how they can be assessed using separate pieces of evidence, will help your learning in general. It will also increase your chances of producing 'exhibits' which could be used for this purpose should you so wish. The GNVQ key skill 'improve own learning and performance' (1996) will be used to develop this understanding.

What are you learning now?

→ Ch 1

What more do you need to learn than the 'facts' about your chosen subject? How are you becoming potentially more *effective*? The first chapter suggested some things that the government and employers think you should be learning – key skills to do with communication, working with others, using numbers, using IT, problem solving and, of course, 'learning to learn' in the applied sense of improving your own learning and performance in any situation. If you have never thought about the wider learning that your student experience offers, it is worth taking time for a brief audit of this. By the end of the book you should have a clearer understanding of the range of possible transferable skills and be able to update and expand your audit. Do not therefore spend too long on the following exercise. Regard it as a rough first draft.

ACTIVITY 3.3

Think about the courses you are studying this year. What broad areas of specialist knowledge do they address? What skills specific to your subject will you also be developing? Which of the above key skills can you develop within your studies? (For example, you can practise communication skills in class discussions, in negotiating extensions to deadlines with your tutor and in writing assignments. You can practise team skills when working with others on this book, or on group projects.)

List the things that you think you are currently learning. Leave space beneath each to write other things, and file this for future use. If there are key skills which you are *not* learning, for example if you have managed to avoid touching a computer or if there is no group work, log these on a separate list. Log also anything which you think you are supposed to be learning, but for some reason are not.

Some difficulty with this exercise is inevitable if you are not yet used to thinking of such a wide range of learning and have not reflected on your own learning before. Don't worry – it will have raised questions in your mind that you will be able to answer later and highlighted areas that you need to think more about.

Kolb's theory

Even for specialist knowledge, an employer would probably be interested in your ability to use, rather than merely recite, what you know. Application is crucial, but something many students find difficult. The skill of applying conceptual frameworks is hardest of all. Yet it is crucial to the sort of learning you need from your studies

Employers expect graduates to be able to *understand* problematic situations in order to respond appropriately. When the context changes you cannot simply do what you successfully did before. To adapt to a new situation you need to understand what you were doing in the old one, and why it worked there.

Organisational life is complex, and you need conceptual frameworks to help you make sense of it. Some of these frameworks or sets of assumptions you will already be using, probably without being aware of them. Kolb recognised the importance of these 'theories' and of the role of conscious reflection in their development. He suggested (Kolb *et al.*, 1984) a model of how ideas and experience are integrated, with learning a circular rather than a one-off process of making sense of things. You do something, reflect on your experience, try to conceptualise it and then test these concepts through more experience. Figure 3.1 shows a simplified version of this process.

Several points come out of this simple model. First, learning is shown as an *active* process. Action generates 'experience' of the results of action, which is food for reflection. This reflection involves trying to make sense of experience in the light of existing ideas and understanding. 'Theorising' involves changing your ideas in order to make better sense of the experience. You then do something to test your improved theories, applying them in another context and seeing whether experience of the results of your action is as expected. By going round the loop again and

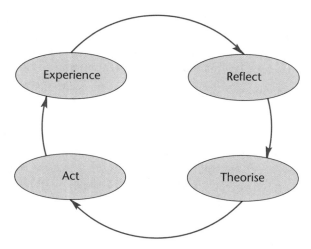

Fig. 3.1 Learning as a continuous process (adapted from Kolb)

again as you have new experiences, you can continue to develop your understanding.

If parts of the process are missing, learning will not take place. You could do something ineffectively for years if you never stop and think about how you might do it better. Experience without reflection will teach you nothing. A friend works for an appallingly bad manager. For decades he has never questioned the ways in which he operates. Indeed he is completely unaware of the 'theories' or assumptions on which his behaviour is based. As far as he is concerned, the way he thinks is the only possible way: anyone who disagrees with him has to be stupid or perverse.

One belief is that a subordinate should account to his manager for every moment. Yet the job is one which requires thinking, networking and other 'invisible' activities for success. The 'control is all' assumption of this boss is making it impossible for my friend to perform. He and the rest of the team are currently actively seeking other jobs, purely because of this ineffective boss and his faulty assumptions.

Theory unlinked to past experience and untested in new contexts is equally unlikely to contribute to competence development too. (In the 1980s most of those on MBA programmes were recent graduates. They tended to be avoided like the plague by most employers.) This is why work experience is a crucial part of an undergraduate business studies degree.

LEARNING STYLES

So if learning is to be effective, and it is vital for your studies and for your subsequent career that it is, feedback and reflection on experience are vital. You need to work to ensure that you get feedback on what you do, and on how you think, and to constantly reflect on your practice and the experience that results. But although this much is true for everyone, people vary in the way they learn, and it is essential to understand your own learning style. There are many different approaches to classifying learning styles. For example, Drucker (1999), suggested that some people learn best by listening, some by reading, some by writing and some by doing.

This may link with the suggestion (see, for example, Andreas and Faulkner's 1996 book on Neuro-Linguistic Programming, or NLP) that people vary in their dominant sense. Some will talk in terms of 'I hear what you are saying', 'Tell me what . . .', 'That sounds as if' . . . For these people, the auditory sense is strongest, and they will presumably learn by listening. Others say things like 'Show me . . .', 'I see what you mean . . .', or 'It looks as if . . .'. For them, vision is strongest, so they presumably would learn best by watching, or perhaps reading. Yet others will say 'It feels as if . . .', 'I can't quite grasp . . .', or 'You need to touch on . . .'. For them, the kinaesthetic sense is important, and presumably they would be the ones who would learn in a 'hands on', or 'doing' fashion.

ACTIVITY 3.4

Observe one or two friends talking for a while, noting whether they use 'seeing', 'hearing', or 'doing' words most. Once you have identified their dominant sense, ask them how they feel they learn best. If possible, then ask them to observe you and identify your own sense dominance. If not, observe yourself – it will be easier once you have sensitised yourself by watching them. Think about the implications of this for your own learning and note them in your file.

Honey and Mumford (1986) suggested that another way of classifying people is in terms of the stages in the Kolb cycle. Although all of the stages are necessary for learning, they suggest that people tend to be happier with some stages of the loop than others. They identified four different *learning styles* which reflect these preferences and developed an inventory to help people to identify their own. There are strengths and weaknesses associated with each style. You can get a 'quick and dirty' approximation of your own preferred style from the following. If you are really interested in your own style you should obtain the full inventory. (Your institution may have rights to use this.)

ACTIVITY 3.5

Think about each of the following statements. Check the one that is most characteristic of your own reaction to a learning situation:

1 I am game to try it – let's get started. ☐
2 I need some time to think about this. ☐
3 What are the basic assumptions? ☐
4 What is the use of this? ☐

Activists

If you chose **1** you may tend towards activism. If so, you are probably open-minded and love new experiences, get bored easily, are highly sociable, love group decisions and bring welcome energy to a task. You are probably not very good at things which require consolidation, or indeed anything which requires sustained effort – even sitting through a lecture may be difficult. Producing a dissertation or other sustained piece of work will be extremely hard for you. You will scorn caution and tend to jump into things without enough thought. Other group members may feel you don't give them a chance in discussions and you may miss opportunities to learn from other people's experience.

Reflectors

If you chose **2** you may be a reflector, preferring to think about all possible angles before reaching a decision, taking a low profile in discussions, cautious and unwilling to leap to premature conclusions. You will thrive on dissertations, provided you do not spend far too long on planning, leaving no time for data collection and writing. You will be a great asset as an observer of others and provide useful feedback, but may not take opportunities to get feedback yourself.

Theorists

If you chose **3** you may be a theorist, approaching problems logically, step by step, analysing and synthesising, establishing basic assumptions, insisting on a rational approach. You probably hate uncertainty and will have trouble with the chapter on creativity, while loving complex problems which have a clear structure. You will hate having to work with problems where you do not have all the information you need, or where some of the factors can be assessed only subjectively. You may find it infuriating to work with people with a strongly activist style. You will love the more theoretical aspects of your courses, but when you come to apply them in a real situation you may be somewhat at a loss.

Pragmatists

If you chose **4** you will love new ideas *provided* you can put them into practice. You will hate open-ended discussion and love problems and the search for a better way of doing things. Theoretical aspects of your courses may leave you cold, but you will really enjoy any skills development as long as there is adequate feedback on performance. You will prefer learning from case study discussions to sitting through lectures and, if you are a part-time student, will benefit greatly from the chance to apply what you are learning to your job. You may tend to leap to practical solutions to problems without thinking about either the conceptual underpinning of what you are doing, or whether a more creative approach might be possible.

Any simple classification of something as complex as learning will be an over-simplification. And the self-assessment questions above are crude. If you want a more accurate picture you need to work through the full inventory. But the strengths and weaknesses identified above suggest that if you have a strong tendency to one learning style you need to be aware of its associated risks and plan ways of coping with these. Furthermore, it is worth seeing whether you can become a more effective learner by developing some of the strengths of your non-preferred styles. Your years as a student offer you an ideal opportunity to do this. The following exercise is designed to help. You will need to do the suggested activities over a period of time, in parallel with other work.

ACTIVITY 3.6

Decide which styles you need to develop. Choose at least six of the following activities and make an action plan for carrying them out. Monitor your progress at regular intervals. Describe your experience of each in your file. This could constitute a useful demonstration of your ability to learn.

To develop activism

1 Do something completely out of character at least once a week (examples: talk to strangers, wear something outrageous, go to a new place).

2 Force yourself to fragment your day, switching deliberately from one activity to another.

3 Force yourself to take a more prominent role in discussions. Determine to say something in the first ten minutes. Volunteer to take the chair or make the next presentation.

4 Practise thinking aloud. Next time you are thinking about a problem, bounce ideas off a friend, trying to get into the habit of speaking without thinking first.

To develop reflection

1 In discussions, practise observing what other people are saying and doing and thinking about why (this will be useful in Chapter 10).

2 Spend some time each evening reflecting on what you have done during the day and what you have learned from it. These notes could usefully be kept in your file.

3 Aim to submit a perfect essay/assignment next time. Do several drafts, trying to get appearance and spelling, as well as content, as good as you possibly can.

4 Select a topic you have covered in your course that really interests you, try to find out as much as possible about it and write a short paper summarising this. (If you have the opportunity to speak about your findings, this will link to work on presentation in Chapter 11.)

5 Before taking any decision, force yourself to draw up as wide as possible a list of pros and cons.

To become more of a theorist

1 Spend at least 30 minutes a day reading something really difficult about one of your subjects, trying to analyse and evaluate the arguments involved.

2 If you hit a problem, whether in your studies or elsewhere, try to identify all the causal factors involved, and work out how they were related and what might have averted the problem.

3 Before taking any action, ensure that you are absolutely clear about what you are trying to achieve. Having clarified your objectives, see what you can do to increase your chances of success.

4 Listen to what people are saying in discussions, trying to identify any dubious assumptions or faulty links in their arguments.

5 Practise asking a series of probing questions, persisting until you get an answer that is clear and logical.

To become more of a pragmatist

1 When you discuss a problem, make sure that before stopping you have agreed what needs to be done, and who will do it, in order to make things better.

2 *Do* the practical exercises in this book!

3 Ensure that you get feedback on the skills you are practising in the exercises.

4 Tackle some practical problem (examples: mending clothes or appliances, choosing and booking a holiday, cooking a meal for friends)

You will find that working through this book will itself help you to develop all four styles to some extent, provided you do all the activities suggested!

IMPROVING LEARNING AND PERFORMANCE BY MANAGING THE LEARNING PROCESS

Expanding the range of learning styles which you can use will improve your ability to learn. So too will an understanding of the ways in which you learn most easily. But you need also to *manage* your learning, using the self-management skills and the classic control model introduced in the last chapter. It is this approach, with its emphasis on identifying learning needs, setting targets and monitoring of progress, that is at the heart of the key skill of 'improving own learning and performance'. As was indicated earlier, the competence approach tries to break skills down into constituent parts. In this case, the skill can be seen as two elements:

→ Ch 2

■ identify targets
■ follow schedule to meet targets.

Targets need to be CSMART objectives (challenging, as well as the other criteria) which are fairly short term (i.e. achievable within three months) but which contribute to your

3

The learning process

achieving longer-term personal or career objectives. They should be based on an accurate assessment of strengths and weaknesses (and adequate evidence), should be agreed with your tutor, supervisor or other appropriate person and regularly reviewed. These agreed targets need to be detailed as an action plan, with dates for achieving them shown. Dates for review of targets need to be included and any revisions as a result of review should be indicated, together with the reasons for change being needed.

Thus a portfolio 'exhibit' to demonstrate that you are competent in this area would have to include not only the action plan and annotations, but also a report which communicated your understanding of this whole process, for example detail on how strengths and weaknesses were identified, who agreed targets and why this person was appropriate. It would need to be clear that targets were indeed CSMART.

To show that you have *implemented* the plan according to schedule, using a combination of pure study and learning activities of different kinds and a range of learning materials, for example some computer-based, prioritising activities in order to make the best progress possible, you would need to report on how you did this. You would need to show that you did indeed meet your targets and that you used support from others effectively, though you were not totally reliant on such support, and that you applied feedback on your performance, from supervisors, other students or colleagues, to help you learn. You would need also to show that you chose activities which were appropriate to the strengths and weaknesses you identified when setting your targets.

Showing that you had done all these things satisfactorily would probably be more complicated than showing that you could set targets and plan. Again, you would need to include a commentary describing and justifying all the aspects outlined above, for example your chosen priorities and learning activities, and the support you sought and obtained.

LEARNING OPPORTUNITIES AND HOW TO EXPLOIT THEM

By now you should realise that learning is a continuous process, with feedback as a key component. Whether you think in terms of the control loop or the Kolb cycle, there is some process of sensing results of actions and modifying thinking and/or behaviour as a result. As almost any situation will offer the scope for such feedback, almost any experience offers the potential for learning. But there is an important first step. You need to want to learn, and this means accepting that you are not yet perfect and all-knowing! This may sound obvious in theory, but can be quite difficult in practice.

→ Ch 9   Chapter 9 makes it clearer why. It is very comfortable to see yourself as competent, and doing an excellent job. If things do go wrong it is easy to blame other people, or outside factors.

Should someone suggest that there might be room for improvement you see it as a slur on your competence and reject their point. (Yes, but . . .) Just stop for a minute to check that you are not already saying that, while this point may relate to others, *you* would never act in this way yourself! It takes a reasonable degree of self-confidence to admit that we are not perfect. And many people are more insecure than they like to admit, even to themselves. People who are unsure of themselves will learn much less in steady-state situations: they will not dare to examine their own behaviour and seek feedback on how they can improve. To make matters worse, they will probably avoid unfamiliar situations. Yet new situations and new challenges normally offer far greater learning opportunities than the steady state. Welcoming the new is an important aspect of creativity.

→ Ch 15

More prosaically, if you actively seek new situations, you are likely to progress faster in any job than the person who stays with the safe, familiar, 'official' role. This is because of the new skills and understanding and confidence that come from taking on the new challenge. Of course you need to understand your strengths and weaknesses. You will lose respect if you push to be allowed to do something way beyond your capacities. Instead, offer to do small extra jobs when a superior is busy, or to cover for a colleague who is sick. Take on a challenging, but realistic, project. Such things will be noticed by those who can influence your progress, as well as providing material for your CV.

If you have always 'played it safe' you can usefully work at improving both your confidence and your motivation to learn. As a student you are in a relatively safe and supportive learning environment. You can take 'risks' very safely. So use the opportunity to experiment with non-preferred learning styles and to practise things you feel unsure about. If you are shy, force yourself to make contributions to group discussions and to make as many presentations as possible. If you hate IT try to use as many of the bells and whistles on your computer as you can. Sign up for an optional course that you think you will find really difficult. Your confidence will be boosted by trying – and succeeding at – something you thought would be almost impossible. And your desire to learn will also grow.

Work experience

Explore the opportunities for gaining work experience as soon as possible if your experience is limited. Practising your transferable skills in a range of different contexts will help you develop them to a higher level. Potential employers will also be impressed. If your course offers the option of a placement year, start thinking about it *now*. If you are already committed to such a year, start thinking about the sort of placement that would offer the greatest learning opportunities. Think about how you can increase your chances of gaining such a position. If your course does not offer this kind of year, you think about how to put your vacations to best use.

By the end of this book you should have a clearer idea of what skills areas are most relevant to you, and be much better at finding learning opportunities. But don't wait until then. Each chapter offers you the chance to reflect on your needs for learning and suggests approaches to meeting these needs. If you think about these, and discuss them with other people, you should be able to take those actions you most need. Indeed the activities you have already done should have started this process. And now that you have a clearer understanding of competence and of the learning process, you should be able to do this even better.

ACTIVITY 3.7

This is part of a major exercise which will produce one or more exhibits for a portfolio, provided that you gather evidence and write an explanatory commentary as outlined above. You need at this stage to think about learning which might be relevant to work. Since you need to show that you have used a variety of learning methods, choose something with a practical component, not purely academic learning. Subsequent chapters of this book offer a range of such areas. Your courses may well offer others, as may industrial placements or vacation work.

Select a relevant skill, assess your strengths and weaknesses using as wide a range of information as possible (past learning, exams, self-diagnostic tests, tutor feedback, etc.) and then *plan* your own development in this area, documenting everything carefully as you go along. If you want to work on an area where the opportunities will not be available for a while, then plan *now* when you will need to start work, log this firmly in your diary and make sure that you do start work, referring to this chapter as necessary, when the time comes.

ACTIVITY 3.8

→ Ch 1

Revisit the work you did on the first exercise in this chapter and the list of transferable skills outlined in Chapter 1. See whether you can add to your file note any learning opportunities that you missed – any situation where you can exercise a relevant skill, either practical or conceptual, and obtain feedback. (You should by now be more aware of possible opportunities.) Now think about whether there are things you are not learning but could be, if you sought the opportunity. The learning style exercises should have provided a starting point for thought.

Learning opportunities might come from adding a feedback and/or reflection dimension to things that you are currently doing, from taking a course that you had perhaps rejected as 'too difficult' or from taking advantage of opportunities outside your course during both term and vacations. Link this to the previous exercise, to see whether you can progress your plans at all by taking a broader view of learning opportunities. You should be starting to get into a mindset of continually asking: 'What can I learn and how best can I learn it?'

ACTIVITY 3.9

Think about the last two weeks. What feedback did you receive on things you did? Did you consider it all carefully? Did you reflect on its implications? How might you have gained more feedback? What things did you not do that might have allowed you to learn? Did you take any decisions that would stop you from taking advantage of future potential learning opportunities?

If possible, discuss your thoughts with two or three other people and plan to do three things differently in the next two weeks to make learning more effective. Review progress and note down your reflections at the end of that period.

ORGANISING YOUR FILE

You may feel that the activities directed at developing a file are just too time-consuming. But remember: you are trying to change the way you operate. And change takes time and energy until it is embedded in your normal way of working. In the last chapter you needed considerable energy to improve your time management. Now you need to apply similar energy levels to developing the habits of reflective practice, of seeking learning opportunities and of using action planning and monitoring to ensure that learning is maximised.

Think back to what you learned about motivation, and apply this to motivating yourself.

- You need a clear goal, and one that will be rewarding to achieve. Remember: you are aiming to manage your learning in order to get a better degree than you otherwise would, and to prepare yourself for a really rewarding career.

- You need to believe that you *can* do it. Proformas are supplied to aid you in building your portfolio. You have the ability – if others can do it, you can. Although the initial time may be a scarce resource, the process is designed to make your learning more effective in future, so should save time overall.

- You need to set yourself manageable milestones and to reward their attainment. Social rewards are powerful – you might like to work with someone on this. (Providing such rewards is the business of a whole industry of Life Coaches, but working with a fellow student who is trying to do the same thing allows you to practice 'co-coaching', and give feedback and mutual support.)

You also need to continually reassess your strengths, weaknesses and development needs. As you learn, you will probably become far more realistic in your assessments. To quote Drucker again,

> *Most people think they know what they are good at. They are usually wrong. More often, people know what they are not good at – and even then more people are wrong than right . . . The only way to discover your strengths is through feedback analysis.*
>
> (from Drucker, P.F. (1999) *Management Challenges for the 21st Century*)

He goes on to explain that this involves writing down expected outcomes of all key actions and decisions and revisiting them a year or so later, comparing what really happened with the expectation and learning from the discrepancies. This can be a powerful tool, and it is well worth adding a section to your file for this. But you could usefully revisit your SWOT at shorter intervals.

By now you should be seeing how you might usefully organise your file. It is important to have an 'at a glance' set of contents/index at the front, so you know how to find things. (I am talking paper, here, as I like to feel things. . . . If you are happy working in html you might prefer a set of electronically linked documents.) It might be useful to highlight any items that you think are particularly good candidates for any official portfolios required for assessment for your qualification, or for a professional institute, or a potential employer.

Then you need a section for your assessment (and reassessments) of your development needs. You need a planning section, with an overall plan and clear way of logging progress, and a set of specific action plans. You might also want to have a learning log section, where you plan each study session, and note key learning points from that session. A section for filing odd resources on learning and self-management could be useful. And you may want to have a section devoted to managing group work. What suits you will depend on the structure of your course, any official file requirements and your preferred learning style. What is important is that you work out a file structure that works for you, and that you use it, and develop it, to maximise your learning.

SUMMARY

This chapter has argued the following:

- Learning, in the sense of developing knowledge, skills and ways of thinking that will make you more effective, is clearly crucial both while you are a student and when you start to work in a world that is highly competitive and rapidly changing.
- Learning is usefully seen as a continuous process dependent on feedback. Seeking situations in which such feedback can be obtained, and using it, will increase learning.
- Learning to understand complex situations (as is expected of graduates) involves trying to make sense of what happens, building new models reflecting this sense and testing them to see if experience confirms them.
- People tend to have preferred learning styles which emphasise one part of this cycle at the expense of others. Developing less preferred styles can make learning more effective.
- Learning will be most effective if it is managed, with learning needs identified and action plans drawn up for what needs to be done for the necessary learning to take place. These plans need to be implemented and progress reviewed, with target adjustment if need be.
- This needs to be supplemented by a constant alertness to the learning opportunities which are available, searching for new ones and willingness to take some risks in order to learn.

Further information

- Andreas, S. and Faulkner, C. (1996) *NLP: The new technology of achievement*, Nicholas Brealey Publishing. This provides a range of exercises designed to increase your motivation and accelerate your learning.
- Honey, P. and Mumford, A. (1986) *The Manual of Learning Styles*, Peter Honey.
- Krishnamurti, J. (1995) *The Book of Life*, HarperCollins. This is a useful introduction to Krishnamurti's thinking, containing extracts from his writings during the period 1933–68. It addresses 'learning for life' in a very different way from the present book, but this different perspective can sometimes sharpen your awareness of existing assumptions and preconceptions.

→ **Part 2**   **STUDY SKILLS**

Introduction to Part 2

In a way the whole of this handbook is about skills for learning. But this part addresses a subset of these, the skills that will particularly help you to learn from, and score good marks in, your academic studies. Is such a section necessary in a book aimed at students in higher education? Surely people who have spent 12 years or more 'studying' will have developed their study skills to a high level. I wish this were true. In my experience few university students have developed *all* of the skills they need to a sufficient level. Many, alas, still have serious shortfalls in several areas. Such students often find their courses unrewarding and experience serious stress. They learn very little. They drop out, gain a poor degree or fail.

This part of the book covers skills which will have an immediate impact on your studies: reading and note taking, basic mathematics, essay writing, using computers, writing assignments and being examined either conventionally or by a *viva*. A quick glance at some of the chapters will probably reassure you that you are already skilled to a high degree in these areas. Indeed, these chapters may seem absurdly basic to you. If so, skip them! Concentrate your energies on those chapters where you have concerns about your level of competence.

Within a single volume it would be impossible to do more than aim to cover the basics. But the basics are *important*. All too often lecturers assume that you are comfortable with the basics of something. If you lack this basic understanding you will learn little from their teaching of more advanced material. Use this book to fill any gaps. If you understand the learning process and are now taking active control of your own learning, this should not be difficult. Take each chapter as the starting point for developing your skills to the necessary level.

To help you do this, each chapter aims to show why the skills it covers are important and to outline any basic ideas you need to 'demystify' the topic. Further readings are suggested in case you feel you need more intensive help. Common sense, with a small amount of hard work, should make you competent even in those areas where you currently regard yourself as 'useless'.

The final chapter in this part concerns something which is not, strictly speaking, a study skill. It addresses the art of doing well, gaining good marks, in assessment. It is therefore about *showing* that you have learned, rather than about learning itself. But gaining a qualification is presumably one of your main objectives and you would want that qualification to be as good as possible. Marks in assessment, whatever form this takes, do not depend solely on how hard you have worked and how much you know. Rather, your grades are strongly influenced by how you *use* what you know in order to satisfy those who are assessing you. So you need to pay attention to the techniques needed to convince assessors that you have learned what they intended.

The skills addressed in this part are very obviously relevant to you while you are a student. But they have a wider relevance too. Each will be of use in almost any job you are likely to be doing after graduation. Given the rate of change in technology, legislation, professional practice and other factors relevant to most careers, you are likely to need to absorb large amounts of information in any graduate-type job. For the foreseeable future, much of this information will come from *reading*. Measurement is an essential part of managerial control, and measurement almost always involves *numbers*. *Communication* with a wide range of people, often in writing, will be equally important, as will be your ability to exploit information technology at your disposal. Even assessment, seemingly all about getting your degree, is important at work. There are many parallels with performance appraisal and assessment for professional qualifications.

→ 4 Reading and note taking

As a student you will spend hundreds of hours reading. This chapter suggests steps you can take to become a more effective reader. This can greatly reduce study time, while improving your understanding and retention of what you read. The skills are equally useful in the workplace.

Learning outcomes

Provided you not only read this chapter but *practise* the skills covered, you should be better able to:

- select appropriate reading material
- use techniques appropriate to that material in order to make most effective use of time
- reduce physical causes of inefficiency
- take useful notes on written or lecture material.

Whatever your preferred learning medium, much of the information you obtain as a student is likely to be from words. You may well spend more time reading than doing anything else. Despite 20 or more years' experience, you may be a far less efficient reader than you think. Increasing your skills in reading and note taking is therefore an important part of becoming more effective as a student. Note taking is equally important for lectures, and will be important for other contexts such as when interviewing, perhaps for a research project. Developing your skills in reading and note taking will mean that you spend less time reading, yet learn more in the process. Reading skills will probably be important throughout your career. Most managers, and those in other graduate-type jobs, claim that they are 'swamped' with reading material. The ability to deal with this material efficiently and effectively will contribute significantly to your likely success at work.

READING SKILLS

Gaining information by reading is one of the most sophisticated skills that we possess. Fine-tuned physical skills are required to use our eyes effectively. A wide range of conceptual skills are necessary too. It is not enough for the eye to focus on the word. The 'meaning' of that word must be interpreted and the 'meaning' of the sentence and paragraph and chapter of which it is a part. Your interpretation will depend upon the context, on other things you have read or experienced, and on your judgement of its acceptability and potential usefulness. Before this, the document in which the word appears must have been found or selected from a range of things on offer. And you will frequently need to respond to what you have read. A letter has to be answered. An essay has to be written. You may have to comment on draft proposals for a change at work, or write a briefing document for your superiors based on what you have read about the latest technological developments in your field, or a marketing plan based on market research reports.

Small wonder that 'read and respond to written materials' is one of the elements in the key skill of 'communication'. And while effective reading is a component of other skills, it itself depends on a number of conceptual skills exercised at different levels of mental activity, in addition to the physical skill of using the eyes. Thus there is a common perception that 'speed reading' techniques, which primarily address the physical side of reading, can allow you to perform miracles. (Woody Allen claimed that after such a course he was able 'to go through *War and Peace* in 20 minutes. It's about Russia.') This chapter addresses much broader issues. Sometimes a superficial scanning will serve your purpose, but much of your reading will need to be more thorough. The chapter's primary aim is to increase the *effectiveness* of your reading, rather than merely its speed. Having said that, physical techniques for increasing speed are important and make a good place to start.

Using your eyes

It is important that you do the following exercise before reading any further.

READING SPEED TEST

This requires you to time how long it takes to read the next section quickly but carefully, without stopping, aiming to remember any significant information contained in the text. There will be a short test to check how much you have absorbed. Read without a break until you are told to look at your watch again. Look at your watch *now* and note your starting time before reading on.

Most readers are unaware of their eye movements while they read, assuming, if they think about it at all, that their eyes are moving steadily along each line before moving to the next. If this were the case, reading at one line per second (which most people would guess to be a reasonable speed) you would cover 600–700 words per minute. At this pace you would find you could easily cope with the volume of reading materials

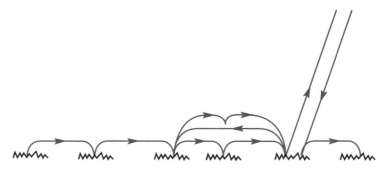

Fig. 4.1 Typical eye movements while reading

you are likely to encounter on your course. Eye movements when reading are far more complex, however. The eye makes a series of extremely rapid jumps along a line, with a significant pause, 0.25 to 1.5 seconds, between each jump. Furthermore, many readers do not move straight along a line, even in this jerky fashion. Instead, as Figure 4.1 shows, they indulge in frequent backward eye jumps, fixating for a second or even a third time on a previous word, and at intervals their eye may wander off the page altogether. With erratic eye movements like this and forward jumps from word to adjacent word, many readers achieve reading speeds of only 100 words per minute. At this rate of reading, the volume of work for your course, or that found in many jobs, is likely to prove an impossible task.

At the purely technical level, it is possible to achieve reading speeds of up to 1000 words per minute by:

- reducing the number of fixations per line, stopping every three to six words rather than every one
- eliminating backward movement and wandering
- reducing the duration of each fixation.

If you wish to reach this sort of speed, you will need to work at it. It will require concentration and considerable practice. But as well as improving your ability to get through your course materials and lessening eye fatigue in the process, such a reduction in eye movements will enable you to deal with reading material at work more quickly. This is important when time is at a premium. Any investment in developing your skills will therefore pay off handsomely. Furthermore, although you might expect comprehension to be reduced by more rapid reading, the reverse may well be the case. The pattern of a sentence and its meaning may emerge much more clearly and be more readily absorbed if the sentence is read in phrases rather than one word at a time. Your interest is more likely to be maintained if ideas are coming at you more quickly and your motivation will be higher if you feel you are making rapid progress, so the rewards of improved reading techniques are many.

If practice is all that is needed, you may wonder why we are all reading so slowly. Surely we have been practising reading most of our lives. But learning involves changing behaviour in the light of feedback. If there is no feedback suggesting the

→ Ch 3

need for improvement, we are likely to establish bad habits more firmly, rather than to develop rapid reading techniques. Breaking such habits is extremely difficult. It takes considerable effort, at least at first, to read at an increased speed. Improvement will be made only through the practice of exercises specifically designed for that purpose. Even when you have developed efficient reading techniques, you may still find that you have to make a point of consciously practising them at intervals, to prevent yourself from falling back into less efficient habits.

READING SPEED CALCULATION

Look at your watch again and note the time _____. Note how long it is since you last noted the time _____. There were approximately 590 words in that piece of text. Divide that figure by the number of minutes elapsed in order to find your reading speed in words per minute. Write this down _____.

TEST EXERCISE 4.1

The activities you have carried out so far have not had 'right' answers, although sometimes the text which followed may have suggested the sort of thing that you might have written. The quiz which follows is the first exercise where your answers can be checked. Answers to test exercises are given at the end of the book.

Now check your comprehension and retention by answering the following questions, saying whether each statement is true or false according to the preceding text. Do not glance back at the text! Cover it so that you cannot. This is a check on what you have understood *and can remember*. Do the whole quiz before checking any of your answers. Remember, the information is for your use. It will tell you whether or not you need to do subsequent exercises. If you look back (or forward) before answering, you will lose this information.

True/false

1 Poor readers fixate once per word. ☐

2 With practice a poor reader can increase from a speed of 100 to 1000 words per minute. ☐

3 A speed reader will fixate only once per line. ☐

4 Once you have mastered speed reading techniques they will become second nature. ☐

5 The only drawback to rapid reading is that it tends to reduce comprehension. ☐

6 The duration of each fixation can range from as little as 0.25 of a second to as much as 1.5 seconds. ☐

The two exercises you have just done will have given you some idea of how well you are reading at present, in terms of both speed and comprehension/retention. If you got more than one of the above questions wrong, you should be aiming to improve your retention while you read. You were specifically directed to remember any significant information in the passage. If all your answers were right and you were reading at 250 words or more (even with a diagram), you may not need to work on your reading skills. This will become a priority only if you are studying a course, or are in a job, with an overwhelming volume of material to be read. If you found your speed to be less than this, or your retention needs to be improved, the following exercises will be extremely helpful in both study and subsequent employment.

Increasing reading speed

The following practice activities have been developed from those suggested by Tony Buzan (2003b). They will enable you to make significant improvements in your reading speed, provided you are prepared to invest the time and effort needed for practice: 20–30 minutes daily for several weeks will probably be required to reach the full speed of which you are capable.

ACTIVITY 4.1

If the speed and comprehension test above suggested that your reading skills need to be developed, the project can provide an excellent portfolio exhibit demonstrating your learning skills. You will need to include your diagnostic information from the previous exercises, as part of your justification for targeting this skill, to set targets for improvement and to keep a record of your progress. Comments in the following text will give pointers to how you can do this, rather than being cast as specific exercises.

Feedback is essential to keep up your motivation, and to enable you to see when your rate of improvement is starting to level off. Keep a graph of your progress. Select a single book (not a set of readings) to control for ease of reading – material varies enormously in difficulty. When you start and every week thereafter, time yourself for five minutes, noting start and finish points in the text. Aim to remember significant content – you can jot down the main points from memory at the end of the five minutes. Check this and give yourself a mark out of 10 to reflect how much you remembered. Count the words you covered. Log both 'scores' in your file.

Many of the following practice activities require you to pace yourself. A metronome is ideal for this, as you can vary the speed of its 'tick'. Failing that, you might be able to find a clock with a loud tick or set your PC to emit beeps at intervals. You will also need to measure intervals – a kitchen timer will be invaluable here.

You need to find suitable practice materials of different text densities. A light novel would be low density. An advanced specialist textbook would be heavy density. The informative parts of a serious Sunday paper, or a periodical like *The Economist* or *New Scientist*, would lie somewhere in between. You can vary your practice materials. It is only your test 'feedback' text that must stay the same.

Your final resource will be an 'eye guide'. You need this in order to coax your eyes to fixate less often and more rapidly. Point with it to where you wish to fixate and move it after the duration of fixation required. A finger will do or some other pointer. Perhaps best when you are studying is a highlighter, as it allows you also to highlight key points of the text as you go along. You need to be careful when merely pointing to keep it just *above* the page to avoid spots before the eyes!

Reading practice activities

1 Muscle exercise

Fixate alternately between the top left-hand and right-hand corners of the page, moving your eyes between them as quickly as possible. Then alternate between top and bottom and between diagonals. Aim to speed up slightly at each session. (If using a metronome, note your speed each time.)

2 Page turning

Practise rapid page turning. Turn pages at a rate of three seconds per page, increasing to two seconds per page after about ten sessions. Move your eyes rapidly down each page, aiming to absorb *something*, though it will not be much at first. Do this for about two minutes at a stretch.

3 Reducing fixations

Practise fixating less often. Start by pointing at every third word, or every second one if you find three too difficult, and moving your pointer every 1.5 seconds. After a few sessions, gradually increase both the speed at which you move the pointer and the distance you move it, until you eventually fixate only once per line, for one second only. It will take a while to achieve this. You might then experiment with more than one line per fixation, but this is unlikely to be possible with the density of materials you need for study.

4 Speed reading

Still using your eye guide, practise reading as fast as you can for one minute, regardless of comprehension. Mark start and finish points. Then read for a further minute, aiming for comprehension of significant points, noting your end point. Count and record words per minute. Do this exercise several times per session, using different density materials each time.

5 Progressive acceleration

Using light- to medium-density material, and starting with your fastest comfortable 'reading with comprehension' speed, increase your speed by about 100 words per minute and read for a minute, then by a further 100 words per minute for a further minute, until after four minutes you are reading for a minute at approximately 500 words per minute faster than your starting speed. Calculate the speed at which your eye guide must move to achieve these speeds. Then read for a further minute, aiming for the fastest 'with comprehension' speed you can achieve. It should be higher than in the previous exercise.

6 Pre-scanning

Using fairly light-density material, start at the beginning of a chapter. Estimate approximately where 10 000 words will take you and insert a marker. Scan read to the marker, taking two to four seconds per page. Then go back to the beginning and read aiming for *some* comprehension, at a minimum of 1500 words per minute. As you get better, increase both the speed and the density of material scanned.

If you practise the above activities regularly, your speed of reading should increase significantly without loss, perhaps even with some gain, of comprehension. But reading effectiveness depends on more than this. You need at the same time to develop study strategies that will help you to choose appropriate things to read, to select appropriate speeds at which to read them, to think about what they contain while you read and to take good notes to supplement recall. It can also be helpful to index these notes for later reference.

SELECTING MATERIALS AND CHOOSING READING SPEEDS

Knowing what to read can be difficult. Some lecturers may present you with a long list of books and articles which are hard to find. After enormous effort you may find that the information in them is dated or of little use. I did hear of one lecturer who had not updated his reading list in 25 years. I hope the story was a campus myth! But even in less extreme cases you may face a problem in knowing what you need to read for an essay, and an even greater one when doing a literature search for a dissertation.

Sometimes you will not know where to start. Sometimes the list may be impossibly long. In this chapter we cover a basic approach to the selection problem. It is a variant of the systematic approach to problem solving covered in detail in Chapter 12, and used in short form in Chapter 2 as the basis for self-management. Greater detail on how to search for and select information is given in Chapter 13.

→ Ch 12
→ Ch 2
→ Ch 13

Define your objectives

What are you trying to achieve? Why do you want to read something on this topic? What do you really need to know? Are you seeking facts, ideas, theories or frameworks to help you develop your understanding as in the Kolb cycle? Are you looking for appropriate techniques or background information? Is the information something you may need for an examination? Is it necessary or potentially useful for a written assignment or clarification of something totally obscure from lectures? Is it merely for your own interest? Until you are clear what you want, you cannot start to look for it (though Chapter 13 explores some ways in which you may need to start with a vague idea and, through looking, find out enough to clarify your objectives).

→ Ch 13

Identify options

What sources exist? How easily can you access them? What does the library have, both on paper and accessible electronically? Until you are comfortable exploring by yourself, staff will usually be very happy to help. Is something so important it is worth buying? If so, is there a second-hand source? What does a bookshop have on the topic? While the extreme case described above is rare, some lecturers update their lists less frequently than they might. There might be something newer and cheaper than a set text, though you would need to check carefully that it was as good or better. Ask teaching staff and other students for guidance, particularly before investing in buying your own copy. If you are generating your own source list, look at references at the end of recent or key papers on the topic. See whether there are other related dissertations in the library. Search key words. Check government publications. If relying on a library, do remember that other people are likely to want the same as you. The early student gets the book!

Identify selection criteria

Coverage relevant to your purpose is obviously crucial. But so are other factors. Is the text recent (or a classic)? By a reputable author? Pitched at the right level? Is it in a reputable, referred journal? Is it based on evidence or opinion? How relevant/adequate is the evidence to your purpose? Are there any other factors which are important to your choice in this instance?

Selection itself

Selection is difficult unless you have access to the possible materials and can scan them briefly. Otherwise you will need to accept advice from tutors, librarians or others with knowledge on the subject. In North America in particular, academic tenure depends largely on the length of an academic's publication list. So there is enormous pressure to publish, regardless of the density of the ideas or the information contained in the book or article. It pays to be sceptical when selecting. It is all too easy to think that everything in print is worthy of your attention. An important graduate skill is to know how to separate that which has value from that which is flawed, whether logically or in terms of evidence used.

Choosing your reading speed

Sometimes you will be looking for a highly specific piece of information. Did this research use a particular technique? What sample was used? What does the author have to say on a particular point? If your purpose is to answer such questions, a full reading of the selected text is unnecessary. Instead, use the index, plus rapid scanning of the material to identify the part you need to read in detail. Just as you can hear your name being mentioned at the other side of a crowded room, so you can bring selective attention to bear on written materials. While scanning the page too rapidly to read it, you can still notice the word or phrase you need. This will require serious concentration, however, and a refusal to be side-tracked. Of course, interesting digressions are what study is all about. Indulge in them whenever you have the time.

The next fastest type of reading after scanning is aimed at getting a picture of the overall pattern of a book, chapter or article. For this, focus first on any contents list, then introductions and summaries, main headings and subheadings. Diagrams and tables of results are useful too. Several rapid passes may help you map the material better than a single slower one.

Slightly slower still is speed reading at your fastest speed. This may be suitable for lengthy materials, where the level of relevance is fairly low, or for background reading. Your aim will be to absorb the main arguments and assess the extent to which these are based on relevant and reliable evidence.

Much of your study will require a slower rate. The exercises you did earlier will still have been useful in eliminating inefficient habits, but where almost every word is relevant and you need to think really hard about the concepts and arguments contained, there will be a limit to how quickly you can work. You will probably need to take notes, both to aid comprehension and for later recall. You may sometimes need to stop reading, think and perhaps consult other sources before progressing.

Slowest of all is reading to learn by heart. If you need to be able to reproduce an equation, a diagram, an argument or a set of categories, then you will need to spend time on every detail, committing these to memory. If you need not only to reproduce but to apply what you are learning, you will need to practise this, preferably across a range of applications. There is not much to be gained (except possibly marks in a simple test) from learning something if you do not also learn how and when to use it.

→ Ch 10
You may find that once you have devoted time to understanding all the details, relationships and possible uses of material, you have in the process learned it. If not, try to devise a mnemonic – this is something which is easier to remember than the thing itself. Acronyms or rhymes are good for this. You can probably already remember the requirements for objectives because SMART is so easy to remember and it is easy to go from that to what the letters stand for. The stages of group formation introduced in Chapter 10 are easily remembered as 'form, storm, norm, perform'. Sometimes rote learning may be more efficient, particularly if frequent fast recall is needed. This is the way multiplication tables were once taught, involving going over and over something until it 'sticks'. Rote learning can decay rather more quickly than rhyme or acronym, so it needs 'refreshing' if it is used for something you will need only occasionally.

NOTES AND ANNOTATIONS USING WORDS AND DIAGRAMS

Note taking is a crucial study skill, but also invaluable at work. You have probably often taken notes to help you remember something afterwards. But note taking is far more than merely a way to extend your memory. It is a key component in active learning. And if you are one of those who learns best by writing, it will be one of your best 'aids'.

Take notes for:
■ concentration
■ understanding
■ retention
■ reference
■ revision.

In writing notes you are – or should be – *organising* material, and therefore organising your thoughts. By extracting themes and key points, and jotting them down in a way that *makes sense* to you, you are interacting with the material. This interaction engages your mind. It stops your attention drifting off. It is *interesting*. It means that you will *absorb* the key points you have extracted, almost without effort. And good notes are likely to be far more useful to you in essay writing or revision than the original material.

'Good notes' are clearly more than a verbatim record of a lecturer's words or a section of text. Of course there will be times when a diagram or piece of text is so important that you will want to copy (or photocopy) the whole thing, or save it from the Internet. Even if you do, it will normally be helpful to take notes on it as well.

As outlined above, the active process of organising material into notes can maintain your concentration and help you sort out the structure of what the author is saying. This means that not only is study more interesting, but you understand the material much better and remember far more than if you merely read it more passively.

Second, good notes can be far more useful for many purposes than the original material. They will be easier for you to understand, as you will have reorganised the material into a form which makes sense to you. You can also include cross-references to other relevant material from other sources, or other courses. If working on paper, you can use colour to emphasise structure and aid memory. Because your notes will normally be much briefer than the originals, they are likely to be much easier to refer to and to revise from. Even with paper notes, you can devise an indexing system so that you can easily find topics. If you are working electronically this becomes very easy to do.

As with everything else, you need to be clear on *why* you are keeping notes. If you are working with borrowed materials which will be crucial for a major project later, you will need to keep more detailed notes and copy quotations and key diagrams, as well as any useful references that you may need to explore and/or quote. With electronic material, there is a strong temptation merely to copy huge chunks. While such copies may have their uses, remember the advantages of notes just mentioned. Without active 'digestion', condensing and restructuring, you are likely to miss major benefits. Keep a full copy 'in case' if you like, but make briefer notes to supplement this. The same applies if you are not restricted in your photocopying. Copies of papers and chapters will not help you merely by sitting on your shelves. If they give you a false sense of achievement they can be a hindrance. They are only any good when you *interact* with them. So how can you do this effectively?

Annotation

If you are working with materials you own, the most basic form of note taking is annotation, highlighting key points or concepts and making brief marginal notes (or an electronic equivalent). This will ensure that you are *thinking* as you read, searching for the key ideas, and that you stay awake! When you return to the materials you will be able to extract key points from the highlighting and your brief marginal notes will remind you of relevant examples from elsewhere, or how you finally sorted out a point in the text that was confusing.

Précis

If you cannot annotate materials because they are not your own, or if you want a more portable form of notes (perhaps as a basis for revision at home over the vacation), then you may want to take notes in the form of a précis or summary, where you write down key points made. If working from annotated materials, you may merely jot down your highlighted words plus marginal comments. But ideally you are aiming to say something more concise than the original *and in your own words*. The translation process will go far to making the meaning sink in. Normally you will want your summary to be organised point by point, even if the original is less clear!

Diagrammatic notes

In taking notes you will often be looking for *relationships* – between ideas in a text or lecture, or between this material and some other. Diagrams are a particularly useful technique for representing relationships, with huge advantages over linear text for this purpose. A number of diagramming techniques will be introduced at different points in the book, but one is worth starting to use already. This is based on the mind-mapping technique, sometimes called brain patterns, described by Tony and Barry Buzan (2003). Variants of this basic form will appear in a variety of contexts and with different names. It is extremely versatile; note taking is just one of its applications.

In drawing a mind map, you start in the centre of the page, with a word or phrase indicating the main idea or central theme, then branch out from this, giving each sub-theme a separate branch. These branches divide further into sub-sub-themes. If you are exploring your own thoughts in this way it is called a mind map. If you are teasing out the content of something else, then it is often called a spray diagram. Figure 4.2 shows an example of a spray diagram on note taking. In the next chapter you will see how a similar diagram can be used to plan the structure of something that you are going to write. Software is now available for drawing mind maps on your PC if you prefer. These look much neater, but may be less memorable.

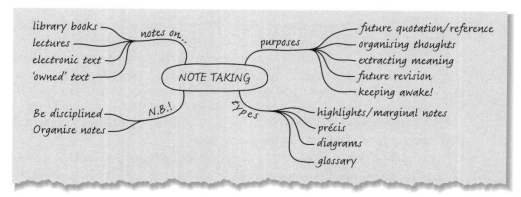

Fig. 4.2 Diagrammatic notes on note taking

Buzan highlights the following advantages of this type of diagram over linear notes:

- the central idea is more clearly defined
- position indicates relative importance – items near the centre are more significant than those nearer the periphery
- proximity and connections show links between key concepts
- recall and review will be more rapid and more effective
- the structure allows for easy addition of new information
- patterns will differ from each other, making them easier to remember
- (for divergent, creative use – covered later) the open-ended nature of the pattern helps the brain make new connections.

Thus you can see how mind maps help you with both the digesting and structuring of material you are studying and its later recall.

→ Ch 3

ACTIVITY 4.2

Return to whatever notes you took on Chapter 3 (or to the chapter itself if you did not take notes). Draw a mind map of the main points. Reflect on the extent to which this helped to make the structure clearer. If working with others, compare diagrams and discuss both your diagrams and the extent to which they helped. Draw mind maps for the next five serious chapters or articles that you read. You should be hooked on the technique by then!

ACTIVITY 4.3

Prepare an exhibit showing that you can select, read and summarise in note form an appropriate chapter or paper. Your exhibit will need to document your objectives, the selection process used, the full reference of the text selected and your summary.

Lecture notes

Lecture notes present a particular challenge, as you have to go at the speed of the lecturer and cannot usually ask for a point to be repeated until you have grasped it. You therefore need to do the best you can at the time and remedy any deficits later. While you do not need to become proficient at shorthand, working out your own abbreviations for frequently repeated words is a great help. If you are taking notes on a lecture, you may eventually become good enough to rely on mind maps, but at first it is better to keep more narrative notes on one page, perhaps trying to build up a mind map in quiet moments on the facing page.

As well as drawing mind maps, try using sketch diagrams. These can sometimes clarify meaning more quickly than words. Space is useful too – leave gaps for things you missed. Leave space too for things which will need expansion if they are ever to make sense to you three months later. Indicate as you go along all the points where your notes are not adequate. Then discipline yourself to make good the deficits *as soon as possible*. You will be able to do this relatively easily within 24 hours, while the event is still fresh in your mind. Check with others whose notes, memories or comprehension may be better than yours. If you wait more than a day, the task will be far more difficult, if not impossible.

Discipline and organisation

However you take your notes, whether in an exercise book, on cards, on punched paper for a ring binder or on a PDA, it is important also to be disciplined about organising them. A series of organised notes can be invaluable. A collection of scruffy pieces of paper scattered all around the house is useless. Part of this organisation should include a good index to your materials, so that you can instantly access notes on a particular topic if an assignment or project requires it. Some sort of page numbering is important too – you need to be able to reorder your notes if the wind blows them about or you lend them to a friend who drops them! If you are keeping electronic notes it is essential to make backup copies at regular intervals. It can be heartbreaking to lose all your notes on a subject, especially if this is shortly before you need to start your revision. PDAs can be lost, stolen or dropped. Hard disks on PCs can fail. So backup frequently, and keep your backup copy safe!

> For good note taking:
> ■ use words and diagrams
> ■ 'organise' content
> ■ 'improve' within 24 hours
> ■ file systematically.

Discipline is also important when it comes to references to any materials you do not own. Keeping a full reference list (use the format in the list of references at the end of this book if you have not been told to use something different) with your notes will save hours of searching perhaps months or even years later, when you need to use it for a paper or dissertation. It may seem a bother at the time, but it is more of a bother to resurrect an elusive reference when everything you can remember about it is insufficient to identify it.

Organised and disciplined notes will have potential uses beyond the particular course to which they relate. They may be a useful resource for a subsequent dissertation or project, or indeed help in a situation at work. Unless you are very pressed for space, it is therefore worth retaining them. It can be infuriating to need something and then realise you threw it away a year ago!

SUMMARY

This chapter has argued the following:

■ Improving your reading skills can make you a far more effective learner, and aid career success.
■ Practice can significantly improve reading speeds.
■ It is possible to increase your reading speed without loss of comprehension.
■ Efficient reading requires you to think more clearly about what you need to read, and why, and about where to find it.

4

Reading and note taking

■ Lecturers, library staff and other students can help you find and select appropriate reading material.

■ Different reading speeds are appropriate for different purposes.

■ Taking notes will increase the effectiveness of your understanding and learning and give you something for future reference.

■ Mind maps can form a useful part of your notes.

■ It is essential to be disciplined in organising and storing your notes.

Further information

■ Buzan, T. (2003a) *The Speed Reading Book*, BBC Publications.

■ Buzan, T. (2003b) *Use Your Head*, BBC Publications.

■ Buzan, T. and Buzan, B. (2003) *The Mind Map Book: Radiant Thinking – Major Evolution in Human Thought*, BBC Publications.

■ Morris, S. and Smith, J. (1998) *Understanding Mind Maps in a Week*, Institute of Management.

■ Rose, C. and Nicholl, M.J. (1997) *Accelerated Learning for the 21st Century*, Piatkus.

■ Russell, L. (1999) *The Accelerated Learning Field Book*, Jossey-Bass Pfeiffer.

→ 5 Basic numbers

If you hate numbers, this chapter is for you. It should make you confident enough to benefit from courses with a quantitative element. If you are comfortable with basic maths, skip it!

Learning outcomes

By the end of this chapter you should:

- see why numbers are important
- understand some of the difficulties you may have had with using numbers in the past
- understand the 'language' of simple maths
- be able to use a calculator to perform simple calculations
- be able to use estimations as a check on your calculations
- understand how to rearrange equations
- have practised manipulating numbers and equations
- feel relatively confident of your ability to do basic arithmetic and algebra.

Number skills are vital for business study (and many other subjects) and for many jobs. Whether you are analysing survey results, claiming your expenses, or project planning with a tight budget, you need numbers. Whether figuring out wallpaper requirements, or deciding between phone providers, you need basic arithmetic. Yet many people doubt their number skills, or are actually frightened of numbers and equations. This chapter aims to reduce such fears and address some of the basic uncertainties causing them. It can't take you from nothing to A-level standard. But it can make the basic principles clear, act as revision of things you have forgotten, and build your confidence.

THE IMPORTANCE OF NUMBERS

It is difficult to over-estimate the importance of numbers. Crosby (1997) argues that the amazing success of European imperialism can be explained only in terms of the shift from qualitative to quantitative perception during the late Middle Ages and Renaissance, the prime use of numbers being for measurement. He gives an interesting quotation (p.109) in illustration:

Wherefore in all great works are Clerks so much desired? Wherefore are Auditors so well fed? What causeth Geometricians so highly to be enhaunced? Why are Astronomers so greatly advanced? Because that by number such things they finde, which else would farre excell mans minde.

(Robert Recorde, 1540)

This might also explain something that puzzled me when I was a psychologist in the Civil Service – the fact that economists on equivalent grades to psychologists, and with equivalent qualifications, were paid significantly more! Consider how many highly paid professions today involve facility with numbers.

Of course, you should already have the basic ability to deal with numbers as a result of your secondary education. If this is the case, check that your judgement is correct by doing Test exercise 5.1 and then move on to the next chapter. If you *can* cheerfully add, subtract, multiply and divide, can cope with fractions, decimals, ratios and percentages and do some basic algebra, you do not need this chapter.

But if you feel unsure about these things, if you hated maths at school, or somehow came to feel you were no good at it, do not worry. This chapter should take away some of your fears. It will redevelop some skills that may have atrophied through lack of use and fill gaps that your education may have left. This chapter is not intended to teach you maths, but rather to show that playing with numbers is not difficult, can often be fun and is an extremely useful skill. It should make you less nervous about any quantitative parts of your course and enable you to use sets of numbers you encounter at work without trauma. Drawing conclusions from numbers, rather than merely playing with them, is dealt with in Chapter 14.

→ Ch 14

This is one of the few topics where 'right' answers to exercises are possible. The answers to the test exercises are given at the end of the book. Write your own answer in the space provided, or on a separate piece of paper, *before* looking at the answer given. It is very easy to think that you know how to do something when in fact you only half know. Spending time on actually working out the examples given and writing down your answers will ensure that you really do master the skills involved. Resist any temptation to cut corners here!

DIAGNOSTIC EXERCISE

TEST EXERCISE 5.1

In order to check whether you need to work through this chapter or can afford to move directly to the next one, answer the following questions, writing down your answers as you go. Do not use a calculator unless the question asks you to. Do not look at the answers given at the end of the book until you have finished the quiz.

(a) Add 273 to 476 and 545, and divide your total by 5. _____

(b) Multiply 27 by 45. _____

(c) Divide 34 546 by 23. _____

(d)   Add 3^2 to 2^3.   _____

(e)   Write 1234.5678 to two places of decimals.   _____

(f)   Write 1234.5678 to three significant figures.   _____

(g)   Write down 75% of 200.   _____

(h)   Write down $^{13}\!/_{25}$ as a percentage.   _____

(i)   If there are 6 tutors and 42 students, what is the ratio of staff to students?   _____

(j)   Divide $^2\!/_3$ by $^9\!/_{16}$.   _____

(k)   Divide $(3a + 4b)(5c - 10d)$ by $5(a + b)(c - 2d)$.   _____

(l)   How many tiles 10 cm square do you need to cover a room 2 m by 3 m?   _____

(m)   Use your calculator to work out $13^2 - 25 + 273 \times 5$.   _____

Now check your answers and decide whether you need to study all of what follows, some of it, or can afford to move directly to the next chapter. If most of your answers were right, but you feel it was as much by luck as good judgement, merely read what follows quickly, doing the examples only in the parts where you feel most uncertain.

ACTIVITY 5.1

If you have decided as a result of the above that you do need to develop some at least of your mathematical skills, and have not yet compiled an 'exhibit' which demonstrates that you can manage your learning, this might be a good topic. Think about what you are likely to need to learn and about any evidence (in addition to answers to the above) of your learning need in this area. Then you will need to set objectives, explore potential resources and so on, keeping a commentary as you go. Refer to Chapter 3 to remind yourself of the process.

→ Ch 3

THE IMPORTANCE OF MATHEMATICAL SKILLS

If numbers are important, then the mathematical skills needed to deal with them are important too. There are many ways of thinking of mathematics. At its simplest it can be seen as a language with a set of symbols instead of words, and a set of rules for combining these symbols. These rules are equivalent to the grammar of a spoken language. At this level it can provide a clear, unambiguous and concise way of describing certain relationships. The section on 'mathematical vocabulary' will enable you to use the language to communicate in this way.

More often, though, you will want either to draw conclusions from numbers or to manipulate them in some way. To work out the cost of something made from several

5

Basic numbers

components, you need to manipulate numbers. To check expenditure against budget, you need numbers. To make sure that you have ordered enough meals for attenders at a conference when you know a certain proportion of those registered will not arrive, you need numbers. Decisions about future actions in organisations will often involve cost–benefit or other calculations. Recently I asked a graduate employer what recruits needed number skills for. He replied: 'Just about everything.' Indeed, it is hard to see how you can measure, control, analyse, forecast, or model, or make sense of the outputs of these processes, without feeling comfortable with basic maths.

Modelling

It is probably worth discussing one of these uses of maths in a little more detail. A model is something constructed for a particular purpose. It represents certain key aspects of the thing modelled in order to allow you to answer questions about it. Models may be used because they are smaller or simpler or cheaper or safer to play with than the real thing. To find out whether a dam design is going to be strong enough for a location you cannot build it and wait to see if it falls down. Nor do you put up a building in order to see whether people like the look of it. Architects make three-dimensional models of proposed buildings, or achieve the same effect on a computer screen. Their clients can decide from these whether something looks right. Engineers perform all sorts of calculations to decide whether, given the strength of the materials, the way they are arranged and the water pressure expected, the dam will be strong enough. Even when deciding whether to fill up at this service station or wait to the next one, you will probably use a simple model. You relate the amount of fuel you estimate is left in the tank to the distance to the next service area, given the fuel consumption of your car at the rate you are likely to be travelling.

Very simple (or very complicated) mathematical equations can be used to give answers to all sorts of 'what if . . .?' questions. What would be the staffing implications of this change in operations? Or of that reduction in absence rates? If fixed costs are this, and variable costs are that, how many items do we need to sell at a given price to break even? What will the profit be if we sell so many hundred more? If interest rates are this, and expected return on investment is that, is it worth borrowing in order to invest? The maths will not tell you how many items you will sell, nor what will happen to interest rates. Provided you have chosen appropriate equations to express the relationship between the relevant factors, it will tell you what is likely to happen in different sets of circumstances. One tool for doing this sort of fairly simple modelling

→ Ch 7   easily is a spreadsheet (discussed in Chapter 7).

When doing this sort of simple modelling and using maths to answer real or hypothetical questions, we are going beyond descriptive language into using techniques derived from mathematics. Some of these techniques are extremely complex and will take you some time to learn. Unless you are going to use them regularly it is better to consult an expert. Others will be well within your grasp once you have learned the basics of arithmetic and algebra covered here. Spreadsheets, introduced in Chapter 7, make it easy to construct simple models on a PC and to use

→ Ch 7   them to answer questions.

SOURCES OF DIFFICULTY

Most small children are perfectly comfortable with numbers once they have learned to count. They can make fairly sophisticated judgements about things like 'fair shares' or what their pocket money will buy. But for a significant proportion of these children something seems to go wrong once they are 'taught' maths. Either they fail to develop their skills further, or they lose even those skills which they have. Furthermore, they develop almost a phobia about anything with a number or an equals sign in it. As soon as they see one, mental shutters clang down. Even totally straightforward explanations of simple operations cannot penetrate. If you are one of these people, take frequent deep breaths as you move through this chapter!

Even if you are not disturbed by the sight of an equation, you may still have suffered from the shift in teaching methods before you entered education. It used to be the fashion to teach mathematics as a series of techniques. These were learned by rote rather than understood. Thus children learned to go through the mechanics of long multiplication or division, with absolutely no understanding of what they were doing. I remember being taught an incredibly complicated method for finding square roots by hand, even though any book of mathematical tables (before the calculator became an everyday item such tables were essential) had lists of square roots and we also knew how to find them from log tables in the same book.

Such a method of learning was difficult, boring and often pointless. But the endless calculations it required gave a great deal of practice in basic arithmetic. The ability to multiply or do long division without a calculator is still useful. It allows quick tests of the answers that your computer or calculator produces and means that you can afford to go out without a calculator on occasion!

The 'discovery' approach to maths teaching which replaced the above was intended to be more interesting. Unfortunately it often left students feeling they were floundering in a foggy mathematical swamp, not knowing where they were going, or how they would get there even if they did. At least with the old-fashioned method students were drilled in the basic techniques to such an extent that they would remember them for the rest of their lives.

Cartoon by Neill Cameron, www.planetdumbass.co.uk

What follows is an attempt at covering these basics. Some practice exercises are included, but they are unlikely to be enough to remedy six or more years of poor teaching. If you are an extreme case, and if you need to pursue courses with a quantitative element, you are well advised to buy a basic maths book which contains lots of examples and answers at the back – and then work through it. Once you start getting things right it can be quite exciting. If on the other hand you are semi-confident, skim the more obvious bits that follow. Pause only on those sections where you feel less sure.

BASIC MATHEMATICAL SIGNS, SYMBOLS AND OPERATIONS

This is where numberphobes may need a few deep breaths before progressing. Put on some relaxing music and then make sure that you understand the meaning of the following basic symbols:

You will know that in 5 + 3 the '+' is telling you to take the sum of 3 and 5, to add them together. For numbers in the thousands or more you might prefer to use a calculator. Note that in addition the order of terms does not matter. 5 + 3 is the same as 3 + 5.

You also know that 5 − 3, or 5 minus 3, means what you get when you take 3 away from 5. Again, even for large numbers, this is easy to do by pressing the right buttons on a calculator. But note, in this case the order *does* matter. If you have £300 in the bank and take out £500, you are not in the same position as if you have £500 and take out £300! In the second case your bank manager will be happy. In the first he or she will not, unless you had previously arranged an overdraft facility. You would have −£200. Negative sums of money, money owing, are often written in brackets, for example '(£200)', in sets of accounts.

What do you do when you want to subtract something that is already negative, i.e. has a '−' sign in front of it? To 'take away' your overdraft, someone would have to give you £200 and, indeed, to subtract a number that is already negative you have to *add* it. Thus 5 − (−3) is 5 + 3, or 8. Note that basic calculators cannot cope with this. You need to apply this rule of signs for yourself and ask the calculator to *add* any negative numbers that are being subtracted.

This indicates multiplication. 5 × 3 means 5 lots of 3, or 15. Again, the obvious calculator buttons will produce the answer if you have forgotten your 'times tables'. As with addition, order does not matter. 5 × 3 is the same as 3 × 5. You need to be careful with negative numbers, however. As with subtraction, two minuses get you back to plus. So count the number of minus signs in the string of numbers you are multiplying. If there is only one of them, or any odd number, then the answer will be negative. If there are no '−' signs, or two, or any even number, the result of the multiplication will be positive. A basic calculator will not read a '−' as a multiplication. Instead it will think it has to subtract. So if using a calculator multiply all the numbers as if they were positive and put the appropriate sign in front of your answer, having worked this out for yourself by counting the number of '−' signs.

Part of the difficulty in working with mixtures of signs on a calculator is that in a string of things to add, subtract, multiply and divide, the signs have different strengths, or priorities. If you see $5 + 3 \times 2$, this means that you should work out the 3×2 first, before adding the 5. Thus you get 11, not 16. Multiplication and division signs are stronger than addition and subtraction signs, so they must be worked out first. Sophisticated calculators are programmed with this rule, but cheap ones usually are not. Check to see whether yours is sophisticated enough by working out something like the example above, before relying on it.

Should you want to multiply large numbers by hand, you need to end up with a number of the right size. So 5×50 will be 250 and 500×50 will be 25 000. In the latter example there were two zeros in the first number, one in the second and three in the answer. If it is not already clear why this should be, you will understand when powers are discussed shortly. If you were multiplying numbers that were not merely hundreds or tens but had units as well (say 521 by 53), you would need to keep clear how many noughts would appear at any stage. So line the numbers up so that the units are underneath each other, thus:

$$
\begin{array}{r}
521 \times \\
53 \\
\hline
\end{array}
$$

Beneath the line, working with each digit at a time and making sure that the answer is in the right (unit, ten or hundred) column, multiply the whole first number by the first digit in the second number then add. So you multiply by the 5 in the 53 first. This is really 50, so place a 0 in the unit column, then multiply the 1 above by the 5, then the 2 (this gives 10, so write down the zero and carry the 1 across to the next column, jotting it down to remember it). 5 multiplied by 5 is 25. Add the 'carried' 1 to give 26 and write it down. In the line below, multiply the 1 by 3, then the 2, then the 5, working across from right to left. Then add the two numbers together. The resulting calculation, done by hand, looks like:

$$
\begin{array}{r}
521 \times \\
53 \\
\hline
26050 \\
\end{array}
\qquad
\begin{array}{r}
521 \times \\
53 \\
\hline
26050 \\
1563 \\
\end{array}
\qquad
\begin{array}{r}
521 \times \\
53 \\
\hline
26050 \\
1563 \\
\hline
27613 \\
\end{array}
$$

$\boxed{\div}$

This indicates division. $5 \div 3$ means what you get when you divide 5 into 3 equal portions. If the second number goes into the first with no problems, for example in the case of 6 ÷ 3, life is simple. If you and your two flatmates have six pies, you can have two pies each. But if you have only five pies and want equal shares, you will be moving into the territory of fractions. You could divide each pie in three and share them out, ending up with five pieces, each ⅓ of a pie. Or you could take one pie each and cut up the two which remained. So you would have 1⅔ pies each. This shows that ⅔ and 1⅔ are different ways of writing the same thing. If you are dividing a large number by a relatively smaller number, then you may not bother about the fraction. Instead, you may merely say what is left – the remainder. If you go out for a meal with five friends and the bill is £43, you might just say that is a bit over £7 each and offer to pay the £1 that is left over when you divide, adding it to your own £7 contribution.

Should you wish to do long division 'by hand', you need to write everything clearly in columns just as you did when multiplying. But instead of working right to left, you work left to right.

Suppose you are dividing 4737 by 21. Write it as:

$$21\overline{)4737}$$

Now ask: 'Will 21 go into 4?' Clearly not. Will it go into 47? Yes, twice. So write a 2 above the 7. But it doesn't go exactly. What is left over? Two 21s are 42, so write this beneath the 47 and subtract. This gives you 5. (Less than 21: if it had given you something bigger than 21, you would know you had made a mistake in the first number you wrote down since it should have been bigger!) This 5 is sitting in the hundreds column. It means 500. 'Bring down' the next available digit, the 3, and write it beside the 5. Don't worry that this is really 530. Treat it as 53. See how many 21s you can get into this. Two, again. So write down another 2, above the 3. This stands for 20 because it is in the tens column. That is why it didn't matter that it was 530. The columns mean that things end up standing for the right thing, even though you conveniently forget what they stand for while working out the sum. Write down the 42 and subtract from the 53. This gives you 11. 'Bring down' the final digit, the 7. How many 21s in 117? Five. So write down the 5 in the last place above the line and work out what 5 multiplied by 21 is: 105. Write this below 117 and subtract, giving you the remainder which is 12. So the answer is 225 with a remainder of 12, or 225 and ¹²⁄₂₁ had you wanted an answer expressed as a fraction. The handworked sum is shown below. You use the same principle, whatever the size of numbers involved.

```
        2                  22                 225
   21 ) 4737          21 ) 4737          21 ) 4737
        42                 42                 42
        ---                ---                ---
         5                 53                 53
                           42                 42
                           ---                ---
                           11                 117
                                              105
                                              ---
                                              12 remainder
```

This is a decimal point. (Note that this is not absolutely standard notation. There are some places where a comma rather than a full stop is used for this purpose.) You will be used to seeing figures written in decimals and know already that 1.5 is the same as 1½. The decimal point tells you where the whole number ends and the fraction starts. Adding fractions is quite difficult. How could you express the sum of ⁵⁄₇ and ¾, for example? (Answer – turn them both into 28ths and then add, which is possible, but a bit messy.) But if you express both as decimals then it is easy. Press 5 ÷ 7 =, and then 3 ÷ 4 =, on your calculator to see what each is as a decimal. Then add both on the calculator. (I get 1.4642857.) You will have noticed that ¾ used only two figures, while ⁵⁄₇ filled up your display with assorted numbers. This is because 100 can be divided into 4 parts, each of 25, but it does not divide by 7. For another nice display, divide 5 by 3 on your calculator to get the decimal solution to the pie problem.

In interpreting figures to the right of the decimal you use the same rule as for figures to the left. You know that the first place to the left of the point represents units, the next tens, the next hundreds, and so on. Starting at the point and moving right, you are still using a factor of ten with each move. The first figure to the right represents tenths, the next hundredths and so on.

If you are working with a calculator, all you need to do to work with decimals is to make sure that when you are entering a number and get to the decimal point, you press the · key and then continue entering the decimal part of the number. The calculator is happy to work with such numbers. However, if you need to work out what the fraction is as a decimal first and then add or subtract, the calculator will get confused. You probably found this a minute ago. The trick is to use the memory. When the calculator has turned each fraction into a decimal, press M+ (or M- for a negative number). When you have entered all decimals in the memory press MR to recall the total from the memory.

If you are adding by hand, you need to make sure that all the decimal points are lined up so that you start adding tens to tens, hundreds to hundreds and tenths to tenths. Thus if adding 101.75 to 1.003, you would write:

$$
\begin{array}{r}
101.75 \ + \\
1.003 \\
\hline
102.753
\end{array}
$$

%

This means percentage or per cent, or a fraction expressed in 1/100ths. Thus 1 is 100/100 or 100%, half is 50/100 or 50% etc. This is very similar to working in the first two numbers to the right of the decimal point and has the same advantages as using decimals. While it is very hard to see how ¹¹⁄₁₃, ²⁷⁄₃₁ and ⁵⁄₇ relate to each other, if you express them as percentages you can easily tell which is the biggest, or add or subtract them. You used your calculator before to find out what fractions were in decimals. You can do this again and take the first two figures. But it is much simpler to press, e.g.

. Start with something you know, like ½, to check that this works on your calculator.

You have already been using this button on your calculator in the above examples. In a minute, when we look at simple algebra, we shall explore its meaning further. Equations always contain this equals sign. Basically it tells you that everything on one side of it is the same as everything on the other side.

This means to the power of 2 or squared. Numbers in small type, up in the air to the right of a number or letter, mean that it has been multiplied by itself, the number of terms in the multiplication being given by the small 'power' number. Thus 2^2 means 2×2, and 3^2 means 3×3. We could call it '3 squared' or '3 to the power 2'. If the small number is a 3, we talk about something being 'cubed' or 'to the power 3'. 4^3 is $4 \times 4 \times 4$ or 64. After cubed there are no more special terms, so we always talk of 'to the power'.

Now, think what happens when you multiply different powers of the same number. What do you think you will get if you multiply 10^2 by 10^3? Try it. This is 100 by 1000, or 100 000, or 10^5. Thus you could have got it by adding the power numbers, or indices, together. This always works. You can always write down the answer to a multiplication between two powers of the same number as that number to the sum of the powers. $3^2 \times 3^5 = 3^7$. Remember this. It has all sorts of uses. By the same token you can divide a power of a number by another power of the same number by *subtracting* the second index from the first. Thus $2^3 \div 2^2 = 2$ and $10^{12} \div 10^8 = 10^4$.

There are two curious indices, or powers: the power 0 and the power 1. Try to work out what these must mean, using as a clue the fact that to multiply powers you add indices. Raising a number to the power 1 must mean using that number as it stands. 5^2 is the product of 5^1 and 5^1. 5^3 is $5^2 \times 5$, or $5^2 \times 5^1$. By the same token, $5^0 \times 5^2$ should give you 5^2. The only number that will have this effect is 1, so any number to the power nought must mean 1.

$\boxed{\surd}$

This is a square root sign. A square root is the number which when multiplied by itself gives you the number in front of which you wrote the square root sign. Thus $\sqrt{9}$ is the number which, when squared, gives 9, i.e. 3. Press $\boxed{8}\,\boxed{1}\,\boxed{\surd}$ on your calculator to find the square root of 81. You should be able to work out the index number, or power, of a square root. Stop for a minute and try. (Some computers need $\boxed{\surd}\,\boxed{8}\,\boxed{1}$.)

If you are stuck, remember that to multiply two powers you *add* the index numbers. And the index for a number itself is ^{1}. The thing which you add to itself to get one is ½. Thus $\sqrt{4} \times \sqrt{4} = 4 = 4^{½} \times 4^{½}$.

Just as you can find squares, cubes, fourth powers, etc., so you can find cube roots, fourth roots, etc. in a similar way to finding square roots. Cube roots are written $\sqrt[3]{}$ or ⅓, fourth roots as $\sqrt[4]{}$. Work out $\sqrt[4]{16}$ on your calculator.

There is no fourth root key. But you know that a fourth root is the square root of a square root, and can therefore press $\boxed{1}\boxed{6}\boxed{\surd}\boxed{\surd}$ giving the answer 2. If this still seems a bit confusing, set yourself some practice examples. Find some powers of numbers on your calculator by repeatedly multiplying the number by itself, counting how often so you know which power it is. Write yourself a question to find the appropriate root of this number, noting the answer separately. Put the questions to one side for a few days, then do them 'blind', checking the answer only when you have finished. Or forget about saving the answer and check on your calculator by multiplying up.

Other mathematical signs

The above list covers what a basic calculator can do. Scientific calculators will offer you a much wider range of options, including the ability to do mixed additions and multiplications without getting muddled and other things scientists do frequently. Financial calculators offer similar benefits in the area of accounting and finance. As well as costing more, these require a time investment if you are to exploit their facilities fully. If you are going to do a lot of specialist calculations when away from a PC, the appropriate calculator (or even better, a palm-top computer) may be a good investment. But a simple calculator is probably best while you are developing your basic skills. It offers less to confuse you!

You will frequently meet the following signs in equations (or sometimes on more complex calculators).

$\boxed{x}$

This could be any other letter, usually italicised. This is referred to as a 'variable' and when it appears in an equation it represents something which can take a number of values, or whose value you do not know. Although you may be disconcerted to see an equation with a mixture of letters and numbers, the letters are very easy to deal with. You treat them just as you would numbers, moving them around in the same way (more of this later). Of course, if you want, say, to multiply 2 by x, you cannot simply write in a new number as you would if multiplying, say, 2 by 3. But you can write $2x$ and carry on quite happily like that. Indeed, it is really much simpler to play with letters than numbers, as well as far more useful on many occasions, which explains why you see them in equations so often. (More of this later, in the discussion of equations.)

$\boxed{\Sigma}$

This is the Greek letter sigma, used to indicate the sum of something. It is often written as $\sum_{n=1}^{r} x_n$. This means that x has a number of values, which have been called, for convenience, x_1 to x_r. You are to add all these values, from x_1 to x_r. Thus you could express a year's sales figures as the sum of the totals of month 1 to month 12, or x_1 to x_{12}. You would write this as $\sum_{n=1}^{12} x_n$. But if you were only interested in sales for the second quarter, you could write $\sum_{n=4}^{6} x_n$. This notation may look clumsy and forbidding (and is a nightmare when it comes to layout) but is often an extremely economical way of expressing something in an equation. And because it is a standard convention, anyone slightly familiar with mathematics will find it easy to understand.

This means 'function'. If we say $y = f(x)$ we mean that y varies in some way as x varies, or it is a function of x. Thus if the area of a carpet varies with both the width and the length of the piece, its area is a function of both of these. If you called the area a, the width w and the length l, you could write $a = f(l, w)$. If you knew that you were always buying from a roll that was 3 metres wide, the area would merely depend on the length bought, or $a = f(l)$. Indeed, it would have been perfectly correct to write $a = f(l)$ in the first case, too, because area did depend on the length. The fact that it also depends on width (or in another case, other variables) does not have to be mentioned. You might choose not to mention all the variables, for various reasons, or indeed might not know what some of them are.

This simply means 'not equal to'. If you write $x \neq y$ you are saying that x cannot take the same value as y, whatever else it may or may not be able to do.

This means 'less than'. If $x < y$ then it means that x must be less than y.

This means, not surprisingly, 'greater than'. So $x > y$ means x has to be greater than y. It is fairly easy to remember which sign is which – the fat side of the wedge points to the bigger number in either case, and the thin side or point to the smaller number.

This means 'less than or equal to'. Thus in $x \leq y$, x cannot be greater than y, but could be either the same as y or smaller.

Obviously, this means 'greater than, or equal to'.

These are brackets and are extremely important in equations. If things are within a bracket, it means that they must be treated as a whole. For example, $2(7 + 6x + y)$ means $14 + 12x + 2y$, because you have to multiply every term within the bracket by the 2 outside.

The above constitutes a very basic mathematical vocabulary. Use the following test exercise to check your understanding of the points covered. Answers are given at the end of the book.

Where you have a wrong answer, work out why. Was it a careless error – when you do it again it actually gives the right answer? If so, take more care in future! But if this is not the case, and what you are doing gives the same (wrong) answer again, go back to the relevant definitions and examples and find out why.

TEST EXERCISE 5.2

(a) Write the following as decimals:

$\frac{3}{4}$ $\frac{21}{7}$ $1\frac{1}{3}$ $\frac{15}{7}$ $\frac{9}{11}$ $\frac{6}{8}$

_____   _____   _____   _____   _____   _____

(b) Write the following as percentages:

2 $\frac{3}{4}$ $1\frac{1}{3}$ $\frac{10}{11}$ $\frac{1}{4}$ $\frac{2}{3}$

_____   _____   _____   _____   _____   _____

(c) Write down the value of:

2^3 14^2 3^4 $3^2 \times 3^2$ 12^3 1^4 6^0

_____   _____   _____   _____   _____   _____   _____

(d) Write as a power of a single number:

$2^2 \times 2^5$ $3^4 \times 3^2$ $10^3 \times 10^5 \div 10^8$ $17^6 \times 17^3$ $21^{21} \div 21^3$ $x^y \div x^2$ $x^3 \times x^2$ $z^{2x} \times z^{2y}$

_____   _____   _____   _____   _____   _____   _____   _____

(e) Use your calculator to work out the following, writing your answer using only two places of decimals:

$\sqrt{16}$ $\sqrt{144}$ $\sqrt{36}$ $\sqrt{38}$ $\sqrt{2}$ $\sqrt{10}$

_____   _____   _____   _____   _____   _____

(f) Write each of the following as a power of a number, rather than using a root sign:

$\sqrt{2^{16}}$ $\sqrt{10^4}$ $\sqrt[3]{3^2}$ $\sqrt{(x^2 y^2}$ $\sqrt[7]{z^{14}}$

_____   _____   _____   _____   _____

(g) If $x_1, x_2, x_3, \ldots x_r$ represent the numbers 1, 2, 3, . . .r, write down the value of

$\sum_{r=1}^{3} x_r$ _____

(h) Which of the following are true?

(i) $7 \neq 7$ (ii) $3 \geqslant 1$ (iii) $5 > -5$ (iv) $3 < -5$ (v) $x^2 > x$ when $x = 1$?

_____   _____   _____   _____   _____

(i) Write each of the following in a way that does not use brackets:

$2(x + y)$ $3(x - y)$ $(x - y) - (x - y)$ $(x - y) - (x - 2y)$

_____   _____   _____   _____

(j) Work out:

$5 + 2 \times 4$ $3 \times 6 - 5 + 4$ $x + x \times x \div y$ $1.2 \times 3.4 - 1.2 \div 6.1$

_____   _____   _____   _____

UNITS

Numbers can indicate the quantity of almost anything. Even in a number, as you have already seen, the digits stand for different things depending on where they are placed in relation to the decimal point (or to the last digit if the number is whole). So '5' might mean five hundred, five million, five-tenths or whatever, as discussed above. Obviously, to make sense of any number you need to know what it stands for. And in doing things with the number, you need always to keep this in mind. You cannot add apples to oranges, though you can refer to both as pieces of fruit and come up with a meaningful answer. Thus in adding numbers 'by hand' you needed to be sure that you aligned them properly so that you were adding tens to tens, hundreds to hundreds, etc.

In dividing things by other things, it is just as important to be clear what units the answer is in. Thus if you are concerned about fuel consumption you might use the Imperial system and divide distance in miles by petrol used in gallons, and express your answer in miles per gallon. Or you might be resolutely metric and measure distance in kilometres and petrol in litres, and talk of kilometres per litre. But if you had done one, and your friend had done the other, you would not know which of you had the more efficient car (or driving style). And if a third friend had done the easiest calculation and divided miles (because that is what his car's instruments measured) by litres (because that is what the pump measures), producing a nasty hybrid unit, you could not relate his answer to either of yours.

In choosing units to work with, it makes sense to select those which are most straightforward to use and to communicate to others. Note that these may not always be the same. Metric systems, because dividing by ten is so easy, are usually the easiest to use for measures. But if you were selling cars to people who thought in miles per gallon, metric measures might not communicate best. Ease will depend on the size of units. You would use metres rather than centimetres as your main unit in measuring either carpets or short races, because the number of metres will be manageable, whereas numbers of centimetres would be huge and kilometres would require you to be using fractions all the time. A marathon, however, would be measured in miles. Choice of unit will be important later, when you are manipulating numbers and representing them in ways that make their significance clear.

ESTIMATING AND ROUNDING

You have seen, in trying out basic arithmetic operations, that a calculator makes the whole thing absurdly easy. But it is very easy to press a wrong button in the middle of a calculation. And sometimes it is not obvious what button to press. We once took four calculators which were lying around the house and tried to add 50 per cent to 100 by pressing $\boxed{1}\boxed{0}\boxed{0}\boxed{+}\boxed{5}\boxed{0}\boxed{\%}$. The 'answers' were 150, 200, 250 and 300!

Similarly, when you get on to modelling, you may make a simple mistake either with an equation or with some of the data you put into the model. In either case you really need to know that this has happened. If you have worked out very roughly what sort of answer you are likely to get, alarm bells will start to ring if the answer is wildly different. This will not alert you to faults where the answer is only slightly adrift, but it will save you from many an embarrassing situation.

The technique of getting a rough idea of what to expect is called *estimating*. For example, if you are adding up ten numbers, each of which is between 700 and 900, you might estimate that the answer will be about 8000. If it is more than 9000 or less than 7000 you know that something has gone wrong. Whatever calculation you are doing, it is worth getting a ballpark figure in your head, so that you know if some extra noughts have crept in somewhere, or you inadvertently inserted an unwanted decimal point, or pressed ÷ rather than −.

TEST EXERCISE 5.3

Estimate the value of the following before working them out on your calculator.

	Estimate	*Answer*
(a) 2734 + 5955	_____	_____
(b) 40 569 ÷ 9	_____	_____
(c) 25% of 39 400 113	_____	_____
(d) 95 + 15% of 113	_____	_____

To estimate you were probably working to the nearest hundred or thousand to get a rough idea of the expected answer. This technique, called *rounding*, is enormously useful. You will remember that when you used your calculator to work out 1⅔ it filled up its display capacity with 6s. You will not usually work to many places of decimals; total accuracy is seldom that important. It is not worth the inconvenience of working to many decimal places. Worse, to do this implies a spurious accuracy which may cause people to doubt your grasp of what the results really mean.

Suppose that your project involved using a questionnaire to obtain a measure of job satisfaction. Respondents were asked to rate a number of aspects of their jobs on a scale of 1 to 5. If you wanted to work with average scores in this case it would be totally absurd to use more than one decimal place, as the ratings themselves are subjective and the scale crude.

When you have decided how many decimal places you want (or whether you are going to round to the nearest number of tens, or hundreds, or whatever) you need to decide the value of that last number, be it tens, tenths or millions, by looking at the first number that you are discarding. Thus if you want to round 178 to the nearest 10 you will be discarding the 8. But 8 is greater than 5, so 178 is closer to 180 than to 170. You should therefore round it to 180. 172 would round to 170, while opinions differ about 175. Whether you round this up or down doesn't matter, but if you are rounding a set of numbers you should adopt the same principle throughout. Rounding fractional numbers is just the same: 21.178 would be 21.18 to two decimal places, or 21.2 to one decimal place.

TEST EXERCISE 5.4

Round the following to two places of decimals:

(a) 1.2674   (b) 12.9763   (c) 129.763   (d) 129 763.557

_____   _____   _____   _____

You will see from the above exercise that rounding to, say, two decimal places does not make the same sort of sense with numbers of different orders of magnitude. If you are talking of numbers in the hundreds of thousands then decimal places will often be of little interest, while for a small number or a fraction they may make a huge difference. For example, 0.02 is twice as big as 0.01. Therefore, rather than rounding to a specific number of decimal places, or to tens or whatever, it may make more sense to give a specified number of *significant figures*. This is the number of figures from the first (non-zero in the case of decimals) digit to that which you round. Thus 673.457 is 670 to two significant figures, and 0.0050789 is 0.00508 to three significant figures, or 0.0051 to two significant figures.

TEST EXERCISE 5.5

Give the following to three significant figures:

(a) 137.3   (b) 0.00078635   (c) 3976.77   (d) 1.0008762

_____   _____   _____   _____

FRACTIONS, RATIOS AND PERCENTAGES

Decimals are a form of fraction, but a splendidly simple one to use. Decimal notation was not really worked out in systematic form until the sixteenth century. Before that, unwieldy fractions such as $\frac{197}{280}$ or worse (according to Crosby, already quoted) $\frac{3345312}{4320864}$ made life exceedingly difficult. Indeed Luca Pacioli, the famous Renaissance bookkeeper who popularised double-entry bookkeeping, said that 'many merchants disregard fractions in computing and give any money left over to the house'. There was clearly a need, from the customer's view at least, for a workable system for dealing with fractions!

The decimal system provides this. Working in tenths and hundredths is as easy as working with hundreds, tens and units, provided you take reasonable care to keep the decimal point in the right place. Percentages (i.e. hundredths) offer the same advantages of ease of working. As you saw with the case of $\frac{2}{3}$, you cannot always express a fraction exactly as a decimal (or percentage). But by using enough places of decimals you can get as close as you want. Sometimes, however, you need to be given, or need to work with, the fractions themselves. A brief revision of these topics is therefore in order.

TEST EXERCISE 5.6

To see how happy you are with percentages, try the following:

The university bookshop is offering books at 80 per cent of their original selling price. You decide to buy two books, which cost £27.00 and £23.00. You also have an introductory voucher which offers you a 5 per cent reduction on anything you buy. What should you end up paying, and should you ask for your 5 per cent discount before or after the 20 per cent discount is deducted?

As you have already seen, it is easy to use a calculator to turn fractions into decimals, but this is no help if you are working with equations that include letters (we shall cover these shortly). And there are other times when you may not *want* to turn a fraction into a decimal. You therefore need to know the basic rules for dealing with fractions. Sometimes they will make a calculation so easy that you don't need your calculator.

> **Rule 1** You can multiply or divide the top and bottom of a fraction by the same thing, be it number, letter, or mixture of both, without changing the value of the fraction.

Imagine cutting a cake into two, four, six or eight pieces. How many pieces would constitute half the cake in each case? From this you can see that ½ is the same as ²⁄₄ or ³⁄₆ or ⁴⁄₈ or, for that matter, ⁶⁰⁰⁰⁄₁₂ ₀₀₀.

Similarly, when you start to play with equations, you can write $\frac{2x}{6x}$ as ⅓ or $\frac{2(3+y)}{3(3+y)}$ as ⅔. This operation is called *cancelling* and is extremly useful for simplifying fractions, so that they are much easier to work with.

TEST EXERCISE 5.7

Simplify the following fractions by dividing top and bottom by the same thing, i.e. by a factor common to both:

(a) ²⁰⁄₃₀ _____

(b) ⁷⁵⁄₁₀₀ _____

(c) ⁶⁄₉ _____

(d) ²²⁄₁₁ _____

(e) ¹⁶⁄₁₂ _____

(f) $\frac{3x}{4x}$ _____

(g) $\frac{4(x+1)}{8(x+1)}$ _____

> **Rule 2** To multiply a series of fractions you multiply all the numbers (or letters, or brackets) on top of the horizontal line to get the thing on top – known as the **numerator** – in your answer, and all the things underneath it to get the thing underneath – the **denominator**.

Thus $\frac{2}{3} \times \frac{4}{5} = \frac{8}{15}$ and $\frac{1}{2} \times \frac{3}{4} = \frac{3}{8}$. You can now see how cancelling comes in useful. You can cancel out numbers, letters or whole brackets wherever you see the same in one of the things on top of a line and one of the things below the line anywhere in a string of fractions to be multiplied. They do not have to appear in the same term. Thus $\frac{1}{2} \times \frac{4}{5}$ can be written as $\frac{2}{5}$, since you can divide both the 2 on the bottom and the 4 on the top by two.

TEST EXERCISE 5.8

(a) $\frac{2}{3} \times \frac{3}{4} \times \frac{4}{5} \times \frac{1}{2}$ _____

(b) $\frac{1}{(n+1)} \times \frac{(n+1)}{3}$ _____

(c) $\frac{1}{xy} \times \frac{x}{(1+y)}$ _____

(d) $\frac{1}{2} \times \frac{50}{100}$ _____

(e) $\frac{2y}{14} \times \frac{7}{xy}$ _____

(f) $\frac{2}{15} \times \frac{3x}{4y} \times \frac{y(y+1)}{x}$ _____

(g) $\frac{y}{x} \times \frac{7}{y} \times \frac{x^2y}{14}$ _____

Note that whether or not the bottom line of a fraction is written with a bracket around it, you must treat it as if there were one there. It would be quite correct to write $1 + y$ in (c) above, i.e. *without* a bracket, but you could not divide it by any y that appeared in the top line, as this would not go into the whole expression of $1 + y$. However, if there were a bracket containing $(1 + y)$ in one of the top line terms, you could cancel this with a $1 + y$ phrase by itself, without (or with) a bracket below the line somewhere or, indeed, with such a bracketed term multiplied by something else somewhere below the line.

Following the same rule, you can see that to square a fraction you square the number on the top to get the numerator, and the number below to get the denominator. Thus

$\frac{1}{2}$ squared is $\frac{1}{4}$, $\frac{2}{3}$ cubed would have $2 \times 2 \times 2$ on the top and $3 \times 3 \times 3$ on the bottom, so is $\frac{8}{27}$. Or you could write this as 2^3 over 3^3. Thus there are different ways of writing the same thing. Whenever you are raising a fraction to some power, you have the choice of writing a bracket around the whole fraction and putting the index number at the top right of the bracket, or putting an index number against each part of the fraction, or working the whole thing out. Thus the fifth power of $\frac{2}{7}$ could be written as $(\frac{2}{7})^5$ and the nth power of x/y could be written as $(x/y)^n$.

TEST EXERCISE 5.9

Write out the value of $(\frac{x}{y})^n$

(a) where x is 1, y is 2 and n is 3,

(b) when x is 2, y is 6 and n is 2.

Rule 3 To divide something by a fraction, turn that fraction upside down and multiply by the resulting inversion.

This rule may seem strange at first sight. But stop and think. You have to do something different as $4 \div 2$ cannot be the same as $4 \div \frac{1}{2}$. The inversion does make sense. If $4 \div 2$ means divide the 4 into two equal parts, then $4 \div \frac{1}{2}$ should mean divide 4 into half a part, in which case a whole part would be 8. English was not designed for mathematics, but you can see a sort of sense emerging.

So $4 \div \frac{1}{3}$ would be 12, and $\frac{1}{2} \div \frac{3}{4}$ would be $\frac{4}{6}$ or $\frac{2}{3}$, and $\frac{2(x+1)}{3} \div \frac{2}{x+1} = \frac{(x+1)^2}{3}$

Because you are converting a division into a multiplication by inverting it, you can string together multiplications and divisions of fractions without worry, provided you remember to invert all the things with a division sign in front and then multiply. So $\frac{1}{2} \times \frac{3}{4} \div \frac{5}{7} \times \frac{1}{14} \div \frac{3}{5}$ can be written as $\frac{1}{2} \times \frac{3}{4} \times \frac{7}{5} \times \frac{1}{14} \times \frac{5}{3}$, which cancels down to $\frac{1}{16}$.

Similarly:

$$\frac{(x+y)}{(2y+3)} \times \frac{3}{x} \div \frac{2(x+y)}{(2y+5)} \text{ becomes } \frac{(x+y)}{(2y+3)} \times \frac{3}{x} \times \frac{(2y+5)}{2(x+y)}$$

which, as you can divide both top and bottom by $(x + y)$, cancels down to:

$$\frac{3(2y+5)}{2x(2y+3)}$$

TEST EXERCISE 5.10

Work out the following combined multiplications and divisions. Leave the brackets in as was done in the example above. Don't worry that we have not yet learned how to multiply them out.

(a) $\dfrac{1}{2} \times \dfrac{2(x + y)}{3} \div \dfrac{3(x + y)}{2}$ _____

(b) $\dfrac{x}{y} \times \dfrac{y}{x} \div \dfrac{x}{y} \div \dfrac{2}{3}$ _____

(c) $4 \div (x + 1) \times \dfrac{3}{4} \div \dfrac{(x + 2)}{(x + 4)}$ _____

(d) $\dfrac{3}{4} \div \dfrac{3}{5} \div \dfrac{x(x + 1)}{(y + 1)}$ _____

(e) $1\dfrac{1}{2} \times \dfrac{3}{4} \div \dfrac{y}{x}$ _____

> **Rule 4** You can add or subtract only fractions which share a common denominator.

Go back to your pies. It makes sense to talk about ½ + ⅓ but you could not neatly include this expression in, say, a string of numbers to be multiplied. You cannot say that ½ + ⅓ is ²⁄₂, ⅔ or ⅖. It isn't any of these things. In order to write the addition as something with a single number top and bottom, we need to turn each fraction into something comparable: ½ can be written as ³⁄₆ and ⅓ can be written as ²⁄₆. We can add sixths to sixths, as they are the same thing. So we end up with ⁵⁄₆. Similarly, ½ − ⅓ could be written as ³⁄₆ − ²⁄₆, or ⅙.

If you have letters in your fractions, the principle is the same. If you wish to add ⅗ and $5x/y$, you can turn both into fractions with $5y$ on the bottom line, by multiplying top and bottom of the first by y and top and bottom of the second by 5. This will give you the sum of $3y/5y$ and $25x/5y$ or $(3y + 25x)/5y$. (Turning everything into a percentage is another way of ensuring a common bottom line, or denominator – in this case 100.)

The only remaining thing to note is that you *cannot* cancel between different terms in an addition in the same way as you can for a multiplication. Note also that you cannot cancel between *part* of the numerator and *part* of the denominator unless that part is in a bracket. Thus in the example just given you cannot get rid of either the 5 or the y in the answer above by dividing the $3y$ by y, or the $25x$ by 5. You have to be able to divide every term in the top line by something on the bottom line in order to be able to cancel. Thus if the top line had been $5y + 25x$, you would have been able to cancel the 5 in the bottom with the 5 in $5(y + 5x)$: an alternative way of writing the denominator.

TEST EXERCISE 5.11

Write the following as single fractions:

(a) $\dfrac{3}{4} + \dfrac{7}{8}$ _____

(b) $\dfrac{2}{x} + \dfrac{4}{y}$ _____

(c) $\dfrac{5x}{y} - \dfrac{(2x+1)}{y}$ _____

(d) $\dfrac{2}{3} + \dfrac{3x}{5}$ _____

(e) 50% of ¾ _____

(f) $\dfrac{y(5x+1)}{x} + \dfrac{xy}{(5x+1)}$ _____

(g) $\dfrac{5}{(x-1)} - \dfrac{3}{(x-2)}$ _____

5

Basic numbers

Ratios

Now that you are comfortable with the basic rules for dealing with fractions, whether expressed in letters, numbers or a mixture, you can move on to another way of expressing what are essentially fractions – that is, ratios.

You use ratios when you are more interested in the relative sizes of things. That is, their proportions are of more interest than the absolute differences between them. To say that part A costs 20p more than part B may be more or less impressive, depending on how much they both cost. If part A costs £200.20, the difference is very slight. If it costs 21p, the difference is huge. To say that you need 100 g more flour than fat in making pastry would only be true if you were using 200 g of flour. It is far more useful to say that you need to use half as much fat (in weight) as flour. This is true whether you are catering for an army or cooking for yourself.

Ratios are obtained by dividing one thing by another. Thus in the above, if part A is 21p, the ratio of the cost of A to B is 21:1. If it is £200.20, the ratio is close to 1:1, that is, they cost almost the same. In basic pastry, the ratio of flour to fat is 2:1. You obtain the ratio of A to B by dividing A by B. The ratio of fat to flour is 1:2, or ½. The thing you are finding the ratio *of* comes before the colon, or on top of the fraction. The thing you are finding the ratio of that *to* appears second, or as the denominator. While the colon way of writing ratios is very common if you merely want to say what a ratio *is*, if you want to include the ratio in an equation then writing it as a fraction will enable you to treat it as any other fraction. Since percentages are just another way of writing fractions you can, of course, express ratios as percentages if you want.

TEST EXERCISE 5.12

Imagine that you work for a charity with a budget of £40 000, of which £12 800 is spent on advertising and fundraising.

(a) What percentage of the budget is spent on advertising and fundraising?

_____

(b) What is the ratio of this spending to the total budget?

_____

(c) What is the ratio of the advertising and fundraising budget to the money spent on everything else?

_____

If you are studying management or business, or if you become a senior manager, then you will meet many ratios. Because ratios deal in relative values rather than absolutes, they allow you to make meaningful comparisons between operations of different sizes. Particularly important is the use of certain key ratios to compare an organisation's performance from year to year and to identify emerging trends.

One key ratio of this kind is 'return on capital employed', or ROCE. This is sometimes called 'return on investment', or ROI, as it tells you precisely this. Obviously, if you make a huge investment and your profits are small, you will be less happy than if you get the same profits from a very small investment. The following exercise requires you to work out ROCE (or ROI) for a number of different organisations. For this you need to know what the ratio is:

ROCE (or ROI) = Operating profit before interest and tax/Capital employed.

Remember, too, that figures may be written in brackets to show that they are negative. In such a case the figure in brackets is a loss, not a profit.

TEST EXERCISE 5.13

Calculate ROCE (as a percentage) in the following cases (figures in £K):

	Operating profit	Capital employed	ROCE
(a)	500	4000	_____
(b)	164	83	_____
(c)	4.3	13	_____
(d)	(10)	256	_____

USING EQUATIONS

Equations have countless uses. Take a simple example: you want to borrow money at a certain rate of interest. Instead of paying the interest as it becomes due, you want to add it to the amount borrowed. This is called compound interest. Suppose you borrowed £1000 at 15% interest for five years. At the end of the first year you would owe £1150. Or you could say that your debt at the end of year 1, call this D_1, will be 1.15 × the sum borrowed. At the end of the second year your debt (D_2) will be D_1 × 1.15, or the original sum multiplied by 1.15 squared.

TEST EXERCISE 5.14

Use your calculator to find the debt at the end of the second year and then the debt at the end of the third year.

_____   _____

Now you can see why it is useful to replace numbers by letters. It enables us to write a general, all-purpose formula for how to calculate the amount owed without specifying actual figures. We can say that after any number of years, say n, the balance outstanding will be $(1.15)^n$ × £1000. If you want the debt after ten years, it will be $(1.15)^{10}$ × £1000, and so on.

We can make the formula more general by using a different letter, say A, for the original amount borrowed. It is even more general if we use a further letter, say r, for the interest rate. Thus if D_n is the debt at the end of year n, we can say that $D_n = A(1 + r)^n$.

Armed with this formula you can work out the debt for any loan, at any interest rate, for any length of time. You merely replace the letters by the numbers that apply in a particular case and work out the answer.

TEST EXERCISE 5.15

Work out the amount which will be owed:

(a) At the end of one year on a loan of £2000 at 13% interest.   _____

(b) At the end of two years on a loan of £1500 at 25% interest.   _____

(c) At the end of five years on a loan of £10 000 at 15% interest.   _____

Thus far we have merely substituted values in a given formula in order to work out the amount owing. You can see that this is extremely useful. There are many formulae that will allow you to work out all sorts of things which might be important to you. But sometimes it is not simply a case of plugging in the numbers to get what you want. You might find that, instead of sitting all by itself to the left of the = sign, the 'thing' you are interested in finding the value of may be mixed up in the middle of an equation. Then you will need to move terms around to get the 'thing' by itself. Or, worse, you may wish to find the value of several terms which are all jumbled up in a single equation. In this case you will not be able to find a solution unless you have several equations.

Classical algebra relied heavily on x and y for its variables, but you can use any letter you want. It is usually easier to remember what stands for what if you use letters that relate in some way to what they stand for. Thus in the example above it was easy to remember that D stood for debt, r for rate of interest and A for amount borrowed initially. If you are working things out for yourself this can be a great help. (If working something out in an exam use the letters in the formula as it was taught you, or as it is given in the exam.)

To sort out equations into something that helps you work out what you want, you need to think a little more about just what an equation is. It is easiest if you visualise an equation as something where the two sets of things to be seen each side of the = sign are in balance. For example, look at Figure 5.1.

Here, x on one side balances with $y + 1$ on the other, and we can write it as $x = y + 1$. Seeing it in this way makes it easy to understand what you can and cannot do to an equation. Obviously, if you added something to one pan you would only be in balance if you added the same thing to the other pan. So in this case you could write, for example, $x + 1 = y + 1 + 1 = y + 2$. Or $x + z = y + z + 1$. You could also take the same quantity from both sides and still be in balance.

Thus you could write $x - z = y + 1 - z$, or $x - 1 = y$, or $x - y = 1$. (Can you begin to see how useful this fact is if you want to get one term all by itself on one side of the = sign?)

Similarly, you can multiply both sides by the same thing, or divide by the same thing, and still be in balance. So

$$2x = 2(y + 1), \ zx = z(y + 1), \ \tfrac{1}{2}x = \tfrac{1}{2}(y + 1) \text{ and } x/(y + 1) = 1$$

Indeed, whatever you do, so long as you do the same thing to each side of the equation, you will still have a valid equation. But what you *cannot* do is to do

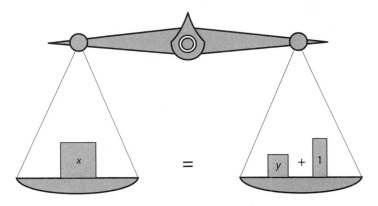

Fig. 5.1 An equation as a balance

something to one side only, or to one side and only part of the other side. Thus you could not double the x and the y, but leave the 1 alone: $2x \neq 2y + 1$ in the example used above. To make sure that you do not inadvertently deal with only part of one side, put brackets around the whole thing before multiplying or dividing.

This is the main rule for manipulating equations. If you have now grasped it – and it is obvious when you think of the balance – you are in a position to do all sorts of things. Suppose you were working with the debt and compound interest example used earlier, but you did not know how much had been borrowed, only the amount owed at the end of the period and the interest rate. You want to find out the original amount borrowed. Suppose that after four years at 20% the debt was £4147.

You could experiment to get close to the answer. Guess at a loan and work out what the debt would be at the end of the period, using the formula as given. If it is too high, try it with a smaller loan and so on, until you hit on a loan which is close enough for your purpose. When you cannot easily sort out an equation, this may be a useful approach. But in this case there is a much easier way. All you need to do is to use what you know about equations to rearrange this one to give you what you want to know, A, on one side of the =, with everything else on the other. Then you need to substitute the numbers which you know for the terms on that side to give you the value of A.

The original equation was:

$$D_n = A(1 + r)^n$$

Don't worry that this is much more complicated looking than the equation in the balance illustration. The principle of doing the same to each side is just the same. Here, we want to stop the A being multiplied by $(1 + r)^n$. If we divide that side of the equation by $(1 + r)^n$, then the two terms will cancel out, giving us A by itself. But remember, we need to divide *both* sides by the same thing, so we need to divide the D_n by $(1 + r)^n$ as well. This gives us the equally valid equation:

$$A = \frac{D_n}{(1 + r)^n}$$

This is a much more useful arrangement of the equation if A is what we are trying to find. We know the values of D_n, r and n, and can put these into the equation, giving A = £4147 divided by $(1.2)^4$, which your calculator should tell you is near enough to £2000. This is quicker and more accurate than the trial and error method.

We shall now do a similar thing with a different equation which looks more like those you find in a conventional algebra text. If you want to find x when you have the equation:

$$y = 7 + 3x + 1/y$$

you want to rearrange things to get the x on a different side from the 'y's, and from the 7. You can take 7 from both sides. And you can take $1/y$ from both sides. This gives you:

$$y - 7 - 1/y = 3x$$

It is usual to have the thing we are looking for on the left, so these two sides can be reversed:

$$3x = y - 7 - 1/y$$

The only thing remaining is to divide both sides by 3, to leave us with a single x on the left:

$$x = \frac{y - 7 - \frac{1}{y}}{3}$$

This would be fine if you knew y and merely wanted to put in its value and work out x. But you might want to include this in a longer equation, where there could be a chance of cancelling some terms out and, with a messy looking thing like this, it would be quite hard to keep track of what you were doing. So it could be tidied up into something with only one fraction. To get rid of the $\frac{1}{y}$ on the top, we need to turn all the terms into $y$ths. (Remember that with fractions you could multiply top and bottom by the same thing, or divide them by the same thing, without changing the value of a fraction: $\frac{1}{2} = \frac{3}{4} = \frac{19}{20}$ etc.). So y can be written as y^2/y, and 7 can be written as $7y/y$. Thus the whole numerator, the bracketed term, can equally well be written as

$$\frac{y^2 - 7y - 1}{y}$$

The whole equation can thus be written as:

$$x = \frac{(y^2 - 7y - 1)}{3y}$$

This makes it easy to work out the value of x. It would be fairly easy to include this 'phrase' in a larger equation if you wished to work out something more complicated.

TEST EXERCISE 5.16

Rearrange the following equations to get x on the left, then work out the values of x if (i) $y = 2$, (ii) $y = -3$, (iii) $y = 0$.

(i)   (ii)   (iii)

(a) $2y = x + 5$

(b) $y + 1 = 3x - 2$

(c) $y + 2x = y - x + 12$

(d) $\frac{y}{4} = \frac{x}{2} + 3$

(e) $xy = 3$

(f) $\frac{x}{y} = y + \frac{1}{2}$

(g) $\frac{y}{(x + 3)} = 4$

h) $\frac{x}{(y + 2y + 1)} = y + 4$

USING BRACKETS

In the above examples it was often necessary to use brackets to remind you that everything on the top or bottom of a fraction needed to be multiplied or divided by the same thing, or that whatever you did to one side of an equation you needed to do to the other. In Test exercise 5.11 above, you could handle the brackets by substituting numbers and working out the bracket before going further. Sometimes, though, you need to work with the brackets without substituting. This is less forbidding than it looks.

You have already seen that a simple multiplication, say $2(a + b)$, means multiplying *everything* in the bracket by the 2: here this simply gives you $2a + 2b$. In the slightly more complicated case of multiplying two brackets, the same underlying principle of multiplying everything in the bracket applies. So in $(a + b)(c + d)$, you need to multiply everything in the second bracket by a and add it to everything multiplied by b. Thus:

$$(a + b)(c + d) = ac + ad + bc + bd$$

Note that wherever two brackets are written side by side like this it means that they are to be multiplied. There is no need to put a $\times$ sign to show this. Work out the value of each side of the above equation substituting $a = 1$, $b = 2$, $c = 3$ and $d = 4$, to check that they are indeed equal.

TEST EXERCISE 5.17

Write without brackets:

(a) $2a(3b + 2c)$

(b) $\dfrac{x(6y - 4z)}{2}$

(c) $3r(s + 2t) + 3s(2r + t)$

(d) $(2x + y)(y + 2)$

(e) $\dfrac{(3z + 4y)(2y + z)}{2(4y + 2z)(a + b)}$

GOING FURTHER

This chapter has introduced the basics of the maths that you are likely to need and should have made you less nervous about learning more. Once you grasp that the underlying principles are really remarkably simple, you should find that 'playing' with

→ Ch 14 equations is fun. Chapter 14, Making sense of data, will show you how you can understand the numbers that your equations or whatever produce, communicate this sense and use your results to aid decision taking.

This chapter has been a long one. Even so, it may be nowhere near as long as you may have felt was necessary! Perhaps you feel that you need more practice before you are really comfortable with working things out and moving equations around. You may need more practice, too, in order to establish the skills sufficiently so that they will stay with you. There is no real substitute for practice – more practice than the limited number of exercises given here can provide.

So make up further equations for yourself, or for each other if working in a group. What equation will tell you how far a car will go on *g* gallons of petrol if it does 56 miles to the gallon? How many miles to the litre will it go if there are 4.5 litres in a gallon? Think of other such useful things to calculate. Or ones which are not useful, but still good practice. Obtain one of the many books which offer examples (but make sure that it gives answers at the end). Knowing that you are competent at manipulating numbers and equations in the simple ways described here will make you more confident in a huge range of situations. It is well worth the effort it may take to practise enough that the skills 'stick'.

→ Ch 14 You will need some of these skills again in Chapter 14, in order to make sense of data. One further area of mathematics, the calculus, will be introduced there, as well as some basic ideas about statistics.

SUMMARY

This chapter has argued the following:

■ Mathematics offers a clear language for describing many relationships and for analysis and modelling in order to inform decisions.

■ Being able to work with numbers and equations is an essential skill in a huge range of academic subjects and is needed for most graduate jobs.

■ Although calculators or computers are wonderful for working things out, it is helpful to be able to get a rough idea of what the answer is. This acts as a check against faulty keying in of data or a flaw in the model.

■ This means that you need to be able to do the basic operations 'by hand', working with simplified numbers of about the right size.

■ Ratios, fractions and percentages can be used to indicate how parts relate to each other or to the whole.

■ Ratios are particularly important in accounting and finance.

■ Equations can be used to find unknown values, or to provide a general formula from which values can be calculated in specific cases.

■ Equations can be simplified or rearranged, using the basic rule that whatever you do to one side you must do to the other.

Further information

- Crosby, A.W. (1997) *The Measure of Reality*, Cambridge University Press. This will not teach you any techniques, but is fascinating background reading, with discussion of the role of numbers and measurement in a wider historical context. Thus it covers not only mathematics and bookkeeping, but also music and painting, over the period 1250–1600.

- Graham, L. and Sargent, D. (1981) *Countdown to Mathematics*, Vol. 1, Addison-Wesley with the Open University Press. This covers much the same ground as this chapter, but at greater length and with many more examples for you to work through, with answers.

- Morris, C. and Thanassoulis, E. (1994) *Essential Mathematics: a Refresher Course for Business and Social Studies*, Macmillan. This also gives straightforward explanations of the topics covered here, together with statistics and calculus relevant to Chapter 14. Again, there are many examples for you to work out and answers at the back.

5

Basic numbers

→ 6 Written communication

Improving your writing, whether it is essays or management reports, will make you far more successful as a student and at work. This chapter will help you to do this!

Learning outcomes

By the end of this chapter you should:

- understand what is required for effective communication
- have assessed whether your grasp of written English is adequate for study and report writing
- be able to write a short letter or memo communicating a particular message
- be able to plan an essay or report
- know how to structure a formal report.

If you can write clearly you have a great advantage in most situations over those who cannot. The written word (whether on paper or a PC screen) is still a major channel for communication. Writing clearly, whether essays, letters, memos or reports, is a key skill, but a rare one. Even native English speakers have difficulty with some of the basics of the English language. Mastering these can help you to become more confident, and more competent, in expressing yourself. Understanding the basic forms of written communication can make you better at structuring your essays or reports. Improving your writing style will make your communication more persuasive. Your grades will benefit markedly.

Note that there are two Helpfiles at the end of this chapter. The first covers the basics of English grammar, the second is designed to give additional help if English is not your first language.

WRITING AS A TRANSFERABLE SKILL

Being able to communicate by writing clearly is important in virtually all aspects of life. As a student, you will probably be assessed on what you *write*, rather than directly on what you *know*. Whether writing essays or exams, your ability to *communicate* the extent of your knowledge and understanding to your assessor is what determines your marks. It is no use knowing everything there is to know if you cannot convey that knowledge to your marker. Expressing yourself in writing is therefore a critical skill for success as a student.

The same skills are helpful on many occasions. Whether you are writing to a landlord about a problem with a flat, to the police explaining why you were parking in a residents' area without a permit, to a prospective employer to enquire about the sort of opportunity that might be available to you on graduation, or to your bank manager to explain why it would be a good idea for you to have a higher overdraft, it is important to get your intended meaning across and to create an appropriate impression.

The ability to write clearly will be equally important once you are working. Often a memo or report that you have written will be your first contact with senior managers. If you create a favourable impression at this stage you may be offered opportunities in future. But if your writing is confused, rambling or ungrammatical this will suggest an inability to *think* clearly. Giving people the impression that you are illiterate/uneducated/woolly-minded can seriously reduce your chance of being chosen for interesting projects. It will not do much for your promotion prospects either. Poor communication because of an inept letter can be costly to both your organisation and your reputation. Being able to express yourself clearly and communicate what you *want* to communicate while creating a good impression is essential for success.

ELEMENTS OF COMMUNICATION

Think of written or spoken examples of communication that you have recently encountered and how you reacted. You are likely to find that you were responding both to the content of the communication and to the way in which it was communicated. Sometimes you may have *misunderstood* a message. The meaning you extracted from what you received was not the meaning intended by the person who was communicating with you. The diagram in Figure 6.1 makes these different elements in communication clear. It provides a very simple framework which acts to draw your attention to the four elements of communication. This helps you to pay attention to each when planning any communication.

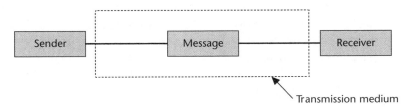

Fig. 6.1 The elements of communication

6

Written communication

Sender

The first and most important point is to be clear about your own objectives. What message(s) are you wanting to convey? Unless you are absolutely clear yourself about this you are unlikely to achieve your objective. Are you aiming to impress, inform and/or influence? You need to know your communication strengths and weaknesses. Are you better at speaking than writing or vice versa? Do you tend to make things too involved or to skip over necessary detail? Do you antagonise people unintentionally or avoid necessary conflict? The more you know about your own characteristics as sender, the more likely you are to be able to achieve your (clarified) objectives. It is worth giving this aspect of your skills serious, and honest, consideration.

Receiver

Who are your intended receivers? What are their objectives and characteristics? Are they happier with some forms of communication than others? Do they expect a particular format or level of language? Will they have particular expectations about you or your message that you need either to meet or to overcome? At work, you may find that one boss expects you to put everything in writing while another is happier with a quick face-to-face meeting. Different lecturers may demand different writing styles or have different attitudes to word limits. Some managers refuse to read anything longer than one page.

At work, there is also often a question as to the best receiver(s) for a given message. Do you tell your boss or his or her senior? Or do you write to one of these but copy it to the other to make sure they don't ignore your message? This whole area is fairly fraught and there is scope for making enemies by copying implicit criticism of one person to a number of others! On the other hand, you can waste considerable energy by communicating with those who choose to ignore you, or by failing to copy messages to people who need to know what you have said.

Message

Are you trying to communicate simple information or an interpretation of, or particular response to, that information? Do 'the facts' speak for themselves and, if so, which facts? Do you need to include numbers and tables in the message and, if so, do they also need explanatory commentary? Are qualitative factors important and, if so, how can they be made convincing? Do you need to use diagrams or other illustrations to make a point more clearly or more compellingly? Remember that for all course assessments you will be trying to convey the message that you know and understand and can use relevant concepts and techniques and have the basic knowledge about your subject that your lecturer expects. At work the 'meta-message' is likely to be slightly different: that you are capable of seeing clearly the essence of a situation and responding effectively, given the context in which it occurs.

Transmission medium

The medium, or channel, which is likely to be most effective will depend on all the other elements of the situation. A short, factual message could be conveyed equally well by e-mail, phone or face to face. A long, complicated argument, based on an analysis of large amounts of data, is likely to need a written report. A sensitive interpersonal issue is probably best handled face to face. A difficult communication which you do not wish to discuss might be easiest via memo or e-mail (a friend recently tendered her resignation by e-mail). For course assessment the medium, written or oral or other, will usually be prescribed.

Few channels are perfect. They tend to distort messages in various ways. A phone line can make words inaudible. And your use of English can similarly obscure or distort your intended message. Poor handwriting in an exam or essay can add to problems. A clearly word-processed, well-laid-out piece of work will normally attract a significantly higher grade than the same material scribbled on scruffy pages. This is not a conscious 'mark for good presentation' effect, but an unconscious alteration of the meta-message. The well-presented work will leave the assessor with an impression of better content and better underlying understanding. An inappropriate style in a job application will reduce your chances of an interview. Scruffy work communications will create a poor impression on your superiors.

→ Ch 11

Given the potential for loss in transmission, it is worth adopting strategies to minimise this. Underlining of key words, inclusion of diagrams or other illustrations to clarify and reinforce written points, and brief introductory statements of complex points you are about to make will all help. So too will summaries of points once made. These points are particularly important in verbal presentations (dealt with in Chapter 11). The formal report structure outlined shortly also serves to minimise this sort of transmission loss. So too, of course, does correct use of English!

Cartoon by Neill Cameron, www.planetdumbass.co.uk

ASSESSING YOUR WRITING SKILLS

Again this is an area where you can obtain some objective evidence on your abilities. But first, look back at your SWOT analysis to see what your initial assessment was, and then use the following activity to think further about how good your skills are in this area.

→ Ch 1

ACTIVITY 6.1

Use the following questionnaire to help you to reassess your written communications skills. Say how often each of the following is true for you. (Score N for never, S for sometimes, O for often, A for always.)

	N	S	O	A
I enjoy having to do a piece of writing.	☐	☐	☐	☐
I think carefully about what I am trying to communicate before starting to write.	☐	☐	☐	☐
I choose words that will be easily understood by the person I am writing to.	☐	☐	☐	☐
I pay attention to the order of my sentences.	☐	☐	☐	☐
I group sentences carefully into paragraphs so each paragraph contains a single idea.	☐	☐	☐	☐
I make sure my writing is legible when handwriting.	☐	☐	☐	☐
I use my PC's spell checker and grammar checker.	☐	☐	☐	☐
When I use the PC checks very few mistakes are shown.	☐	☐	☐	☐
I leave generous margins and spaces between paragraphs to improve appearance and clarity.	☐	☐	☐	☐
I use subheadings to break up long sections of text.	☐	☐	☐	☐
I use diagrams wherever possible to make my meaning clearer.	☐	☐	☐	☐
I re-read what I have written to check that there are no mistakes and my meaning is clear.	☐	☐	☐	☐
If I am writing something important I get someone to check it.	☐	☐	☐	☐
I really enjoy it when people are impressed by what I write.	☐	☐	☐	☐
I get praise from lecturers and others for my written work.	☐	☐	☐	☐

If you have lots of ticks under 'N' or 'S' you should work carefully through this chapter, and perhaps draw up an action plan to continue improving your skills thereafter. Even if your self-assessment suggests your skills are fine, check your competence by trying Test exercise 6.1 before deciding that no further development is necessary. (A version of the above which allows you to obtain a single 'score' and to reassess yourself at intervals is available on the website.)

ACTIVITY 6.2

Collect copies of letters or other things you have written for a non-study and non-social purpose. If you do not have any, save copies of the next few such letters you write. Ideally, work with others to assess the likely effectiveness of these in conveying the intended message, thinking about the message itself, the way it is expressed and the person for whom it is intended. Look out for possible *unintended* messages too. Try to redraft the content to be shorter and/or clearer and/or more likely to produce the response you want.

BASIC ENGLISH

Your parents were probably taught grammar and spelling at school, but you may not have been. The 1970s saw an increasing emphasis on creativity, and a corresponding move away from emphasising language rules in case these should inhibit 'expression'. Government initiatives are now reversing this in the UK, but the full benefits of the literacy strategy are unlikely to be felt by higher education until 2011. As a result, many people under 30 feel fairly insecure with their use of language and many lecturers and employers are frustrated by what they see either as an inability to express thoughts in writing or, worse, an inability to think at all. The following exercise will give you some idea of your own strengths and weaknesses in this area. (You may already have some idea of these from the comments teachers and lecturers have made!) Answers are given at the end of the book, but do the whole exercise before looking.

TEST EXERCISE 6.1

The following sentences contain mistakes. Without using a dictionary or other reference source, write them out correctly. (This may give a different picture from your self-assessment.)

1 The father's going to take his children their, the mother is away on holiday.

_____

2 The dog is compleatly disinterested in it's ball.

_____

3 Studying english is very different to studying engineering.

_____

4 When I recieved them the data surprised me.

_____ →

5   The essay comprised of four separate parts.

    _____

6   He was very unique in having a choice between a career as a rock singer in a leading band or as a brain surgeon.

    _____

7   A range of statistics were available owing to there search of the literature.

    _____

8   I will probably come to see you and he tomorrow.

    _____

9   There were many mistakes in your letter. You're spelling and you're unskillful choice of words.

    _____

10 One can easily improve your writing by redrafting after an interval has elipsed.

    _____

If you had more than two mistakes in your 'correct' versions (either errors which you failed to correct or alterations to text that was already correct) you should probably work through the spelling and grammar helpfile at the end of this chapter. There are further text exercises on the website.

GENERAL POINTS ON STYLE

Even if you write in perfectly correct English, the *style* of your writing may interfere with communication. Style is a difficult thing to define, and tastes in written style may differ almost as much as those in styles of clothing. But just as all winter coats should keep out wind and rain, there are certain general points which can be made about written communication (rather than writing as art). Whether you are writing an essay, a formal letter or a report at work, you are likely to have the same need for simplicity, clarity and absence of emotionality. Other things will depend on the particular form of communication you are using and will be discussed in more detail in connection with that form.

Simplicity and clarity

While it is possible, if you are thoroughly confident in your use of English and can keep control of a whole sequence of subordinate clauses, some of which may describe elements of the main clause, others of which may describe phrases which are already subordinate clauses in themselves, without forgetting which verb belongs to which clause or omitting verbs altogether, to construct a long and complicated sentence that is grammatically correct, the overall effect of complexity is usually far from satisfactory, as the reader soon starts to lose track of the main idea, which may have been introduced several lines earlier, and by the end of the sentence it is extremely likely that he or she will have lost the thread altogether.

Is that clear? Almost certainly it is not. You probably had to re-read the sentence that formed the last paragraph several times to extract its meaning. Yet many students write sentences just as long and all too often their grammar falls apart in the process. If so, then no matter how often I re-read their work I cannot extract what they mean.

TEST EXERCISE 6.2

Try to identify the main clause in the first sentence of the previous paragraph. How many subordinate clauses are there?

Imagine how much harder text is to read if long words are used as well as complex grammar. If you have a predilection for multi-syllabic words, habitually utilising these in preference to equivalent but briefer terms, intending possibly to enhance the impressiveness of your communication by demonstrating the extensiveness of your vocabulary, the capacity for obfuscation is multiplied significantly. So do not indulge yourself! Use short words and short sentences wherever possible.

As a rule of thumb, 25 words or 2½ lines should be plenty for a sentence. Remember that, although a sentence has to be complete, it should also be a single 'unit of meaning'. Unless your meaning is very complex you should be able to express it within 25 words. If you keep your sentences short you are also far more likely to keep your nouns, verbs and objects sorted out. You will be less likely to put plural nouns with singular verbs. You will be less likely to omit verbs, subjects or object altogether. So your meaning will be clearer both because shorter sentences are easier to read, and because they are more likely to be grammatically correct.

Fog Index

There are several ways of measuring the clarity or otherwise of a piece of text. One of the best known is the 'Fog Index'. To calculate this you take six sentences at random from a piece of text (or more, if you want the figure to be more reliable). Number the sentences sequentially, then throw a die, or ask someone to open a book at random and note the page numbers, or use a random number table to determine the sentences to be selected. Do not look at the text while selecting: the result will *not* be random. Count the number of words in your selected sentences and find the average sentence length by dividing number of words by number of sentences. Count the number of words with three or more syllables, divide by the total number of words in the selected text and multiply by 100 to give the percentage of long words. Add your average sentence length to your percentage of long words and multiply the total by

0.4. The answer is the Fog Index for the text in question. If it is greater than 12, the text is 'foggy'. The larger the index, the less clear the text will normally be.

Repeat the above exercise on all course work before you submit it. Try to keep your sentences as short as possible, use subordinate clauses sparingly and use long words only when there is no shorter alternative. You may well find that your grades improve. Once this style is a habit, you are less likely to write ambiguously or unclearly under exam pressure. Again your marks should benefit.

Using paragraphs

Write clearly by using:
- short complete sentences
- few subordinate clauses
- one paragraph per idea
- links between paragraphs.

As well as keeping sentences as short as possible, you need to think about how you split your text into paragraphs. Paragraphs serve to break your writing into units which the reader can absorb at one go. Ideally, a paragraph will be 75–100 words long. More importantly, it will relate to a single topic or idea. Combining disjointed ideas in a single paragraph will confuse your reader.

If paragraphs are too short, your writing can seem disjointed or superficial. Check whether the offending paragraphs need to be expanded or perhaps combined (though only if they are devoted to the same idea). The occasional short paragraph will do no harm. Indeed, it can be used to emphasise a point. But if your entire report or essay consists of very short paragraphs, you might wish to think carefully about whether you are developing your ideas sufficiently.

Over-long paragraphs make text seem heavy and forbidding. See whether you can split them into shorter ones, each containing a single point or idea. A technical report can stand longer paragraphs than a memo or newspaper article and an essay probably falls somewhere between, so the ideal length will depend to some extent on what you are writing. But thinking about carving up paragraphs is a useful way of focusing on the points that you are trying to make and the exercise often generates significant improvements. When you start to think about what you were really trying to say, you can often find a way of saying it better.

However you split your paragraphs, it is important that you link them in some way so they flow from one to the other and you avoid disjointedness. The first part of the previous sentence is an example of such a link. It relates the idea of linking to the earlier idea of splitting. Linking needs to be done with a light touch. You do not want to spend half of each paragraph covering ground covered just before merely in order to establish a link!

At the same time, you need to avoid the floating 'this', one of the greatest enemies of clarity in the essays I mark. In the 'This means . . .' or 'This is . . .' type of link, it is unclear whether the 'this' is the whole previous paragraph, the last sentence or the subject (or even the object) of the last sentence. Whether you use 'this' to link sentences or paragraphs, you should always check that it is absolutely clear to the reader what 'this' is.

Note that it is being suggested only that you express yourself as simply and clearly as possible, given the message that you wish to convey. You should *not* restrict yourself to words of one syllable and sentences so simple that a child of five could understand them. If the ideas themselves are complex, they will need to be expressed in correspondingly complex language. The point is that you should not use unnecessary complexity, either in your course work or when you are producing written communications as part of your job.

Sensational or emotive language

While you want to make whatever you write as interesting as possible, it is best to avoid sounding like a cheap newspaper (unless, of course, you are writing for one). For example, if you had done a survey of health and safety in an organisation, it would be appropriate to describe the situation as 'worrying', 'thoroughly unsatisfactory' or 'in breach of legislation'. It would be inappropriate, whatever your personal feelings, to talk of 'a downright disgrace', 'a thoroughly immoral situation' or 'another example of capitalist managers exploiting the oppressed workers'. It is possible to make your meaning perfectly clear while using restrained language. Indeed, the point may well be better made this way, as you will avoid reducing your credibility through inappropriate language.

Use of the first person

You need to check the expectations of your audience here. For example, I have used the first person ('I') in this book to avoid sounding too distant. I find that 'the author' sounds uncomfortably pretentious, particularly as this is not intended as an academically authoritative text. Rather, it is a collection of my suggestions, for you to use where they seem helpful, and use of 'I' should serve to reinforce this. So the first person, used sparingly, is normally sensible in a letter or memo. However, some organisations do not like reports to use the first person. Some of your tutors may also prefer a more impersonal way of expressing yourself. If you are submitting a paper to a

57 Variety Road
Tintown
Bucks
HB7 3RR
26.4.05

Dr P. Tutor
Dept of Business Studies
University of Wight

Dear Dr Tutor,

Absence at start of term

I am afraid that I was bitten by a snake at the start of the vacation. It is getting better now, but my doctor says I shall not be able to return until the middle of the second week of term. I enclose a certificate from the doctor.

I should be very grateful if you could inform anyone who needs to know, and apologise to those who will be inconvenienced.

Your sincerely

[signature]

ROBIN LEARNER

---

47 Sunny Avenue
Greenlands
Riverton
RV3 5PQ
Tel: 01222 57532

31.5.05

Ms J. Jones
Personnel Department
Bridge Plastics
Industrial Estate
Maintown
M7 6FF

Vacancy for temporary general assistant

Dear Ms Jones

I should like to apply for the temporary general assistant post advertised in the _Maintown Courier_. I am a second-year student at Riverton University, but live in Maintown and am looking for vacation work in July and August.

Before going to university I worked for two years, and my experience includes clerical, secretarial, bar and reception work. I enclose a CV giving details of this and the names of two people willing to act as referees. I am currently studying for a business degree and as part of this have taken a computing course. I am now reasonably competent at both word processing and use of databases.

I shall be at the above address until the end of June, and thereafter living at home, at the address shown on my CV. If you need any further information, please let me know.

Yours sincerely

Chris Student

Chris Student

Fig. 6.2 Possible layouts for a formal letter

learned journal, then 'I' would normally be inappropriate. This is an example of the importance of knowing the expectations of your 'receiver'.

BASIC WRITTEN FORMS

In addition to using correct English and expressing yourself clearly, you may have to keep to a particular form. In writing to your bank manager or a potential employer, you will need to use a formal letter. For a job application you will often be asked to submit a *curriculum vitae* (CV). Your tutors may ask for essays. At work you may have to write memos and reports. Such requirements may be worrying if you are not sure how to use the form. But if you are confident with it, then having a structure provided can make it *easier* to write clearly. CVs are dealt with in the final chapter and the other forms are outlined below. How to decide the *content* within these forms will be dealt with in Chapter 8.

➜ Ch 17, 8

Some guidelines apply to more than one form. In all formal communications it is important to use paper of a reasonably high quality for your final draft, and appropriate envelopes if needed, and to word process or write neatly and clearly. If you make a mistake, start again – your final version should be error free. These aspects of the medium can have a considerable effect on the message that is received.

FORMAL LETTERS

Two possible layouts for formal letters are shown in Figure 6.2, one word-processed, one handwritten. In either case you will see:

■ careful layout on the page, so that there is space around and the effect is balanced

■ sender's address and date of sending at the top right-hand corner (though some company letterheads vary this)

■ recipient's name and/or title with address below this and on the left of the page.

Addressee

Wherever possible, write to a named individual. This is particularly important if you are expecting some effort to be made on your behalf. Suppose that you are writing to enquire about a vacation job in a company that interests you or would like access to the company for research purposes. A letter that starts 'Dear Ms Fortescue' or whatever is far more likely to be read than one which starts 'Dear Sir'. It is usually possible to find out the name of the most appropriate recipient by telephoning first. Often the receptionist will tell you. If not, ask to speak to someone about vacation jobs or whatever and find out from them to whom you should address your letter. Check that you know how to spell the name and write it down straight away – such things seem impossible to forget, but believe me, they are not!

You can further increase your chances of success by speaking to that person on the phone – they are then far more likely to read your letter when it arrives. Failing this, try to find out from the person you do manage to talk to what sorts of skills and experience are seen as important. This will enable you to slant your letter accordingly. If you cannot find a name, at least include an appropriate job title.

Starting your letter

If you are replying to an earlier letter, then it is usual to thank the person at the start, and to include any reference that the original letter quoted, so that the earlier relevant correspondence can be easily found. If you are replying to an advertisement rather than a letter, then still quote the relevant reference. Start a new paragraph for the substance of your message.

Layout

Paragraphs can be separated either by indenting the first line or by leaving an extra line of space. With word-processed letters it is probably now more usual to leave lines, while with handwritten letters indentation is quite common. The examples given show the effect of each.

It is common to leave a slightly larger space between the 'Dear ...' line and subsequent text and again between text and 'Yours ...'. Together with space between the addressee's details and the 'Dear ...' line, this helps you to space the letter nicely on the page.

Epistolary style

As with other writing, you will need to match the style of your letter to your recipient and to your purpose. You do not wish to sound arrogant, demanding or over-familiar if you are writing formally to someone about a job or a favour of some kind. You *do* want to sound clear and to the point, as well as polite, so you will need to balance possibly conflicting demands between clarity and gratitude or whatever. If you are asking for something it is usually enough to say 'I should be grateful if you would ...', perhaps with some explanation of why you are making the request.

Sincere or faithful?

If your computer wants you to use 'Yours truly', ignore it – unless you are in the USA. Both 'Yours sincerely' and 'Yours faithfully' sound slightly archaic, but one or other is expected and many people are uncertain as to which is right. If you are writing to a named person you should end your letter 'Yours sincerely ...'. If you have only a title, and therefore have had to start 'Dear Sir or Madam', then you should end with 'Yours faithfully ...'. Save more friendly endings such as 'With best wishes ... ' for informal letters. Because most signatures are hard to decipher, you should type or print your name beneath your signature. If you are writing in an official capacity, write your position (e.g. Chairman, University Debating Society) beneath your name.

ACTIVITY 6.4

Collect formal letters written to you and check them against the guidelines above. If you have copies of your replies, then check these too and redraft where you can see scope for improvement. (This may be easier if you swap letters with someone else and correct each other's.)

ACTIVITY 6.5

Prepare an exhibit for your portfolio based on two formal letters that you have written. Describe your objectives in writing them and comment on why you adopted the style and content shown. Include copies of the letters themselves and comment on their effectiveness, in terms of the response they generated, noting any lessons learned.

MEMOS

Organisations used to use letters for external communications, but saved time by using memos for internal communications. A memo is really only a simplified letter. With the growth of e-mail it is becoming less widely used in many organisations, but is included here in case you need to write such a document while on a work placement. A standard format is usually provided – a pad of pre-printed memo sheets or a format on your PC – for showing sender, recipient(s), date and subject. Normally a memo would deal with a single subject. Figure 6.3 shows one example. If the name is given in full at the outset, it is normal merely to initial the memo at the end.

MEMORANDUM
From: Group Manager

To: Regional Managers
c.c. Regional Administrators

Date: 11.11 05

Re: *Late delivery of materials in December*

Please note that there is likely to be a problem over materials deliveries from Xxxx during December, possibly continuing to the new year. While every effort is being made to minimise this, you may find that delivery times for orders placed during this month will be approximately 10 days longer than normal.

[signature]

A. Jones

Fig. 6.3 Example of a memo

ESSAYS

→ Ch 8

→ Ch 16

This will be a short section, as there are few 'rules' for the form of an essay. Content is of course more problematic and will be looked at in Chapter 8 when assessment requirements are covered. You will also find the material on report writing later in this chapter and towards the end of Chapter 16 helpful with essay writing. The elements needed for a good essay, at least as far as form goes, are few.

- A *title*, which may be given by the person setting the assignment or, if not, chosen by you to reflect the content.

- An *introduction*, which should 'set the scene' and arouse the reader's interest. Normally it helps to enlarge slightly on the title, so that the topic and scope are clear, explain your objectives in writing the essay, outline the approach you intend to take and briefly preview key points to be covered. (Note: it is a waste of space to use your introduction merely to restate the question to which your essay is an answer. You need to expand or build on it in some way.)

- Any *background information*, if brief, may be included in the introduction. If longer, it could be a separate section immediately after. If very extensive it could be summarised briefly, with the full version appended.

- The *main body*, in which you make the points you feel are necessary to cover the topic of the title. In making these points you will need to include your arguments and describe any evidence on which they are based.

- Your *conclusions*, which provide a satisfactory feeling of completion. This section should look briefly back over what you have said, showing how the points raised answer the question or provide a specific perspective on the title (to which the conclusion needs to refer).

- The *references* which you used in your work, in alphabetical order of first author, giving date and full title of the publication. (More detailed guidelines on referencing are given at the end of this chapter.)

→ Ch 4

An equally important element of your essay, though not a visible part like those above, is its structure. Your arguments should lead firmly and directly from the initial question implicit in the title through to your conclusions. (It may help to try to diagram your points, using arrows to show which logically follows from which. If there are breaks in the logic you need to think again about your structure. Mindmaps can be useful too.)

Essay style

All the earlier general points about written communication are important. You need to be clear about your objectives and meet them by writing in good English, using convincing arguments and evidence. You should avoid colloquialisms and emotive or sensational language, repetition, rambling and pomposity or over-complex or jargon-ridden expression. You should follow a clear structure (this is dealt with in more detail in Chapter 8, together with how to plan your structure) and divide your text carefully into paragraphs.

→ Ch 8

Conciseness will normally be important, not only because it is good stylistically but because you are likely to have been given a word limit for an essay. In an exam being concise is just as important because the time limit has a similar effect. Your marker will usually have a fairly clear idea of how much ground you are expected to cover. If you write in a rambling, long-winded fashion, you will cover only a small fraction of what is expected in the words (or time) allowed. Penalties for going over the word limit will vary from course to course. Penalties for not covering ground in an exam are fairly universal!

Views on use of headings vary slightly. Some people feel that an essay should always consist of continuous, smoothly flowing prose, uninterrupted by any headings. Others feel that for a longer essay it is helpful to use headings for the introduction, main body and conclusion and even appropriate subheadings, if the body contains two or more distinct sections. It is worth asking the person setting the essay for their preference in this. There will also be variations according to subject. Scientific or technical essays may need subdivisions while essays on arts topics may not. Business studies lecturers, accustomed to report formats, normally find subheadings useful.

Lists and very short numbered points are generally seen as unhelpful in essays. Again there will be variations, depending on subject matter and tutor preferences. Sometimes a short list may be very helpful. But normally it will be better to develop each point as you make it, aiming for a flow from one to the next.

Diagrams, tables and other illustrations are also frowned on in some subjects, while considered essential in others. Where a diagram is necessary for your readers' understanding, it is best included at the relevant point, rather than placed at the end as an appendix. Be guided by what is likely to be best for the reader, who will want to follow your arguments as easily as possible, without interruption.

THE SERIOUS SIN OF PLAGIARISM

Plagiarism means passing off the work of others as your own, and is regarded as a serious offence in universities. 'Copying' without attribution, whether from another student's work or from something you found on the Internet, can incur heavy penalties, perhaps leading to expulsion from your university without a qualification and with little likelihood of getting a good reference from your tutors.

Plagiarism is dishonesty of the worst kind – it is stealing other people's thoughts and ideas. If students were not penalised heavily for this, degrees would come to be worthless, negating all the hard work most students put into gaining their (deserved) qualification. It is for this reason that you need to be absolutely clear what it means, and avoid it at all costs, no matter how behind you are, or how tempted for any other reason. Find out what your university's policy is on plagiarism, and make sure that you do not infringe it. Many universities are now using software to detect work that is not your own, so you are increasingly likely to be found out.

There are many possible reasons for plagiarism. These include:

- being unsure of your understanding of an idea so copying the original rather than putting it in your own words
- getting behind, having no time to write an assignment, so 'borrowing' one from a friend or colleague
- getting low grades, so submitting work from a better student or material copied from the Web
- laziness – it is easier to use someone else's work
- misunderstanding what is required – in some educational systems reproducing the (appropriate) original material is acceptable

None of these reasons is acceptable – not even the last one. It is your responsibility to find out what is allowable in your own university (though it is unlikely to differ much from what is said here).

Apart from the risk of being expelled, plagiarism robs you of learning opportunities. You are being asked to write essays to develop and demonstrate your understanding, and to improve your writing skills. Extended use of other people's work will serve neither of these purposes. So use quotations only when necessary to support your argument or if the quotation itself is something which you want to analyse. Do not quote authors when they are saying totally self-evident things. It is not necessary to say things like: 'As Cameron (2005) points out, "Students go to university for many reasons".' This might have been a reasonable point for me to make as part of an introduction to an exploration of these reasons; it is certainly not worth quoting in its own right. (As light relief, you might wish to play 'spot the unnecessary quote' when reading something over-zealously academic and turgid.)

To avoid plagiarism:
- use your own words whenever possible
- quote other people only when necessary
- always indicate clearly that you are quoting
- always give the reference for the material quoted
- never, NEVER use other people's text as if your own.

Quotations need to be clearly indicated as such. Use quotation marks to show the extent of what is being quoted and give the author of the quotation and its date immediately before or after, with the full reference to the source, including page number for an extended quote, in the list of references at the end of your essay. If you are not referring to other works and therefore do not need a list of references at the end, then the complete reference may be given immediately after the quote, or in a footnote on that page.

Remember: copying chunks of other people's work, without saying so, is blatant plagiarism, whether you are quoting published authors or other students' work. Either is unethical. Either will violate university policy. Either can put you at risk of being asked to leave straight away, without obtaining a qualification.

Similarly, you should never claim credit for an idea which originated elsewhere. Although you may not wish to quote the original author exactly, you should still attribute the idea to its originator and refer to the relevant publication in your list of references. 'Combobulation Theory (Blobbs 2002) suggests . . .', 'Blobbs's (2002) ideas about combobulation . . .', or 'As Blobbs (2002) found . . .' are examples of ways of doing this. Where you have not read the original paper, merely the description of Blobb in a textbook by Digester, it is good practice to say 'Blobbs, 2002, as cited by Digester (2005)' and list the Digester reference.

REPORTS

While memos are used for short communications within organisations, management reports are needed for longer ones. Their purpose may be to inform or to persuade, or sometimes a mixture of both, and the exact structure adopted will depend to some extent on which. Even reports written by junior members of staff may be fairly widely disseminated. Such a report may be your first opportunity to make an impression on senior managers when you start work. All the earlier points about clear writing, appropriate style and good presentation are therefore important.

If you have to do a project or dissertation as part of your course you will normally need to submit a report on this for assessment. If so, the structure required will probably be very similar to a management report. The underlying form in either case is similar to that of an essay. However, various devices are used to make the structure much clearer to the reader. A title page, a contents list, an introductory summary and subheadings are the key ones.

> Reports should normally:
> ■ have a clear descriptive title
> ■ indicate author and recipient(s)
> ■ list contents
> ■ use clear subheadings
> ■ include a summary
> ■ list references used.

Managers are busy people and do not want to spend time wading through undifferentiated text, only to find at the end that the whole thing was irrelevant. The title page, contents list and summary allow for a 'cheap' decision (in terms of time) by the recipient as to whether to proceed. By establishing the skeleton of the report in the reader's mind, the summary also makes it easier for the reader to grasp the possibly complex arguments which follow. Subheadings serve to keep the structure clear. (They also serve a useful function in helping the *writer* keep the structure under control.) More detail on the functions of the different parts of a report is given below.

Summary (or Abstract)

A summary is useful for any lengthy document. You are usually required to produce one for a dissertation or thesis. Practice varies as to whether the summary should come at the start or finish. Many organisations insist on it coming at the start, so that the busy manager can decide, having read it, whether or not to continue. Its 'orientation' role is also better served if it is read *before* the report proper. If it is at the end, it may serve better to reinforce what the reader has read, though the conclusions should do this in any case.

Wherever you place your summary, clearly you will *write* it last. It should normally summarise the whole report, rather than merely the recommendations. You should therefore include a brief statement of the original problem and of the main arguments and evidence leading to your conclusions. You cannot do this until the report is finished. The summary should be complete in that it should make sense when read as a stand-alone document.

Title page

The title is important: it needs to be as descriptive as possible. If it is going to appear in a listing of reports, potential readers may select on the basis of title alone. A title page needs to show the report's author(s) and their role or title, if this is significant. It helps to include the intended recipients and you need to give the date the report was circulated. All these will be important if someone is wanting to find a relevant report, or deciding on whether to request a copy of one which is known to be available. Presentation is important in creating a good impression and is served by designing an attractive title page giving this information. For short reports, or those for close colleagues only, the basic information (To: . . ., From: . . ., Report Title, Date) can instead be put at the top of the first page. An example of a title page is given in Figure 6.4.

Contents list

This should show major and minor section headings, preferably numbered. A numbering system such as that given in Figure 6.4 shows which are major sections and which minor. It makes it easy for people discussing the report, or wishing to query some part of it, to identify the part they mean. It also makes cross-referencing within the report easier.

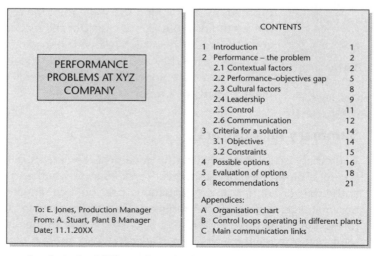

PERFORMANCE
PROBLEMS AT XYZ
COMPANY

To: E. Jones, Production Manager
From: A. Stuart, Plant B Manager
Date; 11.1.20XX

CONTENTS

1   Introduction   1
2   Performance – the problem   2
    2.1 Contextual factors   2
    2.2 Performance–objectives gap   5
    2.3 Cultural factors   8
    2.4 Leadership   9
    2.5 Control   11
    2.6 Commmunication   12
3   Criteria for a solution   14
    3.1 Objectives   14
    3.2 Constraints   15
4   Possible options   16
5   Evaluation of options   18
6   Recommendations   21

Appendices:
A   Organisation chart
B   Control loops operating in different plants
C   Main communication links

Fig. 6.4 Example of student title and contents page

You can see how such a contents list provides a clear indication of what is to come, as well as serving as an index to someone interested in only a part of the report. Page numbers help here, although for a short report they are not essential. Some organisations prefer to number paragraphs rather than sections. This helps with referencing particular parts, but does nothing to reinforce the structure.

Introduction

The introduction to a report is identical in function to the introduction to an essay, but because reports are often longer and more complex, and the topic was not 'set' by the reader, their introductions may have to work harder to achieve their aims. Your reader will usually come to a report with a number of questions:

- Why is this topic important?
- What was the remit of the report writer?
- What method was used (for research)?
- What is the main argument/finding/conclusion?
- On what evidence is this based?
- What are the implications?

If your introduction can answer these questions, at least in outline, your reader will read the subsequent report with greater interest and follow your arguments with greater ease. Of course, if you have included an initial summary, some of these questions will have been answered already and you can concentrate in your introduction on the significance of the topic and the aims of the work reported.

Background information

As with an essay, you may have to provide background information. Often a report will require more background than an essay. You may need a separate section after your introduction. Alternatively you can mention key points in the introduction, with reference to an appendix where more detailed background information can be found for those who want it.

Literature search

→ Ch 13

If your report is a research report, perhaps for a dissertation, you will need to conduct a search of existing research before refining your topic and your approach. Chapter 13 gives guidance on searching the literature. The findings of your search should be written up in a section at this point. Note that this needs to be restricted to relevant literature, that which influenced your work. Do not try to summarise everything that anybody ever wrote that has any connection, no matter how remote, with the broad area in which your topic is located!

Research method

Again, this section is obviously only necessary for dissertations or other research reports, but for these it is absolutely essential. Your reader will wish to know precisely how you went about collecting your data and why, in order to be able to judge the validity of what follows. In justifying your choice of approach you may well need to discuss alternative methodologies that you might have used.

Main section(s)

As with an essay, this is the main substance of your communication. How you write it will depend on your objectives. If you are writing a report on something which has happened, then a suitable structure might be merely to describe the events in logical sequence. If you are writing a progress report, then you might outline achievements to date, and describe work remaining to be done. Cover any problems encountered thus far and ways in which they have been, or will be, overcome and outline the significance of any deviation from planned timescales. If you are writing a position paper, you might want to outline current policy, explain any changes in circumstances since the policy was established and make a case for any change in policy which you think might be required as a consequence. If you are proposing action, you may wish to start with your proposals and then justify them. For a research report you may need to survey prior research, outline and justify your own research design, give the results of your research and then

→ Ch 8

your analysis. (More guidance on planning your structure is given in Chapter 8.)

Whatever structure is appropriate for your objectives, you need to use a system of subheadings to make this structure clear, whether or not you are using a list of contents. If the report is a long one, then it may be helpful to include a short introduction to each main section and possibly a summary concluding statement to each as well. (*Note*: While 'Introduction' is a valid heading 'Main Section" is not. Choose an appropriate one of your own.)

In a report, you should think carefully about how to reinforce the arguments in your text with diagrams, graphical representations of data, such as graphs and charts, and raw data themselves. When deciding how much non-textual material to use, and where to put it, the question is always: 'How will it work best to convince my reader?' If you are unlikely to be believed without evidence, then this evidence needs to be included somewhere.

If the non-textual material is essential for the argument to be understood, then it (or a summary of it) normally needs to go into the text. If your argument can be understood, but may not be accepted without the data, then it may still be necessary to include some of the data in the text. But the bulk of it may be better relegated to an appendix. If a point can be reinforced or made more persuasive by some illustrative material, then again you may be advised to put the illustration in the text. Readers find it inconvenient and annoying to have to keep turning to the end to refer to necessary diagrams. It is even more irritating if there is no mention of the diagram in the text and it is only discovered when the end is reached, far too late for it to be helpful. Always think about how you can best communicate with your reader.

A further advantage of including at least some diagrams in the text is that this breaks up the words, making the text look more attractive and less forbidding. However, it is not normally a good idea to include diagrams only for cosmetic purposes – they should serve a valid purpose in their own right.

Diagrams should be appended rather than included if they are extremely detailed and of interest only to the most dedicated or critical reader, or are working diagrams produced *en route* to final versions. Working diagrams may be of interest to your tutor to show your thought processes, but they would be less likely to warrant inclusion in a management report.

Numerical tables and graphical representations of these such as bar or pie charts, should be treated in a similar fashion. Where they are an important part of your argument they should appear in the text. (If they summarise more extensive information, the full data set could be appended.) Detailed mathematical arguments which support rather than act as the main vehicle for your message might be better placed in appendices. This allows mathematically minded sceptics among your readers to convince themselves, while those who are happy with your condensed version of the data can follow the train of your overall argument without interruption.

Conclusions

Conclusions should:
- flow naturally from earlier arguments
- draw these arguments together
- clarify their implications.

Conclusions should follow naturally from the arguments in the main body of your report. There should be no new material introduced at this stage, nor should any of your conclusions come as a surprise to your readers. Instead, conclusions should draw together the arguments developed in the main section and clarify their implications. It can be difficult to distinguish between conclusions and recommendations – indeed, sometimes they are combined in a single section. This may make sense in a report which is not primarily action-oriented. The distinction may helpfully be thought of in terms of conclusions being to do with the logical outcomes of your arguments and recommendations with taking action in the light of these conclusions and of the conditions prevailing in the real world.

Recommendations

Recommendations should:
- flow naturally from analysis
- be clear proposals for action
- be sensible and realistic.

As with the summary, there is debate as to the best location for recommendations. Action-oriented managers often prefer them at the front: 'Tell me what you want me to do then convince me!' For a more analytical report they may be better placed at the end, as they follow naturally from your analysis and conclusions. If your summary includes a brief statement of your main recommendations, with more detailed recommendations at the end, you should be safe, but check with the report's recipients whether they have preferences.

In a management report, recommendations should be clearly prioritised and the priorities justified. There may not be the resources to implement all of them and those evaluating your report will be checking that your priorities are justified, and realistic, given the prevailing situation.

Appendices

As indicated, detailed supporting evidence or background information can be placed in appendices. Thus you might append a copy of a questionnaire or interview schedule used to collect data, or full monthly production figures for all departments studied, or detailed organisation charts. Where you do this, you normally need to provide a summary of the information in the text and refer to the fuller version so that the interested reader knows where to find it.

Appendices are sometimes used by students as a way of getting around the word limit: being 'optional' to the reader they may not be counted in the length. This is not a good strategy! If material is essential to your argument it should not be in an appendix. If including it in your text makes your report over-long, consider whether the style is too verbose or the scope of the report too wide.

In the interests of clarity, since numbers are used to identify parts of the report, letters are often used to identify appendices. (If you have more than 26 appendices, think carefully about whether they are *all* essential before moving on to AA, etc.)

References

In a report you are likely to draw on a range of sources for ideas, data and methods. Whether these are printed, electronic or even personal communications, they need to be clearly referenced. This will avoid charges of plagiarism, and will enable your reader to go to the original sources for more information (or to check that you have interpreted them correctly). It will also convince your readers that you are familiar with other work on a topic, and that your conclusions are therefore likely to add something to existing debates.

Sometimes you will want to quote directly from your sources (though remember the caution on this earlier in the chapter). Usually you will want to convey their content in your own words. But it is always important to attribute ideas, methods or theories, as well as showing where secondary information was found. You need to do this briefly, efficiently and consistently within your text. Give fuller information, which would allow your reader to locate the original if required, in a list of references at the end. One well-worked-out system for this, widely used in academic writing but acceptable elsewhere, is the Harvard system. It is the system followed in this book, with the exception of location of publisher, which has been omitted. The following guidelines outline how the Harvard system works. Note the importance of mentioning the date you accessed electronic materials. This is because they may be updated frequently.

Guidelines for in-text references

- When referring to something in your text, give author name and date. Thus: 'It has been shown that . . . (Graveson, 1998)' or 'According to Graveson (1998) . . .'.
- If referring generally to several different authors on a topic, refer to them in alphabetical order, thus: 'The theory's generalisability may also be tested in other contexts (Glaser and Straus, 1967; Straus and Corbin, 1990).'
- If referring to something by two authors give both, as in Straus and Corbin above.
- If referring to something by more than two authors use 'et al.', as in 'Buchanan et al., 1988' (from Latin for 'and others').
- If referring to corporate authors, such as a company report, follow the style of 'Hanson Trust plc, 1990'.
- If referring to something with no obvious author, such as a government publication, give the title, e.g. '*Employment Gazette*, 1992'.
- If referring to works by the same author in different years, order by date, earliest first, thus 'Handy, 1987, 1993'.
- If referring to works by the same author in the same year, use a, b, etc. to differentiate, thus 'Handy, 1987a' and, for the next, 'Handy, 1987b'.
- If referring to something you have read about, in some other book, without actually going back to the original, then make this clear, as in 'Glaser and Straus, 1967, cited by Saunders *et al.*, 1997'.
- You need not use initials for in-text references unless you have to distinguish between two different authors with the same surname.
- If quoting word for word, put the quotation in inverted commas and give author surname, date, page number from which quote was taken, as in

  '. . business and management research involves undertaking systematic research to find out about business and management . . .'
  (Saunders *et al.*, 1997: 1)

  though here you might like to reflect on the wisdom of quoting something like this.
- To save giving the same information repeatedly, especially if you are using footnotes as well as references, two common abbreviations are used:
  - *op. cit.* – this is from the Latin for 'in the work cited', so that if you have already given a full reference and wish to refer to the same publication again, you could merely say 'Jones, *op. cit.*'.
  - *ibid.* – again from the Latin, this means the same work and refers to the work referenced immediately before.

6

Written communication

Guidelines for reference lists

- Reference lists should normally include only those sources which have been directly referred to in your text. It is not normal in a report to include other sources which might interest a reader but which have not been referred to. Should you, exceptionally, wish to do this, it is normal to call the list 'Bibliography'.
- References should be in alphabetical order.
- If you have several references by the same author, they should be ordered by date of publication, earliest first.
- If you have used a, b, etc. to differentiate publications by the same author in the same year, then you need to use them in your reference list as well, making sure that they correspond to the articles you intended in your text.
- Give first author, initials, any subsequent authors each with initials, date (in brackets) then:
    - for papers give title of paper in inverted commas, *title of publication in which paper appeared in italics*, journal volume and number (with a colon separating them) then page numbers of paper
    - for a chapter in a book where chapters are written by different people, you would similarly give title in quotes, the word 'in' followed by name(s) of book editor(s), book title in italics, location of publisher, publisher's name, page numbers of chapter
    - for a book you merely give title in italics, location of publisher, publisher's name. Thus:

        Dooley, D., Rook, K. and Catalano, R. (1987) 'Job and non-job stressors and their moderators', *Journal of Occupational Psychology*, 60: 2, 115–32.

        Craig, P.B. (1991) 'Designing and using mail questionnaires', in Smith, N.C. and Dainty, P. (eds) *The Management Research Handbook*, London, Routledge, pp.181–9.

        Saunders, M., Lewis, P. and Thornhill, A. (1997) *Research Methods for Business Students*, London, Pitman Publishing.

- If referencing something found on the Internet you should indicate that this was the source, give the date of access and the full Internet address. Thus:

    Jenkins, M. and Bailey, L. (1995) 'The role of learning centre staff in supporting student learning', *Journal of Learning and Teaching*, 1:1, Spring [online] [cited 29 Mar 1996] Available from the Internet <URL:http://www.chelt.ac.uk/cwis/pubs/ jolt/issue 1.1/page2.htm>.

(Sanders *et al.*, 1997, p. 406).

SUMMARY

This chapter has argued the following:

- Effective written communication requires clarity concerning your objectives in communication, understanding of your recipient's needs and expectations and choice of appropriate content, style and form.

- Correct spelling and grammar and good presentation will create a good impression and make it more likely that your message will be understood and accepted.

- Your writing is more likely to be clear if you keep your language as simple as possible, given the complexity of the message which you are trying to convey.

- You are likely to be able to improve your writing considerably if you set your first draft aside for a day or two before editing/redrafting.

- Although there is some agreement as to the correct form for memos, essays and reports, there is also some variation in preferred style between both tutors and organisations. You should check with your intended recipient what their requirements are.

- Careful and correct referencing is essential.

Further information

- Bentley, T.J. (1978) *Report Writing in Business*, Kogan Page.
- Blamires, H. (2000) *The Penguin Guide to Plain English*, Penguin.
- Bowden, J. (1997) *Writing a Report: a step by step guide to effective report writing*, 4th edn, How To Books.
- Burchfield, R.W. (ed.) (1996) *The New Fowler's Modern English Usage*, 3rd edn, Oxford University Press. A classic – Fowler's first edition appeared in 1926 – which is a sort of enlarged dictionary with hints on how to pronounce and use the words included. A mine of information.
- Giles, K. and Hedge, N. (1994) *the Manager's Good Study Guide,* The Open University.
- Gowers, E. (1954) *The Complete Plain Words*, HMSO, now available from Penguin. This is *the* classic work on the use of English. It has been regularly updated even since the author's death and is well worth acquiring.
- Gravett, S. (1998) *The Right Way to Write Reports*, Elliot Right Way Books.
- Seely, J. (2002) *Writing Reports*. Oxford University Press.
- Truss, L. (2003) *Eats, Shoots & Leaves: the zero tolerance approach to punctuation*, Profile Books. An amusing defence of appropriate punctuation.

6

Written communication

HELPFILE 1
Grammar and spelling

Elements of grammar

Obviously, it is beyond the scope of this chapter to teach you all the complexities of English grammar. But the following rapid overview may help you to avoid some of the more common mistakes and to feel more secure in expressing yourself. You may find it helpful, first, to become more familiar with a number of different parts of speech, serving various functions in a sentence. The most basic (with examples in *italics*) are:

- A **noun**, which names a person, thing or quality (*James, essay, incompetence*).
- A **pronoun**, which stands in for a noun, to save repeating it (*it, he, them*).
- A **verb**, which expresses an action or state of being, past, present, future or possible (*ran, is, will go*).
- An **adjective**, which describes a noun or pronoun (*unhappy, my own, incompetent*).
- An **adverb**, which modifies a verb, adjective or other adverb (ran *quickly, deeply* unhappy, *extremely* well).
- A **conjunction**, which joins or relates words or clauses (rich *and* famous, poor *but* happy, working *despite* his illness).
- A **preposition**, which introduces a phrase and is followed by a noun or pronoun which it 'governs' (put it *in* my pigeon hole, *between* you and me).

Nouns

Nouns can be subjects (the thing 'doing' something) or direct objects (the thing affected by the action). In 'You wrote your essay' *you* is the subject and *essay* is the object. With the verb 'to be' the noun is a complement, i.e. completes the sense of the verb, as in 'You are *a student*'.

Phrases

A phrase is a group of two or more words that acts as a noun, adjective or adverb. (*To write well* requires a basic knowledge of grammar. Students *ignorant of this* will do poorly. You need to learn *every day*.)

Sentences

Sentences need to be complete. Simple sentences contain one finite verb, i.e. a verb with its subject. The finite verb may, depending on its tense (past, future etc.), be several words. And it may have an object, adjectives or adverbs. (I [subject] *should have written* [finite verb] more clearly [adverb].)

Clauses

A clause is a group of words containing a finite verb that forms part of a sentence. The main clause is the backbone of the sentence and could often be used as a sentence in its own right. The subordinate clause, like a phrase, acts as adjective, adverb or noun and depends on the main clause. For example (subordinate clause in *italics*):

- The person *who marks my essays* is not my tutor [adjectival clause, describing person].
- I was very unhappy *when I received that really low grade* [adverb, saying when].
- I worked really hard *so that I would get a good exam mark* [adverb, describing purpose].
- *Why I found it so difficult* is beyond me [noun, subject of 'is'].
- I do not know *whether I shall pass* [noun, object of 'know'].
- The idea *that I might have misinterpreted the question* never entered my head [noun, enlarging on 'idea'].

Spelling (the right word)

Mis-spelling can sometimes totally alter the meaning of a sentence, occasionally with comical effect. Even if the meaning is still clear, spelling mistakes prevent you from creating a good impression in your readers and may make them less likely to accept the message which you are trying to convey. Fortunately, dictionaries and spell checkers exist to help. Use them! This chapter is not intended to save you the expense of a dictionary or the hassle of using the spell checker once you have completed a piece of work. But many spelling errors are correct spellings in themselves, but of a different word from the one you intended. Your spell checker will not identify these as errors. What follows is a list of some of the most common words which are mis-spelled as other valid words.

accept – except

The first means to receive, the second to omit or exclude.

advice – advise

The noun has a *c*, the verb an *s*. It is clear from the pronunciation which is which in this case, but this does not seem to prevent frequent mistakes. In similar pairs, e.g. practice – practise, the pronunciation is no help. You may like to use the 'advice – advise' pair to guide you in such cases.

affect – effect

To affect something is to change it or to have an effect on it. As a noun, affect is used by psychologists to mean 'mood'. As a verb, to effect something means to bring it about. Thus: 'In order to affect the way recruiters treat minority groups, it may be necessary to effect new legislation. The effect of the legislation might, however, be minimal.'

already – all ready

Already means by this time, while all ready, not surprisingly, means that all are ready. Thus: 'Are you all ready? It is lunch time already.'

bare – bear

You bare (or uncover) your head or soul, while a bear has four legs or is a verb meaning to carry.

complement – compliment

A complement completes something, as in cream complementing strawberries. If you are telling someone they are wonderful it is a compliment. If the strawberries and cream were free with the entry ticket, they were complimentary.

council (councillor) – counsel (counsellor)

Council is an assembly, as in student council, while counsel is advice or the legal person who provides it. Thus if you are worried or depressed you might arrange an interview with a counsellor, but if you are protesting about a local authority decision you might write to your elected councillor.

currant – current

Currants grow on bushes and are used in baking. Currents are found in rivers. Current practice means the practice now.

disinterested – uninterested

Not so much a spelling mistake as use of an incorrect word. Disinterested means impartial or unbiased (related to the use of interest in 'interested party'). Uninterested means showing no interest in something. This improper usage is extremely common, but irritates many readers who do know the correct meanings of the words.

ensure – insure

To ensure means to make sure, while to insure means to take (or make) out an insurance policy.

hear – here

Hear has to do with ears, while here means in this place (as in 'here, there and everywhere').

imply – infer

Another confusion rather than mis-spelling. Imply means to hint at. It is done by the 'sender'. Infer means to draw a conclusion or inference and is done by the 'receiver'.

i.e. – e.g. – etc.

These are all abbreviations of Latin phrases: i.e. means 'that is', e.g. means 'for example' and etc. means 'and so on'. They are frequently interchanged, incorrectly. Even if used correctly, etc. is best used sparingly. It can suggest that you haven't bothered to think an argument through. There is a fairly common school of thought (particularly among editors) that none of these abbreviations should be used unless absolutely necessary.

its – it's

This is probably the commonest confusion of all. It's is short for 'it is' – the apostrophe stands for the missing letter. Its means 'belonging to it', i.e. indicates possession. The confusion arises because most possessives have an apostrophe, as in 'The cat's ball'. But these are there because the old English possessive used to be 'The cat his ball', which was shortened to cat's, with the apostrophe, as in other contractions such as 'don't', standing for missing letters. But in the possessive its there are no missing letters, so no apostrophe.

lead – led

The metal is lead, as is the present of the verb: 'I lead a blameless life now'. Led is the past: 'Until I became a student I led a blameless life.'

loose – lose

Loose means 'to unfasten' or 'not tight'. Lose refers to misplacing something or not winning.

moral – morale

When you talk of job satisfaction or the mood of the troops, you mean morale. Every time moral is used in this context (and it very commonly is) it conjures up visions of defrauding the customer, or carryings on behind filing cabinets. Morals have to do with beliefs about right and wrong and with morality.

oral – aural – verbal

Oral has to do with the mouth, so refers to speaking or swallowing medicine. Aural has to do with the ears, while verbal has to do with words, which might be written or spoken.

personal – personnel

Personal means belonging to one or private. Personnel are people, such as employees.

principal – principle

Principal means most important, or head of something like a college. Principle means an idea, or truth, or code of conduct.

stationary – stationery

You buy stationery at a stationers. Stationary means not moving.

their – there – they're

There is the place (here, there, etc.). Their indicates possession (there is nothing missing when this is in the form 'theirs', so no apostrophes are needed). They're is short for 'they are', hence the apostrophe.

6

Written communication - Helpfile

to – too – two

The only times you don't use to are when you mean excessive (too) or when you mean the number (two). So: 'Two of us are going to be too late.'

were – we're – where

Were is the past tense, we're is the shortened version of 'we are', where is the place – think of it getting the answer 'here'.

who's – whose

Another muddling case like its, where you have a possessive without an apostrophe, whose. Who's is short for who is.

your – you're

Again, you're is short for you are, while your indicates that you possess whatever it is.

You will see that by remembering the simple rule that an apostrophe stands for the letters left out, many of the most common errors will be prevented. For the rest, you either need to learn the correct spellings by rote or use mnemonics. For all other words that cause you doubt use your dictionary. And always use your spell checker too, to check for mis-types as well as mis-spellings.

Punctuation

Once your spelling is under control, the only thing left to worry about is getting the punctuation right. Grammar checks on your word processor are some help here, but the following comments might also be useful. Keeping your sentences as short as possible (see the section on style earlier in the chapter) will make correct punctuation easier, but even with short sentences you are likely to need most of the following. The following digest may help. For more, see the hugely popular Truss (2003).

Full stops (.)

You will need one of these at the end of each sentence. Check that the sentence is complete before putting in the full stop. Occasionally a sentence may be a single word, such as: 'No.' But normally you will want to check that the sentence has a verb, that the verb has a noun as subject and another as object (or clauses serving as subject and object) and that the sentence makes sense.

A series of stops (. . .) can be used to indicate either that you are breaking off before finishing something or that you are omitting part of a quotation. This is called an ellipsis.

A full stop is also used to indicate an abbreviation, as in Co., though it is not needed if the abbreviation ends with the last letter of the shortened word, as in Dr or many other titles.

Question marks (?)

These are used instead of a full stop at the end of any sentence which asks a direct question, such as: 'What do you want to do when you graduate?' They are not needed if the question is reported, rather than direct: 'Many students wonder what they will do when they graduate.'

Exclamation marks (!)

These can be used (sparingly) to denote excitement or amazement, or to indicate humour or sarcasm.

Commas (,)

These are used to split up parts of a sentence to make the meaning clearer and allow the reader to draw mental breath. They may split strings of nouns, such as: 'Students need clear objectives, time-management skills and constant reviews of progress if they are to do well.' It would be equally acceptable to have another comma before the final 'and'. In a longer list this would probably be preferable. Commas may also split lists of adjectives or verbs. For example: 'You need to work quickly, efficiently, thoroughly and with sustained concentration.'

They are also used to split the clauses in a complex sentence. I shall not give you an example of this: the book is full of them. No matter how hard I try to practise what I preach, many of my sentences end up being fairly complicated: someone once described it as 'an unfortunate tendency towards the baroque'.

When using commas it is essential to check that you have not placed a comma between a verb and its subject. For example you should not write: 'The courses I am studying, include accountancy and marketing.' In this case courses is the subject of the verb include. An exception to this is when you need to separate off a clause: 'The courses I am studying, particularly those taught by some of the professors in the business school, are extremely interesting.' This is fine and indeed would be hard to understand without the commas.

Inverted commas or quotation marks ("...") or ('...')

Use these whenever you are quoting, whether speech or a section of text. You can use single or double inverted commas, but you should be consistent. Single ones do not require use of the shift key, which may explain their common usage. If you have a quotation within a quotation, for example if a passage of text you quote itself includes a quotation, use double quotation marks for the inner quote if you normally use single or vice versa, so that the two are distinct. Quotation marks may also be used to denote titles of books or articles, though it is equally common to use italics (or underlining, if in a manuscript).

Apostrophes (')

As has been stressed already, these indicate where a word has been shortened by omitting letters, e.g. 'didn't'. An apostrophe is also used to indicate possession where *s* is added to a normal word, as in 'a dog's breakfast'. For plurals, when an *s* is there already, the apostrophe is added after the *s*, as in 'eight weeks' work'. Note that for odd plurals (those where the plural is different from the singular, rather than merely the singular with an *s* added) where you do need to add an *s* to indicate possession, as in 'men's', or 'women's', you put the apostrophe before the added *s*, just as with singular possessives where you are adding an *s*. Remember that where there is a special word to indicate a possessive, there is no apostrophe. After all, you would never write 'hi's', so don't do the equivalent with 'yours', 'theirs', 'its' or 'hers'.

Brackets or parentheses

These are used to separate off something that is an addition or insertion (such as an aside which casts light on what you have said). When they occur as the last part of a sentence, as above, close the bracket *before* adding the full stop. (When a bracket encloses a complete sentence, as here, put the full stop *inside* the bracket.)

Dashes (– . . . –)

These can be used instead of brackets to separate off the same sort of thing or used singly to indicate a break in the train of thought – those occasions when inspiration strikes in mid-sentence.

Semi-colon (;)

This is a weaker form of a full stop. It is used to separate things which could be separate sentences but which are closely linked, thus making the writing less abrupt. Always check before using a semi-colon that what follows it could stand as a sentence in its own right; if it does not, you should probably have used a comma. You can also use semi-colons to separate the items in a list, provided you started the list with a colon. You can use it before the final item in the list, even where this is preceded by 'and', as in: 'You will need many resources for successful study: access to a good library; access to a PC; good tutors; a quiet place to work; and sufficient time.'

Colon (:)

This can be used to introduce a list as in the example above, or in a way similar to a semi-colon to link two clauses that could stand as sentences in their own right. A colon is preferable if the second clause explains the first, if you want to highlight a strong contrast between them or if you are trying to draw particular attention to the connection between them. For example: 'He had no trouble getting on to the course: his father was head of department.'

Capital letters

These are used at the start of each sentence, for names (people, places, months etc.) or for the adjectives derived from them (Elizabethan, French, Mancunian). They are also used for the first and main words of a book or film title (*The Business Student's Handbook*, *The Good, the Bad and the Ugly*).

Common grammatical mistakes

It would be impossible to list all the grammatical mistakes I have seen cropping up in assignments, but the following are some of the most common and they are worth learning how to avoid.

Mixed plurality

A single noun should have an appropriate verb. 'We is' or 'he are' is clearly wrong. Yet this sort of mixing of singular verbs with plural subjects or vice versa is all too common, particularly in cases where a singular noun refers to, or is linked with, a group of some sort. You should say 'one of the students *was* late' and 'the group *was* annoyed' (although 'group' refers to several people, the word itself is singular – 'groups' is the plural). Purists still hold that 'data', being a Latin plural (singular 'datum'), should be treated as a plural, but it is so often used as singular (data is available . . .) that it is almost acceptable. 'A data' still sounds pretty dreadful, though, so if you feel 'datum' is unacceptable, talk of 'a piece of information'.

Incorrect prepositions

Another fault is using incorrect prepositions. It should be 'different *from*' not 'to', 'anxious *about*' not 'of', 'bored *with*' not 'of' and 'centre *on*' not 'round'.

Will I or shall I?

Confusing 'shall' and 'will' is also common. The normal future is 'I shall, you will, he will, we shall, they will'. 'I will' indicates strong determination, as in: 'I shall take several exams next month. I will work very hard between now and then.'

Can I or may I?

'Can' and 'may' are often confused. 'Can' refers to being able to. 'May' means either being permitted or that something is moderately likely to happen. 'I can swim.' That is, I have the necessary skill. 'I may swim here as it is a public beach.' 'It may rain tomorrow.' 'Might' means less likely, but still possible: 'If it rains tomorrow there might be a flood, but I am not expecting it.'

Due or owing?

'Due to' and 'owing to' are problematic. 'Owing to' means because of and usually comes at the start of a sentence. 'Due to' means caused by and usually comes after the verb 'to be'. 'Owing to confusion over meanings, words are often used incorrectly. This is often due to poor teaching of English at school.'

HELPFILE 2
If English is not your native language . . .

If you are about to study in English for the first time, you may be worried about your abilities. This worry is reasonable, but may not be justified. Many students who are non-native English speakers write far better English than my native speakers! However, even if your chosen institution does not insist upon it, it is worth taking one of the standard English tests available to check that you are likely to be able to cope with university level study in the language.

Three areas of competence will be important:

- **Reading** – you will need to read, and understand, a considerable volume of fairly difficult materials.
- **Speaking** – you will need to be able to follow, and contribute to, group discussions.
- **Writing** – you will need to be able to express yourself in written English in assignments, and, under pressure, in examinations.

I shall focus here on written English, although improving this will impact upon speaking and writing too, and one of the ways of improving your writing is to read as extensively as possible. For more detailed treatement of these points, see Giles and Hedge (1994) from which much of what follows is drawn.

To improve your written English you need to improve your vocabulary, and your grammar.

Vocabulary

Although students often worry about vocabulary, the problem is seldom that the students do not use a wide enough range of words. More often, the words are used in a way that leaves their meaning ambiguous. Part of the reason for this lies in the difference between *active* and *passive* vocabulary. Words which you understand when reading in context, but which you do not readily use, are part of your passive vocabulary. Those you use easily are active. (A similar distinction applies to grammatical structures.) It is likely that you will need to extend and consolidate your active, and perhaps also your passive, vocabulary.

To focus your efforts you need to concentrate on frequency, speciality and utility of words. Clearly words which you encounter frequently in your reading and in lectures are ones which you need to know, and probably need to be able to use easily. Log any such words where you are unsure of the meaning, check with dictionaries and native speakers to be sure that you do understand, note down and learn them!

Words which appear in assignments are of particular importance. You must be absolutely sure that you understand what the assignment requires. There is a Helpfile at the end of Chapter 8 which provides a good starting point, but always check any word in an assignment if you are unsure as to exactly what it means. And make sure that you *learn* the meaning of such words. They may well appear in examinations.

→ Ch 8

Beware of terms that resemble words in your own language. For example, the common word 'sensible' in English now means 'showing good sense' (as in 'sensible shoes', i.e. ones that are comfortable for walking in). Yet the similar looking Spanish or Italian *'sensible'* means 'sensitive', a meaning which the English word lost shortly after the time of Jane Austen. If something is not making sense it may be because you are assuming an equivalence that no longer exists.

Dictionaries are not a lot of help, however, for colloquial English. Some assignment writers revel in using such terms, perhaps in the interests of making a scenario sound 'real'. For example a recent reference to 'mothballing' a factory (closing it down, but in a way that it can be opened later if there is a need for it) puzzled one of my (French) students. If the dictionary offers no meaning which makes sense, you have no option but to ask a native English speaker for help.

Many of the words or phrases you encounter will be specialist terms. Some will have originated in the study of management or related subjects, but most will be everyday words that are given a specific meaning when combined (such as transaction costs or value chain). Normal dictionaries are of limited use here – but you should be given definitions for such terms, and you will be on an equal footing with other students, as such specialist terms will be new to them too. You may well not know the equivalent term in your own language (though if you have a management text from home you should easily be able to find it).

To extend your vocabulary, Giles and Hedge suggest the following:

- Write down words and phrases rather than merely repeating in your head – this will help them stick in your memory.

- Try to learn vocabulary in context, so write new words and phrases into a sentence to learn the way they are used.

- Try to group new words with other words that frequently occur with them – for example 'personnel' might be grouped with: personnel manager; personnel department; military personnel; 'all personnel should receive health and safety training'.

- Set aside regular 'slots' in your study schedule for learning vocabulary. Don't make these too long. Little and often is more effective.

- Work out a system for recording your new vocabulary – for example 'groupings' could be shown diagrammatically on cards, to be easily carried around.

→ Ch 9

- Read for language acquisition – this is different from reading for information (also important). Identify problematic words, check the meaning, and if they seem important (in terms of frequency or utility) ensure that you have a correct definition and start a 'grouping' card for them.

- If your course has not yet started, use an introductory management text, together with an interesting book by a 'guru' and the *Financial Times* and/or *The Economist* as the basis for your 'reading for language acquisition'.

Grammar

English grammar is complex and the guidelines above provide the barest starting point. To go further is beyond the scope of this book. It is poorly understood by many in the UK who were educated in the 1970s and 1980s, when grammar was seldom taught in State schools. Study this chapter and the helpfile carefully. If possible, ask someone who is good at English to read your assignments before you submit them. Where they think grammar could be improved, make sure that they explain (if they can) what is wrong and why, so that you understand how to improve things. And ask tutors for as much feedback as possible. Some are reluctant to correct grammar for fear of seeming petty, but will do so if you show that you genuinely want their help.

If you are uncertain about your grammar it is particularly important to keep the structure of your sentences simple.

→ 7 Using information and communication technologies

Developments in information and communication technologies (ICTs) have transformed jobs and organisations in recent decades. Skills in this area are essential for effective study and for success in almost any business. This chapter looks at how you can use the resources available at university to address any skills deficit you may have in this area.

Learning outcomes

By the end of this chapter you should:

- understand the importance of information and communication technologies for organisations
- realise some of the main advantages of developing word-processing skills
- be aware of the uses of spreadsheets, statistical and other useful packages
- appreciate how the Internet is (not) organised and how you can exploit it
- understand the main features of e-mail and its advantages and disadvantages
- appreciate how computer conferencing can help with remote decision taking
- be eager to learn how to use these tools and planning to do so.

During the 1990s developments in ICT dramatically changed the ways organisations handled information, creating new ways of relating to customers and doing business. Teams can now span the globe, holding regular 'virtual' meetings. Spreadsheets are routine. E-mail is often seen as a curse, so much time does it consume. It is hard to imagine a presentation that does not use PowerPoint® overheads. For almost any job you will need to demonstrate IT competence.

The impact of IT on education has been almost as great. It is normal now to word process assignments and to incorporate a range of graphics within them. Spreadsheets and statistical packages are used for analysing data and for drawing graphs to represent the data. These graphs can be pasted into reports or used in a PowerPoint presentation. Most students use the Internet to find information for essays. Computer conferencing allows 'virtual groups' to work on assignments together. If you are already comfortable with all these applications, move on to the next chapter.

If not, identify those areas where you need to increase your ICT skills, and plan to work on these as soon as possible. Most universities offer excellent access to excellent equipment and software and free access to a range of Internet resources. ICT skills will make you more attractive to potential employers. And, as a graduate recruiter told me recently, the fact that you have taken the trouble to develop them is impressive: it demonstrates your motivation, commitment and awareness of organisational requirements.

ORGANISATIONAL IMPACTS OF ICT

→ Ch 13

Information processing is at the heart of management: many organisations now see 'knowledge management' as a core competence. 'Data', 'information' and 'knowledge' are sometimes used interchangeably, but can usefully be seen as a hierarchy. Data are raw facts or numbers. When processed so that they 'answer a question', they become information. Daily sales figures might be data. Monthly figures, plotted on a graph showing the trend, would be information. Knowledge can be seen as the ability to use information as a resource. Knowledge of customer needs and behaviour, knowledge about effective internal processes and knowledge about the market help an organisation to compete effectively. And ICTs are at the heart of collecting, manipulating and storing the information that underpins this knowledge.

Information reduces uncertainty.

Management involves pursuing, and developing, strategy in the face of environmental uncertainties, which information can reduce.

Think of the diagram of the control loop given in Figure 2.1. You could not have a feedback loop without flows of information.

ICT skills feature prominently in many competence frameworks not only because they are so important in employment but also because the academic world is still primarily concerned with the discovery and transmission of knowledge and information.

The ability of computers to store and manipulate vast amounts of information, and their interconnections via the Internet, has transformed the way organisations operate. You can check train or plane times and prices online, and book and pay for a ticket without ever needing to interact with a human being. Your purchasing behaviour is noted and stored and linked to various personal characteristics via the information on your loyalty card(s). At the same time replacement stock will automatically be ordered when necessary to replace your purchases. Goods can be auctioned on the internet, and potential buyers might be anywhere on the planet. The impact on how organisations do business are endless.

The effects of ICT developments within organisations have been as significant as those at the interface with customers. Computerised accounting and budgeting systems depend on spreadsheets. Databases are used to store all sorts of sets of information and many staff are involved in accessing and/or updating these databases. E-mail is the standard channel for many sorts of communication, replacing paper memos and letters. Intranets allow staff throughout organisations to access relevant information.

Most people use only a fraction of the power of their computer systems. If you can make more sophisticated use of ICTs than do your colleagues, you will gain a significant advantage.

7

Using information and communication technologies

IMPROVING YOUR ICT SKILLS

Given the importance of ICT skills, you probably need an action plan to develop them. What follows is designed to help you assess your development needs in the main areas of application, word-processing, spreadsheets, databases, presentation software, e-mail, computer conferencing and Internet search. It should help you to assess the resources available, and to exploit them to best advantage. But this book is *not* a computer course, nor is this chapter designed to support such a course. Sign up for all such courses as are offered; this is no substitute. But it may help you to target your efforts, and to appreciate why such effort is important by helping you to understand the different ways in which ICT can help you and the sorts of package available. This will make it easier for you to learn to use whatever is on offer. First, however, there are certain rules you need to follow, whatever the application you are using.

PC good practice

Helpdesks are good at patiently asking 'and have you actually plugged it in' when asked why a computer is not working. And there are a few almost as basic points of good practice that you need always to remember. They may sound totally obvious. But even the IT-experienced sometimes come close to nervous breakdowns because they have committed one or more basic 'sins'.

Cartoon by Neill Cameron, www.planetdumbass.co.uk

What follows are the basic commandments of good PC use.

> ### The nine PC commandments
>
> **1 Do not offer beer or coffee to your PC**
>
> PCs and partying do not mix. Coffee and other beverages should be kept well away from computers. Spillages do nasty things to the machine's insides which are very expensive to repair.

2 Never take your laptop to a party

Similarly, it is not a good idea to take your laptop with you if you are likely to become 'tired and emotional' or fall asleep on the bus, leaving it behind.

3 Never expose your PC to infection

Any software, whether you bought it, got it free with a magazine or downloaded it from the Internet, is a potential source of a virus which could destroy your hard disk and make it impossible to retrieve what is stored. There is an epidemic of viruses transmitted as attachments to messages. So make sure you have virus protection, update this *frequently*, never open attachments to emails directly – make sure you know what they are and that you need them and that they are from a reliable source, and store them before opening. If your machine starts to behave strangely, stop using it at once and get expert help. If you have recently sent things to other people, warn them of possible infection.

4 Never rely totally on your PC's memory

Computer memory is a wonderful thing, far better in many respects than human memory. But it is vulnerable both to malfunction in the machine and to error on your part. While you are working, what you do is vulnerable to power cuts. With current software you may be able to retrieve it. If you restart your PC and go back into the application you were using, it should open with an automatically saved version of the document you were working on. (If you do not have this feature, save at least every 10 minutes.) When you close a file, always remember to save your work. Even when your work has been saved to the hard disk, you may still lose data if the machine is infected with a virus, lost or stolen. So it is essential to keep a backup of key files. Always date your backups and store them somewhere safe, separate from the machine. Update them regularly and do not keep too many earlier versions. For something important, like your dissertation, become really paranoid and keep two backups in different places.

5 Do not expect your computer to be sensible

Computers are great at obeying instructions and manipulating data. But they will obey stupid instructions just as happily as sensible ones and also act on data which are faulty. Resist the common tendency to believe anything which a computer produces. Remember the 'GIGO' (garbage in, garbage out) principle. You need to *think* – the computer will not do this for you. And you always need to check that your results make sense and, if they do not, explore the reasons for this.

6 Resist getting carried away by what the computer can do

It is so easy to produce reams of figures and to send them to all and sundry that there is a very real risk of data overload. This can reduce the effectiveness of communication: messages will be ignored. Even if a message is read, the real information content may not be perceived if it is buried in a mass of less significant data.

7

Using information and communication technologies

→

7 Never rely on *your* memory – keep clear records of what you are doing

A computer rapidly comes to hold a great many files. While you may understand your filing system, someone else may need to use your files. You might be ill and someone might need to find a copy of a letter you wrote. It is important to find a transparent way of organising and titling your files so that another person can access information. Get into the habit of doing this now – that 'other person' might be you, looking for something after you have forgotten what you originally did! It is equally important, if you are using a spreadsheet or other way of manipulating data, to keep a clear record of how you constructed your model.

8 Never delete carelessly

It is essential to review your files at regular intervals and delete those for which you have no further use. Computers do their best to make thoughtless deletion difficult. They will ask you several times if you really mean to delete that file. Instead of getting into the habit of saying 'Yes' without thinking, do read the file name carefully and make sure that you *do* mean to delete that one. If you make a mistake, use the 'undelete' command at once. If you have made several mistakes, press the 'control' key and 'z' several times to reverse your last instruction, then the one before it, and so on.

9 Never attack your computer

Recent research has shown that a surprising 25 per cent of employees have either physically attacked their computers or come close to it. While computers can on occasion be infuriating, this is not a good response. You may damage the computer, which can be expensive, or damage yourself!

Having marked these commandments, consider the different ways in which ICT can improve the effectiveness of your studies. The main uses you are likely to make of ICT in the near future are for drafting text, analysing data, accessing information and communicating with others. If you are comfortable with at least one software package for each use by the time you graduate, you will have an excellent foundation for developing any further IT skills which a specific job may require.

WORD PROCESSING

If you are not already word processing your assignments, your life could be easier! Assuming that you have access to PCs, it may be fears about skill levels that are deterring you. Assess your skills to identify the problem.

ACTIVITY 7.1

How would you rate your skills in the following area? Score 5 if you think you are really good, 4 if you are fairly good, 3 if a lot of people seem better than you, 2 if you are at a really basic level, and 1 if you are completely incompetent.

Keyboard/typing – speed and accuracy _____

Keyboard – inserting fancy symbols/subscripts/superscripts _____

Editing – moving sections of text within a document _____

Editing – retrieving text deleted in error _____

Editing – using wordcount, spell and grammar checker _____

Formatting – changing font, paragraph spacing, columns of selected text _____

Formatting – presenting text in the form of a table _____

Formatting – highlighting areas of text using borders and shading _____

Formatting – numbering pages, adding headers and footers _____

Graphics – importing diagrams from other applications into a report _____

Graphics – using the 'draw' facility to generate diagrams in text _____

Filing – using systems of file naming and folders to organise stored documents _____

Total score _____

A web version is available to allow repeated assessment and filing.

If you scored less than 48 on the above, or if you had very low scores on any item, you should consider making an action plan for improving your text processing skills. If you are compiling a portfolio evidencing your competence, this would be a good area to use as the basis of an exhibit showing both managing learning and IT skills

It is worth becoming skilled in this area because the ability to alter and rearrange text revolutionises the writing process. It takes much of the *angst* out of the situation because it is so easy to change the text as your thoughts develop or you find something new that you want to include. Starting to write is so easy – just jot down something which may well be rubbish, but which can serve as the raw material which you then refine into something really rather good. This removes a major inhibition for many people who previously could never get their thoughts into a sufficiently perfect form to write them down. Now, initial imperfections are immaterial.

7

Using information and communication technologies

> *My boss really noticed the first report I wrote. I was pretty proud of the analysis I'd done, but it was the presentation and graphics that seemed to make the biggest impression on him'*

Fairly recent graduate in first management position

For good written work you need:
- good keyboard skills
- facility with edit and format commands
- awareness of the tools available
- good filing habits.

One word of caution here: cutting and pasting is seductively simple, but it is all too easy to end up with the same paragraph appearing twice in a document, or for text to flow very strangely once you have moved things around a number of times. If you indulge in drastic editing it is essential to read the finished product through very carefully. If you find that you need to make further changes, read it through carefully yet again once these have been made.

You can easily and impressively improve the appearance of the work you submit. Your computer will almost certainly have a facility for counting words and will try to check grammar and spelling. So you have no excuse for submitting overlength assignments, and only a partial excuse for spelling and grammar

→ Ch 6

faults (though you may need to consult the Helpfile in Chapter 6 as the computer only checks whether a word exists – it may be a 'sound-alike', rather than the word you intended).

You can generate figures and tables on your PC, using the 'draw' facility in Microsoft Word® (there is likely to be something similar in other programs), or PowerPoint or Excel®, and integrate these with your text. You can play with headings and fonts and layout to produce something that looks highly professional. It is likely that if your work *looks* good your tutor will be influenced, subconsciously, to give you higher marks than if it were handwritten or poorly typed. When learning new word-processing skills you will of course need to practise them often in order not to forget them. Continue to practise your skills on your CV when you apply for a job, and for internal reports and other communications when you are working.

Although relatively affordable voice-recognition software is now available, most people still find keyboard skills an advantage. If you are not a good typist it is well worth spending a little time to develop your keyboard skills. It 'hurts' to force yourself to use the right finger for each key, but the pain is short-lived. Once you have mastered correct keying your speed will increase rapidly as soon as you do much typing. (By the time I had finished my thesis I was typing far faster than I could write!)

Identify a few of the really useful features of your word-processing program and learn how to use them. The activity above should have identified any you still need to work on. Any word-processing course offered by your university will cover these basics. If no course is offered try to find a competent friend to start you on the right track. (Trying to learn from the manual and 'help' commands can be frustrating and slow. Most manuals seem to be written for people who already know.) Or save a lot of time by getting hold of one of the more user-friendly books which any bookshop will stock. They tend to have titles like 'X for idiots', X being the package you are trying to use. It is usually best to try to master only one thing at a time. Once you are happy with that, try something else.

PRESENTATION SOFTWARE

Computers make it remarkably easy to produce impressive overheads either for direct projection or for printing on transparencies. Few managers would contemplate giving a presentation without computer generated overheads, usually using PowerPoint. It offers a number of significant advantages, particularly professional appearance and flexibility. You can revise your presentation at the last minute and easily tailor it to a particular audience. You can incorporate relevant tables and graphics. If you are carrying your laptop anyway you do not need to carry anything additional. If not, or as a safeguard against loss, you can e-mail your presentation to whoever is organising the event. You can produce a handout with reduced versions of your slides and room for notes, at the press of a button. The ability to do all this will supplement the presentation skills discussed in Chapter 11.

→ Ch 11

ACTIVITY 7.2

How would you rate your skills in the following? Again, score 5 if you think you are really good, 4 if fairly good, 3 if most people are rather better than you, 2 if your skills are very basic, and 1 if your skills are non-existent.

Generating basic overheads using headings and bullet points   _____

Making each bullet 'fly in' from right or left during the presentation   _____

Drawing graphs or 'box/arrow' diagrams   _____

Rearranging the order of overheads   _____

Using colour to add emphasis   _____

Adding a logo or other identifier to each overhead   _____

Adding sound   _____

Using clip art or other pre-prepared graphics   _____

Total score   _____

Clearly these advantages are such that it is worth developing your skills if the above shows that there is scope for this. There is probably no need to take time going beyond the fairly basic features: PowerPoint can do far more than you are likely to need. You can produce fancy backgrounds and all sorts of animations at the touch of a button, and it is easy to be carried away by this. But beware – few of these elaborations help! Fancy backgrounds distract, and they reduce clarity. Animations may look impressive but are similarly distracting. There will be times when it is extremely useful

7

Using information and communication technologies

to build up a picture a bit at a time. However, when the animation adds nothing, resist the temptation to use it. Words continually flying in from left and right will seldom help your audience to grasp and retain the points you are making. And now that everyone can use PowerPoint, being expert in its use is less impressive than once it might have been. Remember at all times that you are trying to communicate effectively, and use the tools at your disposal to this end alone.

SPREADSHEETS, DATABASES AND STATISTICAL PACKAGES

If you are studying business or management you will almost certainly need to use spreadsheets – they are a basic business tool which has revolutionised simple financial (and other) modelling. They provide a useful secondary function of allowing you to produce charts and graphs which can easily be integrated into a report. Take every advantage your course offers to develop your skills in this area. You can use spreadsheets in many contexts where you want either to display information as a table or to do simple numerical modelling. Using packages such as these requires constant practice if you are to retain your skills. So look out for opportunities to use them. Databases are sets of linked spreadsheets, so similar points apply; this linking makes for ease of manipulation and updating.

> *You don't think that your spreadsheet classes at university are remotely useful to anything – in fact these skills become key in a job, and far more interesting, because of their relevance, than you ever dreamed.*

Biology graduate, managing databases for clinical trials of drugs

It will be a huge advantage to you, as a student and in most jobs, to be comfortable with using both spreadsheets and databases. Spreadsheet software is likely to be the most useful. The Microsoft version is called Excel, but other integrated office software packages will have an equivalent component. The following brief description is intended only for those who are not yet familiar with the basics of Excel; it will help you to start experimenting. If you are in the majority who are already competent with such software, skip it.

A spreadsheet is an arrangement of 'cells', i.e. spaces, arranged in rows and columns, into which you can enter text, numbers and equations to calculate values using the contents of other cells. Thus, as Figure 7.1 shows, I might want to enter last year's course registrations on different courses in the first column, this year's in the second column, and instruct the computer to calculate the percentage. The cell labels are added for clarity – you would not need to tell the spreadsheet what they were as, on the table the spreadsheet offers you, they are already labelled. We can use a cell to enter: **a title** (see top row), a **number**, or a **formula** (see shaded cells).

We can alter the numbers whenever we like, and the formula will automatically calculate the totals and percentages.

	A	B	C	D
1		**Last year**	**This year**	**Percentages**
2	Accounting	100	109	= (C2/B2)* 100
3	Business studies	230	218	= (C3/B3)* 100
4	Computing	200	242	= (C4/B4)* 100
5	Design	50	46	= (C5/B5)* 100
6	**Total**	= B2+B3+B4+B5	= C2+C3+C4+C5	= (C6/B6)* 100

Fig. 7.1 Example of a spreadsheet

You can see that once you have set up a spreadsheet, which can be fairly time-consuming, it saves a lot of time. As in the above example, equations can be set up to reference cell positions rather than particular values, which means that these equations can be copied and pasted and the spreadsheet reused with different sets of data. The time needed to set up a spreadsheet has been reduced by many shortcuts that are now standard features of the software. For example, the need to total a column or row is so common that Excel provides an 'Autosum' function which allows you to instruct a total to appear at a single mouse click. It is also extremely straightforward to calculate percentages, ignore negative values, round numbers to a given level, provide an average, or compute the rate of return on an investment, if you know present and future value.

As indicated earlier, you can use the facility the spreadsheet offers to draw bar charts, pie charts, scatter diagrams and graphs. (Excel provides a 'chart wizard' to make this easy.)

Rather than writing a further chapter (at least) on how to use Excel, when you perhaps have a different package, I shall leave it at this. You should, early in your course if not before, become familiar with using spreadsheets, using whatever training resources are at your disposal. (There is a wealth of material available on the web, if you have no printed material to hand.)

→ Ch 14

While Excel will do simple statistics, a number of statistical packages are available, which can help with the more complex analysis of research results. SPSS (Statistical Package for the Social Sciences) and SAS (Statistical Analysis Software) are in common use. You still need to understand the basic principles of statistics, or else you will not use such packages to good effect. And you will need to be sure that you are going to generate a sufficient volume of data to make the effort of learning to use the package worthwhile. But if you are planning a project which will generate quantities of data, then explore what your institution provides by way of licenses for software and instruction in their use. Take advantage of any opportunities you can find to learn about the packages available, how to choose between them and how to use an appropriate one. For anything beyond the most basic of analysis the investment of time will be well worth it in terms of time saved handling your data. And you will at the same time be developing a highly transferable skill.

THE INTERNET

The Internet is the world's largest computer network, linking millions of networks around the world so that through one you can gain access to any of the others. It allows you to e-mail any other Internet user, to send them files, to join discussion groups on any topic you can imagine, to read newsletters on topics of your choice, to apply for jobs, to shop and to access detailed information on anything you are ever likely to want to know. It is already having a dramatic effect on people's lives. If you devoted your whole life to exploring the Internet you would not touch on more than the tiniest fraction of what is there: there is unimaginably much and it changes all the time. (Although I checked all sites mentioned in the book shortly before my deadline for handover to the editor, it is possible that some will be out of date before you buy this book.)

→ Ch 13

The Internet has been likened to a giant library without a catalogue. You can spend hours and hours wandering around in it, touching on bizarre and wonderful things. You can also find vast quantities of rubbish that no self-respecting library would give shelf space. And unless you know where to look, you may never find what it is that you were looking for in the first place. Chapter 13 comes back to the problem of finding information and the use of keywords to help you find things.

To use the World Wide Web you need to know what 'hypertext' is. Hypertext documents contain links to other documents. If I were to write something about myself in hypertext I might mention my family, my research interests, the institution at which I work and the books I have written. Linked to keywords in each area there might be other documents. If you were interested in my family you might click on that word and their photo would appear on your screen. Or perhaps I might have mentioned each by name and clicking on the name would take you to that person's own biographical statement, with its own keywords on which you might choose to click for more information. Clicking on a book might give you a detailed précis of that book and publication details. Clicking on the publisher might take you into its information, or 'home page', and so on.

The World Wide Web (WWW) is basically a giant hypertext document. Browsers, such as Netscape® and Microsoft Explorer®, will offer you a variety of search engines and sources of information and allow you access to audio, pictures and even video, although downloading these can be fairly slow as the information content is extremely high. You can use 'bookmarks' to allow you to find sites which you visit regularly.

If you develop your skills, you can find material fairly efficiently. I asked some regular users about searches they had recently made. A mathematician gave me the following example:

I wanted to quote Heraclitus on the harmony of opposites, knowing it had something about 'the bow and the lyre'. It took about five minutes to find four different translations of the fragment, so I could pick out the one that I liked best. I searched for 'Heraclitus' and within the thousands of hits searched for 'lyre', which reduced it to about 50. The search engines give a short description of each site so I only looked at about six to find the four translations.

Not quite what one would expect a mathematician to be looking for, but it illustrates the point!

So how can you *efficiently* search the mass of material to be found on the Internet? The main aids are *search engines*, *metasearchers* and *gateways*. If you click on 'search' when connected to the Internet you will probably be offered a choice of search engine. Google is an extremely popular one.

Search engines

A search engine ranges across the web and comes up with links to sites which include mention of your specified search word(s). It can search millions of pages around the world, but much of what it finds will alas be of little or no use. Your chosen word might appear in the name of a restaurant, for example, or be used as bait for some consultancy's advertising of its offerings. Some of the more promising links may no longer work. All this can be highly frustrating. However, you *may* find really useful links in this way. Different search engines will come up with different sets of links, so it is worth using several. Because of this 'metasearchers' have been developed which run simultaneous searches over several engines. Use of one of these may make searching more effective.

Gateways

Search engines wander around the web looking for your search word, but gateways and directories are more organised, checking sites at regular intervals and structuring them so as to make browsing more systematic. This can save a lot of time, but may not throw up all the nuggets that a search engine, if you are patient and lucky, might produce. A search engine gives you access to the equivalent of a mountain of jumbled books, journals, junk mail and even people's diaries. A gateway is more akin to a respectable library. If you are studying a business related subject you will probably find it useful to visit: **www.bized.ac.uk**

→ Ch 13 There is more on using the Internet to search for information in Chapter 13. And online courses are available to improve your search skills (see further sources at the end of the chapter).

ACTIVITY 7.3

If you are not yet happy with using the Internet, find someone who is and get them to show you how. This will not take long. Spend some time on your own playing with it. Then for your next essay, see how much relevant information you can find via the Internet. Once you have done this, assess whether you need to plan to develop your skills further and, if so, develop an action plan for your file...

E-MAIL

If you are not already using e-mail to contact all your scattered friends and relatives, you are in a very small minority, and seriously disadvantaged! When abroad, e-mail can be easier, and cheaper, than phoning home. And when you are at home it provides you with a quick and easy means of contact and at present is probably free – to you as a student, at least. Obviously there are costs, but they are borne by your institution.

Within all but the smallest organisations e-mail has become an almost universal medium for internal communication, replacing typed memos. The advantages of near-instant transmission like a phone call, but asynchronous receipt, and ease of transmitting to all and sundry, are irresistible. In theory, paper should be obsolete, though in most organisations a substantial proportion of e-mail users print paper copies of at least *some* of their e-mail.

Despite its advantages, e-mail can be a significant source of stress at work. Many people already receive 100–200 messages per day. Despite the hours most managers (and others) spend dealing with e-mail, they often do not use it effectively. There is much you can do to reduce the stress potential of e-mail. The following guidelines should help.

Good e-mail practice

Meet people if you can

Phone conversations are easier if you have already met the other person. Similarly, electronic communication is easier once you have had personal contact, although it is possible to build a good relationship without ever meeting. So if possible, continue to meet people at intervals, rather than relying exclusively on e-mail, and use the phone if you need to discuss something and cannot meet.

Watch your language

Because a screen is very impersonal, care needs to be taken with the tone of a message. It is easy to give unintentional offence because there is no body language, no smile or tone of voice to show that your meaning is friendly. Words that you could say with a smile may have a very different effect if read from a screen. Without such care, e-mail exchanges can become more and more heated, a process sometimes referred to as 'flaming'. A particular hazard here is trying to clear e-mail when you are in a hurry. You may be trying to be helpful by sending a brief message late at night before leaving on a business trip. But the recipient may not be aware of this. And your quick reply may come across as terse or offhand.

Never be abusive or threatening on purpose

Messages can almost always be traced back to you and can easily be forwarded to people in authority if someone wants to complain. Even sarcasm is dangerous because of the possibility of misinterpretation.

Be careful what you send

E-mail is reasonably secure provided you keep your password to yourself. But remember that something you write in confidence can easily be forwarded, perhaps to the person about whom you were being less than complimentary. It is therefore safest not to write anything that would be embarrassing or dangerous if it became public. If someone does send you an injudicious e-mail, assume that it was intended to be treated confidentially.

Be careful whom you mail

Address lists can be both a boon and a real hazard. It is wonderful to be able to send a message to everyone it concerns by typing the name of an address list, rather than needing to key in each name individually. It is *not* wonderful to receive dozens of irrelevant messages because a list has been used which contains people to whom the message is of little concern.

When replying to something sent to you as part of a list be careful to target your reply. Some systems reply to everyone on the list unless you instruct them otherwise, which can be a real hazard. Our entire system was clogged up because of a message sent to all remote e-mail users about a forthcoming change. This upset them greatly, and in their fury, about a half of these hundreds of angry souls hit the reply key and sent their message to everyone on the original list. They were then even angrier at the people who had 'replied all' and did the same thing themselves when complaining! Another case resulted in a confidential letter about a third person being copied to that person. And yet another concerned the message 'I didn't realize you were working late too – why don't you come up to my office . . .' followed by a number of seductive suggestions about what might then take place. This message was intended for the sender of the message prompting it, but because it was a reply to one that had a large address list, it ended up in the mail box of just about everyone in the company the next morning, to the deep embarrassment of the two parties concerned.

Make your meaning clear

It is very easy to reply to an e-mail as if the sender had just spoken to you. Thus you might answer a question with something like: 'Fine by me.' If the question was actually sent some time previously, perhaps as one of several e-mails, such terse replies can be puzzling. What is fine? Unless the system automatically appends the original message to the reply (and not all do), it makes it much easier if you send a message which is self-explanatory. 'Friday at 10.00 am is fine by me' or 'I'll see you Friday 10.00 am' would not take you much longer to type and would make it much easier for the other person to understand. Or if someone has asked you several questions you may find it most efficient to edit their original, putting replies after the questions, and then return it.

Always use the 'title' or 'subject' line to show what the message refers to when originating an exchange. Your recipient may have a lot of e-mails to look at and only have time for a few, selected by title. Extracting from a file is also easier if the title gives a clear indication of the content. (Some skill is needed as you may have only a few words to play with. If your title is too long the end of it may not be displayed.)

Keep messages fairly short

Most recipients find it difficult to absorb more than one screen's worth of message. If a message is becoming over-long because you are trying to cover several topics, use a separate message for each. If it is long because it is complex, it is normally better to attach it as a file. If your recipient has a compatible word-processing package he or she can then print it in a form that is easy to read and digest. Unfortunately, if it can't be printed easily there is a strong chance that it will merely be deleted. This may be the case if you are using a later version of a package. If there is doubt, save your document as a rich text format (rtf) file and send that too.

Use capitals with care

In an e-mail CAPITALS COME ACROSS AS SHOUTING. But they are useful occasionally for emphasis, as italics or bold are best avoided – they and other symbols can arrive as something very different on your receiver's machine.

Re-read before you send

Because of all the hazards above, it is important to read back your message before sending to check that it is clear and does not risk conveying meanings you did not intend. For particularly sensitive messages it may be worth first sending the message to yourself in order to see how it comes across on a screen. Although some systems allow you to 'unsend' internal messages, this is not always the case and you are unlikely to be able to retrieve a message sent outside. Even if you send another message titled 'ignore last message', few people will obey your instruction. There is a strong tendency for recipients to plough through messages in the order in which they were received.

Use an appropriate filing system for messages which you need to keep

It is tempting to treat e-mail as a transient medium and delete all messages once answered. This is fine for social use, but dangerous at work, when it may be important to refer to the details of past messages or check the dates they were sent. Nor should you leave all your back mail clogging up the system. Unless you need to access your past mail from different terminals, you can make space for others on the system by filing past mail on your own machine and deleting it from the mailing system. You need to be careful here – things deleted actually stay on the system until you throw away deletions by 'emptying wastebasket' or whatever your system calls it. Do this regularly or you will be cluttering up the system unnecessarily.

COMPUTER CONFERENCING

Many organisations now operate globally, and 'virtual teams' are increasingly common. Team members may be anywhere in the world, and most of their communication will be electronic. I recently met a manager of a 'team' with members on three continents. They were successfully completing a major project. They held very occasional face-to-face meetings, supplemented by frequent e-mails and computer conferencing.

The latter was necessary because, although you can easily create an address list for team members and send messages to all of them, it is quite hard to discuss things via e-mail. Messages will be mixed in with every other message, so it is difficult to follow the thread of a discussion.

Computer conferencing systems create a 'space' for each team and/or topic, and allow you to select only discussion relating to a particular 'thread', that is, messages which are responses to a particular message, or to those responses. Conferences may have few participants, or hundreds. One or more of these members may be given editorial control over messages. This can be important if unhelpful or offensive messages are posted. Many systems still rely on text messages, with attached files if these need to be shared. They are often 'asynchronous', in that you can read messages and post your responses whenever this is convenient. Some systems now offer the possibility of talking to members in real time, and of members sharing screen images, with any person being able to modify text or diagrams as others watch.

If you are a distance learning student you may already be using conferencing. It is an excellent medium for discussion with other students and tutors, no matter where they are. If not, and you get the opportunity to develop e-conferencing skills, do take advantage of it. For example, you might find people who share your research interests but are dispersed around the globe. You could interact with one or two of them by e-mail, attaching copies of draft papers for discussion. But if there are more of you, and particularly if you have several different topics which you want to discuss, it would be much easier to join in a computer conference.

Good practice in conferencing is similar to that for e-mail – you need to be clear, avoid offence, keep messages reasonably short wherever possible and make them as self-contained as you can. Relate them to the contribution that prompted them, either by copying part of it: 'John says . . .' or by linking in another way: 'John's point that . . . is an interesting one. It suggests that . . . '. Remember too that you are working as a group when conferencing, even if the other group members are scattered around the world. So concern with process as well as with the task is important. Points covered in Chapter 10 are therefore highly relevant to this medium.

→ Ch 10

SUMMARY

This chapter has briefly introduced some of the ways in which ICT developments have affected organisations. It has argued the following:

- As a student you are likely to have excellent opportunities for developing IT skills.
- These skills will help you with your studies and make you far more attractive to potential employers when you leave.
- Word-processing skills are of immediate use for essays and other written materials.
- Spreadsheets and other packages for statistical manipulation will be invaluable for modelling and for analysing data.
- Through the Internet you can access vast quantities of information which may be of use to you in assignments and research.

■ E-mail and computer conferencing allow you to communicate instantaneously with people around the world.

Further information

No suggestions for printed books are given here as publications date rapidly. Any good bookshop will offer a selection. You will need to choose publications that meet your need and are within your price range. Many books on the Internet offer exclusively US URLs. If you are not in the USA you might like to look for one which does not. You may find the following web resources useful.

■ **www.amazon.com** (or for UK site, **.co.uk**, a searchable database, mainly of books)

■ **bized.ac.uk** (useful gateway linking management students and teachers with relevant information providers)

■ **www.dogpile.com** (a good meta-search engine)

■ **www.google.com** (a good general search engine)

■ **www.lights.com/publisher** (links to major publishers' web sites)

■ **www.netskills.ac.uk/TONIC/** (a UK online course)

■ **www.niss.ac.uk/lis/opacs.html** (links to UK online public access (library) catalogues)

■ **sosig.ac.uk/roads/subject-listing/World-cat/busgen.html** (links to UK industrial and business sites)

■ **www.tilbrguniversity.nl/services/library/instruction/www/onlinecourse/** (a Netherlands online course on searching)

■ **www.ukonline.gov.uk** (searches UK government and related web sites)

→ 8 Gaining good marks

You probably want to get good marks for your essays, and pass all your exams! Most students worry about not knowing enough, but their marks depend at least as much on how well they can *communicate* their knowledge! This chapter looks at how you can use what you know to the very best effect! Getting good marks is a skill in its own right, and particularly important at university, but constituent parts are transferable.

Learning outcomes

By the end of this chapter you should:

- understand what is involved in the activity of assessing
- appreciate the perspective of those doing the assessment
- be aware of some of the common causes of student failure
- appreciate the importance of taking action immediately there is a threat to success
- be better able to interpret assessment questions correctly
- be better able to plan a structured answer

→ Ch 6   The ability to communicate in writing is essential to gaining good marks. But there are some factors more specific to assessment. You need to understand what is being asked and write an answer to *that question*. This chapter looks at interpreting questions and planning the content and structure of a good answer. It looks at essays, reports, written exams, portfolio assessment and *viva voce* examinations. And it discusses some forms of assessment you may encounter once working: annual appraisal is common, and you may well wish to seek professional accreditation, too.

THE AIMS OF ASSESSMENT

When I am marking essays or exams, I am assessing how well the student has met a specific set of requirements. You need to understand the objectives of your own assessors, and why they use the processes they do. For a little while, then, you need to try to put yourself into the shoes (or head) of the person doing the assessing.

ACTIVITY 8.1

Select one of the courses you are currently studying. If you were the lecturer, what do you think you would be trying to achieve when you set and marked assignments or essays? Write down what you think your objectives would be and, if possible, discuss them with one or two people who are following the same course. Discuss, too, how sure you would be about your judgements when marking and what might make them more, or less, reliable.

What follows is my own perspective as someone who regularly sets assignments for continuous assessment, devises exam questions, marks both and chairs the board which decides who shall pass or fail. However, although I have been involved with many different courses, at several universities, I cannot guarantee to speak for all examiners everywhere. You need to check what I say against the views of your own assessors.

My main objective is fairly simple: to check that students have learned enough from the course to be able to move on to subsequent courses without difficulty and if so award them a pass. I am also concerned to 'maintain standards' – students who pass our courses should not subsequently reflect badly on our institution because of their ignorance or lack of competence. If our graduates are incompetent, or seem to know little, employers (and other universities) will cease to value our degree. This would be a disaster for our students, who have worked hard for their qualification.

By 'learning' I do not mean merely the ability to regurgitate what has been taught. Examinees need to use ideas and techniques appropriately in a given context in order to come to a better understanding of the situation and, usually, of how to respond to it. My final objective is to distinguish between those who have barely learned enough and those who have a high level of mastery of the subject.

Another objective of assessment is to help learning to take place. The act of writing an assignment can lead to a deeper understanding of the material covered and the ways in which it can be used. (It also helps to develop skills in written communication.) Examinations will exert pressure on students to learn the material so that they retain it and can draw on it when necessary long after the course has finished.

Assessment is difficult, as I am painfully aware. Assessing this deeper form of learning in a subject such as management is inevitably subjective. It is easy to test whether someone knows the definition of a particular concept, or can identify the person who came up with a particular theory. It is fairly easy to see whether a person can use a particular formula correctly. It is much harder to be sure whether or not a person can use relevant concepts appropriately, even creatively, in a particular situation. Unless a lengthy case study is used, the context will be described so briefly that it will probably be fairly obvious which concept to use. Word or time limits will work against answers that go into depth. It is easy to be over-impressed by clear writing (rather than particularly clear thinking) and by a high level of word-processing skills. It is easy to under-rate an assignment that looks rushed and scrappy. It may be impossible to make any judgement about the knowledge of someone who totally misinterprets a question.

Much of what follows is intended to help you avoid these difficulties, or even to exploit them to your advantage.

WHY STUDENTS FAIL

Failure is seldom due to intellectual inadequacy. While some people have to work harder than others, almost all those selected for a place on a course should have the ability to pass. You may not, however, have the ability to manage your learning well enough. And there is a small chance that you will have problems such as illness or difficulties in your private life which will put your success at risk. Figure 8.1 is a composite multiple cause diagram for the most common causes of failure, showing how factors can interact.

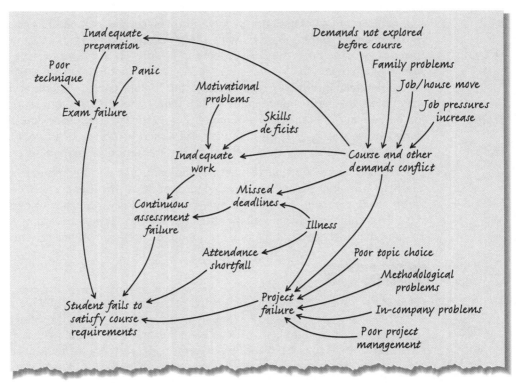

Fig. 8.1 Common causes of student failure (a composite multiple cause diagram)

ACTIVITY 8.2

Think about factors which you feel might threaten your own success. If you cannot find them on Figure 8.1, add them at appropriate points. Highlight all the factors which you think are particularly relevant to you.

The factors shown, and probably those you have added as well, fall into three categories: some factors are beyond your control, some you might be able to do something about with the aid of this book or other assistance, and for some factors you already know the remedy.

Sometimes your success is put at risk by factors beyond your control. You might fall seriously ill, or all your revision notes might be in your car when it is stolen. If so, you need to work out how to minimise the effect of the disaster. Almost always your first step has to be to tell your personal tutor, or someone else in authority. They can help you work out how best to cope with the situation, and can also make sure that the authorities know. Most institutions are prepared to make considerable allowances for students who meet with misfortune of one kind or another. But they cannot do this if they do not know about it. Often there will be deadlines for informing them. But even if not, it is important to tell them *as soon as you possibly can*.

Of course, such disasters are unlikely to affect you and there is no point worrying about them unless they do. Far more likely are circumstances that should have been within your control, but somehow got beyond you. The commonest cause is poor time management. If in the self-assessment above you highlighted this as a threat, and you

→ Ch 2

have not yet developed the skills covered in Chapter 2, you need to work on them urgently, before you fall irremediably behind. You will note from the diagram that dissertation failure forms a major causal strand. If your course requires you to do a dissertation, and your time management is barely adequate for your taught courses,

→ Ch 2

you may be at risk of failure. Use Chapter 2 now to start improving your time management skills so that they are well established before you start your dissertation.

→ Ch 16

You will also need to pay careful attention to Chapter 16 on managing projects.

If 'potentially controllable' factors get beyond control, it is again imperative that you seek help from your supervisor, personal tutor or other member of staff. It is far better to alert them to a possible problem and with their help to avert it, than to persist in denying that things could go wrong until the situation is beyond remedy. Sticking your head in the sand may feel good at the time, but sooner or later you will feel very much worse.

ACTIVITY 8.3

Should things look like getting out of control, see it as an opportunity! Set a specific objective for averting disaster, develop an objectives tree and then develop an action plan for achieving your objective. If you also document the circumstances, the help you seek, remedial actions taken and the outcomes, you will have the basis of an excellent 'exhibit' for the part of your portfolio devoted to 'managing your own learning'.

Motivational problems

Time problems are one major cause of failure, whether generated by circumstances beyond your control or poor management on your part. Motivational problems are another. Indeed, the two may be closely interlinked – either can cause the other. If you think back to the basic principles of motivation, you will realise that your own is likely to flag if:

→ Ch 3

- you feel that effort does not produce performance (this is likely to be due to poor study skills, so revisit Chapter 3), or poor assessment technique; or

- performance does not produce rewards (this may be because your long-term objectives have changed since you chose your course and you no longer want the degree which you are pursuing, or there are too few shorter-term rewards).

There is a further possible reason, not covered by the model. This is that:

- you are depressed generally and have little motivation for anything (if so, try the normal remedies of sleep, healthy food, exercise and talking to friends, and if these don't help within a week or two, or you cannot find the motivation even for these steps, seek medical help).

> **Motivational resources:**
> - **your teachers**
> - **friends**
> - **fellow students**
> - **your academic advisor**
> - **yourself.**

The main sources of motivational 'recharging' are your teachers, your friends on the course, and yourself. If these fail you, then you may need to seek professional help. Institutions vary greatly in the support they offer students, but most will assign students to some sort of personal counsellor or academic advisor, with a backup counselling service for more serious cases. If you experience motivational, or indeed any sort of problems you should not hesitate to take advantage of whatever help is available. This will not be held against you, nor affect your grades in any way other than positively (as your advisor can argue for your circumstances to be taken into consideration when your final marks are decided).

IMPROVING YOUR ASSESSMENT TECHNIQUE

→ Ch 3, 5, 6, 12

To succeed in assessment you need learning, thinking, number and writing skills. There are also some very specific techniques required in the academic context. These are covered in the remainder of the chapter. If you work hard and understand the subject matter but do not do as well as you'd like in essays and exams, study what follows carefully. Remember that in most subjects assessment is an art not a science. Your assessors are making inferences from what you write in answer to the questions set. There is a technique of responding in such a way that they will infer that you are competent. This technique will help you in interviews and when you get a request for a report of some kind on a topic of interest to management. It is therefore well worth developing.

Interpreting questions

A key factor in good exam technique is the art of question interpretation. A common cause of exam failure is that a student appears to have answered a question that bears little resemblance to that which was asked. Perhaps the question, following a description of a particular organisational scenario in, shall we say, Case Study and Co., was:

Analyse the motivational problems in the customer billing department of Case Study and Co. and suggest action which the organisation might take to reduce labour turnover.

ACTIVITY 8.4

Jot down possible headings and subheadings for an answer to the above.

_____

_____

_____

When a question similar to this was set, many students lost marks through poor 'question interpretation' skills. Some seemed to have read the question as 'Tell me everything you know about motivation' and regurgitated all they could remember of the lecture on the subject. Others read it as 'What symptoms are there of low motivation in the above description?' and repeated all the bits of the scenario, in only slightly different words, that relate to motivation. Some realised that they had to *analyse* the situation, but got so carried away by this that they forgot all about the need to offer suggestions for remedial action. (An approach to case study based assessment is given in Chapter 12.)

→ Ch 12

Any misinterpretation of a question can cause huge loss of marks. This sometimes happens with assignments, but it is *much* more common in exams because of the pressure you are under there. If your essays are being returned to you with any suggestion at all that you might be missing some aspects, or misinterpreting others, you need to improve your interpretation skills before your next exam. Make absolutely sure that you now understand what was meant *and* see why you gave an answer that was different in some way from what was required. This is probably the most critical thing for you to address of all those covered in the book, because it can seriously reduce your grades and even cause failure. It will also cause you to waste a huge amount of time and effort in directions that not only gain you few marks, but contribute little to the learning your tutor intended.

Refer to the 'Helpfile' if you meet terms you are not sure about. If you encounter one which is not on the list, or have doubts about the meaning of one which is but seems curious in the context, check its intended meaning with the person setting the assignment. If you are unsure about the meaning of a term used in an examination, avoid that question if you can. If you have to answer that question, say at the outset how you are defining the problematic word. Your markers may accept your interpretation and mark you in the light of that meaning. If you are not explicit in this way, they may merely think that you have not answered the question very well.

DECONSTRUCTING QUESTIONS AND PLANNING ANSWERS

Answering a question, the precise question asked, has several further stages beyond being sure of the meaning of the words used in a question. You need to identify all the separate parts of the question, plan an outline answer covering this, then plan the answer in more detail. For simple questions this is not a problem. But questions are often complex and you may need to practise teasing apart the separate 'building blocks' of which they are composed. A couple of examples follow, of questions that might be asked about the content of this book. There are additional practice interpretation questions on the website. Spend some time on the exercise which follows and look at real questions drawn from your own course.

ACTIVITY 8.5

Before reading on, highlight the key words in the following question and jot down possible headings and subheadings in an answer.

Discuss the adequacy of the control model as a framework for understanding poor student performance. Suggest three steps which you might take to improve your own performance, drawing on this or other appropriate theory.

_____

_____

_____

There are two clear parts here, the evaluation of the control model and the suggested steps for improvement. But within each there are implicit subparts. To evaluate the control model you need to establish what it is – it would be almost essential to include a diagram here, but you would need to describe it in words as well. You would also have to establish what you meant by 'poor performance'. Note that there are different ways in which performance can fail to meet required standards – Figure 8.1 would be a good starting point. Once you have established these two bases, you can start to examine the extent to which the control model helps with the different causes of poor performance. You would probably argue that for some sorts of poor performance it could add considerably to your understanding of the shortfall, as some part of the control loop (establishing standards, perhaps, or monitoring performance against these standards) is usually at fault when this sort of shortfall occurs. But for other causes of poor performance (poor motivation, say, or really serious illness), the control loop might be of limited or no usefulness. Again you would need to say *why*.

The second part of the question requires you to draw on the first, but also to link it to your own situation. Thus you could start by identifying the three ways in which your own performance could most be improved. Perhaps you are poor at managing your time. You tend to hand work in late after a rushed last-minute effort and your 'clear writing' skills are poor. Note that, while your example has to be plausible, you will not be judged on its 'truth'. In an exam it would make sense to pick something that allowed you to show fairly easily that you could apply the ideas, rather than agonising over what were your real performance problems.

You could then show what the control loop would suggest – perhaps the need for interim deadlines to address the time management issue. Then you could refer back to the first part of your answer to establish that some of your shortfall could not be understood in control loop terms and briefly establish some other theory – showing the breadth of your knowledge – which might help. Suppose that you wanted to say that part of the problem was that you couldn't be bothered to practise good time management or work hard at written work. This could be understood in terms of expectancy theory – because you lacked the ability to write well, you knew that effort would not translate into performance anyway. Therefore to improve your performance you would need to work on your writing skills and strengthen this link in the motivational chain.

Given that you are asked only for three suggestions, you might be able to make these based on strengthening various parts of the control loop. But if you had been asked for more, then drawing on at least one other theory would have been advisable. Note that for each suggestion you would need to make it clear how it addressed an underlying reason suggested by the model or theory. Thus to address the second part of the question merely by saying 'The three steps I would take are to work harder, hand in my work on time and try to be neater' would probably gain you no marks at all.

Figure 8.2 shows a mind map for a possible answer to this question.

To take a second example, albeit more briefly: Think briefly about how you would approach this before reading the analysis which follows.

> 'Organisations today are likely to recruit graduates primarily because of the knowledge that they have gained during their degree studies.' To what extent do you agree with this statement?

This question is asking you to demonstrate your understanding of relevant factors in organisations today and link these to employer views about graduates as potential employees. It is also checking your understanding of the whole idea of transferable skills, even though these are not mentioned. Any student who restricted their answer to knowledge, and made no mention of skills, would probably fail.

→ Ch 1 The other implicit instruction is to give a *reasoned* conclusion for agreeing or disagreeing with the question, so you are also being tested on your ability to argue from evidence. You can find plenty of evidence in Chapter 1.

→ Ch 12 Many assignments will require analysis. Some will require you to analyse a case. All the issues discussed in this chapter are relevant to this. But you will also need to understand how to work with cases. Analysis and case working are discussed in Chapter 12.

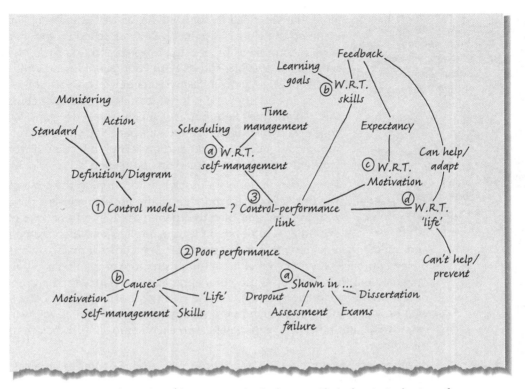

Fig. 8.2 Mind map based on 'deconstruction' of a question about student performance and control

---

ACTIVITY 8.6

Collect samples of essay and exam questions from your own course(s) – lecturers should be able to provide these if you do not already have them. Working with one or two other people if possible, first highlight the 'instruction' words (explain, compare, etc.). Then try to break the questions down into their constituent parts.

Planning an answer

Once you are absolutely clear what the question is asking for, you need to start planning your answer. You were starting to do this in the activities above, but there is more to do than think of the obvious headings suggested by the question. Essay planning is ideally a fairly leisurely process: your ideas need time to develop and cohere. In an exam time is seriously limited. But in either case, planning is an essential stage. Indeed, all the stages of the control loop – setting or clarifying objectives, planning to meet them, marshalling resources, checking progress against schedule and objectives and taking corrective action if necessary – are vital for both essays and exam answers.

→ Ch 2

Essay planning involves:
- noting deadline
- clarifying question requirements
- identifying resources needed
- scheduling activities to:
  - acquire resources
  - extract information
  - plan essay
  - write essay
- monitoring progress.

Note that you need to control time, as well as material. Part of your planning therefore has to involve a work schedule and an essential part of your control will be directed towards ensuring that you keep to this schedule. If possible, spread both your planning and writing over several days, to allow a 'fallow' time between first and final draft of both plan and essay. (This is not feasible in exams, of course.) During this gap you may find that your subconscious develops your ideas considerably without effort on your part. You will also find it easier to spot logical inconsistencies and poor English if you edit your essay after a decent interval, rather than on completion.

There are two popular approaches to planning the content of an essay. The first is to collect together all the possibly relevant things you might wish to cover and then to organise these into some kind of structure. The other is to develop the structure first and then search for the appropriate material to flesh out this structure. Sometimes it may be worth adopting a mixed approach, starting with either a rough structure or reading a few relevant materials and then moving to the other approach which may then prompt developments or additions to the first and so on. If you are already completely happy with how you go about planning (and your grades are as high as you want), stick with what works. But otherwise, experiment with each approach first, before trying the mixed one.

→ Ch 4   In either case, remember the importance (outlined in Chapter 4) of selecting your material carefully with a view to relevance and recency, keeping careful notes as you read and making sure that you keep a record of the full reference of anything you are at all likely to use, as an integral part of your notes. (References are of little use if you cannot marry them up with the relevant notes.)

In an exam you will normally need to keep any 'collecting of materials' to the minimum. Some students find it helpful to jot down single words or short phrases to 'capture' everything they can remember that may be relevant to an answer before it is driven out of their heads by the first thing they start to write. But such notes need to be written very quickly so as not to use time that might be better devoted to analysing the question, planning the structure of your answer and *writing* it.

Mind maps for planning

→ Ch 4   Whichever approach you adopt, you will find that mind maps (mentioned in Chapter 4 and used in the deconstruction example above) can be invaluable. If you have collected notes on a number of relevant books and articles, you can use a mind map to organise the content of these. If you are starting with structure you can represent this as a mind map. In either case, once you have your main 'branches' and 'twigs' established, all that remains is to order the branches in the best way and then for each branch to order the twigs. This gives you the outline of your essay plan. If structure came first, you will then need to search for relevant sources. You may find that these cast new light on the subject. If so, you may need to do some reordering or alter the groupings. If your structure was developed from notes, you may be ready to start writing once you have ordered the branches on your map.

In an exam, a mind map can be a useful way to establish, very quickly, the structure of your answer. While you write, use it as a reference point against which to check your progress. It is a good idea to number the branches in the order you intend to cover them. Sometimes it can be useful to cross off branches when they have been completed. (If you prefer to generate mind maps on a computer, affordable, or sometimes free, software is readily available.)

Your resulting essay plan, however derived, needs to be as brief as possible – a list of section headings or a diagram (with order indicated) is usually enough. Remember to include an introduction and conclusions and, if relevant, recommendations, as well as the structure of the main section. Writing a good answer is much easier if all you have to do is work your way through the stages you have set out for yourself. It is easy to check your plan against the question, to ensure that all the parts you have deconstructed are covered. It is easy to see whether the order you have planned is logical and likely to flow well. It is easy to check your answer, at intervals, against the plan. Writing without a plan and subsequently trying to check your full answer for flow and completeness is far, far more difficult. You should still, for safety's sake, perform a direct check of answer against question at some mid-point and again at the end, to ensure that you answer the question, the whole question and nothing but the question! If you keep this requirement in mind, while you perform both the check via plan and the direct check, you should end up with a good, clear, relevant answer.

TEST EXERCISE 8.1

Draw a mind map and brief essay plan based on the 'reasons for graduate recruitment' question used to exemplify deconstruction of a question.

Rough drafts

Are you prone to procrastination, or more severe 'writer's block'? Do you find it hard to put pen to paper or finger to key? If so, you will find it liberating to write a deliberately rough first draft. Resistance to writing often stems from a fear of not being able to do it well enough, or dread at the sheer size of the task. This latter is a particular problem with long essays or reports.

It helps to set yourself an interim task of completing a quick, very rough draft well in advance of the deadline. This has several advantages:

- The draft will clarify your thoughts greatly, highlighting points where your structure or arguments are weak, or evidence is lacking.

- It will give you raw material to work with. You can then craft this into something far better than you could ever have produced at a first draft.

- It will stir your subconscious into action, as mentioned.

- If you come down with flu or suffer some other disaster, you will have something which you can hand in with an explanatory note if this seems a better strategy than asking for an extension.

Once you have a draft it is usually fairly painless to turn it into something good. It can even be enjoyable – but only if you are prepared to treat the draft as an interim stage in your thoughts and do not become attached to it. Read it in 'critical bystander' mode and discard or seriously modify those parts which do not work. Refer back to Chapter 6 if there are points at which you are unhappy with the quality of your writing, rather than the quality of your thought. Use Part 4 of this book if the content is the problem.

→ Ch 6

Checklist for final drafts

When you have polished your draft into something that you are reasonably happy with, it is still worth performing a final check. Ask yourself:

■ Does the introduction serve to orient the reader adequately?

■ Is there a logical flow through the essay?

■ Is the language clear and appropriate?

■ Have you covered all the parts of the question?

■ Is the proportion of your answer devoted to each part reasonable, given the way the question was phrased?

■ Have you provided enough evidence and clear arguments to convince your reader of each of the points you wanted to make?

■ Have you made use of diagrams or graphs where these really help make your points?

■ Have you used relevant concepts from the course to develop your answer wherever possible?

■ Is there any material which is not really required to answer the question and which could be deleted?

■ Does your conclusion flow naturally from the points you have made earlier?

■ Are you (just) within the word limit?

■ Is your reference list complete?

A version of this is available on the website, for convenience.

You may also find it helpful to ask a friend on a related course to read the essay and tell you of any points that he or she is unhappy about. (If you swap essays with someone on the same course for this purpose, you may find it very difficult not to swap good ideas too, so that your essays come to resemble each other more closely than is safe. Remember, cheating and plagiarism will attract severe penalties.)

→ Ch 6

DOING WELL IN EXAMINATIONS

Once you are good at writing essays to a plan, with a clear structure, and ensuring that you answer all of the questions, you are half-way to doing well in examinations. 'All' you need do beyond that is to manage your time so that you prepare adequately, practise relaxation techniques so that you control any tendency to panic in the exam

Causes of exam failure include:
- inadequate preparation
- poor time management
- answering too few questions
- missing out parts of questions
- misinterpreting the question
- not using course ideas.

and manage your time during the exam itself. Answer the correct number of questions, giving each part of each question an appropriate amount of attention. The basic principles involved are those already covered in the context of managing your learning and written communication. What follows is merely a brief outline of the key points as they relate to the specific context of examinations.

Exam preparation

In one sense, you are preparing for the exam from the moment you begin to study a course. Take notes in a form that will be useful for revision and half your work is already done. However, at some point prior to the exam you will need to focus more specifically on revision and on developing a strategy for gaining good marks. As with much of what is suggested in this book, the action needed is straightforward. But it does require careful planning and good time management. You will probably find the following stages helpful for managing your preparation.

Identify requirements

As with all management, you need to clarify your objectives, in this case by becoming as clear as possible about what will be required of you. Analysing past papers is one of the best means of doing this, unless it is a new course or exam has changed recently. Look for the sorts of questions asked and the most popular topics. Try to put yourself in the examiner's position. It may be easier to set questions on some topics than others. Some topics may be so central to understanding a subject that it is highly likely that they will be included, directly or indirectly, in the exam.

Make sure that you know the format of the paper. How many questions are there? How many of these do you need to answer? Are they equally weighted in terms of marks allowed? How many topics does this mean you can afford not to revise? With a little research you should be able to identify areas of the course which it would be dangerous not to know and some which, if pushed, you could more safely afford to revise less thoroughly. But *always* allow a margin. It is extremely dangerous to think that you can completely predict an exam's content and to revise only the portion of the course you are 'sure' will come up.

Find out from your tutors what *level* of knowledge they expect. Is it fine detail or broad principles? Do you need to remember formulae or will any necessary ones be provided? Find out, too, for subjects where it is an issue, the balance expected between theory and its application. Tailor your revision accordingly.

Find out what you can bring into the exam room and make sure it is in working order. If you need a set of coloured pens, pencil and rubber, invest in new ones: during the exam your mind should be on what you are drawing or writing, not on whether your pens work. Make sure you have a fresh battery in your calculator or perhaps even a spare machine. My apologies if this sounds patronisingly obvious. It is. But many people still omit these simple precautions, with tragic results.

If you have an 'open book' exam and are allowed to take notes or books into the room, think very carefully about the preparation you need in order to make good use

To prepare for exam success:
- identify requirements
- prepare a revision plan
- revise actively
- practise writing answers
- get in good physical shape.

of these materials. You will gain no marks for time spent searching through books for the relevant pages. So produce an index of best references for likely topics. If you are allowed to annotate books, use this facility to make points briefly in margins. Text which is copied is unlikely to gain you any marks at all, but if you copy a relevant note of your own, the examiner will not know.

Prepare a revision plan

The need to prepare a plan in good time should be clear from the earlier discussion of managing your study. A revision plan will help you to balance your efforts and make revision more rewarding, keeping your motivation high. Clarify your objectives and decide on how much revision you need to do. Think about the time you have available and the time you estimate you will need. (Remember to build in a contingency factor here, in case of the unexpected.)

How are you going to revise? Clearly, you cannot read all the books again. Will some parts of the course need more time than others, perhaps because you found them difficult and still do not feel you understand the material? If you have already become used to planning your work actively, this stage should be almost second nature to you by now.

Prepare a chart, showing when you will work on each part of the course. You can do this well in advance, but once actual dates are announced you may need to reschedule to take into account the timing of specific exams. Remember to allow time at the end for overall preparation and for practice with past papers or other dummy questions. Avoid scheduling revision the night before the exam. There are better uses for that time. Your chart should have spaces for you to tick off topics as you progress. This helps to sustain your motivation.

Revise actively

Once you have scheduled your time you need to use it to derive maximum benefit. Mere passive reading of books and notes is unlikely to help. Instead, you need to bear the following questions in mind as you tackle each topic:

- What do I need to *learn by heart* (i.e. be able to reproduce from memory – formulae and diagrams, for example)?
- What do I need to *know* (e.g. concepts, principles and techniques and their significance)?
- What do I need to be able to *do* with the above and in what contexts?

You should already have the answers to these questions, but you need to keep them in mind as you work through your notes and other materials.

Even if your notes were taken with revision in mind, you will still need to take further notes as part of your revision. You may find it helpful to extract on to cards those things which you need to be able to reproduce from memory and learn them (on the bus, in the bath, or wherever you have suitable time at your disposal).

For everything other than rote learning, you should be aiming to *interact* with the materials in as many ways as possible. Draw diagrams of text. Describe diagrams in words. Try to represent relationships with equations. Try to describe equations in words. List possible uses of various techniques. Summarise key parts of the course from memory, then go back to see whether there is anything significant that you have left out. Draw mind maps of possible answers to past questions. Try to invent questions as if you were setting the exam. Then construct outline answers for these. Practise the analysis of requirements and planning of your answer, as suggested earlier for essays.

Aim to do all this fairly quickly. It will keep your brain alert and give you valuable practice in organising your thoughts quickly, a key exam skill. Then go back to course materials and 'mark' your attempts, seeing what you left out and spotting any errors. If you *work* at your revision in this way, rather than sitting in front of your notes and letting your eyes move over them, or merely copying things from one piece of paper to another, you will find that the process is fairly interesting and, more importantly, results in far more learning.

Practise

Unless you are provided with a word processor for the exam there is one very basic skill you may need to practise – that of writing, quickly, for long periods of time, with a pen. If all your writing is at a keyboard, the connection between brain and pen may have withered. This makes it very hard to write fluently in an exam. Your muscles may cramp, and your thoughts will limp along. Prevent this with 'writing practise'. Pick up a pen and write a diary, letters, or first drafts of essays in order to re-establish your skills.

The next thing to practise is writing for as long as an exam, in order to maintain concentration. Unless you habitually write essays in long stretches and by hand, set yourself 'mock exams'. Draft answers to past papers or to questions you set yourself, allowing the same length of time as you will have in the exam. Start, if you like, with single questions and the time that would be allowed for them, before working up to the whole paper. This gives you a good feel for time and the amount you can write in it and will make time management in the exam somewhat easier.

Feedback on your performance is important here, as with everything else. You can check timing easily. You can if necessary mark your own work, putting it aside for a while so that you come to it fresh. Better still, exchange answers with someone else and mark each other's.

Other preparation

Your final task is to be in good shape for the exam. If you are on the verge of caffeine poisoning, have worked through the night or have subsisted on biscuits for a week beforehand, you cannot expect your brain to do you justice in the exam. So it is essential to plan to get enough sleep and exercise during the whole revision period. In particular, use the evening before the exam to do something relaxing and have a reasonably early night. (Walk, hot bath, hot milk, bed is a good sequence.) You can waste all your earlier efforts by not taking your body's needs into account.

During the examination

If you have followed the above advice, have checked the time of the exam carefully (a close relative recently showed up in the afternoon for a morning exam!) and arrived in time to relax before entering the room, you should be in good shape during the exam. You merely need to remember the following points.

Read the paper carefully

Check that the number of questions you have to answer is what you expected. If you have a choice, read all the questions carefully enough to understand what is required before making your choice. It is often better to answer a question you fully understand about something you more or less know, than to attack a question on a topic you have revised extensively, but where you really are not sure what the question wants you to do. Totally open-ended questions are hazardous: they leave you to guess at an appropriate structure for your answer, with the possibility that you will get it wrong. Questions with a number of parts clearly spelled out make it easier for you to feel confident that you understand what the examiner requires.

Manage your time

Work out how much time you can afford to allow for each question and monitor your time usage. You must be disciplined about this. More people have failed because they spent too much time on one question and totally failed to answer one or more others than for any other reason. Remember the Pareto principle: here it suggests that you will get 80% of the marks for a question for 20% of the effort that full marks would require. So keeping to time is far, far more important than aiming for perfection. Move on to the next question when you have used your 'ration' for the current question. You can leave space and come back if you do not use all the time allocated to a subsequent question. Even if you feel forced to choose a question or two on topics where you know your revision to have been inadequate, you should still budget a reasonable time for your attempts. You can gain a surprising number of marks for fairly scant knowledge, if carefully applied to the question Check your watch and your schedule at frequent intervals to ensure that you allocate your time as intended.

Read each selected question very carefully

Remember the techniques covered earlier for deconstructing questions. You will need to do this fairly quickly, but it is essential that you identify and understand the instruction words and that you separate out *all* the implicit parts of the question. Any part that you miss will cost you a significant chunk of marks, as it will get 0 out of whatever was allowed for that part of the question in the marking scheme.

Plan your answer

There is a strong temptation, knowing how scarce time is, to leap straight into answering, without any plan. But this is dangerous. It is easy to miss essential dimensions of an answer or to end up with something which lacks much structure, is out of balance and fails to convince the marker of your grasp of the topic. While you cannot, obviously, afford the leisurely, 'collect everything of potential relevance' approach that may work for essays, you *can* do a quick 'brain dump' of key concepts and points that seem important, each encapsulated in a single word or very short phrase. This captures them so that they do not retreat into the inaccessible parts of your brain once you start writing about something else. You can then spend a few minutes arranging these into a mind map or set of headings and subheadings. Writing your answer will be so much easier once you have done this that you will more than gain back the time you have spent. (This is provided you did not over-indulge in planning – 20 per cent of the available time would seem a reasonable limit for this in most cases.)

A clear structure, with introduction and conclusion and a logical and connected flow between, is essential. It can help to leave space at the start of your answer and add your introduction after you have written the rest. Diagrams may be well worth including. (They need to be clear rather than artistic, so do not spend too much time on making them pretty.)

If you *are* running short of time, do not cross out your notes until your answer is completed. Markers are usually prevented from giving marks for crossed-out work, but will not penalise for notes which are clearly headed as such and *not* crossed out: in case of disaster they may give you some credit for them.

Remember to monitor progress at intervals

The control loop only works if 'outputs' are sampled often enough that you can take corrective action in time to prevent disaster. This means checking your time management every page or so and also checking that you are still answering the question as asked. (Questions have a nasty habit of silently rewriting themselves inside your head into something you would prefer to answer; frequent checking against the original is essential.)

One of your objectives is to demonstrate academic competence, so part of the checking should be that you have noted relevant authors and dates wherever appropriate.

Above all, DON'T PANIC

Most people pass exams. Almost everyone could have passed by following the guidance above. So if anything feels as if it is going wrong, take a few deep breaths and consciously relax your body while reminding yourself of this. Your brain will probably unscramble itself enough to proceed. If you really cannot answer a question then write *something* that has some tenuous relevance. If you run out of clearly relevant things to say and have not used the time, write something more that has at least some bearing on the subject. If you are running out of time despite everything above, stop and jot down some notes in answer to the remaining questions. And if your problems were due to illness on the day, see a doctor, get a certificate and send it in, as soon as the exam is over.

VIVA VOCE EXAMINATIONS

Oral assessment was the earliest examination form of all. You are most likely to encounter it if for some reason the examiners cannot decide your result from your written papers. Perhaps you were on a borderline, or were ill and may not have done yourself justice. Sometimes a few other people are summoned to a *viva* to help examiners establish the range of expected standards. You will normally have a *viva* in which you defend your thesis if you go on to a PhD, and they are fairly common with dissertations too. You may well need to meet your examiner and discuss your portfolio if you are pursuing an NVQ. Such examinations are wonderfully flexible and can be tailored to the needs of an individual candidate. They are also very expensive and it is hard to ensure uniformity of standards, so institutions may keep their use to a minimum.

To do well in a *viva*:
- find out why you are being examined
- prepare accordingly
- check that you understand the questions
- allow yourself time to think
- answer clearly and honestly
- watch responses to your answers
- check you have been understood.

Preparing for a *viva*

Obviously, your first requirement is to know *why* you are being examined. Are you a borderline case and, if so, which borderline? You will probably not be told exactly, but may be able to find out whether you are at risk of failing and can relax slightly if the answer is no. Is there a particular concern which your examiners had? Perhaps you did very poorly on one particular topic, or your dissertation has particular weaknesses? Or perhaps a dissertation is *so* good that the examiners wish to reassure themselves that you produced it unaided!

If the *viva* is to give you a chance to improve on the marks you gained in a written exam, then you should revise in much the same way as you did for the exam itself, as this is another form of test of the same knowledge. You could also usefully reflect on any exam questions you know you answered badly. It is likely that your examiners will focus on the areas where they fear you are weak. Furthermore, if you can demonstrate to them that you are aware of where you went wrong, it will count in your favour. Do not restrict your revision to such areas, however. You may be questioned on any part of the course and, indeed, may not have judged your shortcomings correctly.

If the exam is a routine one in support of a project or thesis, then little preparation should be needed beyond reminding yourself of its contents. If you have sweated blood over writing it, these will probably be indelibly etched in your mind anyway. You might, however, wish to think about your 'reflections' section on lessons learned (assuming there was one – if not, reflect anyway) and about any areas where you know the research was weak so that you can say what you would do about this, given a chance. But much of the exam will probably be directed towards establishing that the work was your own, by looking for the sort of in-depth knowledge you could only have if this were the case.

For a non-routine project *viva*, or in the case of a borderline written exam, try to find out what the concern was, either from your project supervisor or tutor or from your own reflection. Think of ways in which you can reassure your examiner(s) that such weaknesses either were unavoidable, or would be avoided in future because you now fully understand how they arose.

Answering questions

A *viva* is an example of a spoken exchange, where you will be aiming to determine the examiner's concerns and address them concisely. Your goal is to demonstrate your understanding of the material in question. Thus you need the talking and listening skills addressed in Chapter 9. Revisit that chapter before your exam.

→ Ch 9

Listening is crucial. If you fail to understand a question, you will do yourself as much harm as when you misread a question in a written exam. In a *viva* you have the chance to check the meaning of a question with the examiner. Take advantage of this. Clarify the meaning and check that your understanding is correct if you are in any doubt.

Thinking is vital too. Do not feel you have to answer a question the instant the examiner stops asking it. It is perfectly reasonable to spend a short time thinking about how to answer it. If this seems odd, ask: 'Can I think about that for a moment?' You will almost always be told that you can.

Be honest. If there is a weakness in your project, or you answer something and then realise that your answer was inadequate, say so and then go on to do what you can to make good the shortcomings you have revealed. This is far safer than hoping that the examiner didn't notice! Examiners notice a great deal: that is their job.

Take your cues on formality from the examiner. Some are more informal than others. Aim to match their chosen level. But above all, remember that anything you can do to help the *process* of the interview will help. Look directly at the examiner when talking or listening. You can smile where appropriate. The occasion is one for communication, so treat it as such. Check that you have received the right (question) message. Check that your answer is clear to your examiner. If you are at all unsure, ask whether what you have said is enough, or if there is another angle the examiner would like you to explore, or something which should be covered in more depth. They may not always tell you. But often they will and this will enable you to give a more satisfactory answer.

PORTFOLIO ASSESSMENT

If your course includes an element of competence-based assessment, or if you seek such a qualification later in your career, you are likely to be required to produce a portfolio demonstrating that you have the full range of competences covered in that qualification. Your portfolio will consist of a number of 'exhibits' which demonstrate your skills in some way. Your work on the book thus far should have generated some exhibits. Additionally you might need to include letters or reports you have written, work schedules you have drawn up, interview plans and/or reports of the interview, training plans, tape recordings of interactions of one kind or another, testimonials from people for whom you have worked, examples of things you have made . . . the list is endless and what is required will depend on the particular qualification which you are seeking.

→ Ch 1

8

Gaining good marks

But the *principles* of portfolio assessment are fairly uniform. You need to address all, or most of, the aspects of a set of performance standards. The exhibit needs to be relevant, fairly recent, and to demonstrate your own competence rather than that of other people. And you need to have organised, indexed, cross-referenced and justified your contents. The examiner needs to be able to convince him- or herself on the basis of your portfolio (without wasting time or energy) that you would indeed be competent in the vocational area specified.

To convince your examiner, you therefore need to have collected a reasonable set of 'exhibits' and to make a case for their relevance and sufficiency. Different awarding bodies may have different preferences about this. You will need to study the competence framework they use, the contexts in which they want competences to be displayed and the sorts of evidence they want. Then you need to assemble suitable materials, together with a 'story' which explains your situation and the contexts in which the competences are used and an index which clearly links exhibits to competences. This is important because a carefully chosen exhibit can often evidence a number of different competences. A project, for example, could show self-management skills, project management skills, written communication skills, information handling skills and possibly others as well. But you cannot merely hand your project in and expect the assessor to work this out. You need to explain which exhibit shows which competence(s) and why, referencing relevant parts of any lengthy exhibit.

If you have been constructing exhibits as instructed in the exercises, you should already be getting a feel for how to do this. You should also be building a collection of things which will possibly help you gain qualifications after graduation. It is a good habit to treat everything you do which shows you have mastered a new skill, or can use it in a new context, as a potential exhibit. You will find it helps to consolidate your learning to write your case around the material. Leafing through the portfolio can also be a powerful antidote to depression. When you are depressed it is easy to under-estimate yourself. A solid portfolio can counteract this.

SUMMARY

■ Doing well in assessment requires clarity of objectives, planning, monitoring and use of feedback wherever possible. It thus closely resembles management in other contexts.

■ All assessments can usefully be regarded as communication, so written or spoken communications skills are vital.

■ Understanding objectives requires that you deconstruct a question and identify its constituent parts, then plan an answer which addresses all parts of a question, in a reasonable sequence.

■ Both essays and reports need an introduction and a conclusion and clear arguments based on valid evidence between the two. Time management is crucial for written assignments.

- For exams you need a clear revision plan based on identification of the material it is important to cover. Revision needs to be active and to include frequent tests of recall and of ability to draft outline answers to possible questions.

- During an exam it is important to read questions carefully before selecting, to plan your answers and regularly check both your time usage and the continued relevance of what you write to the actual question asked.

- Should anything go wrong to threaten your success, obtain evidence of the problem where possible and notify the authorities as soon as possible.

Further information

- Giles, K. and Hedge, N. (1994) *The Manager's Good Study Guide*, The Open University.
- Race, P. (1999) *How to get a good degree*, Open University Press.
- Stewart, M.A. and O'Toole, F.J. (1998) *30 Days to the GMAT CAT,* Arco. Although this is specifically written to help those taking the GMAT test for entry to US business schools, it is a source of excellent advice on analysis, essay writing and maths, and as such would be helpful for those taking other business studies related exams.

8

Gaining good marks

HELPFILE
Terms commonly used in assessment

Analyse

To examine part by part. Thus if you are asked to analyse a problem situation you would be looking for the roots of the problem, rather than merely describing the symptoms which are presented. You would normally be expected to draw heavily on ideas and frameworks in the course being assessed in order to identify the root causes. The analysis may be the basis for suggesting possible ways forward and deciding between them.

Assess

To judge the importance of something, or say what it is worth, giving your reasons for your verdict.

Comment

This terse instruction may appear after a quotation or other statement. You are required to respond in a way that shows that you understand the topic to which the statement refers. Thus you might need to define any terms contained, explain the significance of the statement and possibly evaluate it (*see* below), or state the extent to which you agree and disagree and give your reasons for this.

Compare

This means that you should look for both similarities and differences between the (usually) two things mentioned. It is very easy to forget one or the other, thus potentially losing half the available marks. It is safest always to think of 'compare' as shorthand for 'compare and contrast'. Sometimes you will be expected to come down in favour of one of the things compared. One possible approach to comparison is to construct a table with one column for each of the items compared and rows for each relevant aspect. This gives an 'at a glance' impression of aspects where entries are the same and those where there are differences. It will not, however, allow much space for discussion and may need to be complemented by a paragraph or two highlighting the significance of key similarities and differences which appear in the table.

Consider

This has a similar meaning to comment, though the emphasis on evaluation is likely to be higher.

Contrast

A subset of 'compare' (*see* above), requiring you to focus only on differences between the things mentioned.

Criticise

To judge the merit of a statement or theory, making clear the basis for your judgement.

This might be in terms of the evidence on which the statement or theory is based, or its internal consistency, or its theoretical, logical or factual underpinning.

Define

To state, precisely, the meaning of a concept. Normally this will be a definition that you have been given in your course. Sometimes there may be competing definitions, in which case you may need to give both (or all, if more than two) and discuss the differences between them. You will often be asked to include examples of the thing to be defined. Even if not asked for, an example may help to convey to the marker that you understand the meaning of the term in question.

Demonstrate

This means you need to show something, usually by giving relevant examples, in order to convince the marker of your understanding of something, or of its relevance or importance.

Describe

To give a detailed account of the thing referred to, again with a view to establishing that you know what is being referred to and understand its significance. Diagrams can often help you describe something and should be included if they add something to your words.

Differentiate

This is similar to 'contrast', again requiring you to describe the differences between the things mentioned.

Discuss

To extract the different themes in a subject and to describe and evaluate them. What are the key factors/aspects? What are the arguments in favour of, and against, each aspect? What evidence is there supporting each side of the argument? What is the significance of each aspect?

Evaluate

This means much the same as 'assess'. If you were asked to evaluate a theory, for example, you would look both at the evidence supporting the theory and at its usefulness.

Examine

This means much the same as 'analyse', though it might require a slightly higher proportion of description in relation to evaluation.

Explain

This can mean to make something clear or to give reasons for something, depending on the context. Frequently you would need to do both in order to answer a question. Remember that your explanation, as with all assessment, is intended to demonstrate your understanding of a concept or argument to your assessor.

8

Gaining good marks – Helpfile

Illustrate

This is similar to 'demonstrate'. It requires you to make clear your understanding of an idea or term by giving concrete examples, or by using a diagram or other figure to add to the word(s) and convey the message that you know what you are talking about.

Interpret

This normally means to make sense of something, to make it clear, usually giving your judgement of the significance of the thing to be interpreted. You might be asked to interpret a set of figures or a graph, in which case you would need to describe in words the significant features, or messages, contained therein.

Justify

This means you must give good reason for something, in terms of logic or evidence. It helps to think of the main objections to whatever it is and then show why they are not valid, as well as thinking of the plus points.

List

This needs to be treated with caution. Strictly it means to give single words or phrases. But sometimes the assessor wants you to give a brief description rather than merely a single word. If in doubt, ask, if it is a written assignment. In an exam, make a reasoned guess from the proportion of the marks allocated to this part of the question and any subsequent instructions. For example, 'List . . . Select two items from your list and describe them in detail' clearly does mean a list pure and simple.

Outline

To give a brief description of the most important features of whatever it is.

Refute

The converse of 'justify', requiring you to make the case *against* something.

Review

To go over a subject carefully, giving as much as you can remember or unearth of what is relevant, though as concisely as is appropriate.

Summarise

Write briefly the main points of something – very similar to 'outline'.

Trace

This requires you to track a sequence of events which led to a specified state. (Multiple cause diagrams may be helpful here if there is more than a single 'track'.)

....?

By this I mean questions which seem to invite the answer 'Yes' or 'No', e.g. 'Do you agree?' after a statement. It is extremely rare for the assessor to expect such a simple answer! Far more often the expectation is that you will discuss the statement and evaluate it.

→ **Part 3** **WORKING WITH OTHERS**

Introduction to Part 3

For almost everyone, work involves communication and collaboration. Structural changes in organisations during the last decade or so have increased the amount and the variety of interaction. Your success will depend on being able to work effectively with colleagues.

Task-related communication is clearly important, but wider aspects of relationships are also important. Many decisions at work are not purely rational. They are influenced by relationships and feelings. If relationships are good, proposals may be interpreted more positively, people will go out of their way to be cooperative, and any inevitable compromise will be reached more easily. You have probably found that you will forgive a good friend who stands you up, but not someone you already dislike. Similarly, you might do a particular favour only for a friend. This partly explains why networking skills are important for management success.

The importance of relationships at work goes beyond issues of success. A job can be one of the most satisfying parts of your life, or it can be sheer purgatory. The quality of relationships between those who work together can in large part determine which. When reading a case for promotion recently, I was struck by the following phrase in one of the references:

> *He's a pleasure to work with – a crucial, yet frequently overlooked attribute of the modern manager.*

Your ability to work well with others affects *their* lives, as well as your own.

Given all this, it is not surprising that in the survey of graduates' work referred to earlier (Harvey *et al.*, 1997), one of the two main categories of attributes sought by employers of graduates was 'interactive attributes'. The authors distinguished the ability to *communicate* with a wide range of people, both formally and informally, the ability to *relate* to these people and the ability to work effectively in *teams*.

Similarly, the graduate recruitment section of a major daily newspaper had adverts seeking graduates who are 'enthusiastic, self-motivated and have excellent communication skills . . .', 'are self-starters with the ability to communicate . . .', 'have excellent communication and interpersonal skills . . . ' and 'have the kind of personality that helps them get on harmoniously and productively with colleagues . . .', to quote but a few.

Clearly, then, interpersonal skills are very important, both if you are to enjoy work and for success. (Note that humans have evolved as highly social animals.) Most selection processes are heavily weighted, intentionally or not, towards assessing interpersonal skills.

Developing your interpersonal skills will help you to benefit from tutors and advisers, and from feedback from fellow students, to do well in group projects, and to make rewarding friendships. There is a body of relevant theory and good practice. You have already met the idea of elements of communication in developing your writing skills. This part of the book develops the ideas in the context of spoken communication, group working and talking to a group.

The first chapter in this part therefore looks at talking and listening, skills which you will use in almost all group working. As part of this, you will explore how to be assertive rather than aggressive or defensive: assertiveness helps you resolve differences of either opinion or objectives. The next chapter looks at the sorts of behaviours which contribute to effective team working. The final chapter looks at formal presentation skills.

→ 9 Talking and listening

The spoken word is perhaps the most powerful communication channel, yet many people are poor talkers and poorer listeners. This chapter shows you how to become better at both, developing skills that will make you a better learner, a better team worker, and more effective in almost all areas of your life. Better communication can transform all your relationships!

Learning outcomes

By the end of this chapter you should:

■ have a clearer idea of your own strengths in the area of one-to-one communication and be able to convey this to a prospective employer

■ be a better listener

■ be better at talking to another person

■ be becoming more assertive if this is necessary

■ be able to influence more effectively

■ be starting to network

■ have developed the habit of reflecting on your interpersonal effectiveness

■ be continuing to learn from your experience so that by the time you graduate you will have developed a still higher level of interpersonal skills.

Most relationships, whether at work or elsewhere, are based on talking and listening. If you are *really* to learn, rather than merely accumulating 'book knowledge', you need to discuss ideas with others. Other people can give you feedback on different aspects of your behaviour: you need to be able to listen to this, and absorb it. You may need to find out more about a situation by talking to the people involved. To convince someone to take action, you may need to talk them through the arguments. You may need to negotiate with people to get what you want. Small wonder that the QAA key skills list includes oral communication skills, and additionally lists talking and listening and negotiation as key interpersonal skills

As with reading, many people do not communicate effectively despite decades of experience. They may say something without thinking about its impact on the other person. They may come across as aggressive, and therefore generate a negative response. Some are so afraid of saying the wrong thing, or of offending the listener,

Cartoon by Neill Cameron, www.planetdumbass.co.uk

that they do not say what they mean. Real communication is a two-way process. And inability to *listen* to the other person causes it to fail. You may be surprised at the extent to which reflection on your own strengths and weaknesses in this area, and feedback from others, can increase your ability to communicate effectively. This will improve the quality of your interpersonal relationships more generally.

THE IMPORTANCE OF INTERPERSONAL SKILLS

In most jobs interaction with others is crucial. Many organisations have restructured around flexible working groups as the main unit, and team work is essential for success. Even if you work in a more conventional and bureaucratic organisation, on projects which are essentially individual, you will still need to interact with others. As a friend who is responsible for systems design for a major US bank said to me:

> *You are always going to have to sell your ideas to your boss, to argue for resources, and to let people know what you have done and why it is important.*

You will be more successful in almost any job if you can talk clearly and confidently, are sufficiently assertive and possess the skills necessary to influence people and negotiate effectively. Whether dealing with clients or customers, your boss or those whom you yourself manage, you have to be able to communicate effectively face to face.

ACTIVITY 9.1

Look back at your initial SWOT. Did you include communication skills as a potential strength? Reassess yourself, using the questions below. If you have any doubts about your skills in this area, reassess yourself at the end of the chapter (a version is available on the web) and develop an action plan for developing your skills. Score each item 1 if it is usually the case, 2 if quite often, 3 if sometimes, 4 if seldom the case, and 5 if almost never.

When I meet new people, much of my attention is on planning my reply rather than really listening to what they are saying   _____

Most people I talk to seem to be rather boring   _____

I find it quite difficult to network with other people   _____

In a group, I don't feel that my contributions have much impact   _____

I tend to get into arguments if people don't see my point of view   _____

I may sound defensive if people give me negative feedback, although it may be because they haven't understood my reasons   _____

I tend to focus more on a person's words than their non-verbal signals   _____

I have no hesitation in telling people they are bad at something   _____

People seem not to hear what I am saying   _____

I feel uncomfortable in social or group work situations   _____

I find it hard to create a good impression in an interview   _____

I find it almost impossible not to interrupt if something someone says prompts a really good idea   _____

Total   _____

Note, this is a very crude questionnaire, but it will act as a starting point for thinking about your interpersonal skills. If you were being strictly honest you are unlikely to get a score much above 50 (unless you are very unaware of your shortcomings). Above 40 is good, but shows room for improvement – file your score if you are planning to work on this area.

Interviews are still the main method of selection for many jobs and one of the methods for almost all others. In an interview it is your talking and listening skills that are primarily being assessed. Thus these skills will help you to get a job, as well as to be effective once you have got it. Appraisal interviews are a major part of the system for assessing performance in most large organisations. Again, your talking and listening skills will be essential. They are essential for the effective team work which is a feature of so many jobs and which will be explored in more detail in the next chapter. Many jobs will involve daily communication with clients and internal and external customers.

→ Ch 10

9

Talking and listening

Good communication with those who work for you is essential to being an effective manager. Indeed it is hard to imagine just how much improving your skills in this area can contribute to success at work.

Indeed, communication on a daily basis, with all those with whom you have contact both at work and at home, will be an essential element in your life. Work on these skills will impact on your social life, and improve your relationships with those close to you. While most people are aware of the importance of talking, its equally vital complement, listening, is often ignored.

ACTIVE LISTENING

When you are talking to someone, do you often have the feeling that they are not really listening to you? They do not remember what you have said, or they think you have said or intended something that you did not, or they interrupt you in mid-sentence with some barely related statement that they have obviously been dying to make for some time. Now, be honest with yourself and think about how often you do exactly the same thing!

→ Ch 6 You will remember the basic communication model from Chapter 6, with its key elements of sender, message, communication channel and receiver. If someone is talking to you, perhaps very clearly and cogently, but you are not really listening, then communication has failed: the receiver is not functioning.

ACTIVITY 9.2

Think of a recent social situation at which you were present and at which people were not listening to each other. If possible, think also of a work-related situation (job or study) in which again communication was failing because you or someone else was not listening. Why do people seemingly persist in such non-communication? List as many reasons as you can for the talker continuing to talk, and the listener not listening, in the situation(s) you have just identified. If you are working through this chapter with others, once you have written your lists compare them with those made by one or two other people and discuss any similarities and differences.

This exercise may well have given you some difficulty. When put like that, why *do* people persistently not communicate? Your list might include:

- failure to realise that the other person is not actually listening
- a desire to be seen by others to be talking – this can make you seem a lively person at a party
- enjoyment of the sound of your own voice
- the conviction that the other person must find what you are saying riveting
- the realisation that *you* are sorting out your thoughts by talking, even if you are having no effect on the thought processes of the other person

- a wish to stop the other person from talking – they may be boring, or you don't understand them and don't like to be found out in this
- a simple lack of interest in the other person
- a desire to be the centre of attention
- the dread of silence.

You may have come up with many of the above, plus a variety of other reasons. Your list and mine can probably be broken down into a small number of categories. Some reasons represent more or less sensible behaviour, such as trying to avoid boredom or exploring your own thoughts and where they lead. Some are defensive, such as avoiding being made to look stupid by not understanding. Some are aggressive, such as exerting your will on others. Some represent lack of perception. Some have to do with communicating something other than the message contained in the words spoken.

The skill of being heard when speaking, rather than having your words fall on unreceptive ears or minds, will be dealt with shortly. First, we shall look in more detail at the motivations for not listening.

Your list of possible reasons for 'people hearing without listening' or, more accurately if less poetically, *not* hearing because of this might include:

- lack of interest in either the person speaking or what they are saying
- fear about how to respond and thoughts about this taking up most of your awareness
- inability to concentrate
- inability to understand what is being said, or to perceive the emotions leading to its expression
- desire *not* to hear – for example things that reflect badly on the listener or are inconsistent with strongly held ideas.

Not listening wastes time and energy – both yours and those of the speaker. It makes for negative feelings between you. It may cause you to miss a real opportunity to find out something useful or interesting. You may lose the chance to build a good relationship, or to give or receive support (both of which can be rewarding). You will also, of course, be wasting the opportunity to develop your listening skills.

Identifying purposes

If you wish to avoid these negative aspects and use one-to-one exchanges to good effect, then you need first to think about the purpose of the exchange, what the positive outcomes might be and then how you can develop the skills needed to achieve these.

9

Talking and listening

ACTIVITY 9.3

Think about some *good* conversations that you have recently had and the sorts of benefits which you were deriving from them. List these. Now think about exchanges which you have had which have been unsatisfactory. Aim for about six such conversations. Split these into those which might have been useful or rewarding if they had gone differently and those which were probably doomed to be a waste of time from the start. Reflect on this, and consider whether talking and listening is an area which you need to work on. If so, develop an action plan for your file.

You should have been able to identify positive potential in at least some of the bad experiences. Few of us know so much that we have nothing to learn from someone else or cannot derive comfort from support and sympathy. Most of us find it intellectually stimulating to exchange ideas and explore areas of disagreement. Of course, it does take two to play. Very occasionally you will meet people who seem incapable of ever taking part in a two-way conversation. In such cases, it may be best to cut your losses and find a tactful way of stopping the exchange. But take care not to do this too soon. Some of the most unpromising beginnings turn into useful exchanges.

Active listening helps you:
- build relationships
- learn
- develop ideas
- work better together.

For conversations which were rewarding, or which had the potential to be so, the outcomes might have included:

- enjoyment at sharing ideas
- discovering new information
- agreement to some future action on your part
- laughter
- an increased sense of self-worth
- a clearer understanding of one or more of your own ideas
- a possible way of resolving a problem
- reduced worry about something that was troubling you
- satisfaction at feeling that you have helped someone
- plans to do things together in future
- a clearer sense of purpose regarding a shared task.

The list could be much longer. You probably identified outcomes that were not on the list, as the range of possible interchanges is almost infinite. But again, a smaller number of broad categories will probably contain most if not all of your outcomes. The first is *satisfaction of social needs*: you will remember from Chapter 2 that these form an important part of human motivation and contribute to your feelings of well-being.

→ Ch 2

The second category will concern *information transfer*. We learn a great deal from conversations with other people. This is one of the reasons that networking is so important. The information could include simple facts, names of further contacts or other potentially useful resources you might be able to access. But more tenuous information can be just as useful. You may get a better idea of what is important to someone, and find out what is likely to upset them. You may discover their position on some issue of future concern to you.

The third category has to do with *developing ideas*. While much of this can be done in a solitary fashion, most people enjoy testing ideas against other people. Apart from the fun, this is an important way of identifying unconscious assumptions which you have made. These may seem so obviously true to you that you do not question them: they may be far less obviously true to others. Inappropriate assumptions may be leading you astray. If the ideas need to be accepted by a group of people, then developing them in the group is important. More of this in Part 4.

→ Ch 12, 13, 15, 16

The fourth category has to do with *planning and managing of tasks*, for which communication is essential, whether at work or in relation to study. For shared tasks the need is obvious. For solitary ones, you will still almost certainly need to communicate – often by talking – to make sure that you understand the task fully. You will also need to renegotiate deadlines or resources if things turn out differently from what is expected.

Listening skills

To achieve any of these categories of outcomes from conversations, both participants need to be skilled listeners. If you are listening actively you will do the following.

Listen better by:
- suspending judgement
- concentrating on the speaker
- watching body language
- avoiding interruptions
- seeking clarification
- acknowledging feelings
- allowing silence
- encouraging and prompting
- avoiding opinions
- not offering 'solutions'.

Suspend judgement

It is vital to keep an open mind while you are listening. If you have already judged a situation and come to an opinion you are likely to hear only those things which are consistent with your existing opinion. This will severely restrict what you learn from the exchange. Instead, try hard to approach the situation as one where what the other person knows and says is the important thing.

Concentrate on the speaker

Focus on what the speaker is saying and how they are saying it. This will take all your attention – you cannot afford to think about their hair, the weather, what you are going to say next, or anything else. Is there a logical thread? Are there inconsistencies? If something sounds wrong to you, is it because you and the speaker have different basic assumptions? If the speaker is giving 'facts', what is the evidence for these? Similarly, what underlies opinions? What feelings are being expressed?

Watch body language

This can tell you as much as the words. Unease may be expressed, for example, by restless hand or body movements, looking away or inappropriate smiling. Where words and body are at odds, remember this for later probing. (When speakers are having a good conversation you will often find that their body language becomes similar, so that one mirrors the other. Two people may face each other over a bar, one with their left elbow resting on it, the other with their right elbow. Or if seated opposite each other they may cross their legs at roughly the same time, one the left leg, one the right, so that again one looks like the mirror image of the other.)

Show your interest

Eye contact, smiles, an 'open' posture help. Don't cross arms or legs – this shows a degree of 'closedness' to the other person. Nods and expressions of agreement from time to time help to demonstrate interest. But it is possible to do all of these without hearing a word the other person is saying. Reinforce these general cues, therefore, by more specific ones. Paraphrasing what the other person has said at key points shows that content has registered with you. 'So what you are saying is . . .' or 'It sounds as if . . .' shows that something has registered. It also allows you to check that you are receiving the message intended. Such reflections are useful for the speaker too. Sometimes they may not have realised just what they *were* saying, or perhaps were unaware of some of its implications.

Avoid interruptions

This is really an extension of the point above. If you are interested, you will interrupt only when the thing said is so interesting that you cannot control your excitement. But interruptions are such a frequent way in which listening fails that they are worth separate mention. Note that talking into a silence, but still breaking the speaker's 'train of thought', is a form of interruption.

Seek clarification

If you are not sure that you understand what someone is saying, or if it seems inconsistent with something said earlier, ask questions exploring this. Use questions such as 'Do you mean . . .?' or 'How does this fit with . . .?' or 'I don't quite understand why . . .' to help clarify things.

Recognise feelings

It was suggested earlier that you note feelings. It can be useful to show the other person that you have done this. 'I can see how angry this makes you . . .' or 'Yes, it is quite scary when . . .' or 'That really upset you, didn't it . . .' can convey that you have heard, and accepted, the feelings that are being communicated as well as the words. If, for example, you are trying to give support to someone who is worried, or who has had a bad experience, it is very important to accept, and show that you have accepted, their feelings.

Allow silence

If the speaker is trying to communicate something difficult, they may need time to organise their thoughts or to work out how best to express them. It is important that you do not rush in to fill silences for fear of embarrassment. Instead, show by your body language that you are comfortable and allow the person the thinking time they need. A good interviewer will always allow a candidate this thinking time.

Encourage and prompt

If a person *is* finding things difficult, and a pause does not seem to be the answer, you might want to ask a gently probing question: 'That's really interesting. What happened next?' or 'How did you feel about that?' or 'So what options do you think you have?'

Direct the conversation only when necessary

If you are trying to listen, to learn and perhaps to help the speaker, then taking charge of the conversation should be done only with caution. Sometimes the speaker will be going round in circles. If so, you may need to summarise the argument in question and suggest another avenue. Sometimes the conversation will raise a question or issue that had not previously occurred to you. If so you may want to lead into this topic. It is usually better to steer with a light hand. Being too directive will carry the message that you are more concerned with your perspective than that of the speaker. (Of course, in a more formal interview, where you have a clear agenda, you *will* need to be rather more directive.)

Avoid expressing opinions and judgements

There is another important reason for suspending judgement. It stops you expressing opinions. If someone feels that you are making negative judgements they will soon stop talking. Being too full of praise is not always helpful either. While support is good, agreeing with everything a person says may make them less likely to question their perspective. Helping someone to see things differently might be a positive outcome of a conversation. There is a further hazard. We almost all have a strong need to be approved. Expressing judgement will slant the conversation even if it does not stop it. The speaker will start to say things in order to gain your approval, which is unlikely to be helpful. This is particularly likely if the listener has a higher status than the speaker, for example if you are listening to someone who reports to you at work.

Be wary of suggesting solutions

If the conversation is a joint problem-solving situation there will be a time when suggested solutions may be helpful. Even then it is possible to start looking for solutions too soon, before the problem is fully understood. (When you have read Chapter 12 the reasons for this will be clearer.) If you are trying to help someone else to solve their problem, suggested solutions, even if asked for, are likely to get a 'Yes, but . . . ' response. This will be followed by a series of reasons why the solution is impossible or inappropriate. It is more useful to help the other person to find their own solution. This will be one which they will accept and therefore have the motivation to implement.

→ Ch 12

This somewhat lengthy list should make it clear why listening is a full-time job. It should also make it clear that becoming a proficient listener is not something that you are likely to achieve overnight. You will need to overturn at least some habits of a lifetime unless you are exceptional and blessed with the skills already. Breaking habits is extremely difficult. To make progress you need first to become much more aware of the dimensions of listening and then to start reflecting actively on how you score on these dimensions – a difficult task when listening itself leaves little if any spare brain capacity!

ACTIVITY 9.4

To heighten your awareness of the various dimensions, start listening carefully to other people's conversations. Make a rough assessment of how well they are communicating. Watch their body language and listen for a little while before coming to this judgement. Then try to find out what is contributing to the effectiveness or otherwise of the interchange. Score the participants on the dimensions described above. Are they expressing interest? How? How is lack of interest being communicated? How are silences handled? What sort of probes seem to be effective in encouraging the speaker? You can do this on a bus, in a pub, at a party or anywhere that people interact. If several of you are doing it, compare notes afterwards.

ACTIVITY 9.5

Once you are sensitised to the aspects of effective listening, start to observe your own behaviour. You can do this by reflecting on conversations as soon as possible after they take place. Once you have done this often enough to be alert to some of your bad habits, identify some purposeful exchanges where you know in advance that listening will be important. Think about both your objectives in the exchange and those of the other person. During the exchange try to think before you speak and to reduce the incidence of bad habits such as interruption or passing judgement. Try also to increase the incidence of good listening behaviour, such as encouragement, close concentration, paraphrasing or recognition of feelings.

GIVING AND RECEIVING FEEDBACK

Giving and receiving feedback are among the most crucial of all interpersonal skills. You will remember from earlier discussions that feedback was essential for both learning and motivation (both of these are specific examples of the more general control loop). Much of this feedback will come from other people. In the work context you will often need to be guided by feedback from a superior and to help your own subordinates improve by use of constructive comment. Performance appraisal interviews are a formal version of this. In many organisations these will be linked to both pay and career prospects. More informal feedback from colleagues will contribute to your learning almost daily, and your feedback will help others. While you are looking for a job you can improve future performance by seeking feedback from interviews where you were not successful.

Talking and listening are of course central to much feedback. You will need to practise these skills in this context if you are to develop the skills covered in this book. Feedback from tutors and other students is an essential part of the process. Talking and listening skills themselves are no exception to the rule that skills development requires feedback. You need to use your talking and listening skills to obtain feedback on your talking and listening skills. You even need feedback on how well you give and receive feedback! It is therefore important to look at what helps and hinders effective use of feedback before going further.

If it is to be effective, feedback involves more than the talking and listening skills already covered. You need to understand some points specific to the feedback situation if you are to overcome the difficulty most people have in both giving and receiving feedback. One important point is that we typically find it very hard to accept criticism – a common response is to deny or explain away any problems. The more insecure people feel, the stronger will be this tendency. Some people simply do not seem to *hear* criticism. They will claim never to have been told that anything was wrong, though their superior may be convinced that the points have been strongly made on more than one occasion. Many people find it equally difficult to give feedback. Curiously, it seems as difficult to praise as to point out where improvements would help.

Guidelines for giving feedback

The following good practice guidelines should help overcome the difficulties. The examples are drawn from situations where feedback is being given on contributions to a discussion group (see next chapter), but the principles themselves apply in any feedback situation. To give effective feedback you should do the following.

To give useful feedback:
- avoid appearing superior
- emphasise good points
- focus on behaviour not person
- be specific.

Avoid appearing 'superior'

Ideally, feedback is a reciprocal process, where *each* party has something to learn. You do not need to be 'better' than the person to whom you offer feedback. You merely offer a different perspective.

Focus on good points as well as bad

It is often suggested that there should be two things to praise for every point made suggesting a need for improvement. This makes the whole exchange more positive and reduces the tendency to reject suggestions because of insecurity. Also, people are not necessarily aware of some of their strengths and it is important that in trying to change their behaviour they do not lose these.

Focus on the behaviour, not the person

Focusing on the behaviour makes the feedback less personal and therefore less threatening. Do not say 'You are bad at . . .' but 'Your comment about . . . seemed to make . . . look uneasy.' Rather than 'You are incredibly talkative' say 'According to my log, you were talking for roughly half of the time.' Rather than say 'You are a really aggressive person' say 'When you said . . . I felt as if I was being personally attacked.'

Be as specific as possible

Say things like 'Did you realise that you interrupted Robin 15 times?' or 'Were you aware that each time someone interrupted you, you stopped talking, and that after the first ten minutes you made no further contribution?' or 'When there was that long silence, you showed you were comfortable with it by smiling and by your relaxed

9 Talking and listening

posture.' If you are focusing on behaviour not the person, you will almost inevitably find that you are being more specific, but give as much information as you can if you want to be as helpful as possible.

Guidelines for receiving and using feedback

In receiving feedback you are exercising your skills very much for your own benefit. To benefit from feedback you need to do the following.

> To benefit from feedback:
> - listen actively
> - appreciate the help
> - clarify what is meant
> - use several sources
> - accept implications
> - identify steps forward
> - monitor progress.

Listen carefully

Listen to what is being said, rather than immediately trying to think of excuses. Watch out for any responses you make which start with 'Yes, but . . .'! You are trying to learn from the feedback rather than justify your normal way of operating.

Be appreciative

Remember that the person giving the feedback may be finding it very difficult and that they are doing it for your benefit.

Seek clarification

Seeking clarification is necessary if you are unclear about quite what is being said (but in a positive, not confrontational way). Say 'That's interesting. But I'm not quite sure if you mean . . . or . . .'.

Use several sources

Remember that observing and giving feedback is a subjective activity. There may be different opinions. No one person is necessarily right (or wrong). But if several are saying the same thing it is worth taking seriously. Try to find other sorts of information to support (or otherwise) the view of the person giving feedback.

Accept your imperfections

No-one is perfect, so there is no need for you to pretend to yourself or others that you are. But by taking feedback seriously you can become very much better.

Try to identify positive steps you can take to improve

Simply giving yourself a mental slap across the wrists every time you interrupt might be one way. Disciplining yourself to check your understanding of the previous point by giving a brief summary before making a new point might be another. Obviously, you would not want to do things like this for ever, but doing it each time you talk until the habit is established can help you to do it on appropriate occasions thereafter.

ACTIVITY 9.6

Revisit your outline file entry and work out a detailed action plan for improving your spoken communication skills, remembering to include target and review dates

Check your progress at intervals

Either repeat the observation exercise to see whether you are developing your targeted skills, or make a habit of reflecting, perhaps weekly, and noting progress (or lack of it) in your learning file. If you feel you are not getting better at this important skill, seek feedback from others.

ACTIVITY 9.7

In reflecting on your own practice in the previous exercise, feedback was through the filter of your own perceptions, which may be less than perfect. Ideally, you need feedback from others. For this you will need the cooperation of at least one other person. Agree to have a session where you will focus on listening and to take turns at being the listener. Think of a topic which would be helpful to talk through, but which is not too sensitive or emotionally painful. Examples might be whether to live in college or private accommodation next year, whether to seek (or accept) a particular industrial placement, or whether to stand for office in a society. Or you could usefully revisit some of the ideas introduced earlier: your work expectations; your progress towards developing key skills thus far; learning objectives for your degree and any blocks encountered towards achieving them.

Agree that for a specific time – say, 10 minutes – the listener will aim to help the speaker in sorting out their thoughts. Then at the end of that period, discuss the effectiveness of the listening. How helpful did the speaker find it? What was most, and what least, helpful in the listener's behaviour? Were there points at which either felt uncomfortable? Why was this? After the discussion, exchange roles and start again.

ACTIVITY 9.8

As giving feedback and receiving it are skills in themselves, you need to extend the previous exercise. Once you have done it often enough to feel comfortable with the feedback aspect, add a further level of 'feedback on feedback', with the speaker and the listener giving observers feedback on their comments. Again, the goal will be to identify useful and less useful aspects of behaviour.

A note of caution

Observing and giving feedback is a very subjective activity and one requiring considerable skill. Done without sensitivity it can on occasion be painful, even damaging to the recipient. You need therefore to be very careful about how you do it. The exercise where you get 'feedback on feedback' can be extremely helpful. And when you are receiving feedback, while you should not be unnecessarily defensive, treat it as an opinion. Rather than believing every word of feedback, take it as information for your use, to be combined with the opinions of others and any other relevant information – for example, your own reflections on situations and exchanges in the past and their outcomes and your observations of other exchanges.

TALKING

The simple act of talking to another person is one in which a huge range of skills can be observed. Many of the dimensions will have been implicit in the discussion of listening, but briefly they are as follows.

Talking clearly – audibility

The need for audibility is self-evident, yet three friends of mine spring to mind. One mumbles so that the ends of words are totally inaudible. I frequently have to guess at the meaning or ask for a sentence to be repeated. Another has such an exaggerated accent that again I am concentrating so much on what the words are that I lose the meaning of the sentence. The third speaks so fast that my brain cannot keep up. Conversation with any of these is exhausting for me, probably unsatisfactory for them, and I am sure that there are many points that I miss. It is worth checking that your speech itself is an adequate channel for your message.

Talking clearly – content

Again, clear content is fairly obvious. If your message is muddled it has little chance of communicating anything. A colleague of mine, let us call him Albert, speaks at great length and with a huge degree of enthusiasm. Unfortunately, I seldom know what he is saying as he never finishes a sentence, leaving me trying to unravel a long string of half-ideas. Another colleague explained that the problem was that Albert's brain is always a minute ahead of his mouth, which is struggling to keep up. Listeners struggle more!

> Good 'talkers':
> ■ speak clearly
> ■ check listener reaction
> ■ meet listeners' needs
> ■ listen.

Another threat to clarity of speech is unclear thinking. This is not a problem if the whole point of the conversation is to try to clarify something. But if in speaking you are attempting to convey something specific, then it is a serious impediment. If there *is* a message which you are trying to communicate, make sure that you have sorted out just what it is before starting.

Checking you are being heard

Watch your listener's reactions. If there are signs that their attention is wandering, try to find out why and adjust your talking accordingly.

Being alert to the listener's objectives

Even if you are speaking to pass on straightforward information, your success will depend on how well you make the other person want to receive it. This will in turn depend on how well you relate what you are saying to your listener's objectives. Links which are clear to you may be far less evident to them. If the exchange is less one-directional it is even more important to be sensitive to the other person's objectives and make sure that they are meeting these to the same extent as you are serving your own needs. Note that the listener will probably be hoping to get social rewards as well as information from the conversation: smiles, explicit verbal 'strokes' (such as genuine compliments which make a person feel good) and other social rewards are important.

Listening as well as talking

The above points mean that listening is crucial. It is unlikely that you will be able to see how a person is responding, adjust what you are saying accordingly, perceive or meet your listener's objectives very well or achieve anything at all if you do not listen.

ACTIVITY 9.9

Repeat the listening exercises with and without observers, and with feedback on feedback, with the focus of observation and discussion shifted to talking rather than listening.

ASSERTIVENESS

Often you will find yourself in a situation where you and the person with whom you are talking want quite different things. Your friend wants to go to see a film, while you

To become more assertive:
- believe in your rights
- express them calmly but firmly
- prepare for any likely conflict.

are keen on a concert. Your flatmates are planning to move out without giving agreed notice, while you want them to stay or at least to keep paying their share of the rent until suitable replacements can be found. Your landlord suddenly demands a contribution to maintenance when nothing was said about this when you moved in. Your tutor gives you an assignment without making quite clear what is required.

One option in any of these situations is to get really angry and shout or be rude. Another is to agree meekly, but feel very unhappy about the situation. Think about which of these would be your most likely reaction. Neither approach is ideal. If you take the aggressive line, you may find that the other person also becomes aggressive and the situation can escalate. Even if you eventually get what you want, future relations with the other person may be soured or even broken off. With a departing flatmate, this may not matter. If the disagreement is with someone at work, with whom you need to cooperate in future, such an outcome may be disastrous.

If you take the 'avoid conflict at all costs' line and go along with the other person's wishes or demands, life may be more peaceful, but it is still far from ideal. If you end up seeing a film that doesn't appeal to you, it is not the end of the world. But if you submit quietly to your landlord's demands, you may be seriously out of pocket and may find yourself being asked for even more in future. If you accept the assignment without query, you may spend hours worrying about it, or working on something that is not at all what was wanted. If you fail to make your feelings known at work, you may end up overloaded, doing work for which you have not had the necessary training, missing out on the chance of working on a project that really appeals to you, or taking the blame for things which were nothing to do with you. You may frequently be seething with resentment, something which can be bad for your health in the long term. Avoidance can be as counterproductive as aggression.

Self-esteem

Assertiveness is about dealing with differences in what people want from a situation in such a way that both parties' rights are respected. How you *perceive* these rights is crucial. A classic book on interpersonal skills is Harris's (1973) *I'm OK, You're OK*. This was based on Berne's Transactional Analysis approach to psychiatry. The title reflects the position that we can see both ourselves and others as either 'OK' or 'not OK'. These perceptions will have a profound effect on how we interact with others. If we see ourselves as 'not OK', and others as 'OK', we may be over-compliant and avoid the slightest hint of conflict. This is because we are trying to persuade others that we *are* worthy of their approval. The belief that 'I'm OK, you're not OK' may lead to aggression and domination. The belief that 'I'm not OK, you're not OK' can lead to either aggression or withdrawal. Only the 'I'm OK, you're OK' position allows for assertion.

This makes the point very clearly that self-esteem and esteem for others is crucial to assertiveness. You will remember that esteem was one of the five major need categories identified by Maslow. It may be helpful at this point to think about your own level of self-esteem. It will affect your interpersonal skills generally, and influence how others view you.

ACTIVITY 9.10

Check the extent to which you agree or disagree with the following statements:

		Disagree				Strongly agree
		1	2	3	4	5
1	Most people are more confident than I am.	☐	☐	☐	☐	☐
2	Although I'm not perfect, I'm pretty good.	☐	☐	☐	☐	☐
3	If I were more attractive people would think more of me.	☐	☐	☐	☐	☐
4	I wish I had a better brain.	☐	☐	☐	☐	☐
5	Most people seem to know more than I do.	☐	☐	☐	☐	☐
6	If I disagree with someone, I'm probably right.	☐	☐	☐	☐	☐
7	I think that I'm likely to be as successful as most of my friends.	☐	☐	☐	☐	☐
8	I am uneasy about talking to strangers as they are unlikely to be interested in anything I say.	☐	☐	☐	☐	☐

		Disagree				Strongly agree
		1	2	3	4	5
9	If someone insults me I feel dreadful.	☐	☐	☐	☐	☐
10	In class I tend to avoid saying anything in case I'm wrong.	☐	☐	☐	☐	☐
11	There are some people I'd like as friends, but I don't think they would want to be friends with me.	☐	☐	☐	☐	☐
12	If I want to get to know someone better I suggest that we do something together.	☐	☐	☐	☐	☐

For questions 2, 6, 7 and 12 reverse the scoring, thus 1 becomes 5, and 2 becomes 4 and vice versa. Then add up your scores. The higher your score, the lower your self-esteem. If it is above 30, you might want to think about how you could reduce it. Try getting your friends to say how they would expect you to score, given how *they* regard you. This may help!

Assertion or aggression?

Where there *are* inevitable differences in interest, you need to learn to be assertive, rather than either aggressive or avoiding. An assertive approach requires that you accept that there is a conflict. Having accepted this, you neither try to impose your needs or views on the other person through verbal aggression, nor simply accept the views of the other person perhaps because they are being aggressive. Instead, you state *your* perspective and *your* needs, because you believe that these are as valuable as those of the person with whom you are in disagreement. Of course, this is rather less simple than it sounds.

If someone starts to be aggressive to you, it is very easy either to go into the same mode yourself or to back down completely. And it is difficult in many situations to accept that your own perspective *is* as valuable as the other person's. They may be more experienced, more senior, seem so much more confident, or seem to feel so much more strongly about something than you do. In order to develop assertiveness skills you need first to start believing in your own rights. The section which follows will help you with this. Once you have come to believe in your own needs, you need to practise saying the sorts of things that will express your perspective in a clear, firm but non-aggressive way. Assertiveness is a skill which can be learned, but as with any skill you need practice and feedback on your performance. The chapter concludes with exercises which will help.

Before going further, you need to check that you have understood the difference between aggression, assertion and avoidance and thought about your own most frequent response to conflict.

9

Talking and listening

TEST EXERCISE 9.1

Classify each of the following responses as aggression, assertion or avoidance:

(a) You always blame me for not washing up. It was you who last cooked a meal.

(b) Of course I don't mind. I'll see if I can find something you can use as an ashtray.

(c) Why are you always so critical?

(d) I feel really fed up that I have to wash your dishes every day before I can cook. I have someone coming to supper tonight. I'd feel much less fraught if you washed your things up before they come.

(e) Well, if you all want to buy a video I suppose I'll pay my share.

(f) I'd love to go out with you. But I only have £20 to last the month. So we'd have to go somewhere very cheap.

(g) OK. If you all think the answer is to increase the marketing budget, I guess I'll go along with that.

(h) I'm afraid I am still not sure who the notional addressee of this report is supposed to be, nor quite what they would use it for. Could you explain a bit more?

(i) If you are all too busy to do any of the work for this group project, I suppose I'll have to find the time for it.

(j) No, that's all right. You borrow it. I'll find something else to wear to the party.

(k) You are right. I didn't realise that I interrupt so often. I must be more alert to that in future.

(l) What do you mean, I always interrupt? You should hear how often *you* do it!

(m) No, I'll work late Saturday night. My flight doesn't go until 7.00 am the following morning.

You should be able to see from the above few examples how wide a range of situations offer scope for assertiveness. Now you need to think about how you react to such situations.

ACTIVITY 9.11

Think of about five recent situations in which you wanted something different from what others wanted. Jot down each of the situations. Now think about whether you got what you wanted or whether you had to compromise or give in totally to the other person's wishes. Think about how happy or otherwise you were in each case. Classify your behaviour as aggressive, assertive or avoiding in each instance. Discuss with others, if possible, to see whether there are some sorts of situations where aggression or avoidance seems particularly likely and why this might be.

This exercise should have given you an idea of the extent to which you might benefit from becoming more assertive. You should have seen how often you are not as assertive as you might be and become aware of some of the disadvantages of an aggressive or avoiding response. For example, although you may have in the end gained your point by aggression, this may have damaged your relationship with the person concerned and make future disagreements both more likely and more heated. Or the other person may have become defensive and failed to point out something you needed to know. Avoidance may have led to resentment on your part and reduced your chances of getting your own needs met in future, as well as on the occasion in question. If the disagreement was over an approach to a problem and you had a clearer view of the situation than did others, avoidance may well have led to a worse solution for everyone than if you had persisted until your position was appreciated.

So how can you become more assertive? How can you, first of all, realise what your rights are and then behave in a way that ensures that they are taken into account?

Believing in your rights

Too many of us under-value our rights and underestimate the worth of our own contributions. If you wish to become more assertive, you need to *believe* that you do indeed have rights such as the following. Thinking hard about them may help your self-esteem.

The right to ask for what you want or to make clear what you do not want

Your wants and needs in a situation, whether for housework to be fairly shared or for a point in a lecture to be explained so that you understand it, are valid information. Suppose that at work you feel unfairly overloaded with routine work, so unable to exercise your particular skills. Others may be completely unaware that you feel this, if you say nothing. Even if they have some idea that you are unsatisfied, they will find it much easier to ignore your rights if you do not state them.

The right to be listened to and respected

There is no reason why you should be of less worth than anyone else. Others may *sound* confident and knowledgeable, but in reality know less than you do. If someone fails to give you respect then it is not because you do not deserve it. It is more likely to be because of failure on their part. One of the great benefits of team working, as a student or in a job, is that it brings together a range of perspectives. If you do not listen to some of these perspectives, or if others do not listen to you, then part of this valuable diversity is lost. So do not keep quiet because your view seems to be different from others: this is the very reason that you should contribute.

The right not to know or not to understand

No one is omniscient. People who think they know everything, but don't, tend to be a danger. It is far better to recognise areas of ignorance or lack of understanding, explain your position and ask for help from those who do know. Sometimes you may be the only person to admit to general ignorance. Or you may have seen a flaw in others' reasoning or have queried an unwarranted assumption. Sometimes when something has been clarified for you, you may be the one who can take a new perspective on the information, precisely because you are less familiar with it than others were.

The right to make mistakes

Infallibility is as unlikely as omniscience. Trying to conceal mistakes can take considerable effort and sometimes make things even worse. Instead, face up to them and learn from them. Some enlightened organisations have as their motto: 'It is OK to make mistakes – once.' They realise that mistakes are an inevitable part of learning.

The right to change your mind

All too often people stick to their initial position come what may, feeling in some way that it would show weakness to change. But this point is linked to the previous one. If you are genuinely pushing forward your understanding of a problem, you may realise that an earlier interpretation was wrong, perhaps because you now have new information. A group can be blocked, and never move on, if a position is defended to the death by its original protagonists, regardless of subsequent debate. Sometimes you can make a major contribution to a group simply by changing your position and explaining why. Whether this happens when you are working with other students, or in a team once you start a job, such change is a sign of strength, not of weakness.

ACTIVITY 9.12

Go back to the situations identified earlier, in which you were unsatisfied with the outcome. Try to identify which rights you had under-valued in each case.

Speaking assertively

Believing in your rights is a large part of becoming more assertive, but finding ways of expressing them is essential if this belief is to be turned into action. Some of this expression has to do with the form of words used. Assertive speech tends to be characterised by:

- clarity
- acceptance of feelings as valid data
- calmness, rather than emotion
- firmness
- refusal to be side-tracked
- pursuit of a positive and constructive solution rather than a 'win'.

Look back at the responses which you classifed as assertive or otherwise in Test exercise 9.1 and at any past examples where you were assertive yourself to see the extent to which they indeed showed these features.

Guidelines for assertiveness

To be more assertive you should aim to:

- use phrases such as 'I think . . .' or 'I prefer . . .' rather than 'You . . .' or 'He . . .'
- use words such as 'could' and 'might' rather than 'can't' or 'shouldn't'
- check that you have understood before responding (remember active listening) – 'I think your argument is . . .'
- ask for more detail if you are unsure – 'Could you give me another example?'
- acknowledge the other person's feelings – 'I know that you are unhappy about . . .'
- say what you feel – 'I feel really frustrated at . . .'
- calmly repeat things, possibly using the same words each time, when it is clear that you are not being listened to (try it – it is amazingly effective)
- avoid apology (unless justified).

9

Talking and listening

ACTIVITY 9.13

Go back to the examples you identified earlier and choose two or three where you were less assertive than in retrospect you would have liked to be. 'Rewrite the script', showing how the exchange might have gone, using phrases similar to those above. If working with a group, act out some of these scripts to see how they 'feel' and comment on the extent to which the words come across as assertive rather than aggressive. File your reflections on this activity.

Acting assertively

As with all talking and listening, body language is important. If you avoid eye contact, if you hide your mouth with your hand and slump back in your chair or lean away from the other person, you will find it very hard to use assertive forms of words. Even if you do, their effect will be lessened. If you raise your voice, glare at the other person, clench your fists or thump the table, or get too close to the person, the effect will be one of aggression no matter how carefully you choose your words. So make sure that your body language matches your words in being straightforward, confident, open and unthreatening.

ACTIVITY 9.14

Observe people in conflict situations. (You may find that you have disagreements in group discussions that provide material for observation, but shops, pubs and society meetings can often be a rich source of further instances to observe.) Focus on the body language used, note examples of assertive, aggressive and avoiding postures and gestures and observe the amount of eye contact.

Preparing to be assertive

Sometimes you will unexpectedly find yourself in a situation where you need to be assertive. If so, you will need to rely on skills and habits developed earlier. Even then, you may want time to think. It is often acceptable, and extremely useful, to ask for thinking time so that you prepare yourself a little, rather than saying things while in a state of mild shock. A response such as 'This is a total surprise. I had no idea you were feeling like this. Can you give me five minutes to think about it?' can lead to a much more constructive outcome to the encounter.

Sometimes you will know in advance that a situation will need to be confronted or that conflict is inevitable. If so, it is important that you prepare yourself. Think clearly about what you want to achieve and why. If you know that you tend to under-value your rights, discuss the situation with a friend or supportive colleague (if at work) to reinforce your beliefs. Think about the other person's possible response and how you might react to this. If possible, act out the encounter with your friend or colleague beforehand, trying a range of approaches but aiming always to be calm and assertive and to face up to issues without aggression.

Assertiveness skills take time to develop. So does the skill of knowing when to be assertive. Aggression has its (limited) place and sometimes avoidance has too. But there will be a wide range of situations where the firm but cool, assertive response will be the most effective. If you have prepared beforehand (if possible), if you use the sorts of phrases outlined and if you *think* about it afterwards, reflecting on your success or otherwise with a view to further improvement in future, you should be well on the way to developing an important interpersonal skill, of use in most areas of your life.

Because learning to be assertive is so important, you may want to read further on the subject. Suggested readings are at the end of the chapter. Because it is very much a skill, and therefore benefits from practice and feedback, you may wish to consider a short practical course if you feel you are seriously unassertive. Certainly, this is one area where you could usefully include materials in your portfolio. A common question in interviews is: 'Think about a time when you were in conflict/disagreed with someone. How did you handle this?' If you have some examples in your portfolio of positive outcomes of conflict that arose because you handled it in an assertive way, with details of how you did this, you should be well placed to answer such questions.

ACTIVITY 9.15

During the next month or so, note carefully the situations where assertiveness is appropriate and describe them for your portfolio. Detail the situation and the aims of the parties involved. If you had a chance to prepare, describe how you did this. Give a brief summary of the exchange, including examples of assertive phrases used and any body language noted. Include your reflections on the extent to which you succeeded, not in terms of winning regardless but in terms of your views having contributed to the outcome and a feeling that the outcome was fair to both parties. Note any things which you wish you had done or said differently. Repeat the exercise in three months to note progress.

NETWORKING

Networking refers to the activity of making, maintaining and using personal contacts for professional purposes. Such contacts are invaluable for *all* areas of life. Think about how often you have discovered something important from someone you knew, rather than through official channels. I found my house not through an estate agent, but via a friend who told me that a friend of hers was thinking of moving and it sounded like an ideal house. A recent graduate found his (very good) present job by talking to someone in a café. In a pub conversation someone said that they wanted a room to rent and someone else said: 'I don't think Sandy has found a new lodger yet.'

> Networking is strongly associated with management success.

Most jobs are advertised and specified selection procedures are followed. Yet they frequently go to someone who knew of the vacancy in advance and who had contacted relevant people, or exploited existing contacts, before the interview. And despite legislation, not all jobs are advertised. There are many ways of starting to work for an organisation which may grow into jobs if the original project is well handled. For those who are, as is increasingly the case, working for small organisations or for themselves, these informal routes are often the most important ones. One writer on networking (Hart, 1996) claims, though without giving the evidence for this, that networking can be 12 times as effective in getting a new job as answering advertisements.

Networking is valued differently in different cultures. In the UK, some people see it as slightly 'unsporting' actively to develop and exploit personal relationships. In Japan, it is seen as a vital activity in business. Indeed, Japanese managers in the 1980s were sent to major US business schools to study for an MBA, not because their superiors felt that the Americans could teach them anything about business, but because of the contacts that they would make with future senior US managers.

→ Ch 1

Networking is not limited to finding new jobs. It also seems to be of value in progressing within an organisation once you have found the job. The US study by Luthans *et al.* (1988), referred to in Chapter 1, showed that those managers who were *effective* (i.e. had satisfied subordinates who performed well) were not necessarily the same as those managers who were *successful* (i.e. were promoted rapidly). Indeed, only 10 per cent of managers were in the top third on both counts, slightly less than you would expect if the two factors were totally unrelated to each other. If organisational life in the USA resembles that elsewhere, and if being successful is something worth aiming for, it is worth looking at the key characteristics associated with success in this study.

The successful managers devoted more time to interacting with outsiders, chatting, joking, passing on rumours, complaining, paying attention to both customers and suppliers, attending external meetings and taking part in activities in the local community. In other words, they spent a lot of time on developing networks of primarily social contacts way beyond their immediate work group, but clearly of value to their careers. Note that these exchanges do not need to involve face-to-face contact all the time, though this helps at the start. The phone can be a useful channel, e-mail is often used in this way to sustain a relationship once established and even letters can sometimes be used.

9

Talking and listening

So how can you develop networking skills while you are studying? There is a heavy overlap with the skills of talking, listening and the 'valuing yourself' aspect of assertiveness. These lie at the heart of networking, and thus in developing these skills you will inevitably be starting to build a network. By making a point of trying to practise these skills with as many people as possible, you will be starting to maximise the networking potential of your time as a student and to build the foundation of a network that you can develop after graduating. This will be greatly helped if you appreciate just how important networking is. After all, other people will be succeeding because they are networking and may well be including you in their networks. As it is ideally a mutual activity rather than exploitation in the bad sense, you should therefore overcome any inhibitions you may have about becoming good at networking yourself.

ACTIVITY 9.16

A useful point is to establish the extent of your current potential network. List all the people you know well enough to ask, for example, if they know of any accommodation coming vacant, or someone who is thinking of selling a ten-year-old car. (It doesn't matter if they would be likely to know the answer, just whether you would feel comfortable asking them for neutral information of such a kind.) If you are working with a group, compare lists and see whether this prompts any additions. Check that you have included people you know at home, as well as where you are studying, and those you know through all the activities in which you take part. File this list, in order to refer to it at intervals and add to it.

ACTIVITY 9.17

Test your network. See whether the assertion that such networks are more useful than official channels is right. Think of some information that would be useful to you and select from your list of potential network members those who might be able to give that information, or might know people who could. This does not have to be information about a job – it could be anything which you could in theory find from an advertisement. See how quickly you can get the same (or better) information just by talking to people.

ACTIVITY 9.18

Draw up an action plan for maintaining your network. Think about opportunities for developing your relationships with people on your potential list. Could you make a point of having an exchange with them the next time you see them? Remember, Luthans listed joking, social chat, exchanging rumours and complaining among effective networking behaviours. List the people you might have a chance to talk to in the next two weeks. List those you do manage to talk to. (You will be practising your talking and listening skills in the process.) Reflect after each contact on how effective the interaction was in strengthening your relationship and what else you might need to do. Add these comments to your list.

ACTIVITY 9.19

Draw up an action plan for developing your network. This requires you to extend it to other people. Think about activities you can take part in and people you can get to know in order that your net spreads more widely. Plan, take the action and reflect on whether you have achieved what you intended. If not, think what else you need to do and act accordingly. Members of your network need to be aware of your interests and strengths, so that they will think of you if asked about someone suited to an opportunity that would appeal to you, or will pass on information which you would find useful without your needing to ask them first. This may help them as well as you. Similarly, you need to know as much as possible about them – the more mutual such relationships are, the stronger and more effective they will be. Again, log thoughts and compare progress with your list and notes already made.

ACTIVITY 9.20

Identify opportunities to use your network. In future, whenever you need to find something out, think about who in your network can help and approach them. Also, help any people who approach you as best you can. Log your reflections on the process. If your network is too limited to be of use, think about who else you need to be able to talk to and deliberately approach them. You will be surprised how often people who do not know you at the start will be willing to tell you things if you make clear why you are asking and that their help would be appreciated. Once they have helped you they will be part of your network.

ACTIVITY 9.21

Monitor your progress. Refer to your list at intervals. If working in a study group, discuss your progress with other members and try to help each other to become more effective in this way. Until you have developed the networking habit, checks will need to be fairly frequent. Later you will need to check that you have not neglected anyone and have had at least some contact with them (even if only sending them a Christmas card) during the last year.

ACTIVITY 9.22

You should by now be far more aware of the components of effective interpersonal skills, and be ready to reassess your own skills level. Revisit the first activity in the chapter, and reassess yourself, In the light of this, organise your action plans for progressing the different elements into a separate section of your file, prioritise them, and draw up an overall action plan to become more effective in this area.

SUMMARY

This chapter has argued the following:

■ Spoken communication is an essential part of virtually all aspects of life and work. It serves to satisfy social needs, for information transfer, for developing ideas and for planning and managing shared tasks.

■ Speaking and listening skills are equally important. Understanding and practice with feedback are necessary to develop these.

■ Giving and receiving feedback skills depend on speaking and listening. They are vital for learning.

■ Assertiveness, rather than avoidance or aggression, is important in the resolution of conflicting objectives. Assertiveness depends on knowing (and believing in) your own rights and speaking and acting in a way which asserts them. Again, practice is important.

■ Networking is making, maintaining and using personal contacts, usually for professional purposes. The skills involved overlap heavily with those of talking, listening and assertiveness.

Further information

■ Andreas, S. and Faulkner, C. (1996) *NLP: The new technology of achievement*, Nicholas Brealey. This contains useful ideas for effective listening and establishing rapport

■ Back, K. and Back, K. (1999) *Assertiveness at Work*, 3rd edn, McGraw-Hill.

■ Burley-Allen, M. (1995) *Managing assertively – a self teaching guide*, 3rd edn, Wiley. This has lots of exercises, quizzes, etc.

■ Caunt, J. (2001) *Stay Confident*, The Sunday Times/Kogan Page. Although this is aimed at those in work, it is likely to be useful to those studying and includes brief coverage of networking, stress management and building supportive relationships.

■ Hart, R. (1996) *Effective Networking for Professional Success*, Kogan Page.

→ 10 Working in groups

Team working is a key skill on the QAA list, and features in almost every job. Students are frequently asked to work on group assignments, and belonging to an informal study group can make a huge difference to your enjoyment of your course, and your performance on it. This chapter will help you acquire the skills you need to work well in, and learn from, teams and groups.

Learning outcomes

By the end of this chapter you should:

- appreciate the importance of group working
- have identified your strengths and weaknesses as a team member and identified any development needs
- be able to identify the roles and behaviours needed to manage group tasks and processes
- understand the importance of clear group objectives
- be aware of the importance of motivation in group work
- be able to identify things that may go wrong in groups and take avoiding action
- be able to make an effective contribution to formal and informal group discussion
- understand the need to monitor group progress
- be able to demonstrate the contribution that you have made to a group project or endeavour.

→ Ch 1   Your trawl of graduate recruitment adverts (Chapter 1) should have convinced you that potential employers are looking for 'good team workers'. Organisational restructuring has greatly increased the importance of both teamwork and networking. Team decisions, reflecting a variety of inputs, can be far better than the decisions of any individual. Commitment to decisions is higher if people were involved in taking the decision. Conversely, ineffective groups can waste time, become demotivated, generate resentment and produce poor quality work.

You will almost certainly experience group assignments, both in order to develop your
→ Ch 12   skills and because some things are learned more effectively through discussion. Case study
→ Ch 16   work (discussed in Chapter 12) and projects (Chapter 16) will almost certainly involve

group work. Developing your team-working skills will help you to get better grades, and to learn more effectively. If you are doing your degree by distance learning you may be part of a 'virtual' student group. 'Virtual team-working skills' are often necessary at work, too.

Your success in both study and employment will depend on your skill in working with others. It can be hugely satisfying to work in an effective team. Sadly, if you lack these skills not only is your team likely to be less successful, but your working life, and the lives of those with whom you work, may be frustrating and stressful. You will have many opportunities to develop your skills while you are a student, both as part of your course, and in your social life, any work placements, and vacation jobs. Grasp these opportunities and exploit them to advance your development.

TEAM WORKING IN ORGANISATIONS

There are many different sorts of groups which form in organisations. Teams, as opposed to more informal groups, are deliberately formed for a purpose, to perform particular tasks or projects. They have a common goal, and this goal cannot be pursued unless the team members work together.

Teams are essential when inputs from a number of different perspectives or different skills are necessary and where commitment to outcome is important. Teams can be given a considerable degree of autonomy. Output may well be specified and measured by higher management. But the team can be free to decide how best to achieve that output, given prevailing conditions. This way of working offers considerable flexibility, as the team can respond to changes in those conditions far more rapidly than could a group of individuals working on the instructions of those higher in the organisation. Where decisions are taken only after reference up (and up) the chain of command they can be very slow. Autonomous team working also provides ideal conditions for high levels of motivation. No wonder team working is so widely adopted.

> Successful team working needs:
> ■ clear, shared goals
> ■ agreed ways of working
> ■ effective communication
> ■ support and cooperation between members
> ■ monitoring of progress.

The nature of such teams will differ greatly, however. Each team's goals will be different. A committee is charged with taking decisions and perhaps seeing that those decisions are implemented. A work group might have the task of producing a particular component or providing a specified service. A project team might be charged with developing an original idea into concrete plans, or with putting those plans into action. Responsibility within the team will also vary. Some teams may have a specified leader who may or may not also have managerial authority. Others may have no such leadership structure. Some teams will contain a wide variety of expertise, while others may consist of people with very similar skills.

But whatever the team structure, and regardless of whether the task is sharing information and negotiating a decision, gathering information and making plans, or performing a physical task that requires the skills or labour of more than one person, effective working together is essential for success. And while some of the skills required will be more important than others in any situation, the requirements for success are remarkably similar across the spectrum. Success will depend on:

- clarity of goals and acceptance of these among team members
- agreement over ways of working towards these goals
- effective communication between team members
- support and cooperation within the team rather than competition
- arrangements for monitoring progress and taking corrective action if necessary.

These factors are not, of course, always present. Calling a group a team does not guarantee success. 'Team' is an emotionally loaded word, standing for all sorts of positive things. Organisations often label groups of people 'teams' and think that this is all they need to do. If you have already experienced a rocky time in some of the groups you work with in class, you know that the label is not enough. Thought needs to be given to the success factors above and the skills which underpin them need to be present in the 'team' members.

Key factors in team success

Looking at the list above, it is clear that the elements contributing to success can be grouped into three broad classes of factors, as has been done in Figure 10.1 (see page 223). Three sets of skills are important:

→ Ch 1, 2
- **Managing the task** – clear objectives, monitoring progress towards them and taking corrective action are as important for team working as for managing yourself. The principles are just the same, although applied in a group context.

- **Managing the process** – this is the part that is new. People need to stay committed to the team's goals, motivated to contribute to achieving them. Attention therefore needs to be paid to their support and encouragement. This will be a major topic in this chapter.

→ Ch 9
- **Communication** – this will be vital for managing both task and process. You have already developed the basic skills of talking and listening (and being assertive where necessary). Their application in a group context is very similar to their use one to one. By practising communication skills in group work, you will become better at communicating in other contexts.

Whatever the type of task a team is addressing, success will depend upon a combination of communication skills and management skills relating to both task and process. The emphasis will differ depending on the nature of the task, as the following exploration of the different contexts for group working shows.

DISCUSSION GROUPS

Because they are a natural extension of the previous chapter, and because almost any group will at times need to have informal discussions about the task, it makes sense to focus first on informal group discussions. You will probably be familiar with these from seminar or study groups.

ACTIVITY 10.1

Reflect on a recent group discussion in which you found it satisfactory to take part and another which you have not enjoyed and/or to which you felt you made little contribution. List at least three ways in which the 'good' group differed from the 'bad' group. If possible, compare your list with other people's.

You will probably find that some of your 'bad' experiences have to do with poor task management. Quotes overheard after meetings with this problem include:

> We've been talking for over an hour and I still don't know what we are meant to be doing!

> Why can't they see that the real problem is . . .

> If they hadn't spent 80% of the time talking about the cost of photocopying we might have had time to discuss what was wrong with the business strategy.

> I wish we had spent some time thinking about what we had to do and how long we had to do it in . . .

> Nobody came up with a single sensible idea.

> Jane had a brilliant idea, but no-one could see how good it was.

> Juan raised a really good issue to pursue, but everyone seemed to want to keep talking about the impossibility of getting anywhere.

> We had a brilliant meeting, and agreed lots of action points, but then no-one actually did anything.

Other 'bad' experiences may have had more to do with poor process management – lack of attention to group needs, perhaps conflict or even aggression between some members. Such meetings produce reactions like:

> I'm useless in groups – I don't seem to have any good ideas at all.

> I felt really bad about the way everyone laughed at Srini.

> I was pretty sure I could see what was wrong, but I was afraid I might be missing something somewhere, so I didn't like to say.

> Everyone was talking across everyone else, and I couldn't get a word in edgeways.

> Gerhard had got it into his head that he was the only person who understood the problem, and he just shouted at anyone who thought that there might be another view.

Informal discussion groups do not necessarily have a 'leader'. All members of the group may be on an equal footing and between them need to ensure that the discussion goes somewhere and that members stay involved. But some of the issues reflected in the quotes above suggest a chair might have been useful. Informal groups without chairs will only work well if most of the members play their part in contributing to both task needs and group needs, and avoiding behaviours which get in their way. This means keeping a focus on what the group is trying to do, contributing to this yourself and helping others to make a contribution, valuing other members and their contributions and not letting your own or others' needs unrelated to the task (for attention, dominance or whatever) get in the way of what the group is doing. (Even if there is a chair, and especially if the chair is not particularly skilled, it will help if you behave in this way.)

Behaviours which help and hinder discussion groups

If you are aware of which behaviours help and which hinder, you will become more aware of your own strengths and weaknesses in this context. The following lists of the most important behaviours in each category may help you reflect on the part you play in group work and to become more effective in future.

Behaviours serving task needs

- Clarifying objectives.
- Seeking information from group members.
- Giving relevant information.
- Proposing ideas.
- Building on ideas or proposals contributed by others.
- Summarising progress so far.
- Evaluating progress against objectives.
- Time keeping.
- Identifying someone to assume responsibility for ensuring that any agreed action is taken.
- Setting up some way of reviewing progress after the meeting.

Behaviours serving group needs

- Encouraging members to contribute.
- Rewarding contributions with praise or agreement.
- Checking that you have understood a point by summarising that understanding before giving reasons for disagreeing.
- Helping to resolve conflicts without either party feeling rejected.
- Changing your own position in the light of arguments or information given by others.
- Helping to control those who talk too much (again in a positive way).
- Praising group progress towards objectives.
- Dissuading group members from negative behaviours (see below).

Behaviours interfering with task or group needs

- Talking too much or otherwise focusing attention on yourself for the sake of it.
- Reacting emotionally to points raised.
- Attacking others' points by ridicule or other unreasoned statement (e.g. 'it won't work').
- Not listening to others.
- Interrupting others or talking at the same time as them.
- Introducing a totally different point in the midst of productive discussion of something else.
- Chatting with others privately during the meeting.
- Using humour to excess (a little can oil the wheels!).
- Introducing red herrings.
- Withdrawing ostentatiously from the group (e.g. turning away, pushing chair back, crossing arms, determined silence . . .).

	JEFF	SABINE	LING PEI	ASAD	YIANI	CLARK	JO
Clarifying objectives							✓✓✓
Giving/seeking info.					✓✓✓✓✓		
Proposing/developing			✓✓✓	✓✓✓		✓✓✓✓	
Summarising	✓						✓✓✓✓✓
Timekeeping	✓✓✓						✓
Encouraging/rewarding							
Conflict reduction		✓✓✓✓					✓✓✓
'Gate keeping'							✓✓✓✓✓
Interrupting/overtaking			✓✓✓✓ ✓✓✓	✓✓✓✓✓✓		✓✓✓✓	
Attack/defence			✓✓	✓✓✓			
Changing the subject					✓✓		
Excessive humour		✓✓				✓✓	
Withdrawal		✓			✓		

Fig. 10.1 Example of a simplified form used in recording behaviours in a group

10

Working in groups

How do you behave?

The lists above are quite long: you will find it difficult at first to keep all the behaviours in mind. But they cover much of what helps and hinders group discussion. The more aware you are of your own and others' use of these behaviours, the better you will be at group discussion. It is probably best to look at the way other people are behaving before working on your own habits. A useful first step is to observe discussions without taking part in them. (If you cannot officially act as observer, choose a meeting in which it will not matter if you adopt a low profile and take notes surreptitiously.) You may want to use a form to help with this. Figure 10.1 gives an example of one such form already completed. At first you may wish to concentrate on one category of behaviour, as this simplifies the task. Two other people can observe the remaining categories.

ACTIVITY 10.2

Use a form such as that shown in Figure 10.1 to record the sorts of contributions members make to a discussion (a blank is available as a web resource). Reflect on the extent to which the pattern of ticks which emerges explains the effectiveness or otherwise of the group.

ACTIVITY 10.3

Ask someone else to use a similar form to record your own contribution to group work and give you feedback on the sorts of behaviours you used most and any reflection on your effectiveness in the light of this. Such feedback can be a powerful tool in helping you become more effective. If any of the desirable behaviours seem lacking, practise using them in subsequent meetings. For example, decide that you will try to ensure that even the quietest members are encouraged enough to make a contribution, or make a point of summarising the discussion each time progress seems to have been made so that points are not lost. If you are behaving in a way which interferes with the group, think about why you may be doing this and try to notice (and silently rebuke yourself) each time you do this in future. It should eventually become less frequent. Devise an action plan for becoming more effective.

ACTIVITY 10.4

After a while, perhaps a few months, repeat the above exercise to see whether you have shifted your behaviours in the intended direction. File your comments for future review.

FORMAL MEETINGS

Many managers complain that they spend far too much time in meetings. Formal meetings may seem intimidating until you are used to them. There are rituals to do with approving minutes, making remarks through the chair and identifying 'voting members'. You may feel unwilling to contribute because you feel unsure about the 'rules' or wonder how on earth to take minutes if charged with this task. However, the 'rules' are really only an attempt to avoid some of the things that commonly go wrong in informal discussions. The actual skills involved are much the same, as becomes clear when you understand what the ritual is intended to serve.

Cartoon by Neill Cameron, www.planetdumbass.co.uk

Membership lists

Particularly where a meeting is intended to take significant decisions (about costs, policy, progress on an important contract and so on), the informality of a discussion group is not enough. It is important that the right people are at the meeting, so a formal membership list will need to be agreed. Otherwise there may be complaints that the decision was improperly taken. Indeed, if some key players are not there to contribute their information, a bad decision may be taken.

Attendance

Since there was a reason for members to be on the list, it is important that they attend. Normally the minutes of the meeting will log those present, so that they cannot later disclaim responsibility for decisions. Absentees, who should have given apologies in advance, can also be contacted by anyone who feels the need to 'fill them in' on something which happened. The secretary may also wish to arrange for absentees to send a representative in their place. (This representative would not usually be able to vote and would be minuted as 'in attendance' rather than 'present'.)

Chair

In an informal group, members usually share responsibility for the behaviours necessary to progress the task and manage the process. They are expected to exercise self-discipline and avoid the unhelpful behaviours listed above. In formal meetings, the overall responsibility for all this is vested in the person chairing the meeting. With a skilled chair this can work wonderfully. People are asked to make contributions at relevant points, the discussion is gently 'managed' to ensure that it is kept to the point, progress is summarised at intervals, conflicts are tactfully explored and resolved and, when as much progress has been made as is likely, the point is drawn to a close and the next item on the agenda is taken so that the meeting finishes on time, with all items having been properly covered. Unfortunately, not all chairs are good at all these behaviours. (Some, indeed, do not seem to be good at any of them!) They may have been chosen for their seniority or some other reason rather than their skills. Provided other group members quietly adopt the necessary behaviours to fill the gap, this does not matter. If they sit back and cheerfully take no responsibility, the meeting can be a disaster.

Agenda

People need to know in advance what will be discussed, so that they can consult with those they represent, gather any necessary information and have thought about the issues involved. An agenda lists the time and place of the meeting and the items to be discussed in the order in which they will be addressed and should be sent to all members well in advance of the meeting. The chair of the meeting is normally responsible for putting together the agenda and will need to think about how long items are likely to take. Too long an agenda is to be avoided. Items will be given insufficient attention or the meeting may go on beyond the point at which those present are capable of thinking straight. (Most people cannot concentrate fully for more than two hours.) As meetings take some time to warm up, one or two short items at the start of the agenda may be a good idea. But the most important items should follow immediately after this, when people are at their most alert. Beware the really important item which appears at the very end of a long agenda. This will be one where the chair is hoping to get a decision to go in a particular way and is more likely to achieve this when everyone is exhausted and hungry. It is possible in this case to ask for the item to be taken earlier on the agenda. If you suggest this, giving your reasons, and others present support you, the chair may have to agree.

Papers

In assembling an agenda, it is important to think about how much preparatory information members need beforehand. Small items may not need supporting papers. Their proponents can make a verbal case at the meeting and this will be an adequate basis for discussion. But for any complex case, where there are reasons for and against a proposal and information which people need to have absorbed before they can discuss it, supporting papers need to be written. Clearly, these need to be circulated to members sufficiently in advance of the meeting (ideally with the agenda) for them to be able to study them in detail. If you are asked to write a paper for a meeting, remember that you are trying to make a clear and fair case, without giving unnecessary information. If a paper is too long, it risks not being read properly.

Preparation

Assuming that the chair and secretary have done their preparatory work adequately and circulated agenda and papers in good time, you have an obligation to prepare too. This means setting aside sufficient time to read papers thoroughly, think about them, discuss them with other people who may be involved, gather together any relevant information to which you have access but not everyone else at the meeting does, as well as working out what points you would like to make at the meeting and how best they might be made, given the people who are likely to be there and their possible points of view and counter-arguments. You may not actually make these points, or not in these words, if the discussion goes in an unanticipated direction. Meetings are not best seen as a collection of set speeches. But if you have done this preparation, the points that you *do* make are more likely to be relevant and effective than if you rely on spur-of-the-moment inspiration. (You are also likely to make a better impression on other group members, which may be important if they have the power to influence your future.)

Discussion style

Because the chair is officially responsible for the progress of the meeting, members are normally expected to catch the chair's eye and gain permission to speak. In large meetings this is essential. In smaller ones, provided conduct is reasonably orderly, the chair may let people discuss without this hindrance, only intervening if discussion is becoming disorganised, someone is talking too much or someone else is contributing nothing on an item on which they would be expected to have useful information to offer. The more formal the meeting, the more formal the language that tends to be used in making contributions, but the basics of talking and listening still apply: paying full attention to what others are saying and making sure that you do not under-value it because of prejudice, 'rewarding' their contributions with agreement, expressing your points clearly, avoiding getting emotional about issues, being sufficiently assertive to make points that have a fair chance of being valid and to make them in a positive enough way that they will be heard, avoiding time wasting of any kind.

Minutes

Because it is important to know what decisions were reached, and who was involved in reaching them, minutes are usually taken. In addition to listing those present, minutes need to log the basic reasons for a decision, actions agreed and responsibility for progressing these actions. Minutes will normally be circulated soon after a meeting so that any inaccuracies can be spotted, and the corrected minutes are then approved at the start of the next meeting. As the agreed record of decisions, these minutes are extremely important. There can in theory be no ambiguity about what is now agreed policy and it is clear whose responsibility it is to implement it. The practice, alas, may fall short of this. The person charged with taking the minutes often feels that they need to transcribe almost every word said, so that the minutes become so long that no one has time to read them. Perhaps because of this, the minutes may be put off as an unimportant or difficult job and appear on the day of the next meeting, by which time no one can really remember what happened and some of those who were supposed to have taken action will have totally forgotten about it. Or the minutes may be circulated late on purpose and record what the chair and secretary wanted to have happened, rather than what really did happen. 'Managing by minutes' can be a very effective tool, if an undemocratic one. Indeed, in an episode of *Yes, Minister* it was suggested that the minutes should be written *before* the meeting. If you are taking minutes for the first time, model them on previous minutes. Once you are confident with this, discuss with the chair whether there might be better ways of doing it.

Action notes

For slightly less formal, or more task-oriented meetings, a scaled-down version of minutes may be taken. These will note who was present and log actions agreed and responsibilities for these actions, but no more. Because they are briefer and focus on action, they can be written extremely quickly, even during the meeting, and people can be given a clear statement of their responsibilities the next day.

10

Working in groups

ACTIVITY 10.5

Review the formal groups to which you belong. (If you cannot think of any, try to join at least one during the next few months so that you can practise these skills.) List them and note against each how effective the formal structure is in progressing the group's objectives. If elements seem to be ritualistic, rather than serving their intended purpose, think about ways in which you might be able to contribute to their effectiveness. Draw up a plan for doing this and check your success against this after each meeting you attend.

ACTIVITY 10.6

Find a way of taking at least some responsibility for a meeting. This might be by chairing it (volunteers for this role are often very welcome), acting as secretary or gaining the chair's agreement that you might act as assistant, joining in agenda-setting discussions and taking some of the responsibility for ensuring that the meeting progresses as desired. Put together an 'exhibit' for your file which describes the purpose of the meeting and the ways in which you contributed to achieving this. An annotated agenda showing which items you suggested and why, any papers you wrote and comments on the interventions you made, together with the minutes and a statement from the chair saying how he or she perceived your contribution, might form a clear demonstration of your ability to function in this context.

ACTIVITY 10.7

Chairing a meeting requires you to think of far too many things at once. You will be so involved in task and process that you will have little brain capacity for reflecting on your own performance. If at all possible, the first few times you act as chair ask someone attending the meeting to act as observer for you and to give you feedback afterwards. This can feel very risky, but may be encouraging. You may feel that you totally messed things up, but the observer may have noticed a number of things that you did well. If they *do* see weaknesses, surely it is better to be aware of them and work at improving them. You would not want everyone else to know about them while you remain in blissful ignorance. Such feedback is best given a short while after the meeting, rather than immediately. Chairing is exhausting and frequently traumatic, at least at first, and you are unlikely to be fit for anything, certainly not for constructive feedback, until you have had a recovery period! It can be helpful to write down your own reflections on your performance – what contributed to success and what might, on reflection, have been handled differently – as soon as you feel strong enough and to file these. Comparing your own reactions with feedback from an observer can make future reflection more effective as you will become aware of blind spots, or areas of over- or under-sensitivity.

TASK GROUPS

Task groups are one of the building blocks of organisations. Teams are formed which contain all the skills needed to progress a specific task. Some teams have a designated leader, while in others responsibility for the work is shared equally among all members. The former is the classic 'supervisor responsible for a group of subordinates' structure. It has the apparent merits of clarity of responsibility and of power. If things go wrong, the supervisor will have to answer to his or her superior. But because the supervisor can, in theory at least, discipline any member of the team not pulling their weight, things should not go wrong in the first place.

There are less apparent, but equally real, drawbacks, which parallel issues raised in the discussion of the chairing role above. If 'team' members see all the responsibility as lying with their boss, they will feel none themselves. Their goal will be to avoid being disciplined and any group interaction is likely to be directed not towards progressing the work better, but towards outwitting the boss.

The concept of 'autonomous working groups' (AWGs) was one of the organisational breakthroughs of the 1960s, seen as avoiding many of the problems of assembly lines. AWGs were given collective responsibility for a specified task (in one of the classic experiments, for assembling engines for Volvos) with all the tools and materials needed to do this. Supervisors were no longer in charge, but either seen as resources available for consultation or removed altogether. All decisions about who did what, how quickly and when (including who took holidays when) were the responsibility of the group as a whole. These autonomous groups became very committed to the task and produced measurably higher-quality work. Absenteeism was much lower. There were queues of people wanting to work in this fashion.

There were costs, of course. Assembly lines are a very efficient way of operating: tooling up for group assembly was much more expensive; there was more work in progress at any one time; the training of multiskilled employees was costly. But above all, management felt threatened by the autonomy which the workforce had under this arrangement, even though managers had their roles redefined rather than being made redundant.

In the harsher 1990s the revolution in information technology meant that neither work groups at the bottom of the organisation nor senior management at the top needed layers of intervening managers to filter information up and down. They could now have direct access to it themselves. Such layers were therefore seriously pruned, or removed altogether, and fairly autonomous working groups came into favour again, variously entitled 'flexible work teams', 'cells' or 'high-performance teams'. In professional organisations this has always been a common way of working. You are highly likely, therefore, to find yourself working as a member of a group with some responsibility at least for the group's performance.

→ Ch 12

In the meantime, you should have plenty of opportunities to work in task groups while you are a student. Even groups formed to discuss case studies and present conclusions to the class as a whole are task groups as well as discussion groups if some of the work needs to be subdivided between group members. Collective work on an experiment, or on data collection for a topic, offers further possibilities. Project groups of any nature are likely to share many features with semi-autonomous working groups in organisations and offer excellent scope for practising the necessary skills. (There is more specifically on project work in Chapter 16.)

→ Ch 16

The non-study part of your life may offer further opportunities. You may be raising funds for a good cause, organising a social event, or planning an expedition to some remote part of the globe. Whatever the task the group addresses, the general principles underlying success are the same as those for a group discussion. All group members need to understand the group's objectives, communication will be vital both at this and at every subsequent stage, progress needs to be monitored etc. Unless a formal leader is chosen, group members will need to find some way of ensuring that these aspects are covered all the time.

Additionally, there will need to be discussion about how to split up the work, both in logical terms of subtasks which can be progressed independently and with regard to allocating these responsibilities so that you make best use of the group's resources. Clearly, the more that group members can take on tasks which interest them and which they feel play to their strengths, the better the output is likely to be. This may require a degree of negotiation or even a rearrangement of subtasks if some jobs prove much more popular than others. People will need to understand their responsibilities (see comments on action notes above), will need to use self-management skills to progress their own part of the task (including taking corrective action, perhaps in the form of letting people know if there is a problem and seeking help) and will always need to remember to communicate anything which comes up in the course of their work which would be useful for others to know. This is often problematic: as one's own task assumes great importance, it is easy to forget the wider group and its needs.

ACTIVITY 10.8

List the task groups of which you are already a member and use the ideas above as a basis for reviewing their effectiveness. Note whether you are clear about group objectives and whether others share your interpretation of these (could you all draw up the same list of what would constitute success and failure?). Similarly, how clear are you about your personal (or subgroup) objectives? Do you know whether or not you are on target? If you know you have done less than you should have, do you know why? Does anyone else know you are behind? Might they be able to help if they did? Do you feel committed to the group and the task? Note down ways in which the group as a whole, and you individually as a member of the group, could be more effective.

ACTIVITY 10.9

In the light of the previous review exercise, try to be part of an effective group and to document the experience as an exhibit. You will need to address the following.

- **Understanding of collective goals** – who set them, what constitutes success and what failure, what the constraints are, what the timescales are, how closely group members agree on the goals. (Note that it is important to explore reasons for disagreement: the minority view might be the right one.)

- **Allocation of responsibility for subtasks** – what was done to maximise the extent to which these fit people's strengths and preferences, how the group checked that people understood and agreed to their tasks, whether people were clear on interim goals and the timing for these, whether there are arrangements for checking progress and sharing information on an ongoing basis.

- **Support and encouragement** – are there ways of ensuring that people can seek help from others if things go wrong and can 'reward' each other for interim successes? Particularly for long-term projects, such motivational aspects are extremely important.

Your exhibit might include notes of discussions, highlighting your contributions, quotes from others (including your tutor) on the effectiveness of your own efforts, any plans you drew up for group or individual work with progress noted on them, notes of any corrective action or adaptation of plans that was necessary and reasons for this, and of course, if appropriate, the finished product or tutor comments on this.

VIRTUAL TEAMS

Increasingly, work groups are dispersed geographically, and need to 'meet' electronically. Students on the (distance learning) programme I teach are often members and/or managers of groups which span several continents. Indeed, my students are similarly distributed. Since travel is expensive of time and energy, as well as money, it is important to find ways of working effectively as a 'virtual team', using ICT for many of the team's interactions.

Effective working in a virtual team requires just as much attention to task and process as in a 'normal' group. Some task issues are actually easier. It is very easy to transmit documents between members, for example. It is easy to communicate your comments, perhaps by annotating the original document and then circulating it to the group.

Some aspects, however, are harder. Members need to be just as clear on, and committed to, the team objectives, as with face-to-face teams, and they need to continue to feel involved. When working remotely, this presents a considerable challenge. You cannot make someone feel better with a smile. If you are conferencing synchronously using Microsoft Netmeeting® or other programs which allow a group to talk in real time while sharing screens, you will need to work hard at ensuring that 'airtime' is shared fairly: gatekeeping is essential and you will almost certainly need a member designated to perform this role. If you are working asynchronously in a computer conference this is less of a problem. But it is still very easy for people to feel 'distanced', and to drop out of discussions. You may find the following guidelines for asynchronous conferencing helpful:

Guidelines for asynchronous conferencing

- Meet face to face if at all possible, in order to get to know group members and start to build trust.
- If you cannot meet, allow some 'social' time in the conference for people to feel comfortable together.
- At the same time, post résumés so that people can check who you are if they forget. Include a photo if you can.
- Obtain members' explicit agreement on what is needed to achieve the group task, and how it will be most effective to operate (times of logging on, deadlines for contributions and so on).
- Break tasks down into constituent parts with deadlines, and be absolutely clear who is responsible for doing what.
- Ensure that someone accepts responsibility for reminding people of incipient deadlines.
- Be particularly careful to give feedback in a constructive and supportive way – and pay attention to making people feel their contributions are valued.
- Summarise discussion at regular intervals and check on progress.

Set aside some short periods when people will all try to log on at once and respond quickly to each other – this can be a useful antidote to the more disconnected and 'measured' asynchronous communication

It is particularly difficult to work through the earlier stages of team working remotely. Clarifying objectives, deciding on the roles members will play and agreeing ways of working are much more easily done face to face. These tasks *can* be done electronically, but it is less easy to thrash out complex issues and explore areas of disagreement remotely. Nor is it easy to develop the sense of membership and mutual support essential for effective team working.

Most effective virtual teams go through these early and crucial stages face to face. Once members feel they 'know' each other it is much easier to sustain subsequent progress while working remotely. But it is easier the more familiar you are with remote working. So if you do get the chance to work in this way during your course you should use the opportunity to develop your remote team-working skills.

DEVELOPING EFFECTIVE GROUPS

Some of the classic research on groups is still helpful when we think about how to make a group effective, regardless of the nature of the task. In case you have not covered this research in a social psychology course, some commonly used frameworks are outlined here. These relate to selection of group members, to the stages which groups go through when they first form and to two main hazards of an established group, 'groupthink' and 'scapegoating'. If you are aware of these aspects of group working, it will increase your chances of being a member of an effective group.

Assembling an effective group

You may well have found that your 'bad' group experiences listed at the start of the chapter arose at least partly because the group seemed 'wrong' in some way. It may have been too big or too small to do the task effectively. Some key skills or perspectives may have been lacking. Perhaps the group got on *too* well and developed its own view of the world which was out of kilter with that of other groups working on a wider task. Or perhaps the group got off to a bad start and people dropped out because it wasn't working. You need to understand some of the features common to groups in order to comprehend and avoid such hazards.

Group size

The optimum size of group will depend on the task. If a large number of perspectives or skills need to be included, or a great deal of work is needed within a short timescale, then obviously a large group will be needed. But the larger the discussion group, the less the scope for individual contributions, and the larger the task group, the greater the task of coordination. And larger groups can present logistical problems as members find it difficult to identify times when they are all free. As a general rule of thumb, if you can do the job with between four and eight people, then stick with a group of this size.

Expertise

Linked to the point above is the need to ensure that the group includes the necessary range of expertise. If you are choosing a group to work with on a project, this can be an important point. Again you may feel most comfortable with like-minded people, but the task may be better done if you deliberately choose to work with a more varied group, with a wider range of backgrounds and knowledge.

Motivation

In forming groups, it is important to maximise the extent to which people *want* to do the task. At work they may not have much choice, but even then there will be issues that seem of burning importance to some and insignificant to others. Where possible, the more commitment you have to a task at the outset, the better the group is likely to perform. If you are choosing a group to work with on an assessed project, it is important to try to find others who have similar goals to your own. If you want to get top marks, you will be very unhappy in a group where no one else cares about doing more than scraping a pass. If you want merely to pass, you may feel out of place in a group of people aiming for a first.

Individual behavioural differences

When you looked at the behaviours that were shown in a group and who was using each behaviour, you may well have found some quite clear patterns. Some people often behaved in certain ways and seldom, if ever, in others. You might, for example, be very good at proposing ideas, but never get involved with making sure that they are implemented. Someone else might be quite the reverse, or do these activities sometimes but spend much more time on, say, clarifying objectives and checking progress. Although if you are aware of the behaviours needed you can make a conscious effort to fill any gaps, you are likely to have natural preferences and to be able to behave in these ways without effort.

Noting this variation, Belbin (1981) suggested that, for a group to be fully successful, a number of roles were needed. He was working with groups doing real tasks in organisations, so although there are clear links with the behaviours seen in group discussions, you will also notice some differences. He originally suggested that eight roles could be identified as the box below shows. Later he added a ninth, the specialist.

→ Ch 16

> ### Belbin's team roles
>
> - **Chair,** who acts as coordinator, working primarily through others. The role calls for discipline and balance.
> - **Plant,** who comes up with original ideas, is imaginative and usually very intelligent, but can be careless of detail and resent criticism.
> - **Shaper,** who stimulates others to act.
> - **Monitor–evaluator,** who assesses ideas or proposals.
> - **Resource investigator,** who brings in resources and ideas from outside. While usually extroverted and relaxed, this person is not usually original. Nor is he or she a driver, relying on the team to take up and develop his or her contributions.
> - **Team worker,** who works on process, holding the team together.
> - **Company worker,** who is strong on practical organisation, administration and turning ideas into manageable tasks.
> - **Finisher,** who does the essential (if unpopular) work of checking details and chasing when deadlines approach.

It is fairly clear that for most tasks to be progressed all these roles will be needed. You will probably be able to think of people who seem to be particularly good at some and less good at others. You may even have a clear idea of your own tendencies. (If not, Belbin includes a questionnaire that, by asking you about your approaches to and feelings about certain situations, enables you to identify your perceived preferred roles. Your tutor may have access to the questionnaire, but as with all such things, it is necessary to have permission to use it.)

If you have the luxury of choosing members of a group according to their preferred Belbin roles, then there is considerable evidence to suggest that it is worth doing this. But the fact that you cannot is no excuse for poor performance. Regardless of preferred behaviours, the roles are necessary and the group will have to find ways of ensuring that there is attention to process and that details *are* checked, even if this means, say, that one or two people who do not score highly on 'finisher' or 'team worker' have to make a conscious effort to take these responsibilities.

Myers-Briggs typing

Belbin's is not the only approach to classifying people. One typology which is widely used by organisations for selection and/or team formation is the Myers-Briggs Type Indicator (MBTI). This uses a fairly complex questionnaire (again, your tutor may be able to administer this) to locate you on four separate dimensions.

10

Working in groups

Myers–Briggs dimensions:

- **E or I:** Extravert v Introvert. This assesses whether you are externally or internally driven. In the first case, as an 'E' you will react to things and people, acting before you think. In the second, as an 'I' you will be more internally focused, more reflective.

- **S or N:** Sensing v iNtuition. This looks at what you pay attention to. If you are an 'S' this will be your normal five senses, you will focus on the 'real', take a pragmatic approach. If an 'N' you will use your 'sixth' sense, and be more future-oriented, more of a theorist.

- **T or F:** Thinking v Feeling. This reflects the way you tend to decide or judge. If at the 'T' end, you will reason from principles, using a logical system. If an 'F' you will use heart rather than head, subjectively emphasising values, preferring compassion to justice.

- **J or P:** Judgement v Perception. This looks at the way you live and work. A 'J' will adopt the planned approach, organised, controlled and with clear goals. A 'P' will be more spontaneous, preferring to 'go with the flow'.

Since the dimensions are independent, this gives 16 different types, each of which has distinct characteristics. You will hear people proudly declaiming their 'MBTI type'. Many organisations have found this information useful in helping people to understand why they are finding it difficult to work together. For example, if you are an ISTJ person, you might find an ENFP person to be hopelessly disorganised. While they might find you hopelessly unimaginative and unadventurous. MBTI types can also be used to help assemble a suitable team for a particular purpose – you would not want all Js in on a project requiring high creativity – though you might need one on the team to increase the chances of an output!

ACTIVITY 10.10

If you have not been 'typed' estimate where you might lie on each dimension. Now think of two people with whom you find it difficult to work in a group. Where do you think they might lie? Can you attribute some of this difficulty to their being different 'types' from you? If so, try to think about the strengths their type might contribute, and see whether it helps you to work together more effectively in future.

List the task groups of which you are already a member and use the ideas above as a basis for reviewing their effectiveness.

Group life cycles

Often when groups first work together they are far from effective. Sometimes (perhaps if there are no team workers and lots of plants) arguments can become very heated and destructive. Some members may withdraw from the group altogether, either physically if membership is voluntary or mentally if they have to be there but are hating every minute of it. There may be disagreements about objectives and about how the group is to work, two or three people all wanting to be 'in charge' of the group, some people behaving in ways that others find unacceptable. Tuckman (1965) found that groups commonly go through a sequence of stages in becoming effective. Knowing that this is normal may make the stages easier to bear and enable you to find ways of minimising any negative effects.

The stages are nicely rhyming (this may in part account for the continued use of this framework):

- **Forming.** This is when individuals are trying to establish their identity within the group and find out what the 'rules' are. Behaviour is often tentative at this stage and extreme politeness may prevail, with no one saying what they really mean. A leadership pattern may start to emerge.

- **Storming.** The politeness vanishes and all positions established earlier are challenged. Personal agendas emerge and there may be fierce status battles. This can be an uncomfortable time in a group: sometimes it may disintegrate totally. But if the conflict is constructive it may generate greater cohesion, a realistic commitment to objectives and trust between members.

- **Norming.** Out of the storm, more enduring norms emerge for how the group will operate and what is acceptable behaviour within the group is established.

- **Performing.** Provided that the necessary roles are being filled, the group can now really start to perform well.

Some people suggest that it is important to recognise a fifth stage. For groups that have worked closely together there can be unhappiness, even distress, when the group stops working together. Indeed, some groups keep going long after they have achieved their original goals. It is therefore helpful to talk about a stage of:

- **Adjourning.** Here the process of group dissolution needs to be handled with care, so that members can move on to other things.

MANAGING DIVERSITY AND CONFLICT

A major advantage of teams is that they can draw on a range of expertise and different sets of assumptions and perspectives. But to exploit this advantage you need to be prepared to work constructively with people whose worldview is very different from yours. This diversity can stem from 'type', but also from cultural and other differences. In diverse groups conflicts will sometimes arise, and you need also to have the skills to manage these.

Workforces (and students) are increasingly diverse. Many organisations now operate around the globe. Many workforces even within a single location draw upon an ethnically diverse workforce. You are likely to work with people from a wide range of backgrounds during your career. Furthermore, different professions have different 'cultures' too – different values and different ways of working. Yet many work teams are interdisciplinary. An ability to work effectively in diverse groups is a crucial management skill.

Most people are fairly tribal, and easily adopt an 'us' versus 'them' position: 'We are OK, they are not.' This is the comfortable view as it preserves familiar ways of thinking and doing. It is probably barely conscious. I was once assessing teaching quality in the Midlands and commented afterwards that it seemed odd to see students working in such unmixed subgroups. The four West Indian boys worked together. The three West Indian girls, the five Asians and the three slightly older white women formed the other three groups. The lecturer seemed surprised I'd mentioned it. 'But they always do that,' she said. Yet this was a hugely wasted learning opportunity. Each of these different groups was bringing different viewpoints and experiences to the task. But because these were not being exchanged and debated, there was no learning about how others see the world. None of the students was finding out what was important to other people, or realising how their own perspectives might be limited. Nor were they learning how to manage the inevitable differences of opinion.

Working in mixed groups takes more effort. It becomes even more vital to check understanding at every stage than it is with a homogeneous group. Words may mean slightly different things within different cultures. Some cultures are less assertive than others: their 'agreement' may be mere politeness. Some cultures express themselves very directly, in ways that may seem almost offensive to others but are just the 'normal' way of saying things to those concerned. Some cultures treat deadlines differently from others.

If you get the opportunity to work in groups from a range of backgrounds, seize it. The potential for learning about others, and about yourself, is great. But to realise this potential you will probably need to make 'understanding each other's viewpoints and backgrounds' an explicit team objective, and to check progress on this regularly. You will also need to pay particular attention to setting 'group rules' – agreed ways of operating. These may need to include procedures for ensuring that less assertive members contribute at regular intervals, and regular checks on how people are feeling about how other members respond to their contributions. You will also need to accept and examine conflict.

10

Working in groups

When conflict *does* arise you need to handle it as a phenomenon to be explored, rather than as a personal threat. Be assertive, not aggressive. In particular, aim to explore the situation rather than judge right and wrong. What exactly is the *nature* of the disagreement? Are people perceiving *facts* differently, disagreeing about *ways of working*, operating with conflicting *values* or bringing different sets of *assumptions* to the situation? If the latter, are these assumptions based on different experiences, perhaps in different contexts? By exploring questions such as these you may as a team come to a much more comprehensive understanding of the task and its context.

It may also be useful to explore why people feel so strongly about a point on which they disagree. This is a potential minefield, so you need to tread carefully. Think honestly about your own feelings first. Do you feel threatened? Undervalued? Are cherished values being called into question? Do you carry 'baggage' in the form of ingrained negative attitudes about certain groups of people? Where possible, check your feelings against the facts. For example, 'You are always saying my contributions are rubbish' might not match the perception of others in the group. Could you have an observer sit outside a discussion and check how your contributions are actually received?

By exploring such issues for yourself you may come to a much clearer understanding of your own attitudes. By exploring the issues – carefully – with others, you may come to see both how they perceive you, and the strengths and weaknesses of their, and your own, ways of thinking.

Feelings are dangerous territory. But an ability to appreciate how others are feeling, and how they are *likely* to feel if you say or do something, is an important

→ Ch 9   management skill. You can go a long way towards increasing your interpersonal sensitivity by treating conflict within groups as a learning experience. Use your talking, listening and assertiveness skills, focus on the behaviour not the person, refuse to 'give up' until an issue is dealt with, and accept that your view may not always be the only, or even the best one. Check your progress at regular intervals as a group, and try to capture what the various members feel they have learned.

Groups which work too well

Mention of groups which work too well may sound like a contradiction in terms and so it is. But if the group *process* is going well, and teams become really close, there are three related things that can go wrong with the *task*. All are variants of the hazard already hinted at, of the group becoming the main focus, with the wider task vanishing from awareness.

Dominance of sub-objectives

If sub-objectives predominate the group may end up in competition with other groups which are supposedly working towards the same wider objective. It becomes too committed to its own task, and to 'winning' in some way (e.g. getting the highest production output), and it forgets that it is part of a wider endeavour. Yet often compromise and collaboration might progress the wider task better than competition.

→ Ch 12   (There is more of this in Chapter 12 when systems ideas are introduced.)

Groupthink

Where 'groupthink' exists the group develops such a good feeling about itself, with members reinforcing each other's good opinion, that all indications that anything is wrong are disregarded. Any member brave enough to suggest that there is a problem will be made to feel a traitor to the group. This phenomenon is common in organisations. You will often find a board of a company refusing to believe that the signs of major problems are more than temporary blips, even though it is blindingly obvious to everyone outside this group that there is a significant disaster looming. You may find the same thing in project groups where members get on very well together and are sure that they are doing brilliantly, despite evidence to the contrary. If they know what 'groupthink' is, you may be able to make progress by asking if they think it is happening. But the tendency is a strong one.

Scapegoating

If things do go wrong, and this is finally so obvious that the group has to accept it, its members may still try to preserve their positive feelings about the group by finding one individual to accept all the blame. A group that realises that its presentation on a case study was the worst in the class may blame something outside the group, for example the tutor for giving unclear instructions, or a task that was harder than that given to other groups, or a single member of the group (perhaps the one who was trying to alert them to problems earlier).

There are two negative consequences of scapegoating. First, the scapegoat, if he or she is a group member, may be unhappy and lose self-confidence. Second, the group will not learn what went wrong if it does not accept responsibility for there having been a problem. This is common in work situations. A single person will be sacked when a problem arises. Yet often it is the system that is at fault and many people in that position would have behaved in the same way. Indeed, they will go on to behave in that way in future if the real cause of problems is not investigated.

Guidelines for effective team working

- Select members with appropriate skills, knowledge, and, if possible, a mix of preferred team roles and types.
- If working remotely, try to have an early face-to-face meeting.
- Ensure that all members understand and accept the objectives.
- Pay attention to both task and process.
- Accept that feelings may run high during early storming, and when working in a mixed group.
- Explore the reasons for disagreements and conflict.
- Value all contributions.
- Review both task progress and group process at regular intervals.
- Reward success.

SUMMARY

This chapter has argued the following:

- Team-working skills are essential in employment, aid learning, and can be developed in many ways while you are a student.
- All teams need to manage both task and process and good communication is essential.
- To work effectively in a team, you need to apply your personal management and communication skills in a group context and understand the requirements for effective teams.
- To be effective in a formal group, you need to understand the role of agendas, minutes and a formal chair; this understanding is also relevant to informal groups.
- In establishing a group, group members should be chosen to cover the necessary range of expertise and of roles. Sometimes it will be necessary to agree on ways of dealing with missing expertise, or handling non-preferred roles.
- A new group can feel uncomfortable, but later performance will actually benefit from early conflict, provided that this is firmly faced and prevented from being damaging.
- Conflict needs to be handled by focus on the issue not the person, using assertiveness skills to identify the source of the conflict.
- A 'mixed' group can produce better task outcomes and help you increase your interpersonal sensitivity.
- Groups are at risk of becoming too cohesive and inward looking, competing with others when they should be cooperating, ignoring external signs that things are going wrong and blaming a scapegoat when things have gone badly, rather than accepting responsibility as a group and learning from the experience.
- This is a rich and varied area of activity, with many dimensions. You will need to observe others and yourself in groups and ask others to observe you and give feedback if you are to develop your skills.

Further information

- Baguley, P. (1992) *Teams and Team-Working*, Teach Yourself Books, Hodder & Stoughton.
- Belbin, R.M. (1993) *Team Roles at Work*, Butterworth-Heinemann.
- Hardingham, A. (1995) *Working in Teams*, Institute of Personnel Development.

→ 11 Presenting to others

Many people are terrified of presenting to a group at first, but with practice come to enjoy it. This chapter looks at the necessary skills, and suggests ways in which you can improve. You may not become a brilliant presenter – such people are rare. But you can become good enough to get good marks and impress employers.

Learning outcomes

By the end of this chapter you should:

- be alert to the things that can go wrong with presentations
- have assessed your own strengths and weaknesses in this area
- be able to structure a presentation in a way that is appropriate to your audience
- be developing your delivery technique
- be using visual aids to good effect
- be confident in handling questions from your audience
- be able to control nervousness.

The final face-to-face communication skill you need is that of making a presentation to a group of others. Poor presentations can be an ordeal for speaker and audience: good ones can be a delight for both. Furthermore, both good and bad presentations are *remembered*. Whether you are presenting your research results to a group of potential collaborators, talking to a group of senior managers in your own organisation, making a pitch to a potential major client or giving an after-dinner speech for a professional association, it is important to make a good impression. You may pay an invisible price for years to come if you do not. On the other hand, if you do well, unexpected opportunities may come your way far into the future. You will also have an immediate feeling of power and euphoria from having had your audience exactly where you want them.

→ Ch 2, 6, 9

This chapter addresses the problem of nervousness and the skills that you need. Again, these overlap with skills already covered. Being clear about your objectives, understanding your listeners' (albeit now in the plural) needs, expressing yourself appropriately and clearly and checking understanding will be as important as in one-to-one talking or in making a contribution to a group discussion. But additionally you need to know how to ensure that your audience can see and hear you, to gain and hold their attention and to use visual aids to good effect.

THE RISKS IN PRESENTATION

Presentations, like written papers or reports, need to be carefully ordered. They need a clear message and should, where possible, use graphs, tables or other illustrations to reinforce the verbal argument. However, the fact that you and your audience are operating in real time makes the risks far greater. If something is difficult to express in writing, you can keep trying until you get it right. If your reader finds that concentration has lapsed, they can go and make a cup of tea, then try reading again from where they 'switched off'. In a live presentation, neither presenter nor audience has a second chance.

There is normally less interchange between speaker and listeners in a formal presentation than in one-to-one or group discussion. Keeping the audience awake, interested and involved is therefore a considerable challenge. You probably know all too well how easy it is to stop concentrating in a lecture and have found sitting still and being 'talked at' a fairly stressful experience. Unfortunately, the older you get, the harder it becomes to be a member of an audience.

As in other areas, the best way to become more aware of what is required is to look at what other people do less than well. You can then look at how those who are more competent do the same thing. Once you are more alert to the different dimensions required, you will be better able to reflect on, and develop, your own skills.

ACTIVITY 11.1

Think of an unsatisfactory presentation that you have attended recently (lectures are fair game here, as well as presentations by fellow students). List all the factors which contributed to your dissatisfaction. Now think of an experience of a good presentation. List any additional features which distinguished this. (You can go on to do this again at the next presentation you attend.)

Good features: _____

_____

Bad features: _____

_____

If your experience is anything like mine, your list of bad practice might include the following:

- The speaker was inaudible, mumbling, whispering or going too fast.
- Visual aids were illegible, whether overhead transparencies (OHTs) with minute print or computer projection too small and faint to be seen.
- The speaker faced away from the audience, perhaps while writing on board or flipchart.

- The speech was a hypnotic monotone making sleep irresistible, probably with no visual aids at all.
- Handouts were distributed during the presentation, so that you read these rather than listening.
- The content was jumbled, or incomprehensible, or already familiar to you.
- Questions were barely relevant, but they diverted the speaker from the main point.
- Timekeeping was poor and the speaker went on long beyond the scheduled end.
- Questions deteriorated into argument between the speaker and a single member of the audience.

The remainder of the chapter will address these common faults, as well as covering features which may well have appeared on your list of 'good' points.

→ Ch 1

11

Presenting to others

ACTIVITY 11.2

Did you mention presentation skills as a strength in your SWOT in Chapter 1? If not, use the following questionnaire to assess your skill level (score 5 if the statement is completely true, 4 if mostly true, 3 if it is neither true nor untrue, 2 if it is not very true, and 1 if it is totally untrue)

I have lots of experience in giving presentations   _____

The presentations I give are usually very well received   _____

I always think carefully about what I need to communicate, and how best to do it to any particular audience   _____

I am good at thinking of how to use visual aids to reinforce my message   _____

I am confident in using PowerPoint to produce effective overheads   _____

I think it is really important to watch the audience, and modify a presentation if it does not seem to be working.   _____

Total: _____

If your score is 25 or above you should not need this chapter – assuming your assessment of your skills is accurate. Below this, you might think about developing an action plan to improve aspects of your skills.

STRUCTURE

The importance of structure was emphasised in the context of written communications, but it is even more important in a presentation. It is very easy for your audience to lose the thread of what you are saying and very hard for them to find it again if they do. They cannot go back and read the difficult bit again. So the classic advice of 'Say what you are going to say, say it, then tell them what you have said' still holds good.

Introduction

Good presentations:
- have a clear structure
- are clearly signposted
- are clearly delivered
- use varied visual aids
- interest the audience
- do not over-run.

You need to settle your audience, so say who you are, what you are aiming to achieve, how long you will be talking and how you plan to operate. Do you want to save all questions except those for clarification to the end, for example, or are you happy to take questions at any point? Will you be handing out copies of your OHTs at the end or do people need to take notes? Once the ground rules have been established, you then need to outline the main points that you will be covering during your presentation. If you can say something that catches your audience's attention at the outset and makes them *want* to hear what follows, then the presentation is likely to go well.

Main presentation

As with a written report, you need to make clear what situation or topic you are addressing and use evidence to support the arguments you are making. Because of the difficulty of following a spoken argument, you need to make your structure absolutely clear and give your audience as much help as possible on this: 'What I have established thus far is . . . (brief summary). The next point I want to make is . . .'. If you give such pointers at regular intervals, perhaps with OHTs to reinforce them, your audience will find it easier to maintain concentration and to stay with your argument.

Conclusion

This is the 'tell them what you have said' section. You need to summarise the points you have made, again using visual aids to reinforce them if possible. If you are making a proposal, then it is worth emphasising the main points of this again. It is also good practice to thank the audience for their patience and invite questions or discussion.

DELIVERY TECHNIQUE

If you do come across good presenters, study them carefully to see if there are ways in which you could improve your own performance. Even if you are not exposed to skilled practitioners, the following guidelines will give you a good foundation.

Relate to your audience

Talking to a point on the back wall, in an impersonal style, will put an unhelpful distance between you and your audience. Try to sound human in your introduction. Look at people. Say things in the way that they are most likely to understand. Check with them that you are on the right lines: 'Was that point clear?' 'Can you all see this slide?' 'Am I going too fast?'

Make it easy for people to hear

Speak clearly, without gabbling, and vary your tone. Use short sentences and straightforward language, avoiding unnecessary jargon. Use 'spoken language' not 'written language'. If you have ever heard someone (literally) read a paper they have written, you will probably be all too aware of the difference. If not, try reading part of a journal article out loud, then rephrase it using words you would normally use in talking. Avoid turning your back on your audience (whiteboards are a real hazard here) or being hidden by equipment.

Try to be interesting

Vary your pace and use a variety of visual aids if there are appropriate ones. Even something as simple as showing a pile of ten books on a subject can reinforce the point that there has been a lot written on it. Occasional humour can be useful, but don't overdo it (unless you are making an after-dinner speech, when a high proportion of jokes seems to be the norm). Above all, make the relevance of what you are saying clear. It may be less obvious to your audience why something is significant than it is to you: you need to *work* at making sure that they see it too.

Beware of becoming bogged down in detail

It is far harder to absorb detail from a spoken presentation than from a written report. More often, it merely obscures the main point. Try to give only as much detail as you need to make your point. If a fine detail is crucial, it is probably better to give this as a handout for later perusal.

Avoid giving handouts while you speak

The distribution of handouts distracts people, and you will lose your audience. It doesn't matter how often you say of a handout 'don't read this now' – the temptation to look at it immediately seems universally irresistible. If you distribute handouts before you start, early arrivals will have something to do while they wait. It will also be clear to them how many additional notes (if any) they need to take. Handouts distributed at the end can be a good way of concluding, but you need to tell people at the outset that you are going to do this, otherwise they can feel annoyed if they have taken careful notes which the handout makes superfluous.

Keep your notes brief

Particularly if you are new to giving presentations, you are likely to be tempted to write out the whole thing. Then you know you can avoid grinding to a stop, because all you have to do is keep reading. Writing it out can be very helpful and the reassurance of knowing you *could* read it if absolutely necessary is very comforting. But try to keep that as an emergency measure. Even if you do write out a 'full text' version, you should also write briefer notes from which, barring the onset of total panic, you will actually speak.

These notes should indicate the key points to be made, in order. Such notes are ideally made on index cards. Number them or join them with a treasury tag just in case you drop them. Trying frantically to reorder a hopeless jumble of cards while facing an audience can be deeply embarrassing! Indicate in your notes each point at which you need to use a visual aid. And cross-refer to your transcript so that you can easily switch to that if necessary. (After a few presentations, when you have never used the full notes, you will probably feel confident enough to dispense with them.)

Watch your audience

You need feedback on your delivery and people may not tell you in words. But you will be able to see, if you look, whether a glaze of incomprehension is stealing over your audience. If so, you may need to slow down and explain more, or perhaps check understanding by asking a question. If eyelids are drooping, you may be going too slowly already or have under-estimated the prior knowledge of people there. Or you may need to vary your delivery more. If people are tense, tapping feet or fingers with restrained force, you are seriously getting on their nerves and need to find out why. As soon as you pick up signals that all is not well, try to work out why. Unless you are fairly sure what you are doing wrong, *ask* what the problem is. And adapt your presentation in the light of the answers.

Be honest

Trying to fool people seldom works. If there is a weakness in your case admit it, rather than hoping that no one will notice. If they do notice, they will not think well of you for seemingly failing to spot the weakness yourself. But if you admit to it and have formed a good relationship with your audience, they may help you to strengthen the point. Similarly, pretending to know something when in fact you don't may make you look foolish. But admitting your ignorance may allow someone in the audience who does know to contribute their knowledge – to everyone's advantage.

Manage your time

Inexperienced presenters are often surprised at how little it is possible to communicate in a specified time. This is because they do not allow for speech being slower than reading, for questions of clarification, for introductions, for interim summaries or for use of visual aids. It is important to judge how long a presentation will take and adjust it if a dry run shows that your guess is wrong. Aim to undershoot slightly. It is generally better to risk allowing slightly too long for questions than to run out of time, and to finish a little early rather than over-running.

EFFECTIVE VISUAL AIDS

Communication will be far more effective in either writing or speaking if you use images to reinforce your words. Visual aids have already been mentioned several times:

this should have indicated that they are essential in formal presentations of any length or complexity. Such aids have three main functions. They can help the audience *understand* a point, they can help the audience *remember* a point and they can keep your audience *awake*. To make good use of visual aids, you need to think about how each of your points could be reinforced by an action, an object or a picture, and then how best to achieve this reinforcement. The best visual aid to use will depend on both the point you are making and the audience to whom you are making it.

> **Visual aids can:**
> ■ reinforce key points
> ■ clarify meaning
> ■ aid retention
> ■ keep audience awake!

Some things can be conveyed far more effectively by means other than words alone. Relationships are more clearly shown in diagrams, while trends are clearly demonstrated in graphs. Other chapters cover representing data visually and diagramming other aspects of a situation, also incorporating the results in written reports. The same principles apply, though within the restrictions of what can be seen from a distance. Revise these principles if you are in doubt. But although you will probably use visual aids similar to those suitable for a report for most of your points, your scope in a spoken presentation is potentially far wider.

Video clips of products, processes, people or places can be hugely effective. Concrete objects can also make a lasting impression. To take an example, when I am running open events to attract potential Open University students, one thing I need to explain is how distance learning works. It is not always obvious that a subject like management can be studied effectively at a distance. So I *show* the audience a course pack, with all the videos, disks, audiotapes and written units. I *show* them course assignments, covered in teaching comments from the tutor. I may *show* them extracts from teaching videos or a video of a tutorial. This allows me to convey far more about the course than would a mere description. If I wanted to make a point about the volume of reading on a conventional course, I might show the audience a pile of the books on the recommended reading list.

I have seen speakers hold up broken items to make a point about quality, or a new product to make a different point. Stephen Pinker held up a comb to make a point about the innate distastefulness of using a comb to stir coffee. Such images make a lasting impression – though the point they demonstrated is not always clearly remembered. If the image is too strong, then it may over-shadow the point (what *was* the significance of this particular distaste?). But this slight caution aside, apart from points which are made better by use of visual aids, people also tend to remember what they see better than what they hear. It is therefore worth using visual aids even to reinforce points which can be made adequately in words in order to aid their retention.

It is also important to incorporate variety to keep people awake and interested. For any presentation longer than, say, half an hour, it is worth using a range of visual aids for this reason alone. You can use some diagrams on prepared OHTs or slides, draw others on a board or flipchart at an appropriate point (do this quickly and avoid talking while drawing) and, if you have the facilities, use video clips and dynamic PC-generated diagrams as well.

If your talk is shorter, you do not need to work so hard at keeping people's attention and too much variety in visual aids can be counterproductive. It is better to reserve them for points that are best made visually, plus those which you really wish to emphasise. More will be a distraction.

Presentation packages

→ Ch 4

It is now normal to drive your presentation from your PC. Indeed it would seem unprofessional in many situations to use anything else. PowerPoint is virtually the standard in management presentations, although other packages are available, and some prefer these. The main advantage of a package such as PowerPoint is its flexibility. Suppose you are talking with potential clients prior to a presentation and discover that they have concerns that you had not realised when you prepared your presentation. In a couple of minutes you can add a slide or two to address these. You can easily edit the slides you used on one occasion to provide a slightly modified presentation for another occasion. You can easily incorporate charts and graphs from a report into your presentation, or diagrams from your presentation into a report.

Because you will almost certainly need to give presentations at work using this technology, you should use the opportunities provided by your course to become proficient in using PowerPoint or a similar package. It is remarkably easy to produce basic bullet point slides, and not much harder to animate them, colour them, and add sound effects and clip art. Aim to become proficient at all these as a minimum.

While it is good to explore the possibilities and experiment with what you can do while you have the chance, remember that you should use the facilities advisedly when presenting at work. Your aim is not usually to show how good you are with IT, but to communicate. Over-complexity, too many animations and sound effects and too many slides may actually interfere with communication. Fancy backgrounds distract, and reduce clarity. Animations may look impressive, but are similarly distracting. While it is sometimes extremely useful to build up a picture a bit at a time, you should restrict use of the facility to such times. Words continually flying in from left and right will seldom help your audience to grasp and retain the points you are making. And now that everyone can use PowerPoint, being expert in its use is less impressive than once it might have been. Remember at all times that you are trying to communicate effectively, and use the tools at your disposal to this end alone.

There are less obvious, but perhaps more serious hazards with PowerPoint in terms of the way that it can easily constrain your presentation to an endless series of bullet points. As Naughton (2003) pointed out, it was conceived in a software sales environment. So it tends to turn everything into a sales pitch. There was a version of the Gettysburg address doing the e-mail rounds a while ago that demonstrated this limitation (see **www.norvig.com/Gettysburg**). But Tufte, a Yale professor and expert on visual communication, goes further in his criticism, arguing (in 'The Cognitive Style of PowerPoint', available from **www.edwardtufte.com**) that PowerPoint's ready-made templates tend to weaken verbal and spatial reasoning and corrupt statistical analysis. He attributes the Columbia disaster to a slide that led Nasa to overlook the destructive potential of the crucial loose tile.

General requirements for visual aids

Whether or not you are using computer-driven visual aids, there are a number of points to bear in mind.

It may sound blindingly obvious, but many people ignore the requirement for an audience to be able to *see* visual aids if they are to be of use. Even experienced speakers have been known to show OHTs which are photocopies of a full-page table in a book, with perhaps 200 numbers in invisibly small type. The amount of effective information you can convey on a slide is surprisingly small. Experiment with handwriting your drafts of overheads on acetate, then see whether you can read them from the back row. PowerPoint allows you to add points one at a time. If using an OHP you may find it helpful to build up information using a series of OHTs which can be placed one on top of the other. Thus by adding them one at a time you build up the complexity of the picture to a point which would be impossible to grasp if you started with this. Either way it is probably best to aim at no more than four points per slide.

Colour can either enhance or hinder clarity. Think about how you use it. I was once provided with a set of very tasteful, but totally useless, OHTs in shades of blue on blue, the words invisible from more than three paces. PowerPoint slides can be equally illegible if you are not careful. Use both colour and light/dark contrast to enhance legibility and emphasise key points and be careful about fancy backgrounds. They may look good in themselves, but obscure your message.

This is not to argue for refusing to use anything but the hand-scrawled, barely legible exhibits that are still often used. They have their place in 'transient' presentations, for example on group work, where all you are seeking is to convey your thought processes to fellow students. But they would be inappropriate for a formal presentation to a client.

If you are doing an informal presentation to your class, do not have a PowerPoint projector and are discouraged from using the copier, then you can prepare flipchart sheets in the same way as slides and ask a fellow student to be responsible for displaying the right one on cue. (Trying to talk and manage a flipchart is possible, but not easy. It helps considerably to split the responsibility.)

If you are still using OHTs, another obvious point (well, I wish it *were* obvious) is always to use photocopying, not write-on, acetate in a copier. Photocopier acetate is firmer and the box should be clearly labelled as suitable for copying. The write-on sort melts in the machine, making a mess which only the engineer can sort out, and which will make you unpopular all round.

ACTIVITY 11.3

You can easily assemble an exhibit for your portfolio that addresses both your ability to use images and your ability to read and respond to materials. Take as the basis for this a presentation you make in class, perhaps summarising something you have studied. Your presentation needs to include appropriate visual aids. You also need a way of obtaining feedback from your tutor and/or those present. The exhibit should include the notes for your talk and copies of the images used, together with a description of how you selected both content and images, feedback on their effectiveness and what you would do differently next time in the light of this feedback.

HANDLING QUESTIONS

Sometimes questions are helpful, but I have seen them wreck a presentation completely. Until you are fairly experienced, and feel confident that you can handle questions during your talk, it is safer to take substantive questions at the end. Make it clear at the outset that during your presentation you will deal only with requests for clarification and that there will be time for questions at the end. Otherwise, you risk being completely side-tracked from your main argument or disconcerted by challenges to what you are saying before you have completed your case. If you want to postpone a question, either take a note of it so that you do not forget or, better still, ask the questioner to ask it again at the end. This means that your brain is not distracted by trying to remember the question while giving the talk.

When you do accept a question, your listening skills will be important. It is hard to listen carefully when you are nervous, particularly if someone is asking a complex multiple question. If this happens, jot down the key parts of the question, otherwise it is easy to answer the first part and forget all the rest. If you are at all uncertain what the question means, clarify this with the questioner. You may feel that it makes you look stupid if you don't understand. But if the questioner is far from clear it is sensible to pick up on this. You may tie yourself in knots if you try to answer a question that you have only partially understood: this does not look all that impressive either.

If a question challenges what you have said, resist the temptation to become either defensive or aggressive. Take the contrasting view seriously, looking for ways to develop your position in the light of it, unless you are convinced that the questioner really has missed the point of what you were saying or is misinformed. If the point has been missed by the questioner, it is possible that others missed it too and finding another way of making it may be helpful. But if you cannot quickly satisfy the questioner, it is usually better to suggest that you discuss it after the presentation is finished, rather than get into an argument that will be of little interest to most of the audience.

People ask questions for many reasons. In work presentations, there will be some who are trying to make an impression on the audience, perhaps with a view to establishing themselves as a rival expert or advertising their own business. Or they may simply like being the centre of attention. Where questions are clearly being asked in the questioner's personal interest, it is simplest to thank them for raising their point, agree with as much of the point as you can, perhaps suggest a discussion outside the meeting and move on to the next question.

If questions reveal a genuine weakness in your presentation, it is usually better to accept this and ask for suggestions from the questioner and the audience for ways around the difficulty. You may find that someone can suggest a way forward. If, however, the difficulty seems to you to be much less significant than the questioner is suggesting, you will need to make sure that the audience does not end up devaluing the bulk of what you have said.

CONTROLLING YOUR NERVES

It is natural to be nervous when standing up in front of a group of people. The adrenaline it generates can give your performance an excitement that it would otherwise lack, so do not aim to become totally blasé about it. But excess nerves can be a liability, drying your throat and making you physically and verbally clumsy. If you think that you are worrying more than is reasonable, there are several things that can help considerably. Get as much practice as you can. Concentrate on exposing yourself to similar situations, practise deliberate relaxation, and prepare for each specific presentation.

> Increase your confidence in presenting by:
> ■ frequent practice
> ■ relaxation techniques
> ■ thorough preparation.

If you *are* over-nervous, you probably avoid all situations where you need to talk in front of people. But the best way to reduce nervousness is to seek out such situations and force yourself to talk. Find the least threatening situations first – talking to a small group of students before addressing the whole class, getting used to the class before giving a paper at a conference . . .. But *do* it. Each time you will feel less nervous.

This is one form of practice which 'desensitises' you to the general trauma of the situation. Another form is to have one or more 'practice runs' of a specific presentation. This will mean that you are confident about the structure of the talk, have practised some of the phrases you will use, know where to use your OHTs or other visual aids and have checked how long it takes, so that you are not worried about having too much or too little material.

→ Ch 2   Relaxation techniques, discussed as part of stress management in Chapter 2, can help reduce this sort of stress too, though you need to be familiar with the techniques for best effect. If you have not yet practised them, a short period of deep breathing will help. And a *small* alcoholic drink can sometimes be useful.

But your best weapon against nerves is the knowledge that you have done everything possible to prepare for the event, that you have carefully researched your subject and audience, your talk is well structured and your notes are well organised, your visual aids well chosen and you have at your fingertips supporting evidence and examples. Dry runs, described above, can be part of your preparation. Remember, a presentation is a challenge, but it can be exciting and rewarding, and can provoke interesting discussion on a subject dear to your heart. Preparation is so important that more detail is given below.

Even if you have prepared, you may well experience an initial onrush of nerves when you stand up. To get you over this, make sure that you have your introductory remarks written out in full, preferably learned by heart. Take a sip of water and a deep breath, go over your introduction and by then you will have calmed down enough to enjoy yourself.

PREPARATION

Preparation is the key to successful presentation and you cannot afford to cut corners if you want to do well. You need to have thought carefully about what to include, how to structure it and how to add impact to your arguments by examples and visual aids.

11

Presenting to others

For important presentations, you will want to rehearse your arguments several times. Much of this can be done piecemeal, for example while exercising or in a waiting room, *sotto voce*. But you will need one full-scale, real-time rehearsal to check timing, use of aids and flow of arguments. Ideally, find colleagues or friends to act as an audience for this and ask them to give you feedback afterwards. If this is impossible, then tape yourself and replay the tape after a decent interval, listening critically and noting points where you need to change something.

If you are giving a presentation at work, to clients or potential customers, or a paper at a conference, your preparation needs to extend to ensuring that the location is set up as you want it, temperature is appropriate and equipment working well. You do not want to be hunting for porters or chasing around for a fresh bulb for the projector while half the audience has arrived and is watching your increasing panic. So arrive early and make all the necessary checks.

Preparation for your *next* presentation should be informed by feedback from the last, so it is important to capture as much feedback as possible. Make a note of your immediate reactions in the light of audience response. Do this as soon as possible after the event, noting points for future action. And if possible, have a friend in the audience charged with giving you their reactions and suggestions. You may even be able to design and distribute a short questionnaire for the audience to complete on leaving. If the presentation is one of a series, this can be extremely useful in helping you to adjust future events to meet audience needs more effectively. If you are preparing an exhibit on your presentation skills, it will be important to include all such feedback.

SUMMARY

This chapter has argued the following:

- Presentation skills are an important part of communication in the work context and may indeed be tested during selection procedures.
- During your studies you will have many opportunities to develop these skills and they may even influence some of your marks.
- Successful presentation depends on adequate preparation. You need to be clear on your objectives and those of your audience, and structure is even more important than with written communications.
- Good visual aids help audience concentration, comprehension and retention. Using PowerPoint or a similar package to project slides from your PC is flexible and looks professional.
- Audibility, visibility and ability to pace your delivery to suit your audience and your content are essential.
- Questions can be an asset or a disruption. Substantive ones are probably best taken at the end.
- Extreme nervousness can be disabling but lower levels can help. Practice, relaxation and preparation will help you to reduce excessive nerves.

Further information

- Bradley, A. (2000) *Successful Presentation Skills*, 2nd edn, Kogan Page.
- Collins, J./Video Arts (1998) *Making Effective Presentations*, Kogan Page.
- Conradi, M. and Hall, R. (2001) *That Presentation Sensation*, Financial Times Prentice Hall.
- Leech, T. (2001) *Say it like Shakespeare*, McGraw-Hill – this gives an interestingly different slant on presenting.
- Manchester Open Learning (1993) *Making Effective Presentations*, Kogan Page.
- Williams, J.S. (1995) *The Right Way to Make Effective Presentations*, Eliot Right Way Books.

11

Presenting to others

→ **Part 4** # CONCEPTUAL SKILLS

Introduction to Part 4

This part of the book explores what is meant by the 'trained mind' that employers so often say they are looking for in graduates. By now you should have become a more effective learner. You will be better at absorbing the specialist skills and knowledge your course covers because of these learning skills. You will also be developing your interpersonal skills. These are important for real-life problem solving. Most problems are better addressed in teams. The perspectives and information that other people bring to bear on the situation are vital for gaining a thorough understanding of the problem.

But there is a third aspect to effective problem solving. You need to be able to bring conceptual skills to problem situations – the skills which help you explore different aspects of a problem, and test different sets of assumptions about it. You need to play mental games, experimenting with different ways of making sense of the complex situation that is problematic. This mental flexibility is essential if you are to avoid the trap of treating what is complex as if it were simple. You need it, too, to cope with what may seem conflicting and inadequate 'information' about the situation. Most importantly, you need to be able to break out of the mindset that may be stopping you from seeing a solution.

Although this part of the book is about problem solving, much of it addresses those problems which you cannot 'solve' in the sense of logically working through to a solution that is unarguably 'correct'. Such solutions are possible only if you know what you are trying to do, have all the information needed to decide between alternative solutions and can therefore by a logical process decide on the best. So committed do we tend to be to this kind of approach that it is adopted in situations where it is impossible to use it properly. The 'problem' is viewed from a narrow perspective that gives the illusion that it can be treated rationally. But remember Procrustes, the legendary Greek robber who stretched or shortened his captives to fit an iron bed. If you treat problems in this way, ignoring the parts which are cut off to make them easier to solve, you risk finding a 'solution' which makes things worse. The following chapters are designed to help you to avoid this trap and to accept that, for many situations, complexity is inevitable. But there are useful techniques that can help you to explore this complexity. And there are further techniques which can help you find creative approaches to resistant problems.

These skills will help you with any complex 'non-scientific' analysis that you need for your courses. Case study analyses are obvious examples of this. So, too, are almost any significant management or social science-related projects. If you can develop your problem-solving skills before you graduate, you will have a significant advantage over work colleagues who lack them. You will quickly be noticed as someone with high-flier potential!

→ 12 Complexity, cases and diagrams

Perhaps the most useful skill of all those you will learn during your studies is the ability to first accept, and then make some sort of sense of, the complexity inherent in problem situations. This is the point of many of the theories and frameworks that you will be taught. Yet it is a point that many students find extremely difficult to grasp. This chapter should help you see why you are learning much of what you are learning, and show you how to put it to good effect in analysing cases during your course, and making sense of situations in real life.

Learning outcomes

By the end of this chapter you should:

- appreciate both the advantages and the limitations of a rational, systematic and logical approach
- be becoming more logical in your own thinking
- be able to locate this rational approach within a wider framework for exploring problem situations and making sense of them
- be using diagrams as a tool for problem exploration and interpretation
- be starting to use mental modelling and experimentation as part of an approach to problems
- have developed a systematic approach to case study analysis.

→ Ch 1

Organisations are complex, and the problem situations that arise in them are highly so. Graduates are attractive to employers in large part because they are believed to have the ability to think their way through such problems. Well developed 'cognitive skills' are perhaps the most important goal of higher education. Demonstrating these skills at interview, and in your job, will greatly help your career. Education tends to emphasise logic and rationality, and being logical is important. But real life often seems fairly chaotic and full of uncertainty, so you need additional skills to deal with complexity.

While many problems *are* amenable to a logical approach, with access to all the information needed to work out the solution, many are not. Key players may be unable to agree what the problem *is*, let alone what would constitute a solution. Even if they agree on the problem, it may seem to defy solution. I am not suggesting you should be *illogical*, but you may need to go beyond the strictly logical framework to find a totally new way through the situation. Playing mental games can help you find a *non-obvious* way of thinking about the situation. Once this shift of perspective has been achieved, logic can be more effectively used.

So you need to develop different, and rarer conceptual skills with which to supplement your logical thinking. Combining a rational approach with the mental agility needed to go beyond the rational should enable you to deal with problems that have defeated lesser brains. This chapter looks at the more rational ways of approaching problems, with particular emphasis on how they can be applied to working with case studies. Ways of becoming more creative are discussed in Chapter 15.

→ Ch 15

RATIONAL APPROACHES

In describing key *cognitive skills,* the QAA talks in terms of analysis and synthesis, and of the ability to identify assumptions, to evaluate statements in terms of evidence, and to check the logic of an argument. Society quite reasonably places a high value on logic and rationality. Treating a faulty assumption as an unquestionable fact can prevent problems being solved, or generate 'solutions'; that magnify the original problem. For example, a Business School whose MBA applications were falling lowered its prices because 'lower prices will increase demand'. While this assumption may be true in many cases, their MBA was already about the cheapest available: indeed people were applying elsewhere because the already low price was interpreted as meaning low quality!

Rationality is based on interpreting the world in terms of simple cause and effect – the underlying model is that the world runs as a well-ordered machine. There are two problems with this. First, people are often less good at thinking rationally than they think they are. Secondly, the model may be faulty! This chapter is intended to make you better at being rational, as well as more aware of its limitations.

Almost everyone would say they were rational. Yet *irrational* approaches to problems abound. You may be less rational than you think! This may seem curious – the classic approach to rational decision taking makes the whole thing sound absurdly simple.

The steps in rational problem solving are widely described as:

- define the problem
- generate possible solutions
- select best solution
- implement solution.

Almost any manager would claim that this was how they operated. Yet if you observe a group of people working on a problem you are likely to find a very different picture emerging. In a classic work on the subject, Kepner and Tregoe (1965) graphically describe the irrational and unsystematic behaviour which they observed in discussions of organisational problems. The cost of some of the poor decisions which they observed as a consequence of this behaviour was enormous.

Managers tended not to follow an orderly sequence of steps such as that above. Instead, they jumped all over the place, leaping to solutions before establishing the nature of the problem. If they thought at all about reasons for the problem, they made *assumptions* about causes, rather than exploring them. As one fairly senior manager said recently: 'If only I could teach my managers that the correct sequence is "Ready, aim, fire". They shoot before they are even ready, never mind about taking aim.' The following exercise should show you that this is fairly universal behaviour.

ACTIVITY 12.1

Next time you are discussing a case study or other complex quasi-problem, focus on the task contributions and sort them into the following categories suggested by Kepner and Tregoe:

- non-relevant information
- problem (what is wrong)
- cause (what made it wrong)
- action (what to do about it).

Plot the subject of discussion as time progresses using a chart similar to Figure 12.1. Even better, if you are in real problem-solving discussions and can afford to take a back seat for a while, observe the way the problem is addressed, using the same categories. If no such opportunities present themselves in the near future, get a group together to discuss a problem which all can relate to – anything from NHS underfunding to rowdy behaviour in the union. The topic doesn't matter provided it is not too simple and is an issue of some concern to all members.

Jumpy discussions like this have led to plans for a major research programme by a department that had already spent its research budget, a decision to sack a number of staff for non-performance when the job they were meant to be doing (and had spent years learning to do) had been made impossible by restructuring and conflicting objectives, and a decision to develop a new version of a product when the problem with the old product was that demand had been reduced almost to zero by totally new technology. In each of

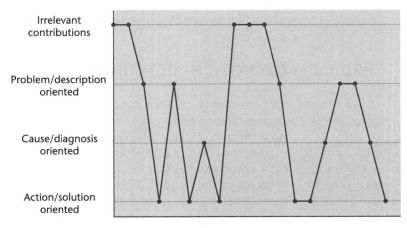

Fig. 12.1 Kepner–Tregoe-type chart of discussion flow

these cases, a bad decision was taken because of lack of systematic consideration of the problem and its causes and the choice, in consequence, of totally inappropriate action.

There is sometimes a good reason to 'iterate', that is, to make several loops through the stages of addressing a problem. (For example, because as you start to understand aspects of the situation you may realise that your earlier diagnosis was faulty.) But many discussions are inadvertently unsystematic, rather than deliberately iterative. And you will almost certainly have observed inadequacies in understanding what the problem *is*, and subsequently what caused it, because of this unsystematic approach.

An analytical approach

→ Ch 8

The rational approach to problem solving is supposed to be analytical as well as systematic. 'Analyse' is a term very frequently used in assessment, and something you will frequently need to do as a manager. You will remember from the Chapter 8 Helpfile that analysis was about examining something 'part by part'. In taking an analytical approach to problems you are trying to make sense of complexity by teasing out different elements in the situation. By looking at these separately and in combination you can advance your understanding of the problem.

Jumping straight to 'Action' is *not* an analytical approach. If you want to be analytical you need to put a lot of effort into exploring the problem in more detail, looking for key elements, and problem themes. Proper diagnosis is absolutely crucial. And you also need to separate out different causal strands – few problems have a clear and simple cause. It is much more common for a wide range of different factors to be involved. Each of these may be fairly insignificant if taken alone, but in combination they produce something highly significant.

A good analysis will explore all these different factors and the different causal chains to which they contribute, drawing upon what you have learned about relevant concepts and relationships between them in your course. This will normally be followed by a *synthesis* which pulls this together into a coherent picture pointing the way forward. In the jumpy discussions described above, this analysis–synthesis sequence is clearly missing. And things often start to go wrong from the very beginning, if the essential first stage of ensuring that the problem was clearly defined was omitted.

PROBLEM DEFINITION: DESCRIPTION AND DIAGNOSIS

So to become more effective at problem solving, you need to devote a large part of your energies to understanding the problem and its causes. Somehow you need to resist the almost irresistible tendency to start suggesting solutions as soon as the first hint of a problem. The more complicated the problem (and almost all problems involving people are complicated), the more important is the stage of problem definition. At the same time, the more difficult it will be. And all too often this difficulty will contribute to the tendency to skimp on problem definition.

Unless you fully understand the problem, your 'solution' may make things worse.

Problem definition has two main constituents, description and diagnosis. You normally start with some unhappiness about a situation. Someone is 'hurting', or has judged

→ Ch 2   that what *is* falls short of what *should be* (remember the control loop). Problem definition will depend on exploring both the 'is' and the 'should be' and the gap between them. This is the description stage. You then need to explore the reasons for this, the diagnostic stage. It is essential that these two parts of definition are addressed thoroughly before you go on to subsequent stages of deciding how to bridge the gap and actually taking the necessary action.

Diagnosis, establishing the 'why', is important. If you do not understand why a problem has arisen and address only its symptoms, your 'solution' may well make things worse, not better. Medical examples make this clear. Taking aspirin because you have a headache may help, at least for a while. If you have a temperature it will bring it down. But both are possibly symptoms of something that is the real problem. Indeed, a raised temperature is probably part of your body's way of fighting an infection. To lower the temperature will make it harder to throw off the infection. Only if the temperature is high enough to be a problem in its own right does it make sense to take aspirin or paracetamol to reduce it. And if you think you have 'solved' a serious infection such as meningitis by taking aspirin and do not seek the urgent help that you need, the 'solution' has been downright dangerous. A doctor would look at other aspects of what is wrong with you. Do you have a stiff neck, hate looking at light, have a persistent rash? He or she would also explore possible causes of the pattern of symptoms (hangover, contact with infected person, sunstroke . . .).

DESCRIPTION AS A BASIS FOR DIAGNOSIS

There is clearly, therefore, a need to gather adequate information on which to base diagnosis during the prior stage of problem description. You should by now be more aware of the importance of adequate description. But if you are working with a group who are less alert to this, you may need to 'educate' them. Ideally, discuss the importance of thorough diagnosis before you start to talk about the problem. If this is impossible, or if despite your efforts you think that discussion has moved on prematurely, say why you are uneasy and ask questions that will elicit more information.

Useful questions about a problem situation include:

- What should be happening, when and where?
- What *is* happening (or not happening), when and where?
- Who thinks that this is a problem and why?
- What do other key people think about it?
- What related things are *not* problematic?
- What is the wider context within which all this is happening?
- Who or what can influence the problem situation?
- Who or what is influenced by it?
- What constraints are there in the situation that will restrict possible actions?

(A version of this is available on the website.)

12

Complexity, cases and diagrams

In complex problem situations you are likely to need to include a great deal of 'soft' information. Facts and figures will be useful, but the feelings and beliefs that people have about a problem may be even more significant. Such problems are far better tackled by a group: discussion will allow these softer aspects to emerge. A carefully chosen group, representing a number of different perspectives on a problem and a range of expertise, can be a rich source of information about the nature of the problem. (If you are working alone, then you will probably need to arrange to talk to all these people individually, but this may be more time-consuming and it will be hard for you to elicit as much as would emerge in a good discussion.)

Descriptive diagrams

→ Ch 4

One way of checking that you have explored all the aspects of a problem is to try to represent these diagrammatically. For example, you might use mind maps (described in Chapter 4) as a tool. Suppose that customers are cancelling orders and complaining of both quality and delivery problems. The main branches of a diagram in this case might be cash, quality and delivery. You might then look for more detail to fill in twigs on each of these branches. What aspects of quality are they complaining about, which stages in the manufacture–delivery chain are going wrong? Try also to explore what is *not* going wrong, as this information will be vital to you in ruling out some of the possible causes of the problem when you start your diagnosis.

Another useful way of exploring a problem is to use a technique called 'rich picturing', developed by Peter Checkland (1981). This is ideal for group exploration of a problem, as it allows you to build up a composite of the ideas of different group members about key aspects in the problem situation. A rich picture consists of all the elements that are seen as possible constituents of the *problématique* – the complex of factors which result in a problem for someone. To make it easier to grasp these at a glance, they are represented pictorially. Note that drawing skills are unimportant – the aim is to make the pictures 'talk', not to be artistic. As the relationships between factors are likely to be at least as important as the factors themselves, these relationships are shown too. Normally arrows or lines are used for this, with some symbol attached to show the nature of the relationship: £££ or $$$ signs are traditionally used for financial links, crossed swords for conflict and so on. But it does not really matter what convention is adopted, as long as it is one that 'speaks' to all members of the group. Figure 12.2 shows an example of a rich picture exploring some of the pressures on academic staff. You might wish to draw a similar picture representing pressures on students.

Drawing such diagrams may seem eccentric at first, but if you try it a few times you will be surprised at how helpful it is and how it allows people to build a shared understanding of what is involved in the problem. If the cartoon aspect seems too bizarre, at least attempt a non-pictorial diagram showing key factors and the relationships between them. Such 'relationship diagrams', which use only words and lines rather than pictures, are less fun, but they are still extremely useful at representing patterns of relationships which would be impossible to convey in mere prose. Figure 12.3 shows an example of a more restrained relationship diagram.

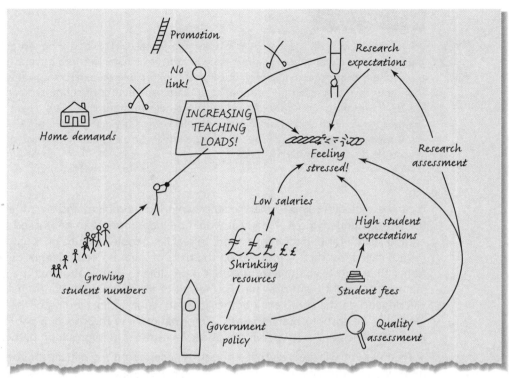

Fig. 12.2 Rich picture exploring factors affecting pressure on teaching staff

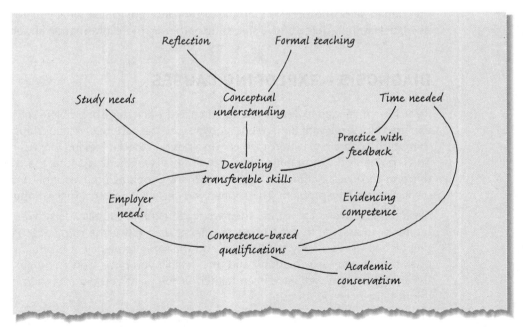

Fig. 12.3 Relationship diagram showing factors relevant to developing transferable skills

12

Complexity, cases and diagrams

ACTIVITY 12.2

Experiment with different ways of exploring a problem. This might be a problem presented in a case study or a real issue of concern to one or more of your group. (This exercise is best done in a group, but if this is impossible the exercise is still worth doing on your own.) First, simply use the list of diagnostic questions suggested earlier as a basis for interrogating a situation. Add any other questions that seem to you to be appropriate. Then try writing down a problem summary using diagrams as an aid to representing the situation. Think about the effectiveness of each approach and if possible discuss this with others.

It can be difficult to know when to stop exploring a problem and start thinking about the reasons underlying it. Clearly, it would be inappropriate to get locked into a never-ending search for perfect information. In real life people seem to do what Simon (1960) called 'satisfice' – proceed on the basis of what is deemed 'enough' information, rather than gather all the information it is possible to gather about all the complicated factors that might be of relevance, in pursuit of *the* optimal solution. What is enough will depend on the complexity of the situation, your understanding of the factors involved, the cost of obtaining further information, and the cost of a poor decision. Expensive decisions are deserving of more investment in information gathering.

Sometimes you will discover that 'enough' is *not* enough! You initially thought that you had enough information and understood what was going on. But your work on a later stage, say exploration of causes, will raise questions that you cannot answer, perhaps because you are starting to look at the problem differently. This is when the iteration mentioned before becomes important and you attempt to seek what you now know you need, deliberately going back a stage and gathering more information about the situation.

DIAGNOSIS – EXPLORING CAUSES

If you have managed to devote enough time to the first stage of problem solving to have explored all the relevant dimensions, and grasped the pattern of relationships and of 'symptoms' contained within it, you are in a position to start looking for possible causes. This is probably the most difficult stage of all. Small wonder that, rather than doing the hard thinking and investigation required, all too many people assume, wrongly, that they 'know' what is causing the problem. This is when you get 'solutions' that make matters worse.

Several things work against us when we try to explore causality. First, we have a strong tendency to assume that if *b* happens *after* *a*, then *a* was the *cause* of *b*. *Post hoc ergo propter hoc* – presumably the Romans had the same tendency. It is often a good way of operating. If you eat something and then feel ill, you put it down to what you ate. And the shellfish might well have been tainted or the plant you discovered in the forest might have been poisonous.

But this form of thinking can be seriously misleading. You might, equally, have caught gastric 'flu from someone in a pub. If you sacrifice a maiden at the winter solstice, and the nights start growing shorter thereafter, it may seem reasonable to believe that the sacrifice halted the departure of the sun. But such reasoning may have led to a lot of unnecessary deaths. ... Such thinking is still common. If a woman is appointed to a job for the first time (or a man to a traditionally female role) and is not a success, this is attributed to gender. Soft drugs have been seen as leading to hard drugs because most users have taken soft drugs previously. Yet it could be argued that most of them also drank milk as children. Further information on history of soft drug usage in the population at large would be needed to make the case.

So while one important line of investigation will always be to explore what changes took place shortly before the problem started to emerge, this is not the only thing you need to know. Before assuming these changes were the cause, you need to understand the connection between the two. An argument can be made in the case of the drugs (assuming the difference is statistically significant – see Chapter 14). But if you really cannot see how the maiden's death influences the sun, you might be wary about this as a causal explanation.

→ Ch 14

Another mistake we commonly make is to see *association* as proof of causation. If we are concerned about one thing and notice that another thing is always present at the same time, we may see the latter as the cause. Again, it may be. But again this is not necessarily the case, even if the relationship is statistically significant. Both might have a common cause (for example a virus causing both spots and headache). Again, you need to work out what the cause really is.

A third fault is to assume that if you have found *a* possible cause you have found *the* cause. Students sometimes ring me to complain about a tutorial which went disastrously wrong. Clearly, a possible cause (and the one the students invariably cite) is incompetence on the part of the tutor. Subsequent enquiry often suggests other possible causes – the student had received a bad grade in a previous assignment, or wanted to be in the limelight, or seems to have unrealistic expectations as s/he has complained about every other tutor too.

Kepner and Tregoe (1965) describe another example of a likely cause not being *the* cause. This involved paper manufacturing, where softwood logs were chipped, chemically treated, boiled to a pulp then fed into a paper-making machine. One day, small pieces of wood started appearing in the finished paper. It was immediately assumed that the pulping machinery was defective and new equipment was bought at huge expense. Only one person questioned the 'obvious' explanation. He looked at the wood chips carefully, found that they were untreated hardwood, not softwood, and traced the problem to faults in a hardwood pipeline transporting the pulp.

In the above example, the experts were so sure that they knew what could cause the problem that they did not trouble to look at the symptoms very carefully. Knowing that *a* possible cause is not necessarily *the* cause may help you to avoid this temptation to skimp on the description stage. You should always question the 'obvious'.

It is just as dangerous to assume that there is only *one* cause of a problem. All too often things go wrong only when a series of unlikely events come together. One part of a plant was shut down for maintenance, another had been badly repaired, the person who understood what needed to be done to adjust a regulator was off sick, someone less qualified adjusted it wrongly and suddenly there was an explosion. Even if we correctly identify one of the causes of a problem and do something about that, similar problems may recur if other contributory factors are not addressed.

Diagnostic diagrams

To overcome these tendencies to an overly narrow approach to diagnosis, diagrams are again useful. One form which is commonly used in quality analysis is the Ishikawa 'fishbone' diagram. This is closely related to a mind map, but tidier! Because the writing is aligned with the normal print on a page, it is easier to read. Because it looks neat, it can look impressive in a report, even if the audience is not very familiar with diagramming as a form of communication.

Fishbone diagrams aim to tease out all the possible sources of problems to enable you to identify those which are actually problematic. Again, you look for main areas and represent these as the main branches or 'bones' and, for each of these, try to identify possible sources of problems. Figure 12.4 gives an example.

Fishbone diagrams are a major tool in quality analysis, with 'bones' representing the stages in a process. They provide a systematic way of exploring all logically possible areas where things might be going wrong. In the manufacturing situations for which they were designed, or situations where the problem occurs within a clear process, they can be invaluable. Many of the situations you will encounter, however, whether in case studies or in real life, will be less obviously structured. The rich picture you drew as your first attempt at describing the situation may show a huge range of different sorts of potential factors and relationships between them.

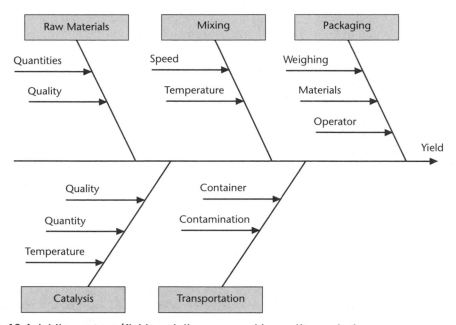

Fig. 12.4 Ishikawa-type 'fishbone' diagram used in quality analysis

→ Ch 8

In such cases, it can be helpful to focus on the *pattern* of causative factors: this is an instant antidote to over-simple views of causation. Fishbone diagrams look at what *might* go wrong. Multiple cause diagrams (similar to that used in Figure 8.1) look at all the relevant things that *actually happened*. They are quite difficult to draw because you start at the end, the problem situation that interests you, and work back in time, looking at all the things that contributed to the situation. 'Multiple contributory factor diagram' might be a better title, if less catchy. In drawing them you need to fight against two temptations – to start at the beginning, and to exclude things that don't cause something, merely contribute to it. Succumbing to either of these will stop you from developing a clear understanding of the whole pattern.

Suppose you wanted to work out why you were doing badly on a course. You would write this – 'doing badly on X' – at the bottom of a piece of paper and put a ring about it. This is the 'event' whose causation you are exploring. You would then ask yourself: 'What is causing this?' Suppose you thought that it was because you hate the subject, fall asleep in lectures, haven't read the set book and haven't submitted the last two essays. At this stage you would add these to your diagram, so that it looked like Figure 12.5(a).

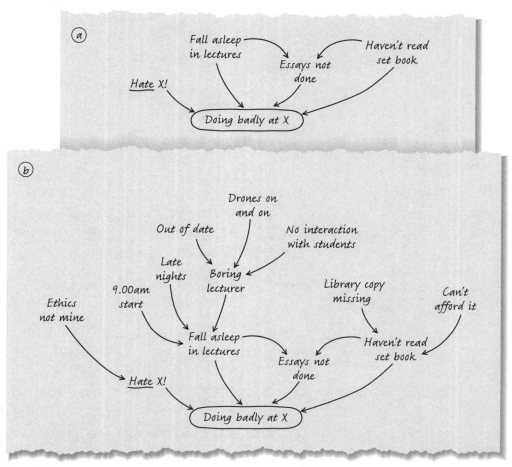

Fig. 12.5 Construction of a multiple cause diagram (a) starting (b) later in the process

You would then ask *why* each of these contributory causes was happening. Perhaps the lectures are at 9am, and the evening before you always go out to the pub until late. Furthermore, the lecturer is incredibly boring and you can't see what he is writing on the board. This is because you are sitting at the back. Why? Because you came in late . . . . Eventually you might end up with a diagram like Figure 12.5(b). This is a fairly trivial example, chosen merely to show the process of working back in time, asking questions about why things happen. Even in this case, you can see that such a diagram could help you to think much more carefully about causes of a problem, because it imposes a discipline on your thoughts and makes you ask questions that might be difficult to answer. Without such a discipline, difficult questions tend to remain unasked.

You may sometimes find that, rather than single, discrete 'chains' of causation, some factors may have several 'effects' which are causes in different chains. In this case you will find a diagram more like Figure 12.6 emerging. But note that you still have a single

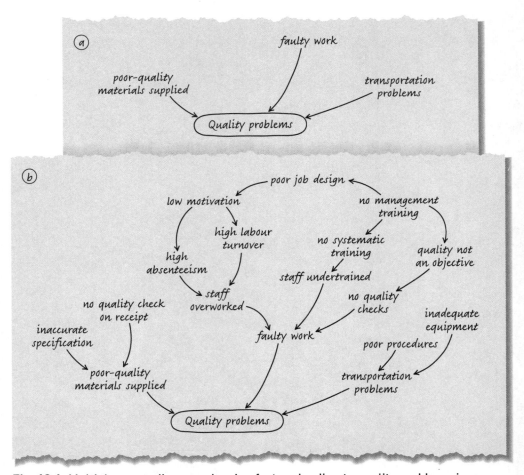

Fig. 12.6 Multiple cause diagram showing factors leading to quality problems in an organisation

end point. Other 'effects' not on the causal chain for the end event are omitted in the interests of clarity. You may sometimes want to explore the likely effects of a proposed change and in this case a multiple *effect* diagram, starting with the change and looking *forwards*, can be useful. But do not mix the two – diagrams depend on simplicity and clarity for their usefulness, and mixing conventions and trying to do too much with one diagram will work against this.

If you are working in a group, and each of you has a slightly different perspective on a problem and different information, working on a multiple cause diagram together can be useful in the same ways as a communal rich picture and can be a useful next step. But you will find it just as useful if you are working alone on any non-trivial problem where an understanding of causes is important.

12

Complexity, cases and diagrams

ACTIVITY 12.3

Think of a problem you are currently facing (or take the next one you encounter). Draw a multiple cause diagram and reflect on the extent to which it helps broaden your understanding. If the problem suits a fishbone approach, then do one of these *before* the multiple cause. Set the diagram aside for a day and then use the following guidelines to check it. If working in a group, have someone else 'read' the diagram back to you to see whether it communicates what you intended. Ask them to perform the checks too. They may be more alert to your shortcomings than you are, therefore a better source of feedback.

Guidelines for drawing a multiple cause diagram

- Start at the *end* (a give-away if you did not start here is that you will probably have a single causal chain, rather than something that looks like a tangled tree with lots of things at the top of the page).
- Each of your arrows should read as '*a* happening contributes to *b* happening' if you have shown *a* → *b*. (Note that it is very easy to reverse arrows inadvertently so that you are showing causes at the arrowhead end, not effects. Beware of this!)
- Each set of arrows should represent all the contributory factors which together 'cause' the event to which they point.
- Your 'causes' should be events not things (machines don't cause problems, but changes in them may do).

(A web version is available for portability.)

There is a logical difference between multiple cause and fishbone diagrams. Fishbones were originally designed to explore *possible* causes of problems, while multiple cause diagrams were intended to explore *actual* causes. But this distinction is a fairly fine one, and because fishbone diagrams are much neater, there is a tendency now to draw multiple cause diagrams in the form of a fishbone. However, this 'tidiness' can make it harder to show where one factor is influencing several causal chains, and may limit your thinking.

Diagrams are intended as an aid to thinking, not a straitjacket. If you are drawing a hybrid 'multiple fish' do try to remember that the main conceptual benefit of a true multiple cause is that it pushes your thinking back through successive 'layers' of causality. Retain this thought process, even if you alter the diagram form.

Models and causality

In drawing diagrams as suggested, you were producing models representing particular aspects of 'reality'. But in constructing these models you are using other models. In attributing causes, you will be drawing on a much wider range of frameworks of assumptions, many of them unconscious. Thus in the politically incorrect example of blaming poor performance on gender of employee, there was an underlying '(wo)men are no good at this' assumption. This was presumably part of a wider set of assumptions, constituting a model, or internal representation, of how (wo)men behave.

McGregor (1957) identified one model of employee motivation which seemed to be commonly held by managers. He called this 'Theory X'. It consists of the assumptions that people are basically lazy, passive, without ambition, disliking responsibility and resistant to change. Such a model would lead you to attribute causes of poor performance to failure of control and direction by the manager and to investigate whether rewards and punishments needed to be manipulated. Contrast this with the rather more complex expectancy theory introduced in Chapter 2 and the sort of explanations which this would lead you to seek for a problem. (McGregor contrasted it with 'Theory Y' – the assumption that people will assume responsibility, and be motivated towards organisational goals, provided that management arranges organisational conditions and methods of operation so that people can achieve their own goals best by directing their efforts towards organisational objectives – a theory directly congruent with expectancy theory.)

→ Ch 2

Models are not reality

If your underlying models do not match key aspects of reality, they may lead you astray. If they are a good match, they may be very helpful. Consider the experience I had with several garages when my car developed a rather frightening electrical fault. Unpredictably – and this might not happen for weeks at a time – using one electrical circuit would cause all the other electrics to fail. Switching on the radio, or even using the brake, would leave me without lights or gauges. After a while, things would function again, but for several days would cut out intermittently. Then for a while the problem would go away.

Three garages failed to diagnose the problem, despite hours spent (at my expense) trying to make it happen so they could 'see what was wrong', i.e. fiddle with the wiring until things came on again. They seemed to have a very simple mental model of my wiring as a lot of connections between parts. They were assuming that all cases of electrical faults were because of a loose connection somewhere. They didn't want to listen to my description of what seemed a fairly bizarre, but informative set of symptoms, nor my suggestion that they focus on parts of the electrics which were common to all the things which went wrong. Fortunately, at the fourth garage there was a mechanic using a more complex underlying model, to which my description of symptoms was relevant. He quickly ruled out most of the wiring as a possible cause, looked at the earthing point (common to all circuits) and found that it was corroded.

It is fairly obvious that a model that fits reality poorly is not much use. But models that are a good *partial* fit can be really dangerous. Their success leads you to equate them with reality. You then expect them to fit it in *all* respects. If they do not, and usually they will not, your predictions may lead you to wrong decisions. One good way of making sure that you remember that a model is *not* reality is to work with several different models at any one time.

This helps if you are *consciously* using models. But many models are unconscious. The mechanics who wanted to twiddle my wires were not aware that they were using a mental model of my electrics. McGregor's managers were not aware of their 'Theory X' or 'Y' of motivation. The problem with unconscious models is that we never work at improving them. We do not use the Kolb cycle to refine them. Such unconscious models will act as hindrance rather than help in situations where they are inappropriate. It is important, therefore, to try to become more aware of the sets of assumptions that we are using. One excellent way is by exploring differences of opinion. Often something will be 'obvious' to you, yet 'obviously' something quite different to someone else because you are working with different sets of assumptions. Only by becoming aware of the difference do you become aware of your own assumptions. This is why groups which work well can achieve far more than individuals. It is why mixed groups can be better than homogeneous ones. And it is why it is so important to manage group process and to ensure that conflict is explored rather than avoided or allowed to escalate to destructive emotional levels.

> Discover your assumptions by:
> - working with people who see things differently
> - exploring disagreements to identify reasons
> - looking at each other's diagrams.

It is also one of the reasons why diagramming is important. It is possible, despite your talking and listening skills, to misinterpret what someone says, because of the slightly different meanings you may attribute to things and the different importance you give them. Also, confusions are often quite hard to spot if you are talking about something complex. Diagrams are much less ambiguous, particularly if you follow a convention and use words and symbols in a particular and agreed way. The convention for multiple causes as described above requires you to use words for events or changes and arrows to point from contributory factors to the events which they help to bring about. If you draw such a diagram, using this convention, and then show it to someone else who is also familiar with the convention, you may be surprised at the sorts of questions that they ask you when they start to 'read' the diagram. Such questions can lead you into areas where your assumptions and underlying models differ, provided that you think carefully about what is prompting the question.

You will almost certainly work with case studies during your course (see next section). One reason for this is to encourage you consciously to use the models that you have been taught as part of your course. Using these models you will be able to suggest possible causes for the symptoms described in the case. Case discussion will also make you more aware of your unconscious models. Your capacity to understand the problem situations that you will encounter at work will be greatly improved if you reduce the extent to which unconscious models are limiting your thinking, or leading you to make inappropriate assumptions about causality.

Guidelines for good diagrams

Although you have met diagrams earlier in the book, this chapter has introduced you to some new ones and to one of the most important uses you are likely to make of them – as a tool for clarifying your thinking about problem situations. (The other main use is to communicate the results of such thoughts, whether in a written report or an oral presentation.) Although a number of comments have been made about diagramming, you may find the following set of guidelines for good practice is a useful summary.

General diagramming guidelines

- **Give yourself space.** Working diagrams should always be spaced out as much as possible. Take large sheets of paper and use the whole sheet. Space will allow easy addition and modification and will make your result much clearer. When using diagrams for communication, you should also avoid cramped diagrams. Adequate space will aid clarity and create a more professional impression.

- **Don't mix diagram types.** It may seem difficult to keep within a single diagramming convention when lots of different aspects of a situation seem important. But a convention helps your reader understand a diagram. And the structure of a convention helps you clarify your thoughts by focusing you on one aspect. So avoid showing 'things' on a dynamic diagram like a multiple cause – save these for a relationship diagram. If you want to show two different aspects, use two diagrams.

- **Seek clarity, not art.** Wanting your diagrams to be artistic rather than merely clear may inhibit you in your use of diagrams and distort your thinking – symmetry may be preferred to usefulness/congruence with features in the situation.

- **Keep diagrams simple.** For the majority of diagrams you are likely to use, it is the pattern that will be of interest and the ability to represent one aspect at least of a whole situation and communicate it. A diagram which is over-cluttered will hide any pattern and communicate very little. So get complex only if it is essential and, even then, start with a simple diagram and build up to a more complex one.

- **Give every diagram a title.** Always give a title to a diagram, saying what it represents and what type of diagram it is. If you are using symbols whose meaning is not clear from the convention, include a key to explain them.

- **Play with diagrams** – be prepared to throw them away. Experiment with different versions of diagrams and different diagram types to develop your thinking about a situation. Remember, diagrams are models and their full value emerges only when you play with them. This will only work if you are prepared to see each model as a hypothesis and cheerfully discard those which are not helpful. This is another reason for not valuing art – if it is too beautiful it is harder to bin it!

(A web version is available for convenience.)

CASE STUDY ANALYSIS

One of the first chances you will have to use your problem-solving skills in a complex situation is likely to be in case study analysis. Case studies have been a popular teaching device since Harvard pioneered the method in its Law School in 1869 and went on to use it for its MBA teaching. They are particularly popular in business studies or other vocational courses. This is because they help to bridge the gap between what you learn on the course and the work situations in which you will eventually apply that learning.

Case studies:
- are interesting
- introduce 'real' situations
- allow application of concepts and techniques
- give practice in handling complexity
- help make you aware of your assumptions
- develop team and communication skills.

A case normally consists of a written description of a situation faced by, or within, an organisation. It may be a brief outline of a scenario, or 100 or more pages of closely written description, supplemented by company accounts, sales figures and other information of possible relevance to the situation. Usually such cases are based on real-life situations encountered by the case author. In writing the case the author will, however, have simplified the situation or been selective in what was described. Sometimes shorter cases are fictional, but even so they will normally make valid points about organisations.

Working on a case, particularly in a small group, will exercise most of the skills you have developed thus far, and indeed some of those covered in chapters yet to come. Case study work therefore presents a rich learning opportunity, where you learn from both the case itself and the process of working on it. Cases can:

- broaden your awareness of organisational situations – particularly valuable if you have little or no experience of organisational life – and give you a chance of looking at things from the perspective of the organisation as a whole;
- give you something on which to practise using the concepts you have been taught as a basis for analysis in order to make sense of fairly complex situations (albeit less complex than those you will meet in real life);
- provide a useful basis for assessment – analysis of a case, although necessarily simplistic, will still be a more useful indication of your understanding of the way in which ideas can be used, and of your analytical skills in the face of complexity, than can many more conventional 'short question' types of assessment;
- develop group-working skills – case study analysis is often done in small groups;
- highlight tacit assumptions about organisations – in discussing cases with others you may find that you disagree: exploring this difficulty will often show that you have different underlying assumptions about people and the way they should (or do) think and behave.

Disadvantages of using cases

The benefits listed above are considerable. But if you are to learn effectively from case studies, you need to be aware that they have limitations. The first is that any case presents a partial picture. It has been 'filtered' by the author. Some things have been

12

Complexity, cases and diagrams

omitted. Others may have been given an emphasis that not all those concerned would agree with. Apart from any conscious selectivity by the author, the information on which the selection was based may have been inadequate or biased. Few interviewees, for example, will admit to their part in something which went wrong, or volunteer information which shows them in a bad light. The slants and omissions may be particularly problematic if the author wrote the case for one purpose and you are being asked to use it for another.

You therefore need to remember all the time that case studies inevitably present a false impression of being 'real'. They are very much creations and as such should be treated with caution. Any conclusions which you draw about 'the world' based on such case studies should be regarded as provisional, to be confirmed by other sources before you trust them. (This caution does not, of course, apply to the analytical, interpersonal and presentational skills which you practise in the course of your work on the case.)

It is worth pointing out that similar cautions apply to computer-based 'business games', which are a sort of interactive case study. Here the outcomes of any decisions you might take will reflect the particular model of organisational functioning espoused by the game's author and built into the computer model. Although many of these authors are experienced managers, and familiar with the theories you are being taught, this is not always the case. Thus although what you learn from the process of taking part will be valid, what you learn from the results of your decisions may not be!

Approaching case study analysis

Many students find being given a case to work on a daunting experience. Sometimes the difficulties encountered mean that they fail to learn as much from the process as they might. Difficulties include deciding what exactly you are meant to be doing, getting the group to work together effectively, coping with time pressures, sorting out a mass of information and structuring it in some way that makes sense. It may also be difficult to draw conclusions from the information and to communicate these via a written report or oral presentation. Coping with, and learning from, the experience of realising that other groups have done better than you is a further challenge. Practically all the skills covered thus far will help you work on cases, and group work on case studies will itself develop those skills further. What has already been covered implies a sensible way of approaching case studies. You need to go through the following stages.

For effective case analysis:
■ clarify and agree objectives
■ manage the process to
  – encourage contributions
  – sustain motivation
■ manage the task by
  – apportioning work
  – coordinating effort
  – monitoring progress.

Clarifying objectives

Case studies are often presented on a 'here it is – get on with it' basis. The first time you encounter a case presented in this way, you may feel totally bemused by the increased responsibility for your own learning. If your tutor has told you little about why you are studying the case, or what you are meant to achieve, you may not know where to start.

When this happens, groups often talk for a long time without really feeling they are getting anywhere. To avoid lengthy and unfocused discussion, you need to be sure that everyone in the group agrees on the objective of the exercise. If it becomes clear that you cannot agree, or that you are all similarly confused, seek help from your tutor. Without clear and agreed objectives you are likely to learn nothing (except the impossibility of getting anywhere without clear and agreed objectives . . .). You need to know what sort of output is required, and when it is required. If you are acting in the role of 'consultants', you need to know who within the case study is your notional client.

Working as a group

→ Ch 10 If the group is newly formed for the purpose of the case, you can expect to go through the stages of group formation described in Chapter 10. Groups working on case studies under pressure will experience many aspects of group behaviour, so it would help to re-read that chapter before you first tackle group-based case work. If the group is to be effective, you will need to ensure that the group *process* is managed so that everyone feels they can contribute and they remain fully committed to the task. In particular, disagreements need to be treated as valuable and their roots explored as a potential source of valuable insights into the scenario. If not this potential benefit will be lost, and disagreements may seriously detract from the motivation of group members. At worst, the group will disintegrate.

The group *task* will also need to be managed so that members make a maximal contribution. Some of the information searching and sorting may need to be split between subgroups to save time. The efforts of such subgroups will need to be coordinated. Time management will be a constant problem and there will probably be a need for frequent reviews of progress and adjusting ways of working in the light of this. Where different group members have different skills, the group may want to split responsibilities in a way that exploits their strengths.

Analysing a complex situation

Case studies typically provide you with an over-abundance of 'information'. Not all of this will be relevant or capable of reducing your uncertainty about what you want to know. Thus they give you a chance to practise turning data into information. (You will
→ Ch 13, 14 therefore need the skills addressed in Chapters 13 and 14 if the case is at all complex.)

First, however, you will want to use the approach described earlier in this chapter to impose some sort of structure on the complexity, so that you can determine what constitutes relevance. The guidelines on page 278 will help.

Communicating results

You may well be asked to make a presentation on the results of your analysis. Re-read
→ Ch 11 Chapter 11 for guidelines on this. Remember to think about your audience's perspective and starting point, to clarify what it is necessary to communicate and then do this in as straightforward a way as possible, using visual aids to reinforce your message. Remember the time you are allowed for presentation and keep within this to allow for questions. It is very easy to over-estimate what you can say in a particular time.

→ Ch 6 If results are to be communicated in the form of a written report, then re-read Chapter 6. Exactly the same communication principles apply as in a spoken presentation. You need

Guidelines for case analysis

- Explore the problem situation, using diagrams such as multiple cause and rich pictures to make sure that the whole group agrees on the 'symptoms' of a problem and on the possible features of the situation relevant to this.

- Based on your understanding of the problem situation, define the problem facing the organisation or protagonist in the case study, probably using course ideas as a framework for diagnosing the underlying causes of the 'symptoms' presented in the case.

- Decide on criteria for a 'solution', or at least for action to improve the situation – here you will need to relate back to the client or protagonist and their objectives and constraints as described in the case or provided by your tutor.

→ Ch 15
- Generate alternatives for action – here you will often find it useful to try some of the creativity techniques you will meet in Chapter 15, although sometimes once you have diagnosed the underlying problem correctly the type of action needed will become fairly obvious.

- Evaluate options by exploring what it would take to implement them, the effects they would be likely to have and checking how well they score against your criteria for a solution.

- Design an implementation strategy (if this is part of your brief) which will meet the needs of the client/protagonist, which will be feasible in cost and other terms and which will be acceptable to other stakeholders in the situation.

(A case is available on the website for practice.)

to have clear in your own mind what you aim to communicate and the perspective of those with whom you are communicating. You need clarity in the way in which you write and to use diagrams and tables to support your writing. This is easy to say, but far from easy to do, until you have had a lot of practice!

Exploiting learning opportunities

You can see from the above that you will need to use almost all your transferable skills to do a good group analysis of a case study. Similarly, the situation allows you a chance to develop these skills, provided that the necessary conditions for learning, namely feedback and reflection, are present. It is worth gaining your group's agreement to a secondary set of objectives, those concerning learning, and to a way of progressing them. You will also need to be open to receiving feedback, from others in the group or the class as a whole and from your tutor. And you need to think about how you can give feedback to others in a way that will help them to learn.

For group skills, you will find it helpful to supplement your personal reflection on the effectiveness of the way you and others are working with periods of group reflection and discussion.

→ Ch 10
Use the list of group behaviours in Chapter 10 and the following list of questions to aid your reflection.

Questions to aid group reflection on process

- How well do people feel the group process is working?
- What behaviours are contributing to aspects that are going well?
- Does anyone feel they are not contributing as much as they would like?
- If yes, what is making contribution difficult for them?
- Is anyone beginning to feel reduced commitment to the task?
- If yes, can they pinpoint the start of this feeling, and the reasons?
- What is sustaining this feeling?
- Has there been any conflict?
- If yes, what was the source of this (e.g. different values or assumptions)?
- How has any conflict been handled?
- Is anyone talking more than their fair share?
- If yes, why do they think they are doing this?
- How do others feel about this?
- What things could the group do differently to improve process in future?

(A web version is available to allow use after each session.)

These process-reflection periods can also be used to take stock of how the task is progressing. Are you managing time effectively? Is everyone happy with the way work is allocated and the methods you are adopting? If things are not going well, *why* are they not going well? Your tutor may be able to help here, if you cannot work out the answers within the group. Ask for assistance on this if you need it.

It is important to take advantage of feedback opportunities such as the above *during* your work on the case. It is easier to learn from the experience while the process and management issues are 'live' than when the detail has been forgotten. It is equally important to take advantage of feedback when you present your results. All too often the competitive nature of presentations by a group to the class as a whole means that 'winning' or justifying 'losing' takes precedence over learning.

If you feel that your group has done well in some way – perhaps because those presenting on behalf of the group are good at this – there is a strong tendency to sit back and congratulate yourselves on success. You may talk about the shortcomings of less successful groups. While it is great to celebrate when things have gone well, you still need to identify the particular aspects that contributed – *why* were you successful? And harder, you still need to think about those aspects where there was still room for improvement, and why. Maybe it was a brilliant presentation, but actually your analysis failed to identify one or two key points that other groups addressed. Why was your analysis not so rigorous? It is much easier to feel smug than to admit to areas of improvement, yet you will learn far less if you do not explore these slightly less comfortable aspects.

If you feel that you have done really badly, there is an even stronger tendency to avoid constructive reflection on your performance. You may scapegoat a group member for having done a bad job presenting or having been disruptive in the group. You may blame the tutor for not having briefed you well enough or helped you out when you were having problems. Or you may cling on to the belief that your work was excellent even if others did not recognise this. However you choose to escape the reality of having done less well than others, the result will be the same – you will fail to learn from the experience and will do no better next time. Nor will you be developing the transferable skills that will serve you well when you start to work.

> It is important therefore to see failure as the richest learning opportunity of all. Mine it for all the lessons it offers with respect to both group processes and the task on which the group was engaged. Learning from doing badly is one of the most useful skills you can develop. Most organisations will tolerate you making a mistake – provided you make it only once!

Failure is a great learning opportunity.

Absolutely the worst sort of colleague is someone who is never wrong. I once had someone like this working for me. He made many mistakes and put a huge amount of effort into covering them up: far more effort than it would have taken to learn to do things properly. Worse, because he was always telling me that things were going well and even fabricating evidence to that effect, I could not take action to avert disaster. He was never going to learn, because he was not open to recognising that there needed to be a change. And as his manager, responsible for the overall job, I was close to a nervous breakdown by the time he was replaced.

ACTIVITY 12.4

Start a section of your file for case study learning, and develop the habit of writing a 'lessons learned' entry for your file after every case you work on. Even if the group does not want to evaluate what happened, you should reflect carefully on your own experience to make sure that you gain what you can from it. Link this to your initial SWOT and any action plans you have made for improving your team-working skills. If preparing an 'exhibit' of your team skills, your reflections and the output of your work – written report, presentation notes or other supporting evidence – can be used to help show that you have the skills in question.

Case-based assignments

Although a major use of cases is for group discussion, you may also find them used as the basis for individual written assignments. If so, you need to draw on both the assessment guidelines in Chapter 8 and the suggestions for group case discussion given earlier. The following guidelines are suggested for cases where there is evidence of a problem and you are asked to analyse the situation and make recommendations.

→ Ch 8

This chapter has looked at both rational thinking and its application to case analysis, but has emphasised the limitations of pure rationality. Mitroff and Linstone (1993) similarly see a real danger in believing in your models – conscious or unconscious. They

Guidelines for case-based assignments

- Read the question carefully, identifying *all* the elements in what it is you are being asked to do.
- Scan the case with the question in mind, highlighting relevant issues or information.
- Note down as many potentially relevant course concepts as you can – aim for as long a list as possible at this stage.
- Read the case again more carefully, concepts in mind, trying to identify the *evidence* of a problem.
- Draft a brief description of key features in the problem situation – it may help to include a relationship diagram or rich picture. Aim to make clear the *evidence* for the problem and its *significance* (cost, potential for future disaster, etc.). Use course ideas in the description where appropriate (e.g. declining market share, high labour turnover).
- Clarify key contextual factors – the relevant factors within and outside the organisation that may contribute to or constrain the situation.
- Diagnose *causes* of problems using course concepts and diagrams to help you understand how the problem situation arose, and what is sustaining it. Be alert to interrelationships between factors – how policy relates to strategy (e.g. how does reward structure relate to required behaviour, how does the marketing mix relate to changing factors in the competitive environment?).
- Draft your analysis of the situation.
- Go back to the brief and contextual factors to work out criteria and constraints for a solution (e.g. time, cost).
- Draw on course concepts to draw up a range of options for improving the situation (e.g. redesigning the reward structure, moving to using distributors for your product).
- Evaluate the options against your criteria.
- Draft recommendations.
- Draft introduction.
- Redraft whole assignment in appropriate format, checking for logic, and clear arguments from evidence through diagnosis/analysis to recommendations. Check too that you have answered all parts of the question.
- List references used.
- Use spell check and grammar check.

call this 'model myopia' and suggest a number of things you can do to reduce this tendency, which you may find useful in conclusion:

- Seek the obvious, but do everything you can to challenge and even ridicule it.
- Question all constraints, the greatest of which is likely to be the mindset of the problem solvers.
- Challenge every assumption – what seems self-evident to some may be less so to others.

- Question the problem scope – what is omitted from the problem statement may be more significant than what is included.

- Ask whether you need to 'solve', 'resolve' or 'dissolve' the problem – a solution is once and for all (and usually elusive), a resolution is good enough for now, and a dissolution is a realisation that the real problem is rather different.

- Question logic itself – it is possible to be logical and *wrong*. Logical solutions to complex problems should always be challenged!

SUMMARY

This chapter has argued the following:

- A systematic approach is needed for complex problems.

- Before solutions can be considered, you need to give due attention to understanding the problem and then exploring causes.

- Diagrams, particularly relationship diagrams and rich pictures, can help you to explore important factors in a problem situation and the relationships between them.

- Complicated problems tend to have complex patterns of causation.

- In attributing causes you will be using both conscious and unconscious models – it may help to become more aware of those which are unconscious.

- Diagrams can help you to think more clearly about a situation and make any confusion or assumptions more clearly apparent to others, provided that you adopt good diagramming practice.

- Case studies are a vehicle for practising the analysis of complex problem situations (as well as for practising most of the transferable skills which are the subject of this book).

- Cases require you to apply knowledge and techniques learned in your course to quasi-real situations.

- Cases increase your awareness of the business (or other) context in which you may eventually find yourself working.

- Difficulties with case studies stem from the need to manage your own learning to a greater extent than with traditional lectures, from possible lack of clarity over objectives, from the overall complexity of the situation described and because much of the case 'information' may be over-detailed or irrelevant, while information you need may be lacking.

- Cases tackled in groups exercise both task- and process-management skills.

- Case study analysis needs to be structured by the use of relevant course concepts. A useful sequence is to explore the situation and symptoms presented, define the problem, diagnosing its causes, decide on criteria, generate options, evaluate them with respect to objectives and criteria, choose one, design an implementation strategy (if required) and communicate your findings or recommendations clearly.

Further information

- Cameron, S. and Pearce, S (1997) *Against the Grain*, Butterworth-Heinemann. This is a fairly gentle introduction to conceptual tools for complexity, particularly relevant to both this chapter and Chapter 15 on creativity, but touching on many of the other topics in the book.

- Easton, G. (1992) *Learning from Case Studies*, 2nd edn, Prentice Hall. This gives much more detailed guidance on case study analysis than is possible here.

- Kneeland, S. (1999) *Thinking Straight*, Pathways.

- Mitroff, I.I. and Linstone, H.A. (1993) *The Unbounded Mind*, Oxford University Press. This is a much more rigorous approach to changing the way you think about complex situations, again relevant both to this chapter and to Chapter 15.

- Pidd, M. (2003) *Tools for thinking: modeling in management science*, 2nd edn, Wiley.

- Senge, P.M. (1990) *The Fifth Discipline*, Century Business.

- Senior, B. (1997) *Organisational Change*, Pitman.

12

Complexity, cases and diagrams

→ 13 Obtaining data and information

Decisions should be based on valid information. This chapter looks at common methods of obtaining data, and at how to turn data into information. It will help you to use existing evidence, to know when further data are needed, and to obtain those data in an appropriate way. This will be invaluable for any project work while you are a student, but equally important when you are a manager needing to make sense of information provided by consultants, or seeking information to determine a way out of a problem situation.

Learning outcomes

This chapter looks at the idea of information itself and some common ways of obtaining it. By the end you should:

- have a clearer idea of what constitutes information
- be aware of the different sorts of data you are likely to need
- have developed a greater understanding of how to search existing literature
- know the requirements that data must meet if they are to be of use
- have an appreciation of how to go about conducting a survey
- appreciate the requirements for effective interviewing.

When faced with a complex problem at work you will almost always need to seek further information, perhaps by talking to people, looking through records or searching the Internet. Who thinks it is a problem? Why? What is it costing? What technology is available? What are competitors doing? Your course will provide you with many opportunities to develop your skills in identifying information requirements, and obtaining and using information, probably culminating in a substantial dissertation or investigative report (addressed in Chapter 16). But long before this you will need to be able to find and use information. Most essays will require you to look for further information about the topic. When you move on to more substantial investigations you will need to identify key research on the subject, refine your question, and seek the information needed to answer it. For a dissertation, the bulk of your effort will be directed towards identifying the information that you need, the best ways of generating it, and then obtaining it.

→ Ch 16

Some information will already exist and can be gathered from library, the Internet or other sources. Some you may need to gather for yourself – surveys and interviews are common approaches. But your conclusions will be wrong if your information is wrong. It is important therefore to understand the nature of information, and how to collect information that is both valid and reliable. Obtaining information costs time and/or money. So you need to decide what is important and then collect it efficiently. Computers can handle huge volumes of data, but unless you understand the difference between data and information you may drown in data, without much information emerging.

INFORMATION VERSUS DATA

The first important distinction to grasp is that between information and data. The words are often used interchangeably, but there is a crucial difference.

- **Data** (literal translation, 'things given') is used to refer to 'facts' or signals collected from the environment in some way and usually expressed in numbers.
- **Information** refers to data that have been organised in a way relevant to your needs, so that they help you to answer a question that concerns you.

> Information is data selected and organised to tell you something you need to know.

Suppose you had access to all the exam marks for all courses in every university in the country. This would be a (large) set of data. But if you wanted to choose a course for next year with a high pass rate, you would find it much more *informative* to be given only the pass rates for the courses you are considering.

This simple example shows that 'more' is not always 'better'. Selecting relevant data and then summarising (more on this in the next chapter) and organising them makes them more useful. Clearly the selection and summarising needed will depend on the question you want to answer. A Funding Council might want to compare mark distributions in particular faculties in every university it funds, so would select differently and would not summarise in terms of pass rates.

As with all other purposeful activity, when seeking information the most important thing is to establish your objectives. You must be clear just what question you are trying to answer. *Why* do you need the data? Seeking data 'because they are there' will not provide you with information. Data become information only when they are organised to help you find the answer to something which you want to know. And *what* you organise, and *how* you do this, inevitably depend on what it is that concerns you.

'Facts' was in quotes in the definition above because data can be more or less 'factual'. Before getting into arguments about what you can and cannot do to data in pursuit of information, you therefore need to be aware of the ways in which the data themselves may be unreliable. (The reliability of the conclusions you draw from data will be discussed in the next chapter.) Reliability will depend to some extent on the type of data concerned, so it is worth considering these types first.

→ Ch 14

Types of data

One important distinction is that between *primary* and *secondary* data. Primary data you collect yourself, by direct observation, measurement, interview, questionnaire or other means. Such data can be tailored to your own requirements (within resource constraints). They can be designed to give you answers to precisely the question which concerns you, using an appropriate sample. You will know the conditions under which data were collected and should have a clear idea of the ways in which inaccuracies or unreliability may have crept in. But there is a price to pay for this. Collecting your own valid data is usually costly. It is much cheaper to exploit data which have already been collected, perhaps for other purposes.

Secondary data are other people's 'facts and figures'. They include the results of surveys carried out by other people, sets of government statistics, company reports or records, reports of research in academic journals, sets of figures available on the Internet and so on. Secondary data can usually be obtained far more quickly and cheaply than primary data. But there are drawbacks. You may not know how much reliance to place on secondary data, particularly if they were collected for purposes other than your own. Even seemingly straightforward figures may be unreliable.

I once came across a set of production figures for a coalmine which were remarkably consistent. It turned out that the 'purpose' for which they were being collected, at least in the eyes of those collecting them, was to keep senior management happy. Any drop in production figures brought a visitation of senior management! So in good weeks some of the coal was stockpiled and not recorded, and in bad weeks some of this stockpile was sent off and included in the production figures. If you had been trying to explore influences of different factors (such as absence) on output, the figures would have been useless to you.

Secondary data may also relate to a different situation from the one which interests you. Suppose the most recent survey you could find of employer views on recruiting computing graduates was five years old. You might reasonably wonder about the extent to which you could draw conclusions about attitudes now. If the survey was recent but had covered only very large manufacturing organisations, while you were interested in small service organisations, you might again be worried.

→ Ch 12

The other important distinction to make is that between *quantitative* and *qualitative* data. Most people think in terms only of quantitative data, sets of numbers derived from relatively unarguable measures. But the last chapter showed that there may be many important 'soft' aspects to a problem situation. Such factors are hard or impossible to quantify. Attitudes and feelings may be important. Differences in how various groups perceive a particular situation may be crucial. Because techniques for structuring and dealing with such qualitative information are less well known than the techniques of basic parametric statistics used for quantitative data, such factors may be omitted altogether.

Data can be:
- primary or secondary
- quantitative or qualitative
- textual, nominal, ordinal, interval or ratio.

Even if qualitative factors are included, numbers may be attributed to them in various ways. These numbers are often treated, unjustifiably, as if they were normal measures. This can lead to totally false conclusions about the meaning of the data. Fortunately, software now exists that can help you with various forms of qualitative analysis. Even without this, provided you are aware of the type of data with which you are dealing and how any numbers have been attributed, you can still make considerable use of qualitative data.

This may become clearer if you consider the classifications usually applied to research data. '*Textual* data' refers to verbal description, for example quotations from an article or interview. Such data can be a splendid source of ideas. Carefully selected quotations can create a vivid picture for the person reading a report. At the start of the book I quoted a couple of friends who recruit graduates in the hope of giving you a feel for how an employer might see things. But you have no idea how much reliance to place on their opinions. My friends may be such unusual people that few other employers share their views. (Note that there *are* occasions when text itself can be the basis of a more quantitative analysis. You could count the number of times advertisements required particular qualifications, or analyse transcripts of wage negotiations to identify the commonest sequences of 'moves' made by negotiators. But this requires fairly specialist techniques and you should seek further advice if contemplating something as complex as this.)

Nominal or *categorical* data are those where some sort of categorisation or classification has been made. You might be able to group your data by country, by income or profession, by star sign, by degree subject or whatever. You could count the number in each category, for example finding out how many chemistry graduates, how many physicists, how many economists, etc. were recruited by a large multinational. For convenience you might number the categories, for example calling chemists category 1, physicists 2, and so on. But it would be a nonsense to try to relate the categories mathematically. In no sense does one physicist equal two chemists.

Ordinal or *ranked* data are those where it *is* possible to tell something about the relationship between categories from their number, but not everything. For example, a graduate recruiter might have four requirements in looking for new staff. When interviewing an applicant, the recruiter might choose to use a five-point scale, from 5 (excellent) to 1 (unacceptable), and rate each interviewee on each criterion using this. You could tell from this that on any of the scales someone ranked 5 was thought to be better than someone ranked 4. But you could not say that the difference between a 5 and a 4 was the same as between a 2 and a 1, or that a 4 was twice as good as a 2. And it would be wrong to do any arithmetic, or use any statistical techniques, on the scores which assumed that the numbers meant more than a ranking.

Interval data are those where the intervals *are* the same. On the Centigrade scale, it would take the same heat to raise a given volume of water from 5° to 10° as from 50° to 55°. But there is no real zero on this scale. It was mere convenience that dictated the freezing point of water as zero. So although you can add or subtract meaningfully on such a scale, you cannot multiply or divide. It does not make sense to say that 40° is twice as hot as 20°. Most questionnaire scores are best treated as either interval or ordinal data.

Ratio data are those where not only are intervals meaningful, but there is a real zero as well, so that you can multiply, divide and describe things in terms of ratios. If you make 40 people redundant this is twice as many as if you had got rid of 20. An inflation rate of 12 per cent is three times a rate of 4 per cent. Such statements are meaningful. Ratio data are the only ones on which you can use any mathematical technique you wish. But even then you have to choose your statistical techniques carefully, as some of these depend on the way in which the data are likely to be distributed. If values clump in different ways, many techniques will not work.

Data deficiencies

Why is it that 'facts' may be less reliable than you think? Data purport to represent reality, but reality does not usually present itself in the form of numbers. Someone has to measure something, or classify something, or record and count something. And they have to decide what to count or measure in the first place. There are all sorts of ways in which the decisions and processes which resulted in a particular set of data can seriously influence that data.

Accuracy and *reliability* of data are obviously vital. If my petrol gauge is totally erratic, then data about fuel consumption would be worth very little. If my eyesight is poor, I may misread the gauge and introduce further errors. If there is scope for judgement and I want one result more than another I may unconsciously influence my measures in the direction I want. This will lead to a biased result. You need to ask, or if possible check, that measures are *reliable*, i.e. that another observer gets the same result. Or that the same observer gets the same result if the measure is taken again. If there *are* differences, they may be random or biased.

Slight random variation is common and with luck errors will cancel each other out. But often inaccuracies are all in one direction. For example, all bad things might be recorded, but no good ones. Or one class of event may be selectively reported. For example, accidents at work are often under-reported. And although there is a system for doctors to notify any adverse reactions to drugs, these too seem to be very seriously under-reported. If there are omissions in data, you do need to check whether they are random or tend to occur in one particular direction. (In the example of 'adverse effect' reporting, this systematic bias has led to considerable delays in identifying drugs with dangerous side-effects.)

> Data need to be:
> ■ accurate
> ■ reliable
> ■ valid
> ■ consistent
> ■ representative.

Validity is also important. Do the data actually measure what they purport to measure? Can you take in-company data at face value, given the various purposes for which it might be collected? Consider the 'measure' of test performance in schools. This might be a measure of teaching effectiveness. But it might be that it reflects the intelligence or social background of the children attending that school. To take an extreme example, if children at a school for those with learning difficulties scored poorly, this would not suggest that the school was unsatisfactory. And lesser variations in ability between intakes in normal schools in different locations could still have a significant influence on test scores. If you were sufficiently unprincipled as to include work done by someone else in your portfolio, would this be valid data on *your* competence?

This issue is important in a number of situations. In surveys and interviews, it is possible to get very different answers depending on how you ask the question. Piaget's classic research offered pre-schoolers two lines of counters and asked which had 'more'. He found that, if four counters were spread out to take more space than a line of five, the children indicated that the line with four had 'more'. It was only many years later that the validity of this test as an indicator of children's concept of number was questioned. Using a line of sweets, rather than counters, and asking them to 'Choose one line' led to the infants taking the line of five every time, no matter how it was arranged!

Indicators or measures?

→ Ch 2

In fact, it is worth noting that many 'measures' are in fact 'indicators' rather than direct measures, and the issue of validity is crucial. Remember the example of 'measuring' paperwork rather than the resulting bank loans which was given in the discussion of measures for control. (Note that control is still the reason for much of the information collected in organisations.) This demonstrated how easy it can be to manipulate an indicator. A direct measure of loans awarded would have been less susceptible to manipulation.

Consistency in measures is also important if you wish to make comparisons. Sometimes data are consciously altered so that the same situation would generate different data when 'measured' again. I think it was during the 1970s/80s that the government changed the way of calculating the unemployment figures something like 19 times in many fewer years. Although good reasons were always given, each change in the way unemployment was measured resulted in a lower employment rate than the previous formula would have generated. Each of the measures was a good indicator of unemployment – in that sense it was valid. Each would have been reliable – a second Civil Servant working out a given year's figures with the prevailing formula would have come up with the same answer. But the changes in method meant that it was impossible to make meaningful comparisons between different years. This is why 'consistency' is such an important accounting principle. There may be different approaches to, say, costing or depreciation, but whichever is adopted it should be used consistently. Otherwise it is impossible for investors to compare financial results from year to year.

Representativeness is also vital. There is always a temptation to use data which are readily available, even if they are not exactly what you would want if you had endless resources. Thus I might ask friends what they think of graduate recruits. It is easy for me to do this. But my few friends are not representative of all employers and drawing sweeping conclusions from what they say would be highly dangerous. Similarly, you would not wish to predict election results from a survey of home owners in two rather exclusive neighbourhoods. It might be easy to ask them because they live near you and are likely to be at home when you knock on their doors. But their voting intentions would be a poor indication of how the population at large was likely to vote.

→ Ch 14

This may seem obvious, yet I have examined far too many student projects where conclusions about hundreds or even thousands of people the world over were drawn from perhaps as few as six interviews conducted in a single branch of one organisation!. How you interpret your data will depend heavily upon the sample from which it is drawn. This topic is dealt with in the next chapter.

From data to information

Much of the next chapter is devoted to how you turn data into information, using graphical techniques and statistics. Indeed, you might prefer to move directly to that and read it before reading the rest of this chapter, which addresses the main ways in which you are likely to obtain data. Either order will work. I have covered topics in the order you would be likely to proceed if doing a research project within an organisation: literature search, interview and questionnaire here and, in the next chapter, analysis and presentation of data. But, equally, you do need to understand how to turn data into information before you plan the data you need. Otherwise you risk collecting data that are incapable of giving you a clear answer to the question which interests you. So you really need to read both chapters before doing anything beyond the very basic. And for anything other than a small project, you probably need to find out much more about statistics and research methodologies than it is possible for this book to cover. Better still, find a good statistician to ask.

LITERATURE SEARCHES: SOURCE TYPES AND THE INTERNET

Throughout your course you are likely to be searching the literature for additional references to supplement or replace those suggested by your lecturer for an essay topic. For a substantial project or dissertation, one of your first activities will be to review the literature. Finding out what has already been done in the area which interests you will first help clarify your research question, second help you work out how to approach your own research and finally to set your research in context when writing your report. If writing a report at work for your manager you will again need to search, though perhaps with a different type of literature and with fewer search tools to help you. In all these searches you will need to act critically, to question assumptions and to evaluate and analyse the sources you find.

As with numerical data, it is possible to classify literature. Here the categories are:

- **primary sources** – the first time something appears, possibly for restricted circulation, e.g. theses, company reports, unpublished manuscripts;
- **secondary sources** – subsequent publication of primary literature, aimed at a wider audience, e.g. books, journals, some government publications;
- **tertiary sources** – search tools designed to help you find the relevant primary and secondary literature, or to provide an introduction to a topic, e.g. indexes, abstracts, bibliographies, citation indexes.

There are several problems with literature searching. These include knowing where to start, knowing where to look and knowing when to stop! A good first step is to get to know your library and the resources it offers.

Libraries contain a wide range of information sources, both traditional print-based and electronic. This information is systematically and consistently organised and there will be people there who are only too happy to explain the systems to you and help you to learn to use them to best effect. If you want a text that is not available immediately, either electronically or in hard copy in your own library, the staff can normally order it for you. While most universities have excellent libraries, for vacation essays you may want to explore your local university or public library too. You can normally obtain reader privileges in any university library if you are a student elsewhere. (This may also be helpful if a nearby university has a better library than your own institution.)

Parameters and keywords

Starting a search requires that you have at least a rough idea of the question you are investigating. (Some of your early reading may help you to rephrase or refine the question.) First, you need to set some parameters to help to define the search area. For a business studies project you would want to know:

■ the subject area, e.g. marketing, impact of legislation, motivation;

■ the language of your search. Note that American and English are different languages! Many words you might wish to use to search indexes are either completely different (car/automobile) or spelt differently (behaviour/behavior, organisation/organization). This is important in electronic searching;

■ the business sector, e.g. manufacturing, not for profit, defence;

■ how far back you want to search, e.g. five years;

■ the type of literature, e.g. refereed journals only.

Then you need to generate a list of *keywords* to drive your search. These are the words which you will look up in indexes or offer a search engine when exploring the Internet. Think about the sorts of words that authors might have used in the title of the kind of article you want to read. Tertiary sources are useful here – a recent review article on your topic can be invaluable. Tutors can help too! You can also use brainstorming (*see* Chapter 15) either individually or in a group to generate possible keywords and phrases. When you have something to start with, you can use that to generate other possible terms. Suppose you have used a keyword and found a useful-sounding item on the database. If you then display the full entry, it will normally show you 'subject headings' or 'descriptors', or some other term relating to the index terms used. Among these there may well be other potentially useful keywords.

→ Ch 15

Another good technique is to construct a relevance tree. This is a close relative of a mind map, though laid out slightly differently. At the top you write the question you are investigating. Branching down from this you write areas which seem important, then move successively downwards, teasing each apart into sub-areas. Figure 13.1 gives an example of a relevance tree. Having spread out the various topics, you can identify those which you need to search immediately, and those which you think may be the main focus of your research. Highlight each category in a different colour, or underline or asterisk – as long as you can immediately see which are the 'urgents' and which the 'importants' at a glance, it doesn't matter how you distinguish them.

As it is inevitable that you will refine your thinking when you start to read more about a subject, you may like to regard your relevance tree as a working document. Update it if you realise that there are different ways of looking at the subject, or when new issues emerge as important.

13

Obtaining data and information

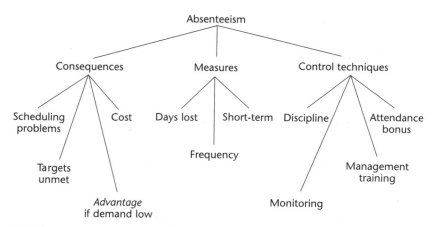

Fig. 13.1 Relevance tree for the early stages of a research project

Using tertiary sources

Indexes used to be available only in print or on microfiche. Now they tend to be on-line, or if not, on CD-ROM. For a keyword (subject or author name) the index will suggest relevant journal articles or other sources, giving you the full reference for each so that you can look it up, or request it if the library does not have it.

Abstracts are indexes which give you not only the reference, but also a brief outline of the content of the article, thus helping you decide whether or not it is relevant for your purpose. They are also available in print or electronic forms. CD-ROM versions are likely to be updated more often than print versions, with many on-line indexes and abstracts updated even more frequently, sometimes daily.

Citation indexes are particularly useful if you find a relevant article and want to know how the ideas in it have been developed subsequently. A citation index will tell you all the other articles which have referred to the original text. (The reference list at the back of the original article will tell you those earlier ones which the author deemed important, so between the two you should have quite a series of items to read.)

You will normally need to use several indexes and abstracts to ensure complete coverage. Consult a librarian. New electronic ones in particular seem to be appearing all the time.

Print indexes normally allow you to search by only a single word or phrase. This can produce an overwhelmingly long list of potentially relevant articles unless your word is newly coined. Even using abstracts to prune the list can be a daunting task.

Electronic indexes offer you the chance to be much more refined in your search, producing a more manageable list of articles, most of which should be relevant if you have chosen your words and *link terms* carefully. These link terms are derived from Boolean logic. You need to understand this and then find out how to communicate them to the particular system you are using. The terms are AND, OR and NOT (though your system could use 1 and 2 or some other way of representing these meanings). Figure 13.2 shows how these relate pictorially. Thus you could ask for 'pay AND appraisal' and

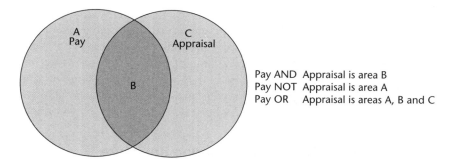

Pay AND   Appraisal is area B
Pay NOT   Appraisal is area A
Pay OR   Appraisal is areas A, B and C

Fig. 13.2 The Boolean logic of searches

the link term 'AND' (or '+' or whatever) would ensure that only references containing both keywords were offered to you. This would be a much shorter list than that generated by either 'pay' or 'appraisal' alone. Asking for 'appraisal NOT financial' would spare you hundreds of references on financial appraisal, but give you all other sorts of appraisal, while 'downsizing OR redundancy' would bring you articles on either topic. (Because there is not yet uniform acceptance of 'AND', 'NOT' and 'OR' for this purpose, you do have to check on the symbols in each index you use.) You can even look for part of a word, thus 'motiv*' might generate references on motivation, motivators, etc.

Internet searches

While indexes on CD-ROM can be invaluable, you will almost certainly want to do much of your literature searching on-line. A good on-line index is more likely to be up to date than a CD-ROM. Many indexes include abstracts. This will enable you to identify journals which look to be worth following up, whether electronically (if your library subscribes), in print (ditto) or by inter-library loan. If this has not already been covered in an introduction to your university's information services, ask your library staff to tell you which of the on-line indexes, abstract services and journals they subscribe to, and suggest those most likely to meet your purposes.

As well as indexes to academic journals there are on-line indexes to newspapers and business reports which you may find useful, together with searchable archives of newspapers. One way of exploring what is available (if you are at a UK university) is to go to the *NISS Information Gateway*: **www.niss.ac.uk/**. This will give you information about the present status of electronically available newspapers and archives (as well as links to all UK university catalogues, a business and industry database and a wide variety of other useful information). Other useful gateways were referred to in Chapter 7. Efficient general search engines such as 'Google' (**www.google.com**) are useful too. Your library staff will advise you.

→ Ch 7

On-line searching has the advantage that you can download relevant text or references directly on to your PC, rather than laboriously copying them from another source. It is important to be disciplined, however, or you could spend hours on fascinating side-tracks.

Note that, if you are searching the Internet for information, it will save time if you save your references into appropriate directories. Otherwise you may end up with a long list

13

Obtaining data and information

of HTML files which can take ages to search. Remember when saving to include the copyright statement of the web page or website and any citation instructions and to note the date on which you last visited the web page, as you need to give this in your references. Bookmark sites if you are not yet sure you will need them. Bibliographic software packages are available to help you organise a large number of references. These make the production of your final reference list a trivial task rather than the nightmare it can be if you have been less than systematic in noting your references.

Getting, reading and evaluating literature

Once you have located relevant sources, 'all' you have to do is read them and decide what they are worth in the context of your question. If your library does not have the publication in question, and it is not available electronically, you will need to ask staff to obtain it. Your library will be charged each time you do this, so in the interests of its budget, request only those items which you are pretty sure you cannot do without.

→ Ch 4   Chapter 4 suggested some ways of evaluating what you read: recency/currency, soundness of methodology, clarity/logic of arguments, adequacy of data and relevance to your particular research question will all be important. It also suggested that you choose a reading speed appropriate to your purpose. Refresh your memory on this if necessary.

Remember the need to note (whether on paper or electronically) not only full bibliographic details, but also a summary of key points of content, and verbatim extracts that are particularly apt or enlightening so that you can quote them. Note too any cross-references or other comments about the article that may make your notes more useful when you are further into your project and therefore further away from having read the original.

INTERVIEWS

One of the most popular ways of generating primary data for student projects is to conduct a series of interviews. This requires you to use the talking and listening skills
→ Ch 9   developed earlier, but you need additionally to know a little about the potential hazards of collecting data in this way.

It sounds wonderfully simple. You merely ask some questions, either standard ones or, even better, anything that on the spur of the moment you are inspired to ask. Provided these fall under a set of fairly broad headings this can be called a 'semi-structured' interview. You record the results, analyse them and you have the answer to your research question. Alas, it is rather more difficult. Although you can learn a great deal from merely talking to people, provided you listen carefully, it is difficult to put together what each person tells you and make collective sense of it. There is also a possibility that they will misunderstand your questions or you will misunderstand their answers. They may even tell you, or at least you may hear, only what you want to hear.

→ Ch 9   Skilful interviewing therefore requires that you add to your talking and listening skills certain other abilities. You need to be able to:

- formulate unambiguous questions which do not indicate, even subtly, the 'right' answer
- avoid giving any other hints as to what you want
- use a style which encourages a person to answer questions freely and to the best of their ability
- probe and clarify if the answer is not sufficiently full or clear
- record interviewees' answers accurately for subsequent analysis.

Of course, as with everything else, you also need to be absolutely clear about what it is that you want to know. And you need to have thought about the number of people to ask and how to choose them, given the question which your project is trying to answer.

Interview types

Before you can do this, you need to think about the type of interview which best suits your purpose:

- **Structured** interviews are those where you work out a set of questions before you start and ask each interviewee exactly the same questions, in the same order, and even in the same tone of voice, so as not inadvertently to bias your results.
- **Semi-structured** interviews are those where you 'know what you want to know', that is, you have a set of themes, issues or topics which you want to explore. But you 'go with the flow' to some extent, approaching these issues in an order that seems appropriate, given the way the conversation is going, dropping issues which seem inappropriate with a particular respondent and adding others which the conversation suggests may be important.
- **Unstructured** or in-depth interviews are even more informal and non-standardised. The interviewee is given free rein to talk about a topic in depth.

Different types of interview will depend both on what you are trying to find out and on where you are in your investigation. At an early stage, while your thoughts are developing, unstructured interviews are likely to be most useful in suggesting issues that seem to be important to the people that you talk to and relationships that seem to exist between these issues. Having this information could help you to formulate a set of questions for a structured interview. While you can gain strong impressions from such interviews, and they may uncover whole areas you had not seen as relevant, they are very difficult to analyse in any systematic way.

If you want to be able to describe tendencies or patterns in a group of responses, then you are likely to need a structured interview. Then you can compare the responses of different groups to the same questions and explore whether responses to one set of questions are related to responses to others. Analysis is usually easy: there is normally only a limited range of answers to any of these questions. You may be able to code answers while the person is talking. Several people can do the interviewing and their sets of answers are easily amalgamated. A structured interview is really a questionnaire which is administered by someone else. It has all the advantages of a questionnaire (see next section, where question design for either is discussed). But if you use an interview, you are more likely to get answers to *all* the questions and a higher response rate – questionnaires go into the bin all too often. Many people, for example senior managers, will agree to be interviewed, but would never complete a questionnaire.

Despite the rather cynical comment earlier, semi-structured interviews can be extremely useful. For example, if you are trying to find out *why* a structured interview gives you certain patterns, you are likely to need a semi-structured interview. Suppose you had used a questionnaire to find out how satisfied people were with their jobs and whether they had applied for jobs elsewhere. You might have found that in most departments people were satisfied, but in two they were not. In one of these unhappy departments everyone was applying for jobs elsewhere, in the other they were not. To find out both why they were unhappy and why they were behaving differently with respect to other jobs, a semi-structured interview would be useful.

Types of question

The exact way in which you phrase your question can have a significant effect on the answers you are given by the interviewee. For semi-structured and unstructured interviews you will need to rely on three main types of question: open, probing and closed.

Open

Open questions allow the interviewee to decide what it is important to include in an answer. Questions which are *too* open can produce long and sometimes irrelevant answers. 'What do you think about the recent redundancies?' might produce anything. 'What methods has your organisation used to make people redundant?' would produce a more focused answer (assuming that it was methods that interested you). 'What', 'who', 'when', 'where', 'why' and 'how' are among the words useful for open questions.

For effective interviewing:
- use active listening
- set the scene carefully
- ask simple, neutral questions
- probe if necessary
- minimise closed questions
- close the interview carefully
- record data immediately.

Closed

Closed questions are those which tend to generate a 'yes' or 'no' answer, for example: 'Were recent redundancies handled well?' This type of question might be very useful either as a starting point, or as a follow-up to clarify your understanding. 'So on balance do you think that the methods chosen were appropriate?' could be useful as a check on your understanding of part of an answer to a more open question. Use such questions sparingly, though. If you use closed questions too early you risk closing a topic before you have found out what you want. If you use them too often your interviewee will tend to give shorter and shorter answers.

Probing

Probing questions are used to explore answers in more depth. If you want to know more than the interviewee has given in an answer, you can say something like: 'That's interesting. Could you tell me more about the reasons for . . .?' or '. . . why the relationship between . . . ?' or whatever it is that you wish to be expanded. Probes are very useful if you realise that you have inadvertently asked a closed question!

Interviewing skills

Once you have selected your respondents, gained their agreement, know what you want to find out, and the sorts of questions you need to ask, there are some basic points to note. These will help you to generate valid data:

Guidelines for interviewing

- Practice active listening and observe body language.

- Manage the start of the interview very carefully – it is crucial to its success. You need to make the person feel comfortable. Thank them for their help and explain again the purpose of the interview and how long it is likely to take. You need to stress confidentiality, making clear whether anyone else will have access to the results of the interview. It usually helps to make clear that the interviewee will not be identifiable in the final report (unless of course they have agreed to be identified). You need to indicate what will happen to the results of your investigation. It is helpful, too, to give an idea of the sort of responses you want (e.g. brief or more discursive, immediate or considered). And you need to explain how you are recording answers (normally notes or tape recorder) and make sure that the person is happy with this.

- Keep questions as short as possible and as simple. If you roll three complex questions into one, it will be hard for your interviewee to make sense of what is required. It will also be hard for you to make sense of what they say! Also, if your question is rambling, your respondents will tend to follow your lead and speak at great length without saying very much. This makes both recording and analysis difficult.

- Use language that your interviewee will understand. It is pointless to use jargon or over-intellectual language with people who are unused to such words.

- Ask neutral questions. It is extremely easy to bias answers by using negatively or positively loaded words in describing some of the options.

- Use closed questions sparingly, only when you mean to.

- Start with questions that the interviewee will find easy, interesting and non-threatening. This will allow them to settle and to feel comfortable with you. Later in the interview you can ask more challenging questions, or touch on sensitive issues, with a good chance of getting a valid response. The same questions, early in an interview, might elicit very little.

- Conclude by thanking the interviewee and giving them the chance to raise any concerns they may have as a result of the interview.

- Record your data as soon as possible after the interview. If you have made notes, sort them out and do any necessary classifying of responses while the interview is still fresh. If you are tape recording, do not let the tapes accumulate. Transcribing takes ages and is best done as you go along in most cases. You may wish to modify later interviews in the light of early responses, so thinking immediately you finish about how the interview has gone and any problems and new thoughts that it prompted is important, particularly at the start of your interviewing.

(This is available on the website.)

FOCUS GROUPS

Thus far the discussion has covered interviews with individuals. But you may want to gather information from a group of people. If so, it can be helpful to use focus groups. This is a technique widely used by organisations, particularly as a way of finding out what is important to customers or potential customers.

To hold a focus group you assemble a small group (usually 6–10 people) whose views are relevant to your research. The group is asked to discuss your chosen topic. The aim is to allow group members to develop their own ideas through unstructured interaction. This can throw up ideas that the research has not considered, and show that other issues are more, or less, important than anticipated.

As the researcher, you facilitate the group. This should be a fairly passive role once the topic has been introduced. You are trying merely to encourage interaction within the group, not to steer it. If the discussion flags you can ask supplementary questions such as 'What about . . .?' If one person dominates you may need to gently subdue them. If some people do not contribute you may need to encourage them. If the discussion veers totally off the point you may need to gently redirect it. You need to avoid steering the discussion too firmly because this will reduce your chances of finding out anything that you do not already know. In industry, focus groups are often run by trained psychologists, but the groups skills you developed in Chapter 10 should help you to make a reasonable job of it.

→ Ch 10

You will need to keep a careful record of the discussion. This can be video- or audio-taped for later analysis. Alternatively, or additionally, notes are taken. If at all possible, find someone to help you with this. It is very hard to take adequate notes while doing a good job of facilitation.

Focus groups can be extremely useful at the start of a project, when you are trying to identify important issues or research questions. But they have the same drawback as informal interviews. The sample is likely to be too small for reliable conclusions. The process of making sense of what was said is also highly subjective, with the researcher struggling to extract meaning from a fairly free-ranging discussion. You will normally need to supplement focus group findings with a more systematic investigation.

QUESTIONNAIRES

Surveys requiring respondents to complete a questionnaire are a popular way of collecting information for all sorts of purposes. You may have received various 'market research' questionnaires through the post or been sent a questionnaire after you bought something or made use of a service. Although you can include open-ended questions on a questionnaire, the fact that you cannot probe or clarify responses can make analysis of responses to these quite difficult. The main strength of questionnaires is that they allow you to identify and describe the extent of variation in answers on particular topics and to look for relationships between positions on one set of questions and positions on another. Thus you could use a survey to establish factual things like the educational qualifications of users of a particular sports facility, or frequency of usage, or attitudinal aspects such as their satisfaction with the various sports on offer. You could also look for relationships, such as between level of education and preferred sport and/or satisfaction levels.

Questionnaire design is crucial, particularly if the respondents are supposed to fill in the questionnaire themselves. (Sometimes questionnaires are administered over the phone or face to face in a structured interview.) You need to have a very clear idea of what you need to know, to ask it in a totally unambiguous way and to make clear how the respondent is to reply.

ACTIVITY 13.1

Imagine that you work in a medical centre and you want to collect information from patients on their alcohol usage. Think about the way in which you and people you know might respond to the following questions and how much information this is likely to give the practice. If possible, ask a few people, using only one of the questions below, followed by informal discussion to check what it means, then ask others all three, in the order shown.

A   Does alcohol play a part in your life?   _____

B   Would you describe yourself as a light, moderate or heavy drinker?   _____

C   How many drinks do you have a week on average? (count a half pint of beer, one glass of wine or a single of spirits as '1')

  0–1 ☐   2–3 ☐   4–7 ☐   8–14 ☐   15–21 ☐   22–35 ☐   36–42 ☐   43+ ☐

You need to be very careful in interpreting answers, as your follow-up discussion may have shown. Question A (taken from a real questionnaire) presumably elicited both 'yes' and 'no' from people with very similar levels of drinking. B may well have elicited some 'light' responses from people who consume rather more than those who see themselves as 'moderate' drinkers. The range of possible drinking levels given in C may make it easier for people to admit to drinking, say, 22 units than if the scale had stopped at 22+, as it makes them appear well within the range on offer, rather than at the extreme. For areas that are often under-reported, like drinking and smoking levels, this may be an important consideration.

You can perhaps see from this why it is important to pilot a questionnaire with a small number of people – try it out and then look at the answers that are given. Do some questions produce the same answer from everybody? If so, they may not be generating much information. Do some questions get omitted? This may be because people do not realise that they must turn the page, or because the question looks like part of the instruction, or because it is not clear what the question means or how to answer it. Talk to those who filled out the questionnaire about whether they had difficulty with any of the questions and probe the meaning of their answers to check that you will be interpreting them correctly. Check, too, that your layout and the way the questions are to be answered make it as easy as possible to analyse the results.

Response rates

It is really important to get a reasonable response rate. What constitutes reasonable will depend on the size of your sample, the complexity of the analysis you want to do and the randomness or otherwise of the 'sample within a sample', those people who *do* fill in the questionnaire.

ACTIVITY 13.2

Suppose that you send a questionnaire to 100 people. You write a pleasant covering letter, explaining what you are doing and why, as well as why their participation is important and that responses will be treated confidentially, but you receive only ten replies.

Think of reasons for people not replying, what this means about the usefulness of the ten you get back and how you might be able to increase the response rate. If possible, discuss this in a group, drawing on your own responses to questionnaires you have received.

You probably came up with reasons such as 'questionnaire looked too long and time consuming', 'first few questions were difficult/intrusive/boring/incomprehensible so didn't go further', 'why should I pay for a stamp to give them information?', 'meant to but somehow didn't get around to it' and so on. Increasing response rate will depend on the reasons – a well-designed, appealing questionnaire will address the first two, an s.a.e. the third. Small incentives such as a prize for the lucky reply and a better prize if the questionnaire is returned within seven days will address two reasons and reminders are also helpful.

It is vital that you *do* ensure a better response rate than this. If you send out 100 questionnaires and get 10 back, you will have very little data to analyse. Worse, you will not know if the 10 were reasonably typical of the 100, or the only 10 who were different in some significant way. For example it might be that the only people who reply to a questionnaire about the quality of nursing care during a recent hospital stay are the tiny minority who had a really bad experience and are still angry enough to want to tell someone about this when the questionnaire arrives. If you assumed they were typical, you could be seriously misled about the quality of care that most patients at the hospital receive.

If you use questionnaires, you are facing a minefield. Plan to spend some time reading about questionnaire design and sampling, or consult an expert, before designing your questionnaire, and never use a questionnaire without first piloting it. Try it out on several people and afterwards ask them to interpret their questions, and comment on any uncertainties or difficulties they had in answering.

DEVELOPING YOUR INFORMATION-GATHERING SKILLS

Although you will probably not need to do a major research project until well into your degree programme, you can be starting to develop the necessary skills long before then. Not only will the information you gather be useful in its own right, but it will mean that, when you do face the challenge of a project, you will approach the information gathering in a more effective way than might otherwise have been the case.

There are two main approaches and you might wish to adopt both. The first requires you to treat information gathering as a series of discrete skills to be developed. Thus you might consider your familiarity with the resources in your university library and how to access them, and seek help in mastering any aspects in which you do not yet feel confident. You could practise searching for information on the Internet. You could set up a series of practice interviews and work with others to design a questionnaire, pilot and refine it and administer it. All these are extremely worthwhile activities. Any or all could constitute exhibits demonstrating 'managing learning' for your portfolio.

→ Ch 3 The second approach involves adopting the 'reflective practitioner' approach outlined in Chapter 3 and making use of the learning cycle model. This means that first you need to be alert to information and its uses – by now you should be a little more so. You then need to think about situations in which you will need actively to seek and use information. Obviously, any project in your degree course is likely to fall into this category. But before this, essays and other course work offer opportunities. And courses may have other smaller-scale investigations which you are required to carry out. Your life will also offer occasions when by seeking information you can take a better decision or action. Your work on specific skills could therefore be supplemented by seeing all such situations in informational terms and using at least some of the ideas here as a framework for finding that information.

Suppose that you want to plan a holiday. You could start by clarifying your objectives for the holiday – an objectives tree could be useful here. Once objectives are established, it will be easier to formulate the question(s) your information needs to answer. The first decisions might be whom to go with and where to go. But even if both of these are already decided, there will still be many questions to answer before you can buy your tickets and book accommodation. Construct a relevance tree and use this to prioritise the information search areas and plan your data search. This might involve finding information about travel routes, exchange rates, local costs, sights (and sites) to visit, medical factors and so on. You might also need to research sources of funding. Information sources might include the library, the Internet, travel agents, past travellers, embassies, friends . . . . Methods might include literature search, semi-structured interviews, writing letters or telephoning people. The information obtained would then need to be organised in a way which makes it easier to take the decision.

ACTIVITY 13.3

Use the following prompts to assess your information-gathering skills. Score 5 if an item is completely true, 4 if it is more true than untrue, 3 if it is somewhere in the middle, 2 if more or less untrue, 1 if totally untrue.

I have explored the library and know how to find any book or journal I need   _____

I know how to access electronic journals subscribed to by the library   _____

I can easily locate sources in the library's catalogue using keywords   _____

I am comfortable using indexes, abstracts and citation indices to identify potential sources   _____

I can easily refine my search to identify only those items most likely to be relevant   _____

I am comfortable with Google® and at least two other good search engines, and can locate relevant sites reasonably efficiently   _____

I have experimented with at least three information gateways relevant to my subject, and now know their strengths and weaknesses   _____

I routinely record and organise my references and can easily locate references or notes on something I have read   _____

I bookmark gateways and other useful sites so that they are easy to return to   _____

I would never use a questionnaire without piloting it to make sure that my intended recipients understood the questions and I understood the meaning of their answers   _____

I would always decide on what the minimum acceptable response rate was before sending out a questionnaire, and do all I could to get maximum returns   _____

I am careful never to draw conclusions beyond those justified by the data   _____

Total   _____

On most of the previous skills assessments a perfect score would suggest optimisim or bending the truth. Here you really should be aiming for a perfect 60 by the end of your degree. Start to plan now to reach that point.

ACTIVITY 13.4

This is an important area, and therefore also a good one to be able to demonstrate if you are building a portfolio. To generate a low-level exhibit, take a simple project – for example finding a holiday job, or deciding on whether to purchase your own PC and if so which one, or whether to do a Master's degree. The topic should be of real interest to you and require a reasonable amount of information in order to take a decision or some action. Clarify your 'research' question, plan the information needed and the best means of obtaining it, obtain the information and take a decision. If you document all of this, commenting on the usefulness of various methods, any possible bias, 'cost' (time and money) of accessing the information and usefulness of what you obtain, you will have a potentially useful exhibit in this area.

You may want, later, to reinforce this exhibit by drawing upon the information skills demonstrated in a final project or dissertation.

SUMMARY

This chapter has argued the following:

■ Data are measures or indicators of some kind derived from a situation. They may be more or less selective, accurate, reliable and valid.

■ Data may be primary or secondary, quantitative or qualitative, textual, nominal, ordinal or ratio. In interpreting data it is important to understand their characteristics.

■ When data are organised in a way that is relevant to a question that concerns you, they become information. In order to obtain useful information, you need to be clear about your objectives and the questions which you are trying to answer.

■ Many quests for information will start with a literature search, using keywords.

■ In generating your own primary data, you may need to use focus groups, questionnaires and interviews; whichever you use, clear communication is crucial, question formulation is critical and it is important to avoid bias.

■ Further reading will be necessary if you wish to rely heavily on either questionnaires or interviews for a major project.

Further information

■ Gill, J. and Johnson, P. (1997) *Research Methods for Managers*, 2nd edn, Paul Chapman Publishing.

■ Jankovicz, A.D. (2000) *Business Research Projects*, 3rd edn, Business Press. This gives excellent practical guidance on projects from undergraduate through to Master's level.

■ Saunders, M., Lewis, P. and Thornhill, A. (2003) *Research Methods for Business Students*, 3rd edn, Financial Times Prentice Hall. This contains considerably more detail on the topics covered here.

■ **www.bized.ac.uk** (useful gateway linking management students and teachers with relevant information providers)

13

Obtaining data and information

- **www.dogpile.co.uk** (useful meta-search engine)
- **www.google.com** (excellent general search engine)
- **www.niss.ac.uk/liss/opacs** (links to UK online public access (library) catalogue)
- **www.ukonline.gov.uk** (searches UK government and related websites)
- **www.sosig.ac.uk/roads/subjectlisting/worldcat/busgen** (links to UK industrial and business sites.)

→ 14 Making sense of data

Raw data are seldom informative. They need interpretation. The interpretation needs to be communicated. This chapter looks at ways of summarising and communicating data. It is all too easy to draw invalid conclusions from seemingly clear sets of figures. A vast range of statistical techniques exists to prevent this. While this chapter can do no more than introduce the basics of statistics, it should help you avoid the dangers of misunderstanding the significance of your results. Such misunderstandings could cause you to fail your dissertation. In an organisation they could prove very expensive indeed.

Learning outcomes

By the end of this chapter you should:

- be able to show sets of figures graphically, interpret graphs and use them to estimate future values
- see how graphs can help you to answer questions
- understand how calculus can help you to solve problems
- be able to summarise sets of figures in terms of central tendency and range
- understand what is meant by probability and significance levels
- appreciate how significance will be linked to the size and distribution of your sample of observations.

Transforming data into information is a delicate art. It is not easy to interpret data and communicate their meaning to others. You may need to reorganise data so that patterns become clear. You need to be able to interpret the implications of these patterns and judge how much reliance to place on any conclusions you draw. You therefore need an understanding of statistical techniques and of the ideas about probability on which they are based. Sadly, such understanding is fairly rare! And its absence leads to flawed decisions. A single chapter cannot turn you into a statistician, but it can give you an appreciation of what statistical techniques can achieve. This should help you with planning any student projects. Perhaps more importantly it will help you to exploit the 'information' with which you are likely to be deluged in any job, and to save you from being led astray by it.

Before introducing you to the basics of statistics the chapter introduces a further area of mathematics, the calculus. You may already know this, or may not need it – in either case, skip it. But I have known not a few students come to grief because a calculus course was taught assuming far more than they knew, making it impossible for them to pass this compulsory subject. In case this is your situation, or you are simply interested in how differential equations can be an aid to answering questions involving numbers and equations, then work through this part of the chapter. In the process you will be able to revise some of the techniques introduced in Chapter 5.

→ Ch 5

'LIES, DAMNED LIES AND STATISTICS'

Statistics is all about making data informative. The quotation in the heading above (attributed to Disraeli) reflects an ignorance of statistics that appears to be as widespread today as it was a century ago. For example, the *Western Daily Press* once claimed that motorists were much less likely to have a car stolen in Bristol than elsewhere because 'New figures from the AA show that, nationally, one car is stolen every 79 seconds, while the figure for Bristol is one car every 35 minutes'! Similar ignorance allowed a national paper to claim that 20 per cent of the population died each year from smoking-related diseases.

This ignorance is often dangerous rather than amusing. Consider the high profile case some years ago of a man accused of murdering his wife. It emerged that the accused had regularly beaten his wife. His defence team presented the jury with the 'statistic' that only 1 in 1000 wife beaters go on to kill their wives. The jury presumably drew the obvious conclusion – that the evidence of wife beating was not really relevant. Yet what was not relevant was that particular 'statistic' – or at least, it was only relevant if combined with information about the chance of the wife being murdered at all and the chances that in any given year a husband will kill his wife. If you use these to work out the chance of a wife beater being guilty of his wife's murder, you find that it is roughly 50:50, significantly higher than the probability of a non-violent husband being responsible.

The problem of knowing what reliance to place on evidence is not limited to the legal profession. You will need to assess all sorts of evidence throughout your life. Whether you have done a lab experiment, conducted a series of structured interviews or are reading a report done for your company by a consultant, you need to know what conclusions you can safely draw from the data. The ability to make sense of numbers and to draw valid conclusions from them is vital in all areas of research and in virtually all organisations. In particular, many organisations are now involved in risk management, for which an understanding of probability is essential.

Because we are amazingly bad at making such judgements without help, a basic understanding of how statistical techniques can be used for assessing significance is invaluable. Such understanding needs to encompass the ideas of sampling, distributions and probability which underlie the techniques, as well as more basic ideas about how to represent numbers in a way that is more accessible than the figures themselves. And while we are looking at graphical representations, we can usefully take a detour into using graphs of equations to solve problems.

DRAWING AND USING GRAPHS

Turning numbers into pictures can make them much easier to grasp. A few people can look at a page covered with rows and rows of figures and instantly grasp what these numbers mean. Most people find it far easier to extract the sense from numbers if they are represented in the form of pictures. Different sorts of graphical representation are appropriate for different sorts of figures. You will probably remember one form, called a graph, from school.

Plotting graphs

The graphs you remember were probably those that showed the relationship between two variables, typically x and y. You drew two axes at right angles. The vertical line you called the y axis, the horizontal x (x is a/cross). Both had numbers along them. The value of y depended on the value of x. You probably had an equation of the form $y =$ (something)x + (something). Perhaps there was a (something)x^2 term as well. For each of the numbers along the x scale you worked out the value of y and put a dot at that height above the x. When you had all the dots, you joined them to form your graph.

Of course, you do not have to have an equation. You can merely observe values of y and plot them against the appropriate x. Figure 14.1 shows such an example, where production is plotted year on year for two factories. You can see that it is easy to spot trends and to make comparisons, whereas if you had been presented, say, with quarterly figures for each factory, each reflecting a degree of seasonal variations from quarter to quarter, it might have been much more difficult.

The graph also allows you to make tentative predictions. Where you have a clear trend, as in both these lines, it is a fair bet that the line will continue, so you could guess at,

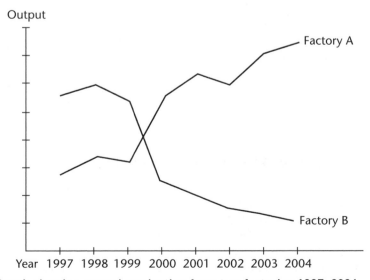

Fig. 14.1 Graph showing annual production from two factories 1997–2004

14

Making sense of data

say, the next two years' output from each factory and use these to inform recruitment strategy or marketing plans. Of course, your estimates would be on an 'other things being equal' basis and other things are not always equal. Clearly, they were not in 2000. But in the absence of any other information, these estimates might be a better basis for planning than assuming that production would stabilise at present values.

Estimating will be easier if the trend is fairly clear. If the line is jumping around somewhat it will be difficult to say exactly where it will end up next. But if there is an underlying trend, then you may still be able to use the graph to get an idea of the area within which future points are likely to lie.

TEST EXERCISE 14.1

Plot graphs of the following sets of figures, leaving room for two more points on the x axis:

(a)

Year	1995	1996	1997	1998	1999	2000	2001	2002	2003	2004
Applicants accepted on to business and management degrees	4800	5000	6000	7500	9000	11 000	11 500	12 500	14 000	15 500

(b)

Year	1990	1991	1992	1993	1994
Rabies cases (Germany)	5500	3800	1500	800	1400

Add your estimated next two points on the graphs you have drawn. (Before looking at the answer you might like to practise using Excel to generate the two graphs.)

In the above exercise you should have realised that it is not always necessary to have your axes meet at the zero point on each scale. If the variation is all within a certain band, then you will not see it very clearly if that band takes up only a tiny fraction of your scale. The line will look almost flat. Sometimes this could be the best way of showing it. Any variations might be insignificant, perhaps the result of measurement errors. It would be wrong to make them look important by stretching the scale. But in other cases the variations might be important. If you were measuring plant growth, small variations in temperature might be crucial and to use a scale starting from zero might be totally inappropriate. You need to think carefully about your axes, about where they cross and where they end in terms of the scale with which you label them, if the meaning of the figures which the graph represents is to be clear. In both cases above there is no data before a certain point, so no need to go back to the year zero, whenever you deem that to be.

Using graphs to answer questions

There are many things you can do with graphs apart from just looking at them for patterns. For example, you can work out from a graph of observations the equation which best represents the relationship between the two variables observed. And you can use graphs of three or more sets of relationships to work out the best values of each of the variables used, if you want to solve a problem such as the best mix of products for a factory where each product has different labour and materials demands, say, and the resources are finite.

Cartoon by Neill Cameron, www.planetdumbass.co.uk

14

Making sense of data

One example of the use of graphs is to find the 'breakeven' point for production. Suppose that you have information about a planned product. First, you know what it will cost to produce. In the simplest case, there will be some costs which you will incur regardless of the number you produce – the fixed costs. These might be buying the machine to do it and hiring an operator for it. Other costs, such as those for materials, will depend on the volume you produce – the variable costs. What you get back will depend on how many products you sell and the price. Assume that you know what you can charge. What will vary is the volume of sales. Managers like to know how many units they need to produce before they will start to make a profit. This is called the breakeven point.

If you plot the costs on one graph, with money on the y axis and number of units on the x axis, and draw another line showing the income to be derived, assuming that you sell this number of products, you should find that (provided the price you plan to charge is greater than the variable cost) the two lines will cross at some point. Figure 14.2 gives an example of a simple breakeven chart, with fixed costs of F. The number

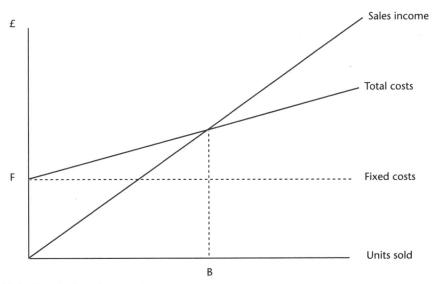

Fig. 14.2 Simple breakeven chart

of units where the two lines cross (*B*) is the breakeven point. If you sell less than this you will lose money. Every sale beyond this will result in profit. You are likely to make a number of dubious assumptions in drawing the graph, not least about the nature of costs – for example once you go into overtime, variable costs are likely to increase – so it needs to be treated with caution. And it will not tell you anything about what price you should charge to maximise returns. Too high a price and very few people may buy your product. Indeed, it will not tell you how many you can sell at *any* price. But it provides a simple example of how you can find answers to questions by drawing graphs, and of how you can use graphs to make a point. Explaining the idea of breakeven to someone is much easier if you show them the graph.

TEST EXERCISE 14.2

Fixed costs are £500. Variable costs are £1 per unit. Price intended is £2 per unit. Find the breakeven point by drawing a graph. Repeat the exercise for a price of £4 per unit.

In Test exercise 14.2 you could have expressed the costs and income as equations. Call the total cost *C*, the fixed cost *F* and the variable cost *V* per unit. Call the income *I* and the price *P* per unit. Then for *x* units:

$$C = F + Vx \text{ and}$$

$$I = Px$$

TEST EXERCISE 14.3

As revision, express the value of *x* at which the lines cross, *B* on your graph, in terms of *F*, *V* and *P*.

The lines in Figure 14.2 are straight, because neither equation has powers of *x* in it (apart from the power 1). If it had x^2, or a higher power, the line would be curved. For example, the materials cost of producing a flat, square product would depend on the square of the length of one side. Draw a graph of this, for practice. Sometimes a curve can rise very steeply indeed – the average waiting time in a simple queue will rise dramatically with increases in the rate at which people are joining. (You will have experienced this sort of effect on motorways when there is a reduction in the number of lanes.) Figure 14.3 shows such a situation.

Other relationships will show an increase then a decrease. One typical example is the relationship between stress levels and performance. At first, an increase in stress helps you to perform better. But eventually stress levels are such that you start to perform less well with every increase until you become totally useless. Figure 14.4 shows an example.

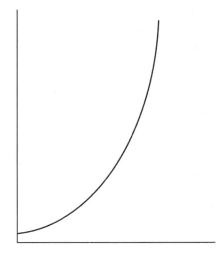

Fig. 14.3 A rapidly increasing curve

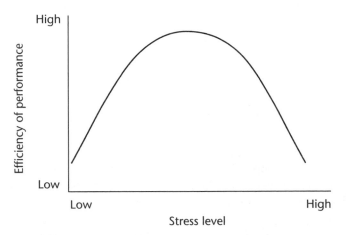

Fig. 14.4 Relationship between stress levels and performance

CALCULUS

There is one further area of mathematics you are likely to need: calculus. If you are seriously unhappy about dealing with numbers and equations, and do not need it, skip it. If you are only slightly uneasy, it may be worth proceeding with it both because it is useful in its own right and because it offers useful revision of some of your earlier number work. It isn't an easy area, but it is the only difficult part of this chapter. The remaining sections are much easier.

If you can plot observed values of variables and then see the shape of the curve which emerges, you can work out the equation of a line which is close to that observed.

Sometimes you will know the equation without needing to draw the curve. Then the *equation*, rather than the plotted curve, can be used to answer certain questions. Two important ones you are likely to ask are:

■ What is the rate at which a value is changing at a certain point?

■ At what point on the curve is a value highest (or lowest)?

For straight lines, the rate of change is constant – for each unit across, the line will go up by the same amount. For curved lines, the rate will be changing all the time. Note though that if you look at shorter and shorter parts of the curve, you will get closer and closer to a straight line. When the part is infinitely small, you will have the rate of change at that point. If you extend this line you can see what that is. This line is the *tangent* of the curve, the line which touches the curve at only one point. Figure 14.5 shows such a tangent.

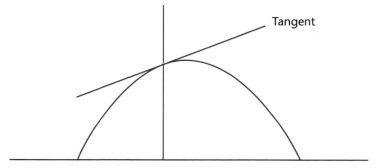

Fig. 14.5 A tangent to a curve

At the optimal point on the stress curve, where performance is highest, the tangent is flat – it has a slope of zero. This would also be the case for a tangent to a U-shaped curve at its *lowest* point. This suggests that, by looking for points at which the rate of change is zero, we can find the answer to the second question.

Doing all this by eye is somewhat imprecise. Calculus, which you may have encountered at school, gives you some rules for working out exact values. You may well be spared the calculus – you can survive as a manager in most situations without it. But if you *are* required to learn it, and find it horrific, or are expected to know it already and have forgotten, just remember that one of its main components, *differentiation*, is about finding rates of change to curves as described above. Use the 'idiot's guide' opposite to work things out and you should not find it too bad.

Idiot's guide to differentiation

1 The slope of the line showing values of some variable y against known values of x (think of that infinitesimally small triangle you could draw which has the same slope as the tangent) is called (usually) 'D Y by D X' and written (usually) dy/dx. The operation of working it out is called 'differentiation of y with respect to x'.

2 If y is some function of a power of x, then dy/dx will be a function of one power lower of x. Thus if y is a function of x squared, dy/dx is a function of x. If y is a function of x cubed, dy/dx will be a function of x squared.

3 This function includes the *number* of the power of the x in the original equation. (My apologies to the 'theorists' among you – there is no room for an explanation. The pragmatists may be satisfied by the next exercise which suggests ways of experimenting to check that this works in practice.) Thus if $y = x^2$, $dy/dx = 2x$. If $y = x^7$, $dy/dx = 7x^6$.

4 If you have several different powers of x in one equation, you apply the same rule to each term. Thus if $y = x^4 + 2x^3$, $dy/dx = 4x^3 + 6x^2$ (remember that there was a 2 in there already).

5 Remember that x is actually x to the power 1, so if $y = x$, $dy/dx = 1$. And if $y = 7x$, $dy/dx = 7$.

6 Remember too that x to the power 0 is 1. Thus any constant terms in your equation, i.e. terms which do not depend on x, can be thought of as an 'x to the nought' term and will be multiplied by zero when you differentiate. They therefore vanish. The fixed costs on your breakeven chart were constant, regardless of x. And, indeed, it is clear that the slope of your total cost line was unaffected by the value of the fixed costs.

7 To find the maximum or minimum of a curve, you work out dy/dx and then find the value of x for which this is zero.

8 Although it is traditional to use y and x, you can obviously differentiate an equation whatever the letters it uses, as long as one letter is used for the value of an equation expressed in terms of the other letter. If the terms are mixed up, with both letters on the same side of the equals sign, you will need to sort out the equation before differentiating.

9 You can work out a second-order derivative by differentiating dy/dx. This would give you the rate at which the rate of change was changing! It is (usually) called d^2y/dx^2. And third- or higher-order derivatives are possible too, by successive differentiation.

(This is also available on the website.)

TEST EXERCISE 14.4

Plot the graph showing y against x in the following cases:

(a) $y = x^2$

(b) $y = 3x + 1$

(c) $y = x^3 + 2x + 2$

You will need to work out a few values in each case: five points should be enough. So use values of x from 1 to 5. Choose a scale for your y, or vertical, axis that allows you to include all the values of y that you get.

Calculate dy/dx in each case.

Now draw the tangents and see how close the slope is to the result of your differentiation.

TEST EXERCISE 14.5

Differentiate the following equations:

(a) $t = 3d^2 + d + 4$ (c) $r = y^2 + 10y - 21$

(b) $y = 2x^4 + x^2 + 5x$ (d) $y = x^7 - 3x^5 + \sqrt{x}$

Integration

Think about the opposite operation to differentiation. It is called *integration* and allows you to find something out about y if you know dy/dx. Try for a minute to think about why you can find out only 'something', not the whole equation for y. The complication lies in the constant which was present in the original, but not in the derivative. Remember that dy/dx for $y = x^2 + 1$, $x^2 + 100$ or $x^2 + 1000$ is $2x$. You have no way of guessing what that constant might be. You therefore need to put something into your answer to remind you of this. Suppose you use K to represent this constant. Then the integral of some function of x, say $2x^2$ (written $\int 2x^2 \, dx$), will be $\frac{2}{3}x^3 + K$.

One important use of integration is to tell you the *area* under a curve. If you know the rate of change of a quantity, the integral is the total of that quantity accumulated. Figure 14.6 shows the number of males of different heights in a particular population. The area under the curve to the left of a particular height value, shaded on the diagram, will be the number of people of that height or less. In case you want to practise integration, Test exercise 14.6 gives you some examples. The idea of area under a curve will be clearer in the simpler examples of distributions shown as histograms which follow shortly. You will be relieved to know that they require no mathematics beyond the ability to count!

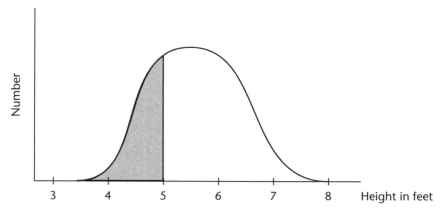

Fig. 14.6 Graph showing height distribution of males in a particular population (shaded area represents those less than 5 ft tall)

TEST EXERCISE 14.6

Find the integrals with respect to x of the following expressions:

(a) $3x^2$

(b) $8x^3 - 12x^2 + 1$

(c) $\frac{1}{x} + 3$

If you need to know more about the calculus than this primer can offer, and there is no basic maths course on offer in your institution, then you will need to buy a book on the subject. But this brief introduction should mean that you feel brave enough to fight your way through such a book if necessary. If you need only a *little* more explanation and practice than it was possible to provide here, Morris and Thanassoulis (1994) is fairly user friendly.

Even if you do not need calculus, being able to plot things in a simple graph will add greatly to your ability to show a pattern from figures and to communicate patterns. If you are writing a report arguing for a need to take action before a situation becomes critical, then including graphs at relevant points to strengthen your argument can be a great help in convincing your reader that you do have a point. And extrapolating from graphs which show a clear trend can be a useful aid to forecasting and therefore planning.

FREQUENCIES AND HISTOGRAMS

Quite often, I find it helpful to chart how frequently various events occur. At our residential schools, we use a questionnaire to assess how successful the school and its various components have been in the students' eyes. This questionnaire also asks

14

Making sense of data

Q13
Please rate your core group tutor on the following items:

	Excellent				Poor
Presentation skills	5	4	3	2	1
Knowledge of course content	5	4	3	2	1
Facilitation skills	5	4	3	2	1

Presentation skills		Course knowledge		Facilitation skills	
5	I	5	IIII	5	I
4	I	4	HHT	4	
3	III	3	II	3	III
2	HHT	2		2	HHT
1	II	1	I	1	IIII

Fig. 14.7 Extract from a student feedback questionnaire, with tally

students to rate tutors on various dimensions using a five-point scale (an extract is shown in Figure 14.7). One easy way to see how each tutor has been viewed by students is to log the distribution of scores awarded on key variables. An example of a tally showing this for one item on the questionnaire and a tutor with 12 students in the group is shown beneath the question. When doing this by hand, it is clearest to tally by drawing four verticals and a fifth diagonal. Adding up groups of five afterwards is then a simple operation.

Such a tally can equally be represented as a *histogram*, where the categories are on the *x* axis and above each is a bar, its height showing the frequency of observations in that category. In the questionnaire example above each score is a category. But if you have a wide range of possible scores, say from 1 to 100, you might wish to group scores into bands and draw a bar for each band of scores. As the bands are 'continuous', i.e. there are no gaps in the scale of scores, you can draw bars touching each other (though of course if one band had no scores, there would be a bar of zero height, which would look like a gap). If you choose the width of band carefully, it will show you the pattern of how the scores are distributed far more clearly than if you tried to show the frequency of each possible score – after all, no single score might have more than two 'scorers' and many might have none at all.

Suppose that two tutors had taught the same course and marked their students on an exam paper common to both groups, and that the results were as follows:

Tutor A: 20, 70, 80, 83, 50, 55, 75, 60, 61, 30, 95, 55, 54, 51, 40, 57, 69, 70, 75, 81

Tutor B: 40, 43, 47, 60, 49, 55, 51, 60, 63, 49, 42, 70, 75, 50, 46, 41, 49, 67, 60, 42

These are a classic example of figures from which it is hard to extract meaning without some sort of organisation. But by representing the figures graphically, in the form of a histogram, it is possible to see clear differences which might prompt a number of questions.

TEST EXERCISE 14.7

On the charts below, draw histograms showing the number of marks in each 10-mark band for each tutor's group of students.

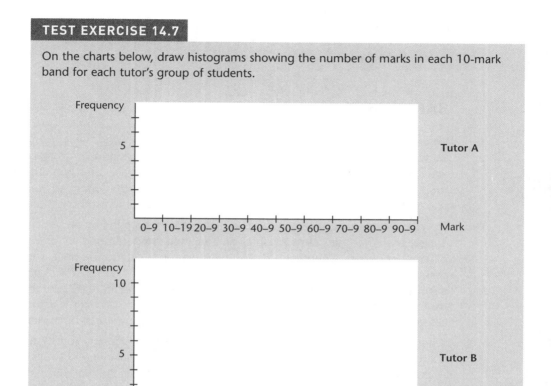

14

Making sense of data

In Test exercise 14.7, each category was of equal size – each represented a band of 10 marks. It is possible to use categories of different sizes – sometimes you might wish to use some categories that cover a wider range than others. Perhaps you could not measure with equal accuracy over the full range of the scale. If you do this, you must remember that the *area* of a bar must correspond to the number of instances. Thus if the first category in the above had been 0–40, then its height would need to be one-quarter that of a bar for a 10-score band with the same number of occurrences. Otherwise a false impression of frequency would be created. For example, suppose there had been 1, 2, 2 and 3 examples in each of the 10-mark bands, thus 8 in the amalgamated band. Whichever way you choose to group the categories, the overall shape should be approximately the same, allowing for the inevitable flattening caused by the broader category. A broad band 8 units high would give a very different picture from that using each separate category, whereas one 2 units high would look fairly similar.

Note that just as using broader categories will lead to flattening of parts of the histogram, increasing the 'stepped' effect, so using narrower bands will lead to a smoothing of the steps, until you approximate to a graph. Thus if instead of two tutor groups' scores you had all the GCSE scores for the country, you could use one-mark categories and end up with something like a graph of frequency of each score.

BAR CHARTS

When plotting a graph you are plotting two 'variables' – things which can take different values on the scales you show on your axes. The scales need to be ordinal scales so that you know how to draw and interpret them. A histogram also uses two ordered scales, though one is frequency. But if you could not order the categories you were counting, you could not use a graph or histogram to make sense of a distribution of values.

Sometimes you may have one variable that is *not* measurable on an ordinal scale. Suppose you had, say, annual rainfall and average temperature data for a series of different countries. Countries are categories, so this is categorical data. You could order them in many different ways – by size, by alphabet, or by geographical position for example. Therefore, plotting rainfall by country, or temperature by country, would not make a lot of sense. You will sometimes see graphs where one axis is actually a set of categories, but this is not good practice: if read as a graph it can be misleading.

Where you have one genuine variable and one set of categories, you should use a bar chart instead. This still gives you a picture of figures and allows you to spot, for example, high and low values very easily, but does not imply that you might be able to find an equation which related the two sets of figures. If you have measured two or three things for each category, you may be able to get a feel for any strong relationships between these by plotting them side by side (*see* Figure 14.8).

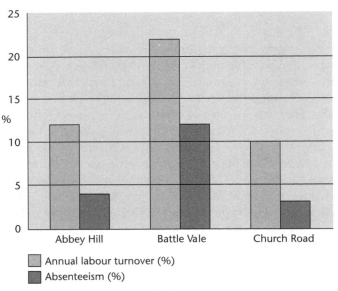

Fig. 14.8 Bar chart showing absence and labour turnover rates at three sites

TEST EXERCISE 14.8

Represent the following information on a bar chart:

Organisation	Percentage of recruits who are:	graduates	female
Anglewide Windows		30	20
Biobreed Technology		60	50
Countrywide Clerical		15	90
Downtown Designers		25	35
Everyman Eateries		10	60

In bar charts as with graphs, you do not need to have your *y* axis start at zero (as the *x* axis is a set of categories, the question of where it starts does not apply). This can help you to make differences clear, as you probably found in Test exercise 14.8. But if you do this, you will need to remember that a bar that is twice as high, say, as another does not represent a value twice as great. There is probably a stronger tendency to assume that it *does* than there is with a graph, so beware.

Sometimes it is necessary to use each interval on the scale to represent an increase in size gained not by adding, but by multiplying. This is known as a *logarithmic* or *exponential* scale. (You can use logarithmic scales for plotting graphs as well.) It allows you to represent a much wider range of values on a single scale than would be possible with an interval scale, yet still to see how things at the small end of the scale relate to each other. You will see an example of such a scale in Figure 14.9.

Because the meaning of a chart (or indeed a graph) depends so much on the scales on the axes, you must always be very careful to make the scale clear when drawing a

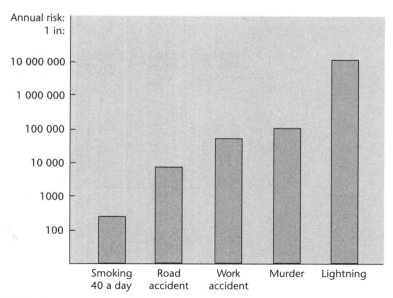

Fig. 14.9 Risk of some causes of death

chart or graph, and to note carefully the scales used when you are reading them. If you are using anything other than a normal interval scale starting at zero, you may wish to alert readers to this in your text, in addition to labelling axes clearly in your diagram. The scope for giving a wrong impression is huge. Look, for example, at the chart in Figure 14.9, which is similar to one which appeared in a reputable scientific periodical. What would you say, at a glance, is most likely to kill you?

It is only when you stop to think that surely lightning *can't* be so much more dangerous than smoking that you realise that the scale is dealing in risks, expressed in such a way that bars for *unlikely* things are taller than bars for *likely* things, which is completely counter-intuitive. A 1 in 10 chance is much bigger than a 1 in 100 chance, yet is lower on the scale. Note this is not because it is a logarithmic scale – it would be the same with a normal one. (In fact, a set of figures seen recently suggested that of 1000 regular smokers aged 20, 250 will die of smoking-related diseases in middle age and a further 250 in old age, compared with 1 by murder and 6 by road accidents – assuming that their smoking habits and crime and road accident rates continue as at present.)

Although the bars have been shown as vertical, you could just as well draw them as horizontals. Indeed, this has the advantage of allowing you to write the bar label in the same direction as the bar itself, which may make both constructing the chart and reading it somewhat easier. The choice is up to you, as long as you make clear what your axes are and thus what the bars represent.

Sometimes bars are used to show proportions. If this is the case, the height of all the bars will be the same, representing 100%. But within the bars there will be different colours or shadings showing the different proportions of the different quantities making up that whole. For example, a survey of a small village over a number of years might show the proportion of owner occupation rising. This could be represented as in Figure 14.10.

Note that it is not possible to tell from this sort of bar chart how *many* of any type of dwelling existed in any year. This is a difference from the other bar charts described.

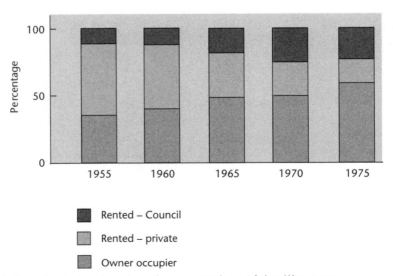

Fig. 14.10 Bar chart showing changing proportions of dwelling types

The village may well have been growing significantly over the period shown, but there is no way of telling this from Figure 14.10. All you can tell from that chart is how the total housing available in any one of the years surveyed was divided between the three categories. You would need to be extremely careful not to draw conclusions about whether actual *numbers* of dwelling in any category are increasing or decreasing.

PIE CHARTS

A popular way of representing this sort of proportional data is a pie chart. This has the advantage over a bar chart that it is clear that the whole pie represents unity. Again, the ease of generating such diagrams on a PC has led to their proliferation in reports, often in glorious colours, sometimes in mock 3D. Such charts have obvious attractions. They look good, far prettier than simple bar charts. They are easy to understand, even for those who have some difficulty with fractions. Such people might have some difficulty in working out how ⅙, ⅓ and ½ relate to each other, but they could see this immediately from a pie chart such as Figure 14.11.

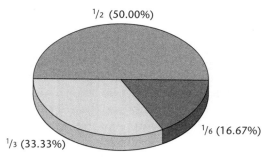

Fig. 14.11 A very simple pie chart

While pie charts are great when they have only a few 'slices', they become difficult both to label and to interpret once they contain a larger number of categories. We are not good at judging fine differences between angles at a glance and it can be quite difficult to see whether one slice is marginally greater than another. This problem is made harder by the 3D effect if used and by the different colours and shadings used to differentiate slices (*see* Figure 14.12). If you have more than four or five categories, it is

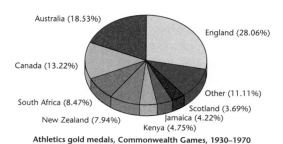

Athletics gold medals, Commonwealth Games, 1930–1970

Fig. 14.12 A pie chart with too many slices

better to use a bar chart, as lengths are easier to judge, though even then it can be difficult.

SUMMARY MEASURES

Graphs are not the only way of giving a summary of a set of numbers. Numerical summaries are possible too. You will be all too familiar with one, the *average*. Whether you are talking about average marks, average rainfall or average wages, you mean the figure you would get if you added all the marks (rainfalls or whatever) together and divided by the number of exam papers, or years for which rainfall measures had been taken or whatever. More generally, you add together all the values you have and divide by the number of values.

TEST EXERCISE 14.9

Estimate the average mark for Tutor A's student group and for Tutor B's student group in Test exercise 14.7, then see how close your estimate was by working it out using a calculator.

When I am doing my rough analysis of questionnaire data, I calculate the average rating tutors have received, as well as obtaining a histogram of distribution of rating. Rather than adding up all the scores on my calculator, which is a fairly error-prone operation as you may have found in the exercise above, I work from the histogram. The formula for doing this can be written using the vocabulary or code introduced in Chapter 5. If you use x to refer to the scores the tutor had, or whatever the measures obtained happen to be, and f for the frequency with which each measure occurred, the formula is:

→ Ch 5

$$\text{mean} = \Sigma fx/\Sigma f$$

Thus you work out the total value of scores in each category – five ratings of 5 would give you 25, while five ratings of 1 would give you only 5. You add all these together and divide by the number of ratings. Think about the histogram. The arithmetic mean is going to be the line on the x axis with an equal area of bar on either side. So the formula is telling you to work out the area of each bar, add them together and divide by the number of bars.

If you are using bands, as in the Tutor A/Tutor B example, then your x will be the mid-point of the band. Thus the mid-point of a 1–5 band would be 3. And the mid-point of a 0–9 band such as we used would be 4.5. It is perfectly OK to work with fractional values of x such as 4.5, but it makes the arithmetic slightly more difficult. If you are planning to use this method and want to calculate in your head, you might want to choose a band size and location that will make the calculation easy.

TEST EXERCISE 14.10

Work out the average value of Tutor A's and Tutor B's groups working from the histogram you drew. You will need to construct for each set of scores a table with columns:

Band value	Number of scores (f)	Band mid-point (x)	fx
0–9	_____	_____	_____
10–19	_____	_____	_____
etc.			

See if you take fewer attempts to get it right using this method!

Sometimes an average, or arithmetic mean, gives a misleading picture of the centre of a distribution. Suppose the numbers were distributed in an odd way. There might, for example, be one or two huge numbers which made the mean come out as higher than any of the other numbers in the group. Say you were working out the average income of inhabitants of a medieval village and included the lord's income alongside those of the peasants. Then an average calculated from the total sum of income would be fairly useless. There are many situations today where you might get a better picture of the middle of a group using some other measure.

Median

There are two other commonly used indicators of central tendency. The first is the *median.* To obtain this you order your numbers by size and count along to the value which is in the middle of the line. This is the median. Thus suppose you had the values 4, 1, 11, 10, 5, 10, 7, 10, 1. You would rearrange these in order to give 1, 1, 4, 5, 7, 10, 10, 10, 11. There are nine measurements, so the middle will be the fifth one. Counting from either end, as it is immaterial which, you reach 7. This is the median of that set of values.

TEST EXERCISE 14.11

Write down the general formula for knowing which term in an ordered series of n terms will be the median.

Your answer to the exercise above will be a whole number when n is odd – after all, in any series with an odd number of terms, as in the example above, one is in the middle. But what if there had been only eight measurements? If n is 8, $(n + 1)/2$ (the answer to the exercise above) is 4.5. Where this happens, it is normal to take a point midway between the two middle numbers as the median. Suppose the 11 in the above example had not been there. Then the fourth term would be 5 and the fifth term 7, so the median in this case would be 6. (For very large distributions, you can ignore this and use either. If you had 100 observations, it would usually be sufficiently accurate to take either the 50th or the 51st observation as the median.)

Mode

The other indicator of the middle of a distribution is the mode. This is the most commonly occurring value. For small sets of numbers it is easy to see what the mode is – in the example above it was obviously 10. For larger sets you will need to tally the values occurring, or draw a histogram. On a histogram you can see it easily, because it is the value of the score or band with the highest bar.

TEST EXERCISE 14.12

Locate the modal mark for Tutor A and Tutor B from your histograms in Exercise 14.7.

TEST EXERCISE 14.13

Find the mean, median and mode for each of the following sets of values:

	Mean	Median	Mode
(a) 5, 5, 3, 2, 6, 7, 9, 11,1	_____	_____	_____
(b) 3, 3, 7, 2, 1, 4, 3, 3, 13, 10	_____	_____	_____

(c) Now experiment with writing lists where mean, median and mode all have different values (no answer given for this part).

MEASURES OF DISPERSION

The way in which the values you have obtained are spread out is important for a number of reasons. You may simply need to know the range you can expect in order to plan for all possible situations. But more often, you will be wanting to know how important differences between groups are, and the importance of differences in means will depend on the variation in the data. Suppose one group you observed had an average value of some measure of 5, and another group had an average of 6, and you wanted to know if this was a significant difference or just happened to have come out that way on the day you measured. If all the values in the first group were between 4.5 and 5.5 and all the values in the second group were between 5.5 and 6.5, you might be surer about the difference than if numbers in each case were scattered about between 1 and 10. You therefore need some measure of this scatter or dispersion.

The bell-shaped curve shown in Figure 14.6 is frequently found in nature. It occurs when you have a large population and you are measuring a continuous variable. The curve may be taller and thinner, or flatter (this will depend upon the scale you are using in any case), but is basically the same shape. So common is it that it is called the 'normal distribution'. Examples of normal distributions range from children's IQ scores to actual dimensions of parts produced on a machine. Many statistical tests assume that a sample is drawn from a population with this distribution. If you have a sample drawn from a population with a different distribution, you may need to use other tests.

Range

There are several measures of dispersion. The simplest is the *range,* the distance from the smallest to the largest measure observed. Thus in Test exercise 14.13, the range in **(a)** is 1–11 and in **(b)** is 1–13. It is the most obvious indicator of the dispersion of the set of figures and the easiest to ascertain. But it has fairly obvious drawbacks. Even more than the mean, it is susceptible to being distorted by one or two maverick figures. This may not be a distortion, if you genuinely need to know the *possible* range. But if you are trying to get a quick picture of the distribution, then it may be misleading. Also you may not *know* the end of a distribution, because you used an 'open' category; for example the question on alcohol consumption in one of the exercises in the last chapter had a '43 +' category. You would have no idea of the highest alcohol consumption in your survey if you had some respondents in this category.

→ Ch 13

Inter-quartile range

One indicator of spread that avoids these problems is derived by developing the idea of the median. Just as the median tells you the position of the middle observation, so you can find the middle of observations to each side of the median, by treating each as a distribution and finding *its* median. These values will represent the positions one-quarter and three-quarters along the distribution and are called the *quartiles*. The distance between the upper and lower quartile is called the *inter-quartile range* and tells you the range within which half your values are likely to lie. It is not distorted by the odd deviant value and is almost as easy to work out as a median.

The idea of quartiles can be extended still further, to deciles and percentiles. For example, you might be designing a car seat and need to know the range of adjustments to build in. It would not be much good to use the inter-quartile range. If you did, the seat would be uncomfortable for half your potential customers. Equally, you would probably not want to design a seat that would suit every adult on the planet. It would be expensive and the small number of potential purchasers who are over 8 ft or under 4 ft do not justify this expense. For many such design situations, percentiles are used, dividing the distribution into hundredths. And traditionally the lower five percentiles and the upper five percentiles are disregarded. If you are at the outlying end of a distribution, say one of the 5% shortest or 5% tallest people, you will have problems finding chairs, cars, kitchen units or whatever to suit.

14

Making sense of data

Standard deviations

If you have done any statistics at all, you will have heard of standard deviations. They are widely used in a variety of situations as a measure of dispersion. If you want to know how representative your mean is, you might reasonably ask: 'How closely do the values observed cluster about this mean?' One way of answering the question would be to work out the difference between each value and the mean, add these values together, and average them. There is a snag to this, which you have probably spotted. By definition the answer will be zero. Some of the numbers will be negative and will cancel out the positives. You could get around this by ignoring the negative signs. But statistics of this kind were developed by mathematicians, who do not feel comfortable with such ideas! So instead, they chose to get rid of the negatives by squaring each deviation. Negative numbers multiplied by negative numbers are positive. The average of these squares will be a positive number. And if you take a square root of this, you will have something close to the average deviation worked out by the obvious 'ignoring signs' method. If $\overline{x}$ is the mean value of x, and n is the number of values, we can write this as a formula:

$$\text{standard deviation} = \sqrt{\frac{\Sigma(x - \overline{x})^2}{n}}$$

or, by working out the bracket and cancelling the ns that result:

$$= \sqrt{\frac{\Sigma x^2}{n} - \overline{x}^2}$$

The second way of writing this is much easier to work out when you want to insert your values of x and n.

This gives you the standard deviation of a whole population if you have measured every member of that population. If you have only a smallish sample, the calculation will give you values that are smaller than you would expect from the population sampled. A better estimate of the standard deviation of this 'parent' population when you have a smallish sample is given if you divide by $n - 1$, rather than n. For a large sample, the difference will be insignificant, as $n - 1$ will be virtually the same as n. Dividing by 8 rather than 9 may make a noticeable difference. Dividing by 81 rather than 80 will not.

If you have a *normal distribution* (*see* Figure 14.6 for an example) of values, 68% of scores/values/measures will lie within 1 standard deviation of the mean and 95% within 2 standard deviations of this.

DRAWING CONCLUSIONS FROM FIGURES

In talking about both graphical representations of data and the numerical descriptors such as means, medians or indicators of dispersion, we are organising data in a way that makes patterns or aspects clearer. But although some things may look 'obvious' from histograms, or from differences between means for different sets of figures, they need to be treated with caution. This is because the world has a habit of producing what we interpret as 'obviously' weird results when there is nothing weird going on at all.

How likely do you think it is, for example, that in a class of 32 students at least two will share a birthday? The chances are about 3 to 1. Or guess the probability that if you toss a coin just six times you will get either six heads or six tails. Most people would assume that this was extremely unlikely, unless the coin was weighted in some way. In fact, the chance is as high as 1 in 32. So if each of the students in the class above toss six coins, you can expect one of them to get six of a kind and should not be surprised if they do. Few people choose consecutive numbers in the lottery, yet it is as likely that there *will* be two consecutive numbers as it is that there will not. Your chance of winning will still be minuscule, but if you choose consecutive numbers and *do* win, your prize will probably be bigger.

In collecting data to inform a decision or test some hypothesis, we can usually afford to look only at a *sample* of the population in which we are interested. If we wanted to know how people were likely to vote, we would not survey every voter. If we wanted to know whether one form of testing predicted later performance better than another form of testing, we would try each out on a reasonable-sized group of people, not on the entire world. If we wanted to know whether a new drug was effective, we would try it on a sample of people with the disease it was supposed to help, rather than on everyone.

In drawing conclusions, as was clear from the last chapter, the nature and size of sample are important. If we did not choose our sample carefully, the data could be unrepresentative. If you tried the drug only with those who were sickest, this would not tell you how well it compared with a drug normally used on people who are not very sick. If you tried it on a tiny number of people, you would also find it hard to be sure what your results implied for the world at large.

Note that in each of these examples the 'data' might also be imperfect. People might say they will vote one way and then either not bother to vote at all, or change their mind at the last minute and vote for some other candidate. Some might hate surveys so much that they deliberately mislead the surveyor.

As we are so prone to go wrong even when assessing the likelihood of simple things like birthday coincidences and results of coin tosses, considerable caution is needed in making inferences from a sample of imperfect data relating to more complex situations. And yet this is the sort of data that we are normally using to provide information. Because this area is so important, a considerable battery of statistical techniques has been developed to help with drawing conclusions about the meaning of sets of numbers. Unfortunately such techniques are often ignored and faulty conclusions are drawn as a result.

LEVELS OF SIGNIFICANCE

To know whether to be surprised at coinciding birthdays or tossed coins, you need to know how likely they were to happen 'by chance'. In knowing whether apparent differences in recovery rates on the old and new drugs mean that the new drug is actually better, you need to know the same thing. How likely is it, given all the other factors that influence recovery, that the difference you observe might have just happened by chance? Statistical tests of significance give you an idea of this. They will indicate how often a result as extreme as yours could happen if there were in fact no difference in the populations from which your samples were drawn, that is, how often you could expect to get this result 'by chance'. You will often see at the end of a table of results in a research paper '$p < 0.05$'. This means that only one time in twenty would you get such a difference if the populations sampled were the same, or so strong a relationship if the two things you were measuring were in fact unrelated in the population from which your sample was drawn.

This can also be expressed as 'a confidence level of 95%' or 'with 95% confidence'. Normally journals are prepared to publish results which are as significant as this, but not results with a lower probability. But beware of two ways in which the meaning of such confidence levels can be affected by how they were derived. The first factor is the prediction or hypothesis you are testing. You might test either 'this drug is better' or 'these two drugs are different in their effect'. When you are predicting the *direction* of the difference, rather than merely hypothesising that there would be a difference of some kind, a smaller actual difference is sufficient to give you a 95% confidence level in your result. Think about the bell curve. The area under both extremes is obviously twice the area under one only. So it is twice as likely that you will get a result that is 'extreme' as that you will get one that is 'at this extreme'. Because you are talking about 'tails' of distributions, significance tests are referred to as 'one-tailed' or 'two-tailed' to differentiate these two cases. It is important to decide *beforehand* whether you are predicting a result at one end or at either end and therefore whether you need a one-tailed or two-tailed test. Otherwise you can rationalise your result – 'well, of course, if you think about it, it had to come out that way' – and end up accepting as significant something which could happen one in ten times, say.

The other slight caution about significance testing is that, while a single very extreme result would be worth taking seriously, if one of 20 results came out this way, by definition this is what you would expect. So it is misleading to work out lots of relationships or differences and throw away all the non-significant results, including in your paper or report only those that came out as significant. And it is equally dubious to draw conclusions from a matrix of results of which something like 1 in 10 or 1 in 20 reaches a significance level of 0.05. (Watch out for this in journals – it is fairly common!)

ACTIVITY 14.1

If you are studying a course that has suggested readings including research papers in journals, look carefully at the significance levels reported, the number of such results tested and, if appropriate, whether one- or two-tailed testing was done. See if you can find examples of papers where conclusions seem to be rather stronger than the numbers warrant.

DEVELOPING YOUR INFERENCE SKILLS

The coverage of statistical inference given here has been an American-style, whistle-stop, 'If it's Tuesday this must be Rome' tour. But it should have introduced you to some very important issues in drawing conclusions from data, alerted you to the ease with which you can draw unwarranted conclusions and made you appreciate that there is a wealth of knowledge about this area on which you can draw and techniques which you can use.

The actual use is fairly easy now, as software is widely available for calculating the relevant statistics. The difficulty is to know how to design your data collection to get usable data from which, using appropriate techniques, you can draw conclusions with confidence. There is also the difficulty of knowing which techniques to use.

Do take advantage of any basic statistics courses which are available. This is an area where a little understanding can pay off handsomely. It will be a great help in planning any research you do, either during your degree, as a postgraduate or in employment. (Even more helpful will be to find a statistician and consult with him/her about your plans at an early stage. This can save you a great deal of wasted effort in gathering data that are unlikely to tell you anything at all.) Even the small amount of understanding of probability and statistics that you now have should make you suitably cynical about many of the conclusions you will find being drawn from data, both in research and when data are used in organisations to inform decision making.

SUMMARY

This chapter has argued the following:

- Graphs and charts are a useful way of making it easy to see patterns and discontinuities in sets of numbers. They can usefully be included in reports to illustrate a point or strengthen an argument.

- Graphs can also be useful for estimating future values, by extending them in the direction in which they are moving.

- Numbers can also usefully be summarised in terms of their central tendency and dispersion, using means, medians and modes for the first, and range, inter-quartile range and standard deviation for the second.

- In drawing conclusions from numbers it is easy to over-estimate the significance of seemingly striking differences and relationships. Statistical tests of significance will provide an antidote to this by indicating the level of confidence you can have in predictions or conclusions.

- It is worth studying at least some basic statistics and, for research design or interpreting figures to inform an important decision, seeking the advice of an expert.

Further information

There are many good books on statistics available. The following are merely suggestions.

- Huff, D. (1991) *How to Lie with Statistics*, Penguin.

- Moroney, M.J. (1951) *Facts from Figures*, Penguin. A classic but very readable introduction.

- Morris, C. (2000) *Quantitative Approaches in Business Studies*, 5th edn, Financial Times Prentice Hall.

- Morris, C. and Thanassoulis, E. (1994) *Essential Mathematics*: *A Refresher Course for Business and Social Studies*, Macmillan. Very gentle going.

- Powell, J. (1991) *Quantitative Decision Making*, Longman.

- Rowntree, D. (1987) *Statistics without Tears: a Primer for Non-mathematicians*, Penguin.

- Stutely, R. (2003) *The Definitive Guide to Managing the Numbers*, Pearson. Very good on spreadsheets (and finance).

- Targett, D. (1983) *Coping with Numbers*, Blackwell. Primarily aimed at managers, but very rigorous and detailed treatment of data communication, statistical methods and decision-making techniques.

→ 15 Increasing your creativity

New situations may need totally new solutions. In a changing world the ability to think creatively, to break out of the 'box' of existing assumptions, is invaluable. People vary in the ease with which they can do this, but this chapter introduces techniques that can help you be more creative.

Learning outcomes

By the end of this chapter you should:

■ understand the place of creativity in problem solving

■ be aware of some of the ways in which creativity is restricted

■ be able to use a range of techniques to increase individual and group creativity.

Earlier it was argued that although it is important to be rational when analysing problems, for complex problems rationality is not enough – it may even be limiting. If a situation is changing rapidly and unpredictably, drawing on past experience and frameworks for thinking about it may not be enough. This is when you need to go *beyond* rationality, question assumptions and look at situations in totally new ways.

Creativity is the ability to think in new ways, to see new patterns and come up with new ideas. The techniques introduced in this chapter will help you become better at identifying, and then breaking away from, the limitations of your existing mindset and assumptions. You can then locate your rationality within a wider, less limiting approach. This will make you a great asset to any project group you join, whether as a student or when you start work.

THE NEED FOR CREATIVITY

Change is now so widespread that organisations have had to make radical changes to their ways of working. Changes over the last 25 years or so have not been the comfortable continuous, 'more-of-the-same' change of the past. Instead there have been major discontinuities. Handy (1989) expressed this well when he said that 'Change is not what it used to be.'

In coping with discontinuous change, and preparing for futures that are hard to guess at, logic and reason are not enough, as we need to go *beyond* what is known. Handy says that we are entering the 'age of unreason', drawing on George Bernard Shaw's observation that all progress depends on the unreasonable man. (Note that this is not the same as irrational!) In such an age, he says, we need *discontinuous thinking*. Others refer to lateral (rather than vertical) thinking, divergent (rather than convergent) thinking, unbounded thinking or, more generally, creativity. All are talking about ways of breaking away from the limitations of traditional mindsets, traditional sets of assumptions, traditional rational approaches to problems. Some suggest that different halves of the brain are used for these different sorts of approach. Logical processes are a left-brain activity, creativity and pattern perception use the right side of the brain.

While definitions vary, creativity is generally taken to mean originality, new ways of seeing, new ideas, the thought processes associated with imagination, insight, intuition, ingenuity, inspiration. The adjective 'creative' can be applied to people, their mental processes and the ideas or other things that they produce.

→ Ch 12

If you think back to the stages of problem solving introduced earlier, perception of a problem in terms of a gap between what is and what should be, the generation of possible ways of bridging that gap, selection of the best of these ways and then making it happen, it is possible to see ways in which creativity can complement rational thinking at almost all stages.

Problem definition

In defining a problem, a fixed mindset can be incredibly limiting. It will limit what you can 'see' in a situation, and seriously constrain your thinking. If poor performance is seen as a 'control problem' by all concerned, only control solutions will be generated. A more creative approach to the initial situation might generate a far broader definition of the problem, indeed might see it as an opportunity. Removing constraints to thinking at the outset is therefore essential if the situation is to be fully exploited. Henry (1991) emphasises the need to reframe the problem from a number of different angles before settling on a problem statement that encapsulates what appear to be the crucial factors. She says that she finds that some 70% of people will end up exploring a *different* problem from that with which they started.

→ Ch 12

The rich pictures which were suggested as a way of mapping possible elements in a problem situation are part of a whole methodology (Checkland, 1981) for approaching 'soft' problems, those where people and their perceptions are important, not everything can be measured and objectives may be less than clear. The next stage in this methodology is to tease out a number of 'problem themes'. Following a methodology such as this, with specified stages which you are to go through in pursuit of a problem, is one way of resisting the temptation to a narrow and premature diagnosis of problem causes. (The pictorial stage also involves the right brain.)

→ Ch 1, 2

To succeed in a changing world you need to do more than merely maintain the status quo. Goals need to be reformulated continually to take account of the changing environment (it is essential to 'move the goalposts'). Forecasting significant changes in this environment (remember Fayol?) will be important. In a situation of discontinuous change, it takes real creativity to conceive of a radically different future, or even to see the implications of a future that is rapidly arriving. Many organisations were slow to grasp the full implications of the ICT revolution. Indeed, it is likely that much of its impact has yet to be dreamed of.

Generating possible solutions

When it comes to choosing the best way forward, the choice will never be better than the best option that was thought of. Although a broad understanding of a problem situation, freed from preconceptions and accepted limits, can in itself go far towards increasing the range of options which suggest themselves, idea-generation techniques can usefully supplement this. On the whole, the wider the range you have to choose from, the greater the probability that one or more of these will offer a way out of a situation which has previously resisted any form of improvement.

Idea generation will often involve successive divergent and convergent stages. For example, in looking for a project topic you might generate a range of broad subject areas (divergent activity) before selecting the area which seemed most promising (convergent). You might then focus on this area, generating a range of ways of approaching it before selecting one and then go through further stages of divergence and convergence before formulating the exact area to be researched. Figure 15.1 shows this diagrammatically.

Implementation

The diagram makes the point that when you have decided which broad option offers you the best way forward, you often have scope for creative implementation. There

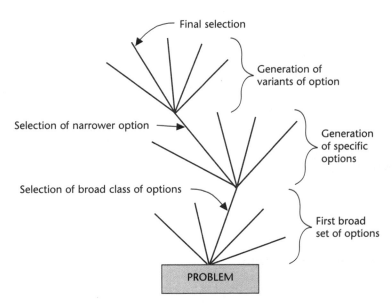

Fig. 15.1 Option selection by successive choice of divergence

may be many ways of taking action to bring about a particular change. Suppose that you have decided to restructure your organisation to make more use of self-directed work teams. You will still have many ways of forming such groups, of involving the group members in that formation and of designing control mechanisms that allow direction without loss of autonomy. If the earlier stages of your attack on the problem adopted a broad perspective, then it is likely that your chosen approach has already broken away from preconceptions and limited frameworks. But this may be further helped by use of the divergent/convergent/divergent sequence described above when planning ways of implementing the changes that have been agreed.

Mintzberg (1976) makes the interesting suggestion that while planning is essentially a left-brain activity (it is, after all, important that a plan does follow a sequence that enables things to be done in a logical order), the implementation of plans, that is, the *managing* that comes after, is essentially a right-brain activity. He bases this claim on his observations of very senior managers at work. These managers seemed to be splitting their attention between a number of different tasks, preferred talking briefly to people to writing at length, seemed to be reading non-verbal aspects of such interactions as well as verbal, looked (if they were good) at the situation as a whole, seeing patterns therein, and relied heavily on intuition.

These observations led Mintzberg to argue that truly effective managers can harness *both* halves of their brain effectively. If true, and if you are planning a career which includes management, this is yet another reason to experiment with the creativity techniques which follow and to use diagramming wherever possible. Both should develop your ability to use your right brain.

BARRIERS TO CREATIVITY

If you are to develop your creativity, you need to understand the pressures *against* you. One of the main barriers to creative thought is the belief that a rational/logical/scientific way of thinking is the *only* way to think. This is because most education is directed towards this view and because it is an extremely useful and productive way of thinking.

→ Ch 12   The inability to be rational and logical is a serious shortcoming. Even the greatest creativity enthusiasts suggest that creative or divergent thinking constitutes no more than 5% of all the thinking that is needed (though I am not sure how such a figure is arrived at). But the quality of the 95% of logical thought will depend on its direction. This will depend on the extent to which a creative interpretation of the original situation was found. The amount of time devoted to creative thought may be small, but in any situation where 'soft' problems are addressed the quality of your output will depend equally on the two types of thought process.

> Being creative for 5 minutes can transform 95 minutes of rational thought.

Setting logic aside

To overcome the 'logic habit' you need to practise deliberately setting aside your ingrained logic, *even though you still need to use it most of the time*. Spend some time

Table 15.1 Creative (lateral) vs logical (vertical) thinking

Lateral	Vertical
Seeks questions	Seeks answers
Diverges	Converges
Explores different views, seeking insight	Asserts best/right view
Restructures	Uses existing structure
Seeks ways an idea might help	Says why an idea won't work
Welcomes discontinuous leaps	Uses logical steps
Welcomes chance intrusions	Concentrates on what is relevant
Open-ended	Closed

indulging in a way of thinking that is in many ways its antithesis. The list of contrasts in Table 15.1, derived mainly from de Bono (1971), shows dimensions in which the two ways of thinking differ.

If you are good at vertical or rational thinking, gain praise for it and are making progress because you are more rational than other people, it will be particularly difficult for you to move to a more lateral approach. The 'vertical' habit will have been strongly reinforced. Out of this, and out of some of the other differences, come more emotional barriers to lateral thinking.

Feeling happier with creativity

Barriers to creativity:
- education
- existing thought habits
- fear of failure or ridicule
- ambiguity avoidance
- inability to play.

It is usually uncomfortable to move away from your 'comfort zone' of established habit. Especially when the habits are familiar ways of thinking and of approaching problems. People are afraid of failing or looking silly. Many are uncomfortable with ambiguity, and like things to be clearly 'right' or 'wrong'. Many have a compulsion to judge ideas, whether their own or others'. They cannot relax enough to play mental games with ideas. This seems so 'unserious' as to be inappropriate. All these feelings get in the way of creativity.

Most education discourages lateral thinking, while encouraging rational, convergent, 'left brain' thought. The left brain is the side where speech, essentially linear, is located. If you seldom use the right side of your brain, the side where lateral thinking and pattern recognition are located, you may feel unhappy with such use. This will make any holistic activity involving parallel rather than sequential processing difficult.

To become more creative:
- value playfulness
- draw
- deliberately break mindsets
- practise techniques.

Creativity techniques are broadly directed at breaking convergent habits by deliberately specifying steps in problem solving when you do things that have the effect of broadening your thinking. They aim to overcome emotional resistance to this by creating a situation in which 'play' is in some way made respectable and/or by encouraging use of the right brain. For example, drawing a rich picture, when you put down everything you can think of as potentially relevant, acts *against* the convergent habit. Involving a group in drawing fairly juvenile cartoon representations makes play respectable and, being non-linear, encourages right-brain involvement. (Indeed most diagrams will aid creativity.) Practising such techniques should help you develop the skills you need if you are to be creative and overcome any emotional resistance to this sort of approach. Indeed, you should become equally happy with using either type of thinking.

TECHNIQUES FOR IMPROVING CREATIVITY

There are many, many techniques for encouraging lateral thinking. Using them will make it more likely that you will come up with new ways of looking at a situation and new approaches to making it less problematic. What follows is a small selection, to give you an idea how they can work. If you want to try a wider range, read some of the books suggested at the end of the chapter.

The first way of overcoming limitations is to try to ensure that nothing is left out. Techniques already introduced in the problem-solving chapter serve this purpose. These include rich pictures, the use of fishbone diagrams and systematic 'questioning', trying to answer the 'who', 'what,' 'when', 'where' and 'why' questions about the problem situation. Aiming for this breadth of understanding of the scenario is equally important for rational and arational or lateral approaches, so it should not be forgotten when aiming for a creative approach. The other techniques given here are more clearly aimed at going beyond rationality.

Brainstorming

You will almost certainly be familiar with this term. But you may not have actually used the technique or you may have used it in a watered-down form which did not allow for much creativity. The intention of brainstorming is to create a situation where people feel free to play. The idea is to disable the judgemental censors within ourselves. These sensors normally kill many ideas before they surface into consciousness. Because it is done in a group, it provides social rewards for this way of operating. It also offers scope for chance associations and discontinuities: one person's ideas will interact with those surfacing in another person. This can lead to a completely new train of thought. The following classic technique is designed to make this easier.

Preparation

The first thing you need is a *lot* of writing surface – a room with boards all round or flipchart paper stuck to several walls. Also appropriate pens and someone prepared to act as scribe and write fast. Although you can brainstorm alone, ideally you need to assemble a group of people to take part. You also need to think about the question you wish to address. Aim for an open, 'ways to . . .' question. If you are looking for a topic to practise on, you could always brainstorm ways of selling more copies of this book, or better titles for it, and let the publisher know! There might be a reward for any adopted.

Rules

Next, you all need to agree to abide by the only 'rule' in brainstorming – that *all* suggestions are treated as valid and written down, and *nobody* voices criticism of any kind, whatever the idea. Silliness is to be welcomed, as one person's silly idea may spark off a productive new train of thought in someone else. After all, you are brainstorming because the sensible ideas have failed to resolve the problem. (This is why the unreasonable person may make progress where reasonable ones have failed.)

Warm-up

Once you have agreed the rules you start to brainstorm a silly problem. You use this to warm up and get into the mood before moving on to the serious issue with which you are concerned. Silly ideas could be anything: uses for a dead cat or for the discarded plastic cups by the drinks machine; stopping a flatmate from breeding snakes; persuading your tutor to give everyone in the class 100%. The more frivolous the topic the more likely you are to loosen up. You might even try thinking up silly topics for warm-ups at brainstorming. Everyone starts to shout out ideas and the scribe writes them large enough that people can read them easily. Reading back over past ideas while others are shouting can prompt further ideas. It doesn't matter if an idea is voiced twice – better risk this than get into judgemental mode. Five minutes should be enough for a warm-up.

Brainstorming the real question – idea generation

Put up fresh paper and start on the real thing. You may want to spend a few minutes in 'private brainstorming' with group members writing down their initial thoughts, or prefer to work in a group from the outset. If you do list privately first you may find it interesting to compare the number of ideas generated by individuals (duplications removed) with those generated by the group. Continue brainstorming until you run out of steam.

Convergence – organising the results

The final stage of brainstorming is the convergent one. A smaller group takes away all the ideas and selects the most promising ones. They may look for themes, grouping related ideas together and then looking for solutions to the problem theme that the solutions suggest. Or they may simply select the best of the original suggestions. If they wish to go through a further creative stage, they can choose the two or three most impossible or the craziest ideas and see if they can think of ways in which they could actually be made to contribute to a solution.

One interesting variant on this approach is negative brainstorming – a good example of upside-down thinking. Instead of brainstorming ways of *doing* something, you brainstorm ways of *not doing* it. This may throw up a whole new set of ideas about a problem situation, highlighting contributory factors to a problem or things that will militate against a solution.

Brainwriting

Brainwriting is a variant of brainstorming which can be used face to face, but is of particular value if you cannot physically meet with others, but can communicate in a virtual group. You sit down alone to write down all your ideas. You then share these with others in your virtual group, which is likely to prompt further ideas. You can then share these, and so on. It is rather quieter and less frenetic than when you are all in the same room shouting out ideas, but can still work. You can even use this alone, coming back to your list at intervals and adding to it. Things that have happened to you in the interval may prompt new reactions to items on the original list. Try sticking it to the wall near the stove, or in the loo so that you will pass by it often. Leave a pen nearby. As you are likely to be more creative when using diagrams, supplement your list by a cumulative rich picture.

ACTIVITY 15.1

In a group, use the brainstorming technique as described above, several times, until you are comfortable with its use. When using it as part of solving a real problem (for example, for identifying possible keywords for a literature search or for suggesting project topics) document it as an exhibit to demonstrate your competence in applying the tool.

Forced associations

Brainstorming works partly by throwing up ideas which may fortuitously associate themselves for some people. Other approaches force such associations as a way of breaking out of a particular mindset. These can be useful if you are working alone, but groups can use them too.

Random words can be used to force associations. Simply stick a pin in a dictionary or newspaper and see what word is selected. Then see what associations you can make between the word and the problem. Suppose your pin penetrated 'plant'. This grows, needs attention, soil, cross-fertilisation, may grow better in some places than others and so on. What thoughts do each of these characteristics of 'plant' prompt about your original topic?

Superheroes can be used in the same way. Each group member nominates a favourite superhero (see the link with fun again) and these are listed on a board. Or list a number yourself if working alone. Any sort of hero is OK; Homer Simpson or Judge Dredd is as valid as Tony Blair, or Mother Theresa. The hero's sponsor is asked to give their characteristics – special powers, weaknesses, idiosyncrasies. Then the group tries to answer the question (again, fairly frivolously): 'How would X approach the problem?'

Greetings cards provide a more pictorial basis for association. Get a group of helpers, ideally people unconnected with the problem, to cut two or three pictures that take their fancy from a magazine or similar and paste them on to a card, writing 'Get well', 'Happy Anniversary' or other greeting. The cards are then given to those working on the problem and used in the same way as random words. Without helpers, it would be possible to use your pin to select a random illustration rather than a word.

Cartoon by Neill Cameron, www.planetdumbass.co.uk

ACTIVITY 15.2

In a small group, experiment with each of these idea-generation techniques, writing a brief description of your experiences and thoughts about contexts in which each might be appropriate, storing this in your file.

Metaphors and analogies

The use of metaphor – talking of something as if it *is* something which it merely resembles – is deeply rooted in our speech and thought. Whether we are saying a politician is a demon, dove or pussy cat, or speaking of light waves, or of 'the machine' when we speak of an organisation, we are using metaphors. This helps us to feel we understand something with which we may be less familiar because we are describing it in terms of something with which we are more familiar, ascribing properties of the second to the first. In so far as the two are similar in their properties, this can be very helpful. But when only *some* of the properties are common, a metaphor may be limiting or misleading. You would not expect a pussy cat politician to lap milk from a saucer, or a dove MP to take wing. Many people, however, *do* unconsciously expect organisations to behave exactly like machines. And this can seriously limit understanding of what is really going on in them. If you take this view and want to introduce a change, you will merely decree that the change should happen. It will be a great surprise to you when it does not, or when what happens is very different from what was intended.

Unconscious use of metaphor can be particularly dangerous, as you will be unaware of many of the assumptions you are making and cannot check their reality. But conscious use of a range of metaphors can work in a similar way to forced associations. The potential is richer, as the metaphor will often carry a wider range of implications. This is discussed in more detail in Cameron and Pearce (1997).

ACTIVITY 15.3

Listen carefully to people talking about a problem and try to identify unconscious use of metaphor from the language they are using. Machine metaphors of organisation are indicated by words like 'cog', 'clockwork', 'tool', 'spanner in the works'. Military metaphors are indicated by 'attack', 'strategy', 'guns', 'heavy armoury', 'captain', 'breach', 'bombshell'. Look for such metaphoric use of language, identify the underlying metaphor, then try to think what such a metaphor will lead the speaker to consider and what to ignore. Look out for more organic words, too, and think about *their* implications. Note your reflections in your file.

The organic metaphor and systems thinking

The commonest alternative to the machine as a metaphor for organisations is that of the organisation as organism. The systems approach uses an analogy with a living organism as the basis for analysis. Organisms have goals and purposes to which their behaviour is directed. They exist in an environment which has a profound influence upon them, but which they can influence in only limited ways. This environment changes, so they need ways of maintaining a steady state in the face of this change. Systems are separated from their environment by some sort of 'boundary'. Although they are entities, they are made up of many components which interrelate. Some of these components (for example the respiratory system, the digestive system) can be seen as systems in their own right. The organism is much more than just the sum of its parts. It needs to be looked at as a whole, with all its parts and their interactions, if it is to be understood. Some of its properties only emerge at the level of the whole organism. This approach has been highly influential in management thought, where the need to look at things as a whole, to consider how their parts are related, and to see how they interact with their environment is now widely recognised. For example, 'systems thinking' is at the heart of Senge's 'Fifth Discipline'. It also underpins much of this book. Mitroff and Linstone (1993) describe 'Unbounded systems thinking: the fifth way of knowing' (the other ways they identify are agreement, logic, multiple realities, and conflict.)

Ideas of control and multiple causality are central to systems thinking. So too is the emphasis on problem definition and diagnosis. The Rich Pictures introduced earlier are part of Checkland's 'soft system methodology'.

→ Ch 12

A systems approach explores:

- the *goal* of the system and how it is measured
- the *components and subsystems* that must be part of the system if it is to achieve this goal
- the *relationships* between these
- any *wider system* of which the system of interest is itself a subsystem
- the external *environment* of the system and its components
- the influences exerted by this environment – for example via resources and constraints
- the *control loops* that maintain internal stability in the face of change.

→ Ch 12

The deliberate use of a systems metaphor can be useful in any problem analysis that involves human activity. If you are working with problems in organisations, it can be another way of ensuring that all aspects of a problem situation are looked at, in much the same way as the fishbone diagram can be used for exploring all aspects of production that might be contributing to quality problems.

Seeking non-obvious systems

While such uses of the systems metaphor are not particularly creative, going beyond the 'obvious' system can aid creativity greatly. If you choose a variety of non-obvious but relevant systems, and describe them in systems terms, this can markedly broaden your perspective and help you to escape from conventional limitations in thinking. The Checkland (1981) methodology starts with rich picturing and then goes on to extract problem themes. It moves from that into identifying *relevant systems* for each theme. These are not intended as blueprints for a solution, they are not systems which, if introduced, would solve the problem. Instead, they are ways of looking at the situation which prompt constructive thought about it. By *mapping* such systems, you can obtain a very simple picture. Yet if you draw such a map you may be surprised at the number of useful questions it can cause you to consider, and the amount of debate which it can prompt among group members.

This is particularly the case if you choose non-obvious systems, having no generally accepted counterpart in reality. Thus a university might obviously be seen as a system to teach young people academic subjects. Less obviously, it might be viewed as a system to allow academics to do research and travel a lot, to keep young people out of the employment market, to allow employers easily to select people with certain skills, or to indoctrinate all the reasonably intelligent people in the country in a particular approach to 'knowledge'. The potential list is endless and each title would generate a different map of the system.

ACTIVITY 15.4

Listen to your own language when you are discussing organisational problems. Is it mainly mechanistic or do organic metaphors (or indeed political or other metaphors) predominate? Consider whether this is helping or limiting your thinking.

ACTIVITY 15.5

For one of the problems you worked with earlier, perhaps the one for which you already have a rich picture and problem themes, try to describe some relevant systems. Find titles in the form 'A system to . . .' which reflect the purpose of the system and what it does. Then try to draw a picture of the system showing components, sub-systems and key environmental factors. Draw a boundary separating the system and environment. Figure 15.2 shows examples of simple maps of different systems.

15

Increasing your creativity

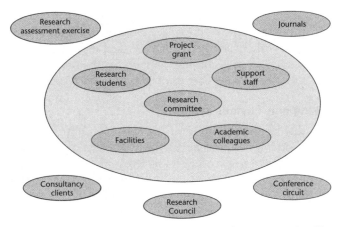

(a) A system to provide an academic with an interesting life

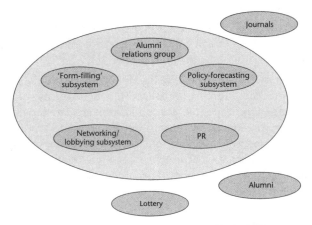

(b) A system for attracting funding to an institution

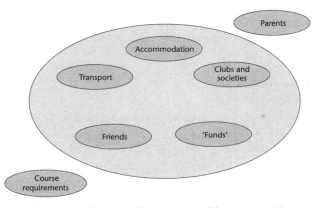

(c) A system for providing an enjoyable time at college

Fig. 15.2 Three simple maps reflecting different systems relevant to higher education

Morgan (1986), in a fascinating development of the idea of metaphor as an aid to understanding organisations in new and creative ways, suggests additional metaphors. In addition to the conventional machine and organism metaphors, we can consider the organisation as brain, culture, psychic prison, product of flux and transformation and instrument of domination. Each of these metaphors suggests a different set of properties, which pose new questions about organisations and from these suggest new insights.

Although most of the problems you will analyse if you are a business student, and most of the problems you will encounter during employment, will have organisational contexts, the use of metaphor is not limited to understanding organisations. Whatever your context, when you are seeking to break out of an existing set of assumptions, it is worth looking for metaphors as an aid to creativity.

Visual metaphors

Time and again, the use of graphic rather than verbal representation has been emphasised and metaphors also lend themselves to this. *Drawing* a metaphor can be surprisingly powerful, tapping into emotions that you were not aware of and highlighting aspects of a situation that you were not aware had any significance for you. This technique is particularly useful for finding out what you would like a future to be, but it has a wide range of applications.

ACTIVITY 15.6

Think of a metaphor for your future life. This could be a journey, a home, a country, a piece of art, whatever suits you. Now *draw it*. Artistic ability is irrelevant. If it worries you that you were bad at drawing at school, draw it as a caveman might, or as a five-year-old child might. You may find that you become surprisingly involved in this endeavour. When you have finished, show your drawing to a friend and ask what it tells them about your hopes and/or fears and/or predictions. Then look at it again yourself and ask *yourself* what it is saying.

ACTIVITY 15.7

Now draw your present life. And then draw a series of intermediate pictures, as if it were a cartoon story of how to get from 'present' to 'future'. (This is called 'storyboarding'.) With your friend, or alone, see what ideas this suggests for action. List these and file the 'story'. It may be useful to you when you work through the final chapter.

Morning pages

A somewhat different approach to creativity in a work context is suggested by Bryon, Cameron and Allen in *The Artist's Way at Work*. This assumes that we are all creative, and can become more creative, becoming happier, healthier and more successful in the process. It offers a range of tools to help this 'creative emergence' which you might like to explore. The first is remarkably simple, and can be surprisingly powerful.

All you need do is wake a little earlier each day, and write (longhand) three A4 pages continuously. Just keep writing, putting down anything that occurs to you. It doesn't matter what. Thoughts about study, work, or anything else, brain dump, to-do lists or whatever. It is *intended* to be messy, disorganised, chaotic. Do not stop to think. Do not re-read. Do not show to anyone else. When you have finished, simply put it away.

It is claimed (and it works for me) that the act of writing creates a safe psychological space, and starts a process of re-ordering: goals and aspirations emerge from the chaos, you will find that you get more done, are more focused, and although they take time (20–40 minutes at first, though you will speed up with practice) they also *create* time at work, and free up a great deal of energy. The result is not instant, but should be felt within a matter of weeks. If you have time before your course starts this is something well worth experimenting with. (It has the added bonus of giving writing practice, so that you will answer exam questions much more fluently!)

→ Ch 8

Dangers of creativity

After such a discussion of the value of creativity, it may seem strange to talk about its dangers. But these stem from the point at which we started, the value and prevalence of a rational approach. These are not negated by the need for creativity as a *part* of any attack on problems or search for opportunities. Rational, convergent thinking needs to be set aside for creativity to have free rein, but it needs to be set aside consciously and temporarily.

The danger of creativity is that it can become so exciting that the rational world, with its all too real constraints, is devalued or ignored while play and fantasy rule supreme. While this may feel wonderful, the results of such 'unanchored' creativity may be disappointing or non-existent. It is from the *combination* of the two forms of thinking, and out of the tension between them, that true progress will come.

By nesting creative thinking within a wider rational approach and by exploiting the strengths of each form of approach, combining play with sheer hard work, you will, with luck and your developing skills, become the flexible, innovative thinker that organisations say they want. But you will still be able to bring your thoughts to fruition and plan carefully for their successful implementation.

FINDING OPPORTUNITIES TO BE CREATIVE

At first sight, your degree course may appear to offer you few opportunities for creativity. Indeed, there may be many occasions where being creative would be seriously discouraged! This will, of course, depend on your subject and on how it is taught. You may not need creativity to apply a specific equation, for example. However, there may be more scope than you think. If you can find new ways of approaching essay topics your originality may lead to high marks.

Of course your interpretation would have to be valid, and you might need to justify its validity, and your logic within this original approach would need to be sound. Remember, to be effective creativity needs to be combined with rationality. There will always be a slight risk of a spectacularly low mark if your tutor is not impressed by your creativity – it is up to you to assess this risk, and decide whether you want to take it.

→ Ch 12

If you are working on case studies, then you can use creative approaches such as the sequence of rich picturing → problem theme → relevant systems, or deliberate use of other metaphors than the system, in the early stages. These may well lead you to a better approach to a problem than you would otherwise have chosen. If you are faced with the requirement to do a dissertation or research project as part of your course, you should find idea-generation techniques helpful in producing a topic and may then be able to use systems ideas or other metaphors as an aid to finding ways of addressing your chosen problem.

→ Ch 16

Practising creativity will not be limited to your course work. During your time as a student you will encounter many problems apart from those posed by your lecturers. If you take these as opportunities for experimenting with the sort of techniques described above, you will be developing skills that will be immensely useful to you in employment, as well as finding better solutions to your immediate problems.

ACTIVITY 15.8

Each time that you hit a problem, try to use at least two of the techniques suggested in this chapter as part of your attempt at solving it. Document your efforts and write down your reflections on the strengths and weaknesses of the approach in that context, together with thoughts about difficulties and how you might have done better. Review this growing 'creative problem solving' part of your file at intervals.

SUMMARY

This chapter has argued the following:

- Creative thinking is in many ways the antithesis of rational thinking and because of this may be difficult for those who have been trained in the latter. While you may need to spend much less time being creative than being rational, they are equally important.
- Creativity depends on becoming comfortable with ambiguity, mental experiment and play, while suspending judgement. Holism rather than linearity, pattern rather than sequence, 'right-brain' rather than 'left-brain' activities, are all important.
- Forced associations and conscious use of metaphor can add to ideas already generated by chance associations.
- Visual representations can be hugely powerful aids to creativity, as in addition to their other advantages they engage the right brain.
- Success will depend on keeping a balance between convergent and divergent thinking and using both halves of the brain effectively.

Further information

- Bryon, M., Cameron, J. and Allen, C. (1998) *The Artist's Way at Work*, Pan Books, for a range of techniques to make you more creative generally.
- Cameron, J. (1992) *The Artist's Way*, Tarcher. This is the source of the ideas in Bryon *et al.*, and addresses creativity in the more general sense. Either is well worth looking at.
- Cameron, S. and Pearce, S. (1997) *Against the Grain*, Butterworth-Heinemann.
- Checkland, P. (1981) *Systems Thinking, Systems Practice*, Wiley. This gives a clear description of how to use a particular methodology.
- de Bono, E. (1971) *Lateral Thinking for Management*, Pelican. This is a classic.
- Handy, C. (1989) *The Age of Unreason*, Business Books.
- Henry, J. (1991) *Creative Management*, Sage.
- Mitroff, I.I. and Linstone, H.A. (1993) *The Unbounded Mind*, Oxford University Press. This is not an easy read, but well worth the effort.
- Morgan, G. (1986) *Images of Organization*, Sage. This is a fascinating and stimulating development of the use of metaphor.
- Senge, P.M. (1990) *The Fifth Discipline*, Century Business.
- Senior, B. (1997) *Organisational Change*, Financial Times Pitman Publishing.

→ **Part 5** # INTEGRATING YOUR SKILLS

Introduction to Part 5

Thus far, the skills you will need for successful study (and frequently for success in employment as well) have been addressed in a fairly piecemeal fashion. Any other approach would have been extremely difficult both to write and to study. This final part of the book looks at how they need to be integrated in order to make you effective as a manager, both of your own future and of projects for which you are given responsibility at work. It also shows how some refinements of the skills already developed can help you meet the specific demands of both these areas.

This part therefore looks first at project management, a term with multiple meanings! Projects can be extremely small, or huge, or anywhere in between. The project you are likely to be asked to do towards the end of your degree course is a small-scale induction to the art of project management. Yet it is likely to share many features with the 'internal consultancy' projects often given to recent graduates, or to managers assessed as having 'high-flier' potential, and the same skills will eventually be relevant to far larger projects involving major investments over a long timescale.

Projects require the same skills as effective self-management but in a context presenting much greater challenges. It may be difficult to establish clear, and agreed, objectives. You will need to plan and coordinate work on a wide range of tasks over a longer timescale. Thus it is vital that you set your own interim deadlines. You can no longer merely respond to the shorter-term deadlines set by others as you may have done thus far. Thus projects demand a high level of discipline and advanced time-management skills. You may also need to work with others and negotiate to secure their cooperation to an extent not previously encountered. If you are doing a group project, the 'working with others' aspect will be similar to working in a task force – a way of organising jobs that is increasingly common in employment.

Then you will need to write a coherent and persuasive report of perhaps 10 000 words, incorporating the analysis of a considerable body of data. This will probably tax you more than anything you have so far written. Again, the ability to do it is often important for project work in employment. For any project directed towards bringing about change, senior management will need to be convinced of the need to implement recommendations. A well-written report may play a key part in persuading them.

The final chapter looks at the specific 'project' of getting the sort of job you want once you graduate. You will need to revisit and redefine your objectives, and to research job opportunities. You will need to apply your written communication skills to making an application and use your 'talking and listening' skills to good effect in interviews. These final two chapters therefore address, and allow you to practise further, most of the skills the book has already introduced. Where a skill is particularly important in this context, further detail is given.

You will need to plan your work on this chapter carefully, as the best time to do the activities will depend on your course, and life, schedule. Some of the project-management skills will be best left until you encounter a project. Some of the job-seeking skills will similarly depend on your being ready to apply for jobs (though they can be addressed in the context of seeking vacation work, or industrial placements). But it is worth looking at these chapters now, to identify those things that you *can* practise in advance. As the first chapter pointed out, to increase your chances of getting a really good job you *need* to take action in advance. So you should draw up your action plan now.

→ 16   Managing projects

Task forces and project teams are a common form of work organisation today. You are likely to spend large parts of your working life leading or working in task forces and project teams. Most courses will include a substantial project or dissertation to help you develop the relevant skills. This chapter will help you to do well in course projects, and to contribute effectively to a range of projects at work.

Learning outcomes

By the end of this chapter you should:

- understand the specific demands of project work and how they relate to skills already covered
- be able to choose a suitable topic for a project or dissertation to meet your course and personal objectives
- be aware of the steps needed to gain access or commitment to a project within an organisation
- know how to draw up an initial research plan
- understand some of the specific requirements of project reports or dissertations.

'Project' can be used in many different ways, but normally includes the idea of some specific task that is non-routine, somewhat complex and discrete. In contrast with the continuous nature of much traditional management, there is a clear goal to *complete* the project by a specified time. This greater clarity brings into sharp focus the managerial roles described earlier. Because they relate to something specific, they are easily identified. Control, in particular, is highly visible. The chapter looks at each stage of project management from the viewpoint both of a course project and the sort of project you may well encounter at work.

PROJECT TEAMS

A project-based form of organisation has many advantages. It allows for devolution of authority – a task force with a clearly defined remit can be left to get on with it, subject to fairly simple controls. The person responsible for the group (or the group as a whole if autonomous) can adapt rapidly to changes in the environment in order to remain on target. It is thus a more flexible structure. People organised in this way are more motivated. A clearly defined and manageable task, as consideration of expectancy theory makes apparent, should allow for closer links between performance and both intrinsic and extrinsic outcomes. In addition to the autonomy already mentioned, the job is high on task identity so feedback is likely to be more clear cut. Objectives can more easily be specified in CSMART terms.

→ Ch 2

Such project teams require their members to have virtually all the skills covered in this book:

- self-management skills to perform their part of the collaborative task effectively
- planning skills to help them contribute to designing the project and the way in which the team will share the work
- interpersonal skills for communication with other team members
- problem-solving skills to address the inevitable snags that will arise
- creativity skills to enable the unforeseen to be envisaged and difficulties which defy resolution by a merely rational approach to be overcome.

These skills will be equally relevant to any project you do as part of your course work.

GROUP PROJECTS

You may well be required as part of your course to do a group project. This is excellent preparation for being part of a project team at work, and will allow you to reinforce the team-working skills addressed in Chapter 10. (Revisit this to check on your skills levels.)

→ Ch 10

Group project work will be more satisfying if:
- members are equally committed
- there is a good mix of strengths
- objectives are clarified and agreed
- meetings are frequent
- attention is paid to process
- efforts are coordinated
- progress is monitored regularly.

The success of the project, and hence your grade, will not be totally under your control. It will depend upon the efforts of others, as well as your own, so it matters who you are working with. Aim to be in a group with others who are prepared to exert the same level of effort as you are, and have a similar level of concern with success. There is nothing worse than being part of a group where you feel you are the only one who actually cares about getting the work done well. It can be fairly difficult, too, if you take a relatively relaxed approach and the others in the group want to work every hour there is in pursuit of perfection.

Managing the group process is equally important. When forming a group it is a good idea to aim for a mix of academic strengths and of preferred team roles. You will do better if at least one in the group is good at analysis, one is good at organising people's contributions, one is good at drafting and so on. This chapter is written primarily from the perspective of work on an individual project. If you are working as part of a team, you need additionally to be absolutely sure that you are all clear as to what you are trying to do and how. At each stage you need to have a clear and *shared* understanding of the group's objectives, of how responsibilities have been allocated and of how progress will be monitored. You will need frequent meetings to share progress so that you continue to move in the same direction, and to build on each other's work.

Coordination will be crucial throughout. Any conflicts need to be addressed as soon as they surface. You will not have time to repair damage later. In particular, you need to be firm about setting, and *meeting*, interim targets. While you may feel sorry for a friend's troubles, whatever they are, and feel it is mean to insist that they keep on schedule regardless, sympathy can be dangerous. So is optimism. You cannot afford to *hope* that a colleague will sort things out in time to catch up with their part of the work. You need as a group to address any such problems and work out ways of handling any slippage as soon as it occurs.

If despite your best efforts not all members play a full role, this needs to be discussed with your tutors. Your report can often usefully indicate the roles played by different group members. If you end up having to do more than your fair share, it is worth documenting this fact, together with the unsuccessful efforts you made to avoid the situation occurring.

Whether you are doing it individually or as part of a team, working on a project which appears to be under control can be highly motivating and the experience deeply satisfying, not least because you will be aware of using a wide range of skills to achieve a challenging objective and because your success or otherwise will be clearly apparent. The converse is that a project which goes less well, whether because you lack the necessary skills or because you fail to exercise them as well as you might, can be a nightmare. Figure 16.1 maps some of the necessary skills on to the stages you are likely to go through in such a project, indicating the chapter numbers where these are covered. This shows clearly the function of project work in integrating a wide range of skills. The discussion which follows looks at the different stages of such a project, expanding on the way in which the skills shown on the diagram are needed. This should help you to manage any project more successfully, whether it is academic or work related.

PROJECT PLANNING

For projects, as with everything else, clarity of objectives is essential. In real projects there are normally three sets of project objectives which will need to be specified. These concern:

- performance
- cost
- time.

For example, a project might have the objective of designing a new IT system to a particular specification, within a specified cost, for implementation in 18 months' time.

For a student project or dissertation, there will be *learning* objectives in addition to the explicit project aims. These will influence the objectives for the project itself. It is worth understanding your tutors' likely perspectives before going further. Although these are

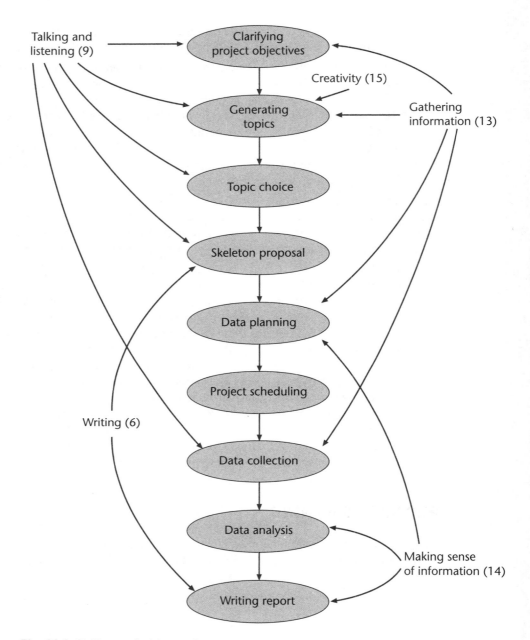

Fig. 16.1 Skills needed for project management
(NB for clarity, project and self-management skills, which are needed at *every* stage, are not shown, nor are the group skills needed at every stage of a group project.)

outlined with respect to management research, you will find close parallels with social science research more generally and indeed with any research. If you are studying something other than management, it should not be too difficult to translate them into something relevant to your own area.

Management research can take a number of different forms. It may aim to:

- resolve theoretical questions
- explore a topic of general interest to managers
- evaluate some aspect of an organisation's performance
- address a practical organisational problem, culminating in a set of recommendations for action
- implement and evaluate changes, based on recommendations as above.

Where your project will lie on this theory–action scale will depend on the practical bias of your course and whether or not you have facilities to cooperate with an organisation in order to address a genuine concern. Your tutors will probably be aiming to provide you with as many of the learning opportunities listed below as practical considerations allow. Such potential learning from projects includes the ability to practise:

- liaison with 'clients', developing negotiation, communication and other interpersonal skills
- diagnostic work on complex situations, using concepts, diagramming and other techniques and talking and listening skills
- problem-formulation and data-planning skills
- evaluation of different methodologies and selection and application of appropriate methodologies
- techniques for planning and scheduling your work
- information-gathering skills including electronic literature search and collection of some form of primary data
- use of IT and other skills for data analysis
- evaluation of information and its limitations
- research skills relevant to a postgraduate degree
- written communication skills needed to integrate data and descriptions into a compelling argument.

Setting clear objectives

Different sets of objectives were outlined above: learning objectives; general objectives which a project must meet to pass; your task objectives for your specific project; the objectives any client may have for the project. It is important to distinguish these sets when clarifying objectives. Clearly, one of your first tasks will be to clarify your tutors' requirements, highlighting the skills on the list above which are most relevant to your situation, adding any others and making sure in general that you know what requirements are specified for the project or dissertation.

16

Managing projects

If you are doing an in-company project as a student, you need to be very careful that the 'client's' objectives for the work are consistent with those of your tutors. You cannot firm up your choice of project until this has been established. If you are doing project work for real, it is equally important to check that client objectives are appropriate. They need to be capable of being met within the resources likely to be available and capable of resolving the problem situation if met.

'Define objectives' is easily said, but less easily done. Clients may be unclear about what they want. Or they may express their objectives clearly, but you may feel that these reflect a faulty diagnosis of the situation or no real diagnosis at all. You may feel that further investigation is necessary before you can be sure that the specified objectives are appropriate.

→ Ch 9

Suppose that your client is demanding a new IT system. You have a strong suspicion that the existing one could more than meet the required specification if staff were only trained to use it properly. If you are in the market for supplying such systems and the existing system was provided by a competitor, you might be tempted to go along with this (although it raises interesting ethical questions). If you are an 'internal supplier' you may do your company better service by questioning the stated objectives, showing what could be achieved by training and perhaps saving hundreds of thousands of pounds. This is just one example of the need to question given objectives. It is for this reason that the diagnostic and investigative skills covered in Chapter 12 are so important.

→ Ch 12

→ Ch 13

Diagnosis is absolutely crucial. In any complex situation, diagnosis is essential to ensure that objectives are clear, appropriate and understood by both you and your client. Talking to those likely to be affected by the project can give you valuable information. And implementation of any proposed changes is likely to be more successful, and less problematic, because of this communication. The plans themselves are likely to be far better because of the information you gained at this stage. Furthermore, people are more likely to cooperate if they feel that they have contributed to planning a change. Changes seen as imposed from above are likely to be strongly resisted.

Although in work contexts you are likely to be given a project, that does not (usually) mean that you have to accept objectives as specified. Clarification and exploration of the context which generated the idea for the project may produce agreement to a slight shift in focus at the outset. This can greatly increase the likelihood of a satisfactory outcome both for the internal or external client and for you as project manager. If your student project is one which is done in-company, and perhaps suggested by the company, your position is very similar to that of undertaking a project as part of your job. If you are doing a library-based project you will have more scope, but ensuring that the objectives are appropriate is perhaps even more of a challenge.

ACTIVITY 16.1

If you have worked, think about changes you experienced at work. Divide these into those where you were involved in planning the change and those where change was imposed. Rate your commitment to making the change work in each case and the extent to which you believed that it was aimed at the right objectives. If you have not worked, find two or three people who are currently working and ask them about *their* experience of change, again trying to distinguish between change with and without involvement in planning. Discuss your findings with others if possible.

FINDING A TOPIC

For organisational projects once you are in employment, you will normally start by clarifying the objectives given to you by someone more senior (remembering that they will often need to be seriously modified). But for student projects there is a prior stage of generating the project topic in the first place. This may be the hardest part of the whole experience. It is also the most important. It is important to consider as wide a range of topics as possible before selecting one: your choice will never be better than the best option you come up with, so you need a good range.

→ Ch 12, 13, 15

Generating possible topics will depend on some of the techniques discussed in Chapters 12, 13 and 15. You may need to be able to look at a situation from a broad perspective in order to identify possible problem themes, you will need to be able to use the library to see what related research has already been done, and you will need to have an understanding of how to collect information and interpret it in order to know which possible topics are capable of being progressed within the resources

→ Ch 9

available to you. You will even need talking and listening skills as covered in Chapter 9, as discussion with tutors and others will be extremely valuable at this stage.

When seeking ideas for projects use:
- tutors
- library
- existing interests
- past projects
- discussions
- brainstorming.

If you are one of those who find it impossible to think of a single topic, there is a strong risk that you will postpone even *thinking* of the project until dangerously late. You will probably hope that if you wait long enough inspiration will miraculously strike. Indeed it may do. But equally, all too often it does not. You may still be looking for a topic at a point when you should be almost at the end of your planning stage. There is then a risk that you will grasp at *any* suggested topic, regardless of its interest, and a further risk that this will turn out to be both difficult and tedious.

So even if you have almost no idea what sort of topic appeals to you, avoid procrastination at all costs. Start to think about it seriously at least six months before your project work is scheduled to begin, if at all possible. If this is not possible, then worry away at the issue of project choice as soon as you can and don't stop thinking about it until you have a topic that you are happy with. Use creativity techniques. Work with others who are similarly uncertain. Look at past projects to find topics that look potentially interesting and which you might explore in a slightly different way, or with a different sample. Talk to people in any organisation to which you have access about issues which are of current concern to them.

ACTIVITY 16.2

List titles of past projects or dissertations that interest you in some way, noting beside each the aspects of the topic which particularly strike you and why.

ACTIVITY 16.3

For one or more broad areas of potential interest, draw mind maps showing all possible questions concerning the area which might be part of, or lead to, a project topic. (Figure 16.2 gives an example of such a diagram.)

Make a project section in your file, and start to file all your project-directed activities and thoughts there.

Topic choice

Once you have a range of possible areas, the process of clarifying objectives and choosing and refining a topic will be absolutely crucial. You may well need to go through an iterative process of broadening and narrowing – generate a range of possible areas and narrow them down on one. Tease apart a range of ways of approaching this or sub-topics within the wider area. Choose one and again pull this

→ Ch 15

apart . . . Figure 15.1 showed this sequence diagrammatically.

Yet again there will be a need for communication – with your tutor to check that your shortlist of proposed topics meets course requirements, with those in any organisations which are hosting the project or allowing you access for research purposes, and with your tutor again (and again) as your ideas progress. You will need to use skills from

→ Ch 13

Chapter 13 to generate keywords, search the literature (including projects by previous students) and refine your research question. The following factors should influence your choice.

Interest

It is important that the topic you choose interests you (and interests your organisation if you are doing a work-based project). You are likely to be investing considerable effort

Project topics need to:
- be interesting
- offer suitable scope
- have symmetrical outcomes
- be feasible
- be low risk.

in your project. If you need organisational facilities for observation or interviewing or access to other data, the organisation will be investing too. If neither you nor the organisation cares overmuch about the outcomes, the labour can be soul-destroying. But if your client organisation does care about the topic, you may gain considerable support and help in your work and find that your final report is used to inform policy. If you are really concerned about the topic too, you will find project work engrossing.

If you are doing a library-based rather than on organisation-based project, then you may be able to make it more interesting by thinking of it as a potential publication. This could perhaps be in a non-academic periodical. By thinking of a potential outlet for something derived from your research, and perhaps making sure that you collect

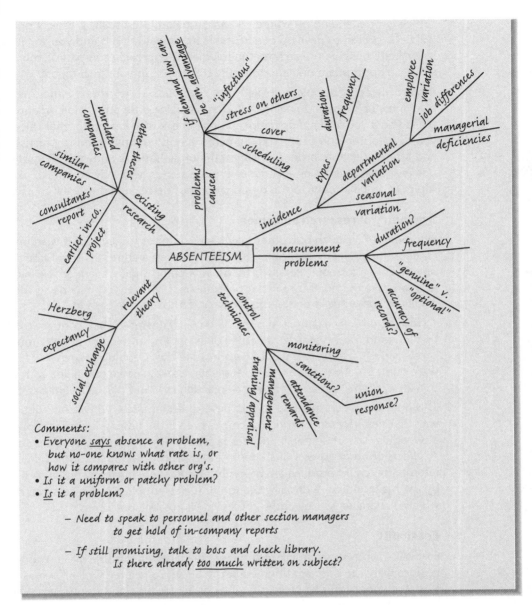

Fig. 16.2 Student's mind map and subsequent thoughts on a possible absenteeism project

additional titbits that would make the derived article more interesting to readers, you might add to the interest value of the project for yourself.

Scope

It is important that your chosen topic is potentially broad enough and deep enough for you to exhibit the range of skills that your tutors expect. Such expectations will vary somewhat depending on where you are studying. But usually a project or dissertation will be expected to develop generalisable investigative skills and you will be expected to evaluate possible research methodologies or approaches as part of your project, to select an appropriate one and to justify this choice in your final report.

A narrowly defined topic is unlikely to allow you to demonstrate either methodological awareness or strategic thinking. If you are working with an outside organisation and it offers you a very narrow operational topic, check with your tutor that this will allow you to meet the university's requirements. If not, you may need to practise your talking and listening skills in order to increase the organisation's understanding of what the university means by a project. Once it understands, you may be able to explore other topics of equal interest to the organisation but better suited to your course needs.

Symmetry of research outcomes

Symmetry of research outcomes may be less familiar to you, but it is an important criterion for choice. What it means is that your research results should be of interest however they turn out. Research to 'prove a point' should therefore be avoided. If it fails to prove the point it may not be of interest. Worse, you may be so keen for your results to come out in one particular direction that bias creeps in.

To take an unlikely example, suppose you were convinced that, contrary to popular opinion (and most research), a degree does not improve job prospects. You might carefully design some research to demonstrate this. Certainly, there would be a stir if you were right. But if you were wrong, and your research came out in line with what people think they 'know' already, the general reaction to your findings might be: 'So what?'

This does not mean that you should never question received wisdom. But do it in a way that generates interesting outcomes even if the basic principle is supported. Look at whether class of degree influences prospects when A level grades are controlled for, or effects of other aspects of students and their courses. Such supplementary information could produce an interesting result even if the obvious view *is* supported by the main finding. Normally, though, it is a safer bet to pick a research question which is characterised by equal interest in all possible outcomes.

Feasibility

Feasibility is obviously crucial. No project manager in industry would want to take on responsibility for a project doomed at the outset to failure. Similarly, you should make sure that your proposed topic is feasible given the time and resources at your disposal. To attempt the impossible shows a distinct lack of judgement. If you have little experience of project work, such judgement may be difficult. A striking feature of most student projects is the extent to which they take longer than expected. All projects have a way of expanding to use at least twice the time and energy expected at all stages from planning to writing up. To allow for this, be cautious in your aims. If ever you feel that your ideas might be even slightly ambitious, talk to your tutor and cut back your plans if so advised.

There are other warning signals that something may not be feasible. If activities will incur significant costs, or need access to data that may be commercially sensitive or require significant investment of time by others over whom you do not have control, be very wary. In general, the world is not sitting there waiting to help students with projects unless very clear advantages are apparent as a result of such cooperation.

Scope for catastrophe

Scope for catastrophe in a project is closely related to feasibility and is just as important. It relates primarily to projects involving organisational involvement. These can be threatened by organisational changes. For example, if redundancies are planned for a group of staff you were planning to interview, you may find that you are suddenly denied access. Your project is also at risk from personnel changes. You may have one champion in the organisation, but only one. If that person leaves, you may find that cooperation is seriously reduced. Real-time projects are another area where you are at serious risk. If your project is linked to events happening in real time in the organisation and these events are put back by a few months, you may find yourself with nothing to study until after your project is due for completion! It is worth 'hazard spotting' for all suggested organisational topics in order to assess the scope for catastrophe associated with each.

Although the techniques you may use at different stages (brainstorming, literature search, discussion at the start, for example) may vary, the general approach you will need for project choice can be summarised by the algorithm shown in Figure 16.3.

> **ACTIVITY 16.4**
>
> When you have settled on one or more likely topics, use the choice algorithm in Figure 16.3 to help with your decision. Note your likely topic, and your initial thoughts about it, in your file.

Once you have a likely topic, you will probably need to do a first rough literature search (unless you have already done one in the process of settling on your topic). This will enable you to check what already exists in terms of investigation of this or similar topics and the methods which have been used in such investigations. From this, you should be able to refine your topic still further.

PROJECT PROPOSALS

Having made your choice, write as clear and detailed a draft project proposal as you can. This will assist you in planning the project and will help your tutor to know just what you have in mind. If you are doing an organisation-based project, it will also ensure that your organisation knows and is happy with the way your thoughts are developing. At this stage your thoughts will not be fully clear. Your final project proposal will need to be completed at the end of your planning stage, but a skeleton will be useful now. You can amend it as much as is necessary in the light of future thinking. At this point, simply outline your intentions under the four headings on page 363, leaving spaces if you are unsure of anything.

16

Managing projects

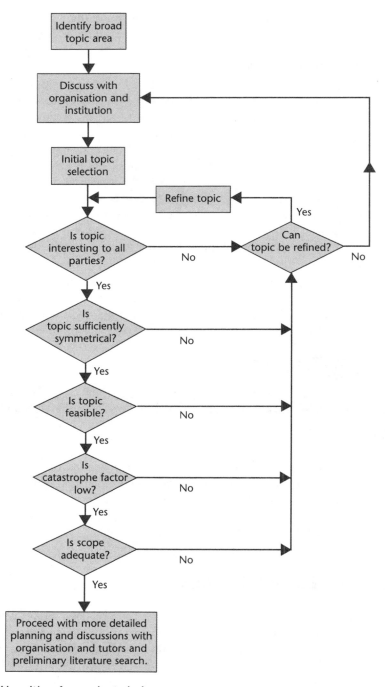

Fig. 16.3 Algorithm for project choice

- **Problem or topic description** – background to the project, its context and significance.
- **Value of investigation** – why would the client organisation or other reader want to know what the project aims to establish?
- **Likely project design** – possible methodology, timescale and the skills likely to be employed.
- **Data requirements** – the information needed and how data will be obtained and analysed.

Gaining client agreement

In real-life consultancy the key skill is maintaining good relationships with the client. If you are doing a project for an organisational client, you need to pay careful attention to this. One factor which is absolutely critical is that you work out a clearly written and *agreed* research proposal. In order to obtain such agreement, it is helpful to discuss your skeleton proposal with any client. If differences of perspective emerge, it will be relatively easy to redirect the project at this early stage in order better to meet both sets of objectives. If this looks impossible, it is even more important to find this out as soon as possible, while there is still time to choose another topic. You should if at all possible obtain written agreement to this proposal and to any necessary access to information. This may seem unnecessarily legalistic, but it can provide an essential protection if your contact in the organisation moves on and is replaced by someone less committed to the project. A written agreement will not prevent all the problems such a change can cause, but can strengthen your case for continued facilities. It is also a useful protection against claims from some quarters that your research has in some way failed to meet its client's objectives. If these objectives now seem different from the agreed project objectives, the written agreement to the proposal can be very helpful.

> A clear proposal, agreed in writing with your client, is essential.

Once the skeleton has been agreed, and you have gone through the stages outlined in the following sections it is useful to develop a clear project brief that you and your client, sponsor and/or supervisor can use as a reference document. Note that this is being discussed ahead of the stage when you will be doing it, for two reasons. First, the same reasons for gaining agreement apply. Second, knowing that you need to produce this document will focus your thinking as you go through the stages that follow. Possible headings for a project brief include:

- project title
- client and researcher names
- date brief agreed
- project start and finish dates
- significant milestones
- key project objectives
- success criteria
- scope of project (including constraints)

- resources needed
- communication arrangements during project
- form of final report.

As with the skeleton proposal, the fuller brief needs to be agreed with key stakeholders.

ACTIVITY 16.5

File your agreed project brief, together with any comments such as areas of continuing concern, or things still to be resolved. Make a plan for progressing these, and gaining agreement with key stakeholders

DATA PLANNING

Detailed and realistic project planning is essential and should begin as soon as you are happy with your project choice, certainly well before you are due to commence any data collection. The first stage is data planning. You cannot fully assess the feasibility of your proposal until you have a detailed plan of what will be involved. This will depend on the data that you decide you need and the approach you decide on for collecting them.

No matter how carefully you have thought about possible topics and used the algorithm to test/refine them, detailed planning may highlight difficulties you had not envisaged. You need to allow time to go through further cycles of topic choice and development should such iteration be necessary. So data planning should commence as early as possible – for most projects, the bulk of your work will consist of data collection and analysis. The adequacy of any report you write and of the conclusions you present therein will depend on the evidence on which these are based. If your information is biased or inaccurate, your conclusions will be worthless.

→ Ch 13, 14   Obviously the type of data sought will depend on your particular project. If you read Chapters 13 and 14 some time before starting your detailed project planning, re-read them with your particular topic firmly in mind. When you have done this, map out the data you will need to address your chosen problem or answer your research question.

ACTIVITY 16.6

When you have decided on the data you will need to collect, and the approach you will take to collecting them, ask yourself the following questions:

- How accurate and reliable will the data be?
- Is the proposed sample large enough to warrant the conclusions you are likely to draw?
- Is your sample sufficiently representative of the population in which you are interested?
- Will any measures actually measure what they purport to measure?
- If they are indicators rather than direct measures, will they be the best available indicators?

Once you are satisfied that the data you propose to collect will be adequate for your purpose and the way in which you propose to collect them is an appropriate one, you are in a position to start detailed scheduling.

PROJECT SCHEDULING

Once a project manager has clarified the performance, cost and time objectives for an organisational project, careful planning is needed to ensure that necessary resources are acquired, tasks identified and scheduled and control systems set in place. Normally completion on time will be crucial, with cost over-runs and other financial penalties if the project is not finished. For a student project or dissertation, the penalties of over-run may be at least as severe – your degree is probably at stake.

→ Ch 2   Chapter 2 introduced the ideas of charts and networks and you might find it helpful to revise these briefly before tackling the more detailed treatment which follows. You need to be clear about the use of Gantt or planning bar charts as planning and scheduling aids. For simple projects, these can simply be drawn. For more complex ones, with many interdependent activities, it would be difficult to work out how to arrange things so that everything gets done in the right order, in the minimum time and without over-straining resources at any point. Networks and critical paths were introduced in Chapter 2 as a logical approach to optimal sequencing. Your project may well be the first time that you need to construct a network 'in anger'. The following more detailed description may help.

Critical path analysis

When you were considering charts and networks as an aid to the relatively straightforward case of managing your study, you probably did not need to draw network diagrams. However, for project management planning is crucial and often complex and constructing a network will help greatly. It is possible to construct networks by hand. Figure 16.4 is an example of such a diagram. But software is readily available for constructing network diagrams and identifying critical paths, and scheduling activities efficiently as a result of these. It is worth using this as a planning aid in any moderately complex situation. (You will be developing another IT-related skill in the process, which could add to your portfolio in this area.)

In either case, you construct the network by looking at each activity, at how long it will take and at what needs to be completed before it can start. You can see that the diagram does indeed look a bit like a net. The diagram is drawn, and read, from left to right. No activity can be started until those to the left of it are complete. There are different ways of drawing networks. (A common minor variant is to write the name of the activity on an arrow, rather than the numbers shown in the diagram.) The example described is merely one common approach. Whichever you choose, as with other diagrams, it is important to use the convention consistently. If you combine aspects of different conventions in a single diagram, you are likely to end up with a muddle. As the whole point of the exercise is clarity, avoid this!

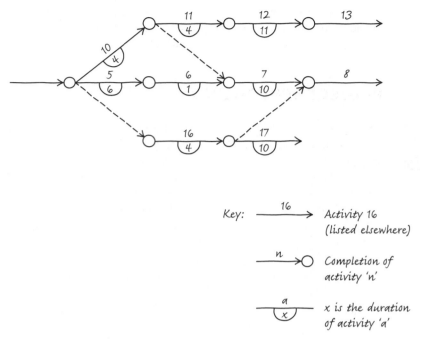

Fig. 16.4 Part of a hand-drawn network

In the diagram shown, activities are identified by a number (key elsewhere) on the arrow, duration of the activity is indicated not by the length of the arrow but by a number in a semicircle beneath the arrow, and 'events', that is, the completion of activities, are indicated by circles. The dotted lines on the chart represent so-called dummy activities, normally of zero duration. Such dummies are necessary to show constraints between activities – something cannot be started until several other activities have been completed. Rather than superimposing these events at the start of the next arrow, which would be hopelessly confusing and impossible to read, the dummy device is used.

Estimating how long it will take to complete various activities can be difficult. Ask advice and then (remembering the 'Topsy' nature of projects) allow some extra. Remember that there will be 'dead' time to be included, time when you are waiting for people to return telephone calls, for surveys to be posted back or for someone else (if you are lucky) to process your data. (Examples in employment might include time for an advertisement you have designed to appear in a specialist journal, or for a training course to be available for staff, or for machinery or materials that you have ordered to be delivered.) 'Dead time' means that you can schedule activities in parallel, as was → Ch 2 shown on the bar chart in Chapter 2, as you can work on one activity when waiting for something that will allow you to progress another.

In order to do this juggling and make full use of your time despite such waits, you need the ideas (*see* Chapter 2 again) of critical paths and floats. To work out the minimum time a project can take, you need to look for the path of longest duration

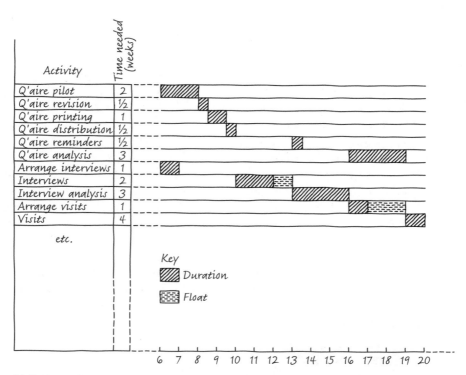

Fig. 16.5 Part of a hand-drawn schedule for project planning

through the network. You get this by adding together the estimated activity times on the arrows forming each pathway through the net. This longest time tells you the earliest at which the end event can be reached. Any delay to any activity on this path will delay completion. Activities on this path are therefore critical, hence critical path analysis. Activities on non-critical paths *can* be delayed without affecting the completion time. This scope for delaying or slack is called 'float'.

To calculate float you work in the reverse direction, from right to left, subtracting activity durations from the time of the last event. This gives you the *latest* permissible start time for achieving each event. The difference between this and the *earliest* possible time for starting the activity is the float. In a bar chart, this can be shown by a shaded area. On a network, you could use, say, a big circle above an event enclosing the earliest event time and a square above events enclosing the latest time. (Remember, for critical events these times coincide.) Figure 16.5 shows part of a hand-drawn schedule for a project where there is some float.

Milestones

You will remember that control needs to be exercised while there is still time to take remedial action if necessary. In planning a project it is necessary to plan for control and the idea used most frequently is that of milestones. In a complex project, with subgroups working on sets of tasks, project managers cannot monitor every activity and all the inevitable adjustments that their subordinates will make to cope with varying circumstances. It is therefore helpful for them to identify points on the critical path at which agreed and recognisable criteria need to have been met. Normally, these criteria would relate to the three sets of objectives distinguished earlier, those to do with task progress and the cost and time taken to achieve this. Your task may be somewhat simpler, but the idea can still be a useful review mechanism and help you sustain motivation.

Some milestones may be set for you. You may be required to submit a project proposal by a given date, a progress report by another and a draft report chapter by a third. But it is worth looking at your critical path and selecting other milestones that relate to completion of significant sub-tasks and highlighting these on your schedule. You will probably find that each time you approach one of these milestones you will need to put in some extra effort in order to prevent slippage. If you do this, you will find the achievement of your deadline deeply satisfying and reassuring and your motivation to do well in the project is likely to be strengthened. If no amount of effort enables you to hit the milestone on target, you know you have a problem! But provided the milestones are sufficiently frequent (say, approximately every 20% of the time allotted for completion, perhaps more often on a really long project) the problem will become apparent while there is still time to do something about it.

ACTIVITY 16.7

Draw up a network for your project, including all the tasks necessary for completion. Identify the critical path and milestones on it. Then convert this into a schedule, drawing a bar chart to represent it and highlighting the milestones. Remember to schedule the final draft of your project proposal and gaining approval to this as either your first or a very early task.

NEGOTIATING ACCESS

If you need to gain access to organisations in order to gather the data you need, then you need to give careful thought to how you will do this and allow considerable time for it in your plans. Some of the reasons for difficulty have already been indicated. Key reasons include:

- lack of interest in your project or failure to understand its relevance
- reluctance to commit organisational resources to anything other than normal work
- nervousness about what may be found (whether political, commercial or personal sensitivity)
- knowledge (which is still secret) about imminent change that makes research invalid or undesirable
- doubts about your competence as a researcher
- worry that research, whatever its findings, may be disruptive or generate expectations which cannot be met.

In order to gain access, you need to slant your approach in a way that best addresses whichever of these reasons are important to your potential 'client'. It will be easiest to do this if you can identify your best contact person and find their views about the topic you propose before you make your request, though this is not always possible. If you cannot, then think about their likely concerns and aim to address these. You will normally find it helpful to do the following:

- *Use existing contacts.* Here your networking skills are important. Whom can you contact through members of your current network? If existing contacts are inadequate, then develop new ones. Initial informal contact by phone or e-mail can be useful.

- *Be very clear about what you want, why and what it will involve.* Few organisations will be willing to agree to something open-ended or unclear. For example, if you want to interview some staff, you will need to say how many of which kind(s) of people you want to interview, how long the interview will take, where and when it would need to be conducted and what will happen to the results. (Confidentiality will usually be a major worry.)

- *Make equally clear the benefits of collaboration to the organisation.* If there are none, you might want to think again about the project.

- *Make a formal request in a way that reinforces your credibility.* A neatly laid-out, word-processed letter, on headed (your college or department) notepaper, giving your tutor as a reference, will help greatly. Even if you have gained informal agreement by other means, you need to confirm this via such a letter.

- *Make replying easy.* A proforma and stamped addressed envelope may seem trivial, but could increase the number of positive replies considerably. A suggestion that you will phone to discuss this after a stated period (if it may be difficult for them to phone you) may also help.

- *Keep to agreements.* If you go outside what was agreed, you may lose access. So if you have sworn not to reveal what individuals say and then tell someone's boss the views they express, you can expect (deservedly) to be denied further access. In the interests of those who may request access for future projects, you should also keep to any agreements about what you will do subsequently. If you promise a copy of the report, for example, make sure that they get one.

MONITORING PROGRESS

Keeping control of your work is very important, given that there may be few interim deadlines imposed by your institution. Your planning chart will be an essential tool throughout your project. Display it prominently, refer to it frequently and modify it if this proves necessary. Although you should be monitoring progress all the time, find some way of ensuring a more formal progress check at each milestone. Perhaps you could schedule meetings with your tutor at these points, or at least agree to send in progress reports.

Any slippage should be treated extremely seriously. Resist the (strong!) temptation to attribute it to 'one-off' factors which will not happen again. Excusing yourself in this

16

Managing projects

way, and adjusting subsequent schedules to allow for the delay that has already occurred, is likely to mean you merely have worse 'slippage' when you reach the next milestone. Instead, you should look very carefully at the possible reasons for the delay and address these causes. Above all, resist the near-universal tendency to see the final deadline as so far away that project work is not urgent. If you are to do a good project, it is urgent from the start. Time will not expand as you approach the deadline!

Unless you are absolutely sure that you *can* get back on track and avoid any similar slippage in future (and this doesn't mean that you *hope* all will magically go more smoothly), you should discuss the situation with your tutor and adjust your plans accordingly. You may need to reduce the scope of your project in some way.

If you are working on a group project, it is very important that the group sets individual as well as group milestones and that the group as a whole meets regularly to review progress against these. If one group member encounters problems, ways of adjusting workloads may need to be found and of supporting the member in difficulty, if the project is to be completed successfully.

Writing a project log

As well as your planning chart, you should keep a detailed record of progress in the form of a project log. In this you should record all project activity, reasons for decisions, times taken, details of what happened, snags encountered and insights gained. This can be enormously helpful when you come to write up your report. It is surprising how things which seemed burned into your memory at the time can fade into oblivion before you come to describe them. Your log can be a source of observations made at the time and will be eminently quotable at appropriate points in your dissertation.

Furthermore, many institutions require students to include in, or with, their report a series of reflections on lessons learned and points where with hindsight it is realised that the project could have been approached better. This is intended to demonstrate that you have indeed learned something about the process of this kind of research and how to be critical of such investigations. (As an examiner, I find such reflections a valuable source of necessary marks for the student whose project has gone wrong for some reason.) Such a reflections section can draw heavily on your log.

Because a project draws on almost every skill covered in this book (and many more), your final report is a potential exhibit for almost any key skill or management competence you are likely to want to demonstrate. It can therefore be a valuable component of your portfolio. You would need to include a covering document with it which made explicit to your assessor the competences demonstrated and how. Again, a detailed project log would be a useful part of the 'story'.

Keeping track of references

→ Ch 13

The importance of noting full references was mentioned earlier, but cannot be stressed too often. Either in your log, or preferably on your computer, or somewhere very safe, you should keep a full record of *all* the sources you have used, even if you are not yet sure if you will need to refer to them. It really is worth using a bibliographic software package if you can. You can waste a huge amount of time hunting for references if your notes are incomplete. And you will probably be doing it just before the project is due while you are struggling to write a substantial report to a tight deadline. The last thing you need at this point is to be distracted by a search for complete references. Avoid this by getting into good habits now!

> **ACTIVITY 16.8**
>
> Look at the references you collected while doing your initial literature search at the topic choice stage. If they are not complete (i.e. with full title, author and publication names, publishers and/or page numbers), properly organised and safely stored, sort them out *now*, either using bibliographic software or by developing a system that you can easily use throughout your project. Then use it!

WRITING A PROJECT REPORT

If you spend some of your career as a consultant, report writing skills will be invaluable. Consultancy is a service, and largely intangible. When people are purchasing a service, they tend to be disproportionately impressed by the few tangible aspects there are, and a report is one of these. A consultant friend of mine freely admits that clients normally read only the first few pages. Yet he sees it as absolutely crucial that the report is fat, glossy and full of colour. It is the 'thwack' factor (when you thwack it down on the table) that gets him future business, he says.

You may not want to go to these lengths (though presentation will still be important). But after data collection and analysis, the most substantial task is likely to be writing your report. This activity can usefully be started much earlier than most people think. It may seem absurd to start drafting when you have scarcely started to collect your data and have little idea of what your eventual conclusions will be. But actually it can be most enlightening to write a skeleton draft based on guesses as to what the results might show. Often this will uncover a need for additional data: you may realise that, even if your results turn out as you expect, they will support only a weak argument. If you find this out at the data-collection stage, you have time to amend your plans accordingly.

→ Ch 12

→ Ch 3

Topic choice is therefore not the only time when iteration can be helpful. As with any complex problem-solving activity, a constant process of thought, experiment and refining of thoughts is necessary. This point is made explicit in many of the systems methodologies which you may be taught during your course. It also reflects the Kolb learning cycle introduced in Chapter 3. It is difficult to make sense of complexity all at once. But we can make a little sense of it, see ways in which our ideas might be improved, try these new ideas, refine them further in the light of experience and so on. Thus step by step we improve our understanding.

The other advantage of starting drafting early is that it is much less frightening to draft what you *know* is only a dummy draft. Sitting at the keyboard towards the end of your project knowing that you have to write 10 000 words or so at a single bite can, in contrast, be a prospect too awful to contemplate. If in consequence you postpone the exercise the task becomes quite impossible. You have no time left for revisions, no time even for proper thought. The resulting dissertation, despite much burning of midnight oil, is a disappointment to you, to your tutors and to any client organisation.

If you have written a skeleton draft at an early stage and are reasonably competent at word processing, writing your report can be relatively stress free. You can flesh out parts of the skeleton as you go along, revise these longer versions, incorporate your references and start analysing your data, all in parallel. Your final draft will gradually, and relatively painlessly, emerge from this process. Revisit Chapter 6 on clear writing at about the time you start to draft. There is more detail on report writing there. And most important, keep backup copies of your work somewhere absolutely safe and update these backups regularly. This is work you *cannot* afford to lose.

→ Ch 6

Style and format

You may be given a specified format, but if not, the following is one which is widely accepted:

- Title page
- 1–2 page summary – you may be required to submit this separately, rather than binding it with your report
- Preface and acknowledgements
- List of contents – numbering should usually reflect major and minor sections, e.g. 4, 4.1, 4.2 (*see* Figure 6.4 for an example)
- List of tables, figures, etc.
- Numbered sections – these should include an initial statement of project aims, a short statement of major findings and recommendations and then detailed descriptions of relevant literature, chosen methodology with justification, data collected, analysis, conclusions and probably reflections
- List of references
- Additional bibliography, if needed
- Appendices.

Style should be clear. You will normally be expected to use academic concepts wherever appropriate, but avoid any unnecessary jargon. Equally, you need to avoid sounding over-colloquial and 'chatty'. A report should be 'considered and careful' in its expression. In particular, do not make unsupported assertions. It should always be clear how your results are derived, or upon what evidence you are basing your statements. (Where there are shortcomings in your evidence and you need to make assumptions, you should say so clearly and discuss any resulting limitations to your conclusions.)

It will be much easier for your reader to absorb your developing argument if you give a short introduction to each section. This should clarify the structure of what you are about to write, and make it easier to grasp your arguments as they are reached.

Large chunks of text can be hard to read, so it helps to include relevant diagrams and tables at appropriate points. This breaks up the text, and is easier for the reader than having to turn repeatedly between text and appendices. (Very detailed or complex diagrams, tables or other information should be included as an appendix – it would interrupt your argument if included in the main text, and only a few of your readers may want to have that level of detail.)

Errors in spelling and grammar can make your meaning unclear, and additionally will make people less likely to believe you know what you are writing about! It is important to check what you have written – use the checks on your PC, and if you are worried that this will not be enough, find a competent friend to read it through as well. Double-check that you have entered figures in tables correctly. It is very easy to make errors that can alter the whole meaning of the table.

You can further improve the impression created by your report by using good quality paper, and thinking about fonts, graphics, use of colour and binding. If a particular binding is specified, make sure that you arrange for this in good time. If there is no specification, think carefully about the best way of presenting your report. Assessments of work are subjective. While content is crucial, presentation can have a strong influence on the mark you receive.

If you do all this and allow yourself sufficient time (twice as long as you imagine you can possibly need) for drafting, your finished dissertation/report can be one of the most satisfying things you have done. It will have uses as an exhibit of your competence in a number of areas when you are seeking employment or a competence-based professional qualification and it may be a source of articles should you wish to start writing for a wider audience. The process of producing it will have developed skills that will be vital in many of the jobs for which you are likely to apply. May I wish you success in your endeavour!

SUMMARY

This chapter has argued the following:

- Work in organisations is increasingly carried out in task or project groups.
- Project management, whether in employment or for projects you are required to do as a student, draws on almost all the skills covered in this book.
- Group projects need to be very carefully managed.
- Clarity of objectives is essential and topic choice should be approached as soon as feasible.
- Through iteration you should aim to select a topic that meets course requirements, is interesting and, if you have a client organisation, meets client needs.
- Detailed project planning is essential and cannot be undertaken until you have a clear idea of how you will proceed and the data that will be required.
- Networks, critical paths, milestones and bar charts are invaluable aids.
- Negotiating access is time-consuming and needs to be done with care, making clear what you want and why and what benefit there will be for the organisation. You need to do this in a way which reinforces your credibility.

- Progress should be monitored carefully and corrective steps taken as soon as any delay occurs – optimism is not enough.
- Drafting should start early, allowing time for insights from drafting to influence data collection. Ongoing redrafting will reduce the pressures of producing a final report.
- The final report should be clear, well presented and in appropriate style, format and binding.
- Project work presents major challenges, but can be a source of substantial learning and satisfaction.

Further information

- Bell, J. (1999) *Doing your Research Project,* 3rd edn, Open University Press.
- Bryman, A. (2001) *Social Research Methods*, Oxford University Press.
- Gill, J. and Johnson, P. (1997) *Research Methods for Manager*, 2nd edn, Paul Chapman Publishing.
- Howard, K. and Peters, J. (1990) 'Managing management research', *Management Decision*, 28: 5. This special issue provides a clear, fairly brief coverage of different types of management research, what is involved and a short but useful bibliography.
- Howard, K. and Sharp, J.A. (1996) *The Management of a Student Research Project*, 2nd edn, Gower. This is aimed at all types of research, not just management, and covers planning, data collection and analysis in far more detail than is possible here.
- Jankowicz, A.D. (2000) *Business Research Projects*, 3rd edn, Business Press.
- Saunders, M., Lewis, P. and Thornhill, A. (2003) *Research Methods for Business Students*, 3rd edn, Financial Times Pitman Publishing. This provides an excellent and more detailed treatment of the topic than is possible here, with useful material on the data-collection methods you are most likely to use in this sort of research and on analysing both quantitative and qualitative data. It also includes a number of case studies.
- White, B. (2003) *Dissertation Skills for Business and Management Students*, Thomson Learning.

→ 17 Into employment

Perhaps the most important and challenging project you face is obtaining a job after graduation. It will take all the skills you have developed thus far. This chapter will help you find jobs you would like to apply for, and increase your chances of getting one. If you are some way from graduating, working through the chapter can also help you apply for vacation jobs and industrial placements.

Learning outcomes

By the end of this chapter you should have:

- reassessed your work objectives
- identified sources of information on ways of meeting these
- drawn up a plan of action to take between now and graduation
- compiled a basic CV
- learned how to write a letter of application
- become more confident about being interviewed.

No job should be seen as permanent these days, so there is no need to seek the 'perfect' job. If you find that your first job is not what you wanted, you can change. But there are costs involved in changing jobs too quickly. The emotional and financial costs will be immediate. But longer term, potential employers will start to doubt your reliability or perseverance if you change too often. It is therefore well worth maximising your chances of finding a job that will suit you for several years, and will give you the experience and learning opportunities you need to prepare you for an even more rewarding job subsequently.

It may take considerable research, and perhaps some creativity, to identify the sort of work that will meet your objectives and to find the kind of organisation offering it. You need communication and ICT skills to find out about job opportunities. You need to manage your learning in order to make yourself a stronger candidate for them by doing things before you graduate. Your written communication skills will be taxed by preparing a compelling letter of application and professional looking *curriculum vitae* (CV). And you need talking and listening skills for an interview. If other assessment methods are used to supplement the interview, 'being assessed' skills will be relevant.

As was pointed out at the start, there can be 50 or more applicants for a good job. You need to put considerable effort into job search, building contacts, developing your skills, and making a good application if you are to be at the head of the queue.

One way of orienting your work to this chapter is to think in terms of three circles, the largest representing all jobs, the second jobs you would like, and the third jobs you could reasonably be offered. Your aim in working through this chapter is to find out more information about the first two circles, so that you can map them and their boundary more clearly. You then need to work on enlarging the third circle, or at least on maximising its overlap with the second. This you can do by developing skills, gaining relevant experience and making contact with target organisations in a positive way. Your career future lies within the third circle. Figure 17.1 illustrates this view. Note that this diagram suggests the category 'jobs you would like but which do not exist'. This will upset logicians, but the point is important. What do the other overlaps (or failures to overlap) suggest?

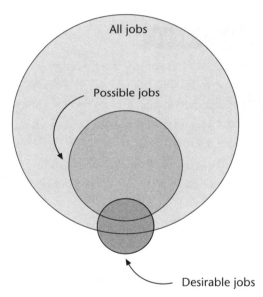

Fig. 17.1 Circles of employment

ACTIVITY 17.1

In order to gain more practice in diagramming, experiment to see whether any of the other techniques described in the book will help you to visualise your task in ways that suggest new lines of attack, or raise useful questions other than that of whether what you want actually exists. Start a 'job seeking' section in your file, and log your thoughts.

17

Into employment

REVIEWING YOUR STRENGTHS

If you are to target realistic jobs, those in the intersection between possible and desirable, you need a clear view of your strengths. Objectives and strengths need to be consistent with each other. If you are working through this chapter during the second or third year of your degree, your skills will have developed considerably. Try to resist temptations towards modesty just as much as you resist over-estimation. If you are working through the chapter earlier in your programme you may find it useful to pull together development needs you have identified while working through the book and construct a unified action plan for improving your employability.

Deciding what you want to do for the next few years is a complex task, the result of which can impact on the rest of your life. As with any complex problem you may need to work on several different strands simultaneously. Here, objectives and strengths and weaknesses need to be worked on in parallel. You also need to iterate, that is, develop thinking done earlier in the light of subsequent insights. As strengths and weaknesses will be of different significance for different jobs, you may need to do several analyses, one for each possible area of work, and to iterate several times, working through this section, then the next, then returning to this and so on as your ideas become clearer.

ACTIVITY 17.2

→ Ch 1

You started to consider your strengths and weaknesses in Chapter 1. Go back to that now. Use the list of key skills outlined there to update your lists of 'Strengths' and 'Weaknesses'. These skills include:

- number
- communication
- information skills
- working with others
- learning
- problem solving.

You may now be able to identify specific relevant skills under these broad headings, for example presentation or report writing under communication skills, networking or leadership under working with others, or facility with particular software packages under information technology. If you have already started to look at advertisements for jobs you might like, this may highlight other areas of strength and weakness. Remember to add experience as well as skills to your list. Again, your trawl of web sites and advertisements should give you an idea of the kinds of experience which you need to be able to offer. For example, this might be to have worked in a particular sector, or a particular function such as sales, or a particular context such as a 'lively creative team'.

Once you have constructed your list of strengths and weaknesses and thought about how important they might be for the sort of jobs you might wish to take, you are in a position to think seriously about the actions you need to take. Some will be short term, some longer, but all will be aimed at increasing relevant strengths and reducing relevant weaknesses so that you will be well positioned to gain a 'desirable' job at the end of your planning period. These plans will need to be revisited and amended at intervals, and the planning horizon extended. This planning process can help you to develop your career throughout your working life.

ACTIVITY 17.3

Develop a draft series of action plans for making yourself more employable by targeting key strengths and weaknesses. Follow them! Monitor progress at regular intervals and update plans regularly.

REASSESSING YOUR OBJECTIVES

Both your life objectives and your career objectives are likely to have altered markedly during your time as a student. Your perspectives will have broadened, you will have made new contacts, and you will be aware of a wider set of options. So in parallel with thinking about your strengths and weaknesses you need to reassess your objectives.

→ Ch 1 Again you should have already started this process at the start of the book, when you began to think about what you might want from a job and to question people about their experience of work, and will have been developing your thoughts about this ever since. If not, start by making a list of the things that are important to you in life as a whole.

What makes you feel satisfied? What would you like to achieve? Once you have answered these overarching questions, narrow down to the area of employment, and consider how this might help you achieve your wider objectives. Draw upon any work experience you have had, and conversations with people about their jobs. Think about which of the skills you listed you really *enjoy* using. If computer-aided careers guidance is available and you have not used it recently, take advantage of it now as a further aid to identifying your interests.

ACTIVITY 17.4

→ Ch 1 Try to imagine yourself five years from now in the 'perfect' job situation. Then look at what it is about that situation that makes it so good for you. What does this tell you about yourself? Revisit the 'hopes and fears' exercise in Chapter 1 and see how they have altered since then. If they have not altered much, or if you found your imagination didn't come up with much, spend some time talking to family, friends, mature students and those who have had vacation jobs in order to find out what they see as the elements of a 'good' job, and use this to refine your thinking.

ACTIVITY 17.5

Develop a hierarchy of objectives related to employment, highlighting those branches which are particularly important to you. Space this out on a large piece of paper and annotate it with thoughts about experiences and jobs which might help you achieve these objectives. (If you hate this degree of freedom, a tabular format is available as a web resource.) File your objectives.

ACTIVITY 17.6

Think about the implications of your objectives and then redraft your SWOT to reflect these, adding in opportunities and threats that the employment market offers, given your particular objectives. (You should revisit this SWOT throughout your work on this chapter, as part of the iterative process, aiming to have it fairly fully worked out by the time you have finished the book. Then revisit it at intervals throughout your career.)

Possibly the most powerful tool of all for making you aware of what you like and do not like, are good at and not good at, want and do not want of a job, is the actual experience of working. Vacation jobs, a placement year, or work before starting your degree, will make exploration of the 'circles of work' much easier. It will always be biased though, by the nature of your experience. If you are still in your first year, think seriously about a placement if you have not already committed yourself to one. If you *are* committed, but have not yet decided what to do with your year in industry, then the work in this chapter, including discussion with your careers service if at all possible, will help. You need to choose a placement likely to contribute to your development of relevant skills. This will enlarge your 'possible' circle.

ACTIVITY 17.7

Construct a series of objectives trees for your goals for the next five years (longer if you can think that far ahead). Focus your hierarchy on broad life objectives, with the job objectives that will serve these slotted in. Spend some time on this, talking through your diagrams with others if possible – they may ask you questions which prompt further thought. You should by now need no persuading that clarity of objectives is all important. File the results when you are satisfied with them.

FINDING OUT ABOUT OPPORTUNITIES

Once you have a clearer idea of your objectives, you can better focus your exploration of the circle representing 'all employment'. You are only really interested in the part of that circle that is relevant to your objectives, therefore potentially in the 'desirable jobs' area. You may not need to explore openings for telephone sanitisers, or sex chat line operators, or many other forms of gainful employment. To focus on the area which is likely to intersect with your requirements is more efficient. However, you need to avoid an uncreative, over-narrow approach: avoid drawing too firm a boundary yet.

You will remember that you need first to formulate your 'research question' and then to identify information sources. At some stage the question is likely to be of the form: 'What sorts of job in which sorts of organisation will offer me . . . and avoid . . .?' But you may need to ask more global questions first or start with something more specific. Use whatever questions seem best to fit your own situation. You may find relevance trees (Chapter 13) useful here. Certainly, if you can identify some keywords this may help you in your later investigations.

➜ Ch 13

ACTIVITY 17.8

Formulate a question or series of questions about theoretical (there is no need yet to be limited by what is *possible*) employment opportunities that will enable you to identify areas for more detailed investigation.

You now need to explore sources of information. Everyone who has ever worked is a potential primary source, as are all employers, so you may need to use secondary or tertiary sources. Probably the best starting point will be your university careers service. Make an appointment with them now, even if you are not yet near the end of your degree. The sooner you can use their expertise to focus your thinking the better, and the sooner you establish the information resources which they have, the longer you will have to take advantage of them. Spend some time seeing what they have that could help you to refine your search, or perhaps to enlarge it to areas which you had not previously considered but which seem to offer unsuspected opportunities.

Another source of information is job advertisements. Collect ones that interest you, even if you are not yet in a position to apply for the jobs they concern. Try to see whether patterns emerge from this. Are there some aspects which many of these advertisements have in common? Does this make you aware of new objectives you could add to your tree? If possible, obtain further particulars for some of the jobs that interest you. Even if you will not be in a position to apply for the job for a year or two, the information will be invaluable in helping you to see what employers think they offer and what they require. Most jobs are now advertised on the Internet. Go to the web sites of organisations you might like to work for and find their job opportunities pages. Look at some of the main recruitment agency pages (you will be able to find these from their advertisements in recruitment pages, or your careers service may provide you with lists of useful URLs).

ACTIVITY 17.9

Practise your Internet search skills by identifying ten sites that you think will be really useful in your job search, making a note of the main advantages of each. If possible, compare lists within a group, and add any which look useful to you that you had missed.

Start to assemble a file on job opportunities which can act as a reference point for future considerations. Guard against premature narrowing by collecting information on a few jobs which do *not* look interesting, as a check on your selection criteria and the boundaries these imply.

Employers who are *not* advertising jobs may still be a source of information. Your search of currently available jobs may help you to identify an area where you would like to work, but where there are no current vacancies. If so, see what you can easily find out about organisations from the Internet and other sources. Contact the personnel department to find out whether they anticipate openings for which you would be eligible, with your degree, to apply.

→ Ch 9

If so, find out more about such openings and about sources of further information about the organisation. Do they have any sort of 'open day'? Do they take on students for vacation work? When vacancies arise, where are they advertised? Could you go for an information interview, just to explore possibilities? This is an application of the networking approach suggested in Chapter 9. You could extend it by exploring your existing network of contacts (family, friends, past employers etc.) to see whether you have any links to this organisation or similar ones. In making contact with someone in an organisation whom you do not yet know, you are likely to get furthest if you make telephone contact first. You will need to draw on your talking and listening skills. As you will be moving into the area of 'extending the possible' here, do not make any such contacts until you have finished this chapter.

If you have yet to do a placement, or if you still have time to arrange relevant vacation jobs, you will have another way of finding out about one organisation in particular (more if you have several vacations still to go) and perhaps working with or for people with experience of other similar organisations and jobs. All this will help to increase your understanding of the sector, of jobs within it, their satisfactions and demands and their likely potential for meeting your own needs and desires.

ACTIVITY 17.10

Start to work seriously on the employment section of your file in which you organise all your information relevant to jobs and their characteristics, their attractions, their requirements and criteria for selection if advertised.

BECOMING MORE ATTRACTIVE TO EMPLOYERS

You should by now be getting a feel for what you need to do to identify promising jobs, the sorts of organisation in which they exist and the things which the employers in question seem to be looking for in applicants for these jobs. How much information you still need and the sources available to you will depend on how clear you are about what you want, how close you are to completing your degree and whether vacation work or placements are still a possibility. Therefore, only you can list the tasks which you need to carry out in order to clarify your objectives, to map the area of the 'employment circle' which is likely to allow you to meet these and to seek detailed information about the sorts of job which you most want.

Once you have listed these tasks, you can think about their duration and the order in which those tasks that depend on prior completion of other tasks must be done. This will enable you to construct a network, identify a critical path, decide on milestone activities and draw up a schedule of tasks.

ACTIVITY 17.11

Construct a network to enable you to draw a bar chart scheduling all the tasks needed to identify the sort of job you want, and if possible make contact with employers or types of employers for whom you would like to work, by the time when you would need to apply for such jobs. (Note: talk to careers guidance people about when this is – it may be sooner than you think.) Monitor your progress against this plan.

Following your action plan should make you much more employable, and increase the size of the intersection between desirable and possible jobs. Four aspects are particularly important:

- identifying skills and competences important to your target jobs and developing these where necessary
- making contact with potential employers
- preparing a good CV and letters of application
- thinking about how you can perform well in selection.

You will need to add these tasks to your schedule. You will be in a better position to do them when most of the tasks already scheduled have been completed.

Contacting potential employers

In addition to developing the general skills which will help you to become a successful candidate, you need to add in activities that will increase your chance of gaining a specific job. These can be scheduled only when you have identified it. As you will see in the following discussion of written applications, CVs and interviews, you are in all cases trying to communicate the extent to which you will meet a potential employer's needs. To do this, you have to put some effort into identifying those needs in each case and finding out as much as you can about a job for which you are preparing an application.

You will normally be sent some information about the company when you request further particulars of the job. If so, study carefully all the information sent to you, trying to work out from it the sort of person, and the sort of skills, that will most fit the job requirements. But try to investigate this further. Seek out other sources of information, from libraries, people you know, the Internet, products or services, shops or branch offices of the organisation in question. If a contact name or telephone number is given for further information, use that as a starting point for finding out as much as possible about the job and competences which would contribute to success in that job. Try to get the names of other people to talk to and arrange a visit if possible.

Organisations are likely to be impressed by the fact that you have clearly gone to considerable lengths to understand their needs and have worked out a good case that you will meet these. If you can go further, and find out more about the sector or industry and about customers and their likely needs, this will put you in an even better position to make an outstanding application and to do well in an interview. Remember to be courteous and professional in your contacts, but not boring. If you can form relationships with people prior to an interview, they may well give you invaluable information and they could even be involved in the selection process. The nature of your contact with them is therefore important.

ACTIVITY 17.12

Pick a job for which you plan to apply. (If you are some way short of graduating, pick one which you might apply for if you were ready.) Find out as much as you can about the job, the organisation and the organisation's competitive environment (customers and competitors), and think about the ways in which you can use this information to identify the strengths which you would want to offer and any weaknesses you might have. See whether you can complete a SWOT on yourself as a product for this *particular* customer, looking at opportunities and threats which the organisation might offer you too.

PREPARING A GOOD *CURRICULUM VITAE* (CV)

Most recruiters will ask you to include a *curriculum vitae* (translated roughly, the course of your life) or CV. This is really a personal data sheet, laid out for ease of reference, so that a potential employer can easily tell your age, status and qualifications, employment history and relevant skills. Once you have a long employment history, you may need to 'version' the CV to emphasise points relevant to the particular job you are seeking. If your experience is limited it should be easy to fit into any limit specified within the job's further particulars without selecting only the relevant points. Even if there is no limit specified, unless you have volumes of relevant experience you should aim to keep your CV to a maximum of two sides of A4. And you should treat briefly, if at all, aspects of marginal relevance.

Remember that this is a written communication and one with which you are seeking to impress as well as inform the reader. Care spent on ensuring that presentation is immaculate is therefore essential. As CVs normally need to be updated at fairly regular intervals, and while you are applying for jobs you will need a seemingly endless supply, this is an obvious application for a PC. A word-processed CV is an obvious demonstration of one (albeit minor) aspect of your IT skills and is far more impressive as well as far more labour saving than a handwritten one. It makes sense, however, to modify the appearance from the standard Microsoft format in order to stand out from the many applicants who will use this.

Layout preferences vary. If you are given a format by your careers service, or one is suggested in further particulars, then use that. Otherwise, take the following format as a starting point:

Name:

Home address   **Term address**

Home tel.   **Term tel.**
                                                       (Required only if applying before graduation)

Marital status (Not strictly necessary unless specifically required)

Dependants (Even more optional)

Date of birth

Nationality (Add work permit status if relevant)

Education:

University (Name of university you are currently at, faculty or school in which you are studying and dates of starting and completing degree)

Courses studied, dates and results

Schools attended (List schools, most recent first, giving name and town)

NB use the above format or similar for education if you have not yet completed your degree. If you have already graduated use the following:

Qualifications (It is normal to start with degrees in chronological order if you have more than one, before covering qualifications at a lower level, if they are recent enough to be relevant)

Date, awarding institution, degree, classification, subject
(list all degrees chronologically, if you are blessed with more than one)

What follows is common to pre- or post-graduation CVs:

Professional qualifications (if any)

A level results (or equivalent)

Subject	Grade	Awarding Body	Date

GCSE results (or equivalent) (Omit once your employment history is substantial)

Subject	Grade	Awarding Body	Date

Employment history (If you have had no paid employment but do have work experience, then list this here, using work experience as the heading. If you have had a number of jobs, emphasise those which are most relevant to the job for which you are applying, making clear the extent of your responsibilities and relevant skills used)

Activities and interests (This is where you have a chance to tailor your CV to a particular job, emphasising things that you have done that demonstrate relevant skills or interests. Aim to make this part as impressive as the facts allow, including anything which makes you sound like an interesting person, or an exceptional one, or which shows you have taken responsibilities or demonstrated initiative in the past. If your first

> draft suggests that your interests are rather restricted and you still have time, develop some fast!)
>
> **Referees:**   **Name**
>
>   **Position**
>
>   **Address**

You will normally be asked to provide at least two referees. These should be people who have some position that will make their opinion of you believable – tutors, past employers or, at a pinch, family friends who have an impressive-sounding job title. These will be contacted by an interested employer and asked about such things as your character and skills. You need to gain your chosen referees' permission before giving their names and addresses, as you are asking them a fairly substantial favour. You must be sure that they are happy to be quoted and will actually respond to requests for references. This means that you need to alert them each time you apply for a job, to check their continued availability and willingness. If they are about to go off to some far-flung research site just at the time you are applying for jobs, find someone else. If you are asked to include referees on an application form which you are sending with the CV, they can obviously be omitted from the latter.

Many employers now accept or even require electronic submission of applications. When you are designing your CV you need to bear this in mind. It is always important to be succinct and to lay things out clearly, but if someone is reading your CV off a screen then clarity is even more important. Avoid being over-sophisticated. Try your design out for both paper and screen reading, as even if you submit it electronically it may be printed for panel members. Think about use of colour and how this will appear on a black and white printer. E-mail it to a friend and ask them to comment on how well it communicates to them using their (preferably different) machine.

ACTIVITY 17.13

Prepare your CV now, aiming for the best possible layout and a maximum of two sides of A4. Aim to emphasise the strengths which you have with respect to employment in general. You can version this basic document to suit specific vacancies when you get to the stage of applying. Compare with other people's, if possible, to see whether you can between you find ways of improving the different CVs. File this 'core' version for reference.

COMPLETING APPLICATION FORMS

Many jobs will send you an application form when you ask for further particulars and will quote a closing date for this to be returned. *Observe this date.* It does not look very organised to miss it and many organisations will simply put all late applications in the bin. If there is a dream job, and you were out of the country or in hospital and couldn't apply, it is worth telephoning, explaining your predicament, stressing your interest and pleading for a late application to be accepted. Otherwise, make sure that you are better organised and apply for things in good time.

Think carefully about the application form and how to complete it. For a paper form it is probably worth making photocopies to practise on. The form you submit has to contribute to the impression you wish to make and therefore has to look tidy and be error free, as well as making maximum use of available questions and space to make you look like a candidate worthy of shortlisting. Remember that you are likely to be in competition with perhaps hundreds of other applicants. If this is the case, most applications will be discarded after a cursory inspection of the form alone. You have to make a good enough impression in your application to survive this preliminary sift. Think about how you can complete the form so as to emphasise your strengths in relation to this particular job. Refer to your SWOT. And remember that you are selling yourself and need to do this professionally.

You should always supplement your CV and any application form with a letter. This, free from the formal constraints of form or CV, is your main chance to convey an impression of what you are like as a person. Use it to emphasise your key strengths, cross-referring where appropriate to the relevant parts of accompanying documents. The letter needs to be properly laid out (look back at Chapter 6), error free, and to show that you have identified what is important to the person recruiting, thought about how you meet these needs and can communicate this clearly. If you can justify your motivation in applying, this will also strengthen your case. 'I am looking for a job which will enable me to use the skills I have already developed in the area of . . ., while offering opportunities to learn/do/gain experience of . . . with a view to moving eventually into . . .' will make your application sound more serious than one from someone who has not mentioned motivation, or mentioned only what they want out of a job. This is a fairly tall order for a short letter, but again is a vital part of standing out from perhaps hundreds of other applicants as a candidate who is worth seeing. (A job application checklist is available as a web resource.)

→ Ch 6

To reach shortlist:
■ research both job and organisation
■ version your CV to fit the job spec.
■ pay attention to presentation
■ make form and letter error free
■ highlight strengths for the job
■ if not successful seek feedback.

If you do not get shortlisted for a job for which you thought you were well qualified, it is worth seeking feedback as to why not. This is not an accusatory 'I want to know why I wasn't shortlisted since I am obviously perfect for the job' letter but a polite request for information. Say that you were very interested in the job and would like to know what you should do to increase your chances of being shortlisted for a similar job in future. You would therefore be extremely grateful if they could find time to give you any relevant information that would help. They are under no obligation to reply, but you may be lucky and receive some helpful advice, or even luckier and get shortlisted if for some reason they do not like the first set of people they interview and decide to see some more.

INTERVIEWS AND ASSESSMENT CENTRES

Considerable research suggests that interviews are not a very good way of choosing new staff. Yet they are still the selection device you are most likely to encounter. They test your talking and listening skills and your ability to think through a question and answer clearly and to the point. From this, interviewers will probably infer a whole raft of other intellectual skills. In an interview a potential employer can also see what you look like and what you sound like, and will guess from this how well you are likely to get on with other employees and any customers with whom you may come into contact. (They will also be able to see your ethnic background, judge social class from accent, and access information on a number of things which should not influence a fair selection process!)

There is a strong tendency for people, particularly if they are untrained as interviewers, to decide on your suitability within the first minute or so of your entering the room. First impressions are therefore crucial. Part of your research prior to the interview should be into the sort of people already working there and what they wear. You should then aim for a slightly smarter version of this, given that the interview is a formal situation. Whether your research suggests leather jacket and jeans or designer suit (assuming you can afford one), it is worth arriving early enough to spend time in the cloakroom repairing the ravages of travel and ensuring that you look calm and tidy by the time you are interviewed.

For interview success:
■ prepare carefully
■ dress appropriately
■ arrive slightly before due
■ behave professionally
■ listen carefully
■ check understanding
■ answer clearly and succinctly
■ observe body language
■ think before speaking
■ seek feedback if unsuccessful.

Perhaps the most important part of your interview preparation is to think very clearly about what the interviewer(s) are likely to be looking for, and how you can answer their questions so as to demonstrate that you are offering precisely these qualities. What qualities did the job specification mention? Are they looking for leadership abilities? For the ability to pay attention to detail? For creativity? For each of the qualities mentioned try to think of occasions when you have demonstrated that you have this quality. What was the situation? How and why did you show the quality? What was the outcome? You can draw on examples from your course, or your leisure activities, as well as on any jobs you have had. Many interviewers are now trained to ask questions in the form 'Can you tell us about a time when. . . .?'. This is likely to generate far more informative answers than 'Would you say you are a good leader?'. But unless you have thought about possible answers to such questions, you may find the interview quite difficult.

ACTIVITY 17.14

List a range of such questions, drawing on the job specifications you have so far received. (Alternatively, look in one of the many books on interviews that are available for ideas.) Review your portfolio. Look at your list of strengths. Talk to your friends about what they think you might say. Then work out a list of examples of 'times when . . .' you have demonstrated the qualities in question.

This mental preparation should have the additional benefit of increasing your confidence in your abilities, which will have a positive impact upon your interview performance. But you should also be aware of, though not apologetic about, any weaknesses, and think about how they could be overcome. Would you need particular support in one part of the job, or training in a specific skill? It is better to admit to fairly obvious shortcomings in your skills and experience than to pretend that they are not there. If you can at the same time propose feasible ways of overcoming these it will demonstrate your commitment to doing well in the job, and may impress your interviewers.

The other almost inevitable question for which you should be prepared is the final: 'And have you any questions you would like to ask us?' Obviously, if concerns have surfaced during the interview you would wish to raise these at this point. You would not wish to accept a job that was not going to make you happy and it is better for all concerned if you raise any concerns at the interview stage, rather than later. An interview is a two-way selection process. You are selecting the organisation just as much as it is selecting you. But if no such concerns surface, it is as well to be armed with an intelligent question or two. 'What pay will I get?', 'When will I hear?' or 'How many holidays are there?' are not questions with which to impress a panel.

Interviewers will be more impressed if you use this opportunity to ask something about the possibility of future developments in the industry that have occurred to you in the course of your research, and their developmental implications for the successful candidate. This or similar questions allow you to show that (a) you have found out a lot about the organisation, (b) you have thought about what this means for the job in question, and (c) you are interested in further development.

During the interview it is important to listen very carefully to the questions asked and to think before answering. If you are not sure what the interviewer wants, ask for clarification. Try not to get bogged down in minutiae. If you are asked for an example of when you showed leadership, give an outline of key demands in the situation and how you rose to them, rather than the whole story of the walking holiday in which you all got lost, and Jim broke his ankle, and you ran ahead and met these really nice people who were able to help you get him off the mountain.

Body language is crucial. One very successful interviewee of my acquaintance swears that his success is due solely to his way of looking at the panel and smiling at them. He claims that, if he can make them feel good about themselves in the interview, they will feel good about him. Certainly, it is important to *look* interested. Thus you need to lean slightly forward, maintain a fairly high level of eye contact with whoever is speaking, or with all members of the panel if you are speaking to them, and to smile a reasonable amount (too much can be rather offputting as it seems false). And you need to avoid defensive postures such as crossing arms, fidgeting or leaning back.

Avoid carrying a lot of clutter into the interview. Even if you have to leave your bag and coat with a secretary, or untended in a waiting area, it is better to do this than drag them into the interview room. If you wish to take in exhibits from your portfolio then pack these, in the order you are likely to need them, in a neat case. Do this only if you are sure that they are relevant and never insist on displaying your exhibits if the interviewers are not enthusiastic about seeing them. Watch for body language cues here, as well as listening to the words.

17

ACTIVITY 17.15

If you are nervous about interviews, and have not experienced many, find someone who will help you to practise beforehand. Think up a range of likely questions with your helper, then role play the interview several times, using the sort of furniture layout you might expect. Ask them to give you feedback on your answers and on your behaviour and the impressions they created, and to suggest different ways of approaching answers. Try out the interview again, incorporating their suggestions. If possible, tape record or video one of your trial interviews and listen to it carefully, looking for ways of improving the impression you give.

Because of the limitations of interviews as a selection device, employers now often use other means of selection as well. Psychometric testing, basic numeracy and literacy tests and group activities carried out under observation are now widely used. This mix of tests and activities is often referred to as an assessment centre.

→ Ch 5, 6, 10

Your course, and your work on this book, should have prepared you fairly well for an assessment centre, but you may want to think about whether further preparation would be useful. Basic skills tests such as basic arithmetic and English usage *are* susceptible to improvement through practice. Bryon (2000) suggests that 12 hours' practice can achieve a 15% improvement in score, the improvement levelling off at around 20% after 20 hours' practice. Your work on Chapters 5 and 6 should have given you some of this improvement already. Similarly, Chapter 10 and your subsequent work on skills development should have prepared you to do well in any group activity exercise. (Employers will often be looking for the ability to take the lead on occasion, though not to dominate, and to cooperate effectively with fellow group members.)

Verbal reasoning and reading comprehension tests are fairly common. Neither has been seriously addressed in this book. If you suspect weaknesses here you might want to buy a book of practice tests and work through them.

There is probably little you can do to prepare for 'personality' type tests. You will not know the score profile that recruiters have decided they are looking for. There will also be checks built into the test. Inconsistencies in answers, or over-idealised ones, will usually be taken as an indication of dishonest answers. It is best therefore to answer as honestly as you can, though without going out of your way to emphasise any extreme aspects of your personality!

The more selection processes you go through, the better you are likely to get and the more relaxed you are likely to be. Role playing and test practice can act as a partial substitute for real interviews. But you might additionally like to apply for one or two jobs which only slightly interest you in order to get some practice at real selection processes before applying for the job which you are desperate to get. If this is not possible, practise stress-reduction exercises before the interview, and remind yourself that the interviewers and assessors are decent people, merely looking for someone who will be competent to do a good job, motivated to perform well, reliable but still fun to work with. And remind yourself that you are a decent person, competent to do a good job, motivated and reliable, and therefore there is no reason why you should not enjoy convincing them of this during the selection process.

As in cases where you are not shortlisted, it can be helpful to ask for feedback if you take part in a selection process, but are unsuccessful. Again this may point up areas where you need to make changes in order to increase your chances of success.

LIFELONG LEARNING

Gaining a job which meets many of your short-term objectives is but a beginning. Successful 'career management' will need to build on this throughout your working life. Particularly in your early career you need to be continually alert to the learning opportunities a job offers, and to the changing shape of the employment scene. Looking at yourself as a 'product', and developing a SWOT analysis of yourself in relation to an employment 'market' needs to be an ongoing process. Your aim needs to be to do the job you are doing as well as you possibly can, and to take advantage of every development opportunity offered, even if a job turns out not to be all you expected. This should enable you to improve your current performance and become a better candidate for a more demanding and still more developmental job. While changing jobs too frequently looks bad on a CV, many successful people have changed jobs every two years or so during their early careers to maximise learning and experience. If a job turns out to be completely wrong for you, perhaps because it was wrongly described during selection, then you might see whether an internal transfer is possible. If not, seek another job elsewhere. One or two such 'mistakes' are allowable on a CV.

It is clear from the above that the skills developed during your degree will continue to be crucial to managing your career. The following guidelines may help.

Guidelines for successful career management

- Review your career objectives at regular intervals.
- Regularly seek information on job opportunities and changing patterns of employment.
- Construct action plans for positioning yourself for future jobs.
- Monitor your progress at regular intervals.
- Reflect daily on the effectiveness of your performance and any learning.
- Keep a learning diary and assemble exhibits of competence.
- Use informal feedback from your superior and more formal feedback from performance appraisal to revise your self-assessment of strengths and weaknesses.
- Network to develop useful contacts and gain information.
- Be a supportive team member at all times – you may on occasion need support yourself.
- Manage your time and stress levels so as to sustain effective performance.
- Use your creativity and skills in handling complexity to turn problems into learning opportunities.
- Accept that setbacks will occur and take each as a new starting point.
- Find discreet ways of ensuring that your successes are recognised as such.

If you can continue to question both your career objectives and your life objectives, act according to your personal values and follow the guidelines above, you should continue learning all your life. You should also enjoy a career that is interesting and rewarding and supports rather than interferes with other aspects of your life. May it prove better than you can possibly imagine!

SUMMARY

This chapter has argued the following:

- You cannot start too soon to think about what you want from a job and the sorts of job which might meet your needs. You should develop an action plan now which includes activities needed to clarify objectives with regard to employment, identify suitable jobs and increase your chances of getting one of them.

- When a suitable opportunity is identified, you need to research the organisation and job and think carefully about how to demonstrate your suitability via application form, CV and covering letter. Each should be specifically tailored to the job in question.

- Your application needs to look professional and be error free.

- Practise for selection tests if you think you need to.

- Prepare for interviews carefully, thinking about the qualities you wish to demonstrate and experience which you can quote in support of these.

- Listen carefully to questions and ask for clarification if you are unsure. Answer clearly and without straying into irrelevant detail. Try to express confidence and interest through your own body language and be sensitive to the body language of others.

- Ask for feedback when you are unsuccessful.

- Once in employment, aim to continue to learn and question, thus increasing your chance of success in future applications.

Further information

- Bloch, S. and Bates, T. (1995) *Employability*, Kogan Page.
- Bolt, L.C. (1999) *Zen and the Art of making a Living*, Penguin Arkana. (This is very American, but has a wealth of useful activities, and includes self-assessment and interview preparation.)
- Bryon, M. (2000) *How to pass Graduate Recruitment Tests*, 2nd edn, Kogan Page.
- Eggert, M. (2000) *The Best Job Hunt Book in the World*, Random House Business Books. (Whether it is the best is arguable, but it offers lots of easy to read advice on CVs, interviews and careers.)
- Golzen, G. and Garner, A. (1992) *Smart Moves*, Penguin.
- Hopson, B. and Scally, M. (1999) *Build your own Rainbow: a workbook for career and life management*, 3rd edn, Management Books 2000. (This is deservedly becoming a classic.)
- Hornby, M. (2000) *3 Easy Steps to the Job You Want*, Pearson Education.
- Hourd, S. (1999) *Creating a successful CV*, Dorling Kindersley. (This is small, cheap, and packed with useful information.)
- Robinson, J. and McConnell, C. (2003) *careers un-ltd*, Pearson.

Answers to test exercises

4.1

1 False. Poor readers fixate more than once on some words. This backtracking is a major cause of slowness and you should have remembered this.
2 True, provided it is specially designed practice.
3 False, according to the text, which claimed three to six fixations per line, although it may well be true as later text will show. You may have *known* that the statement was really true, but it is often necessary to note what is actually *in* a piece of writing, even if it conflicts with what you believe to be true.
4 False. You would still need to practise the techniques at intervals to maintain high speeds.
5 False. Rapid reading may increase comprehension. This was another very important point.
6 True.

5.1

(a) 258.8
(b) 1215
(c) 1502
(d) 17
(e) 1234.57
(f) 1230
(g) 150
(h) 52%
(i) 1:7

(j) $1\frac{5}{7}$ or $\frac{32}{27}$

(k) $\dfrac{3a + 4b}{a + b}$

(l) 600
(m) 1509 (if you got 2085 see p. 87)

5.2

(a) 0.75, 3.0, 1.3333333, 2.1428571, 0.8181818, 0.75
(b) 200%, 75%, 133%, 91%, 25%, 67% (taking the nearest whole percentage as the answer)
(c) 8, 196, 81, 81, 1728, 1, 1
(d) 2^7, 3^6, 10^0, 17^9, 21^{18}, $x^{(y-2)}$, x^5, $z^{2(x+y)}$
(e) 4, 12, 6, 6.16, 1.41, 3.16 (giving answers to two decimal places)
(f) 2^8, 10^2, $3^{\frac{2}{3}}$, xy, z^2
(g) 6
(h) (ii) and (iii)
(i) $2x + 2y$, $3x - 3y$, 0, y
(j) 13, 17, $x + x^2/y$, 3.8832787 (3.88 to two places of decimals)

5.3

(a) My rough guess was 8600, actual figure 8689.

(b) My rough guess was 4100, actual figure 4507.7.
(c) My rough guess was 10 000 000, actual figure 9 850 028.3.
(d) My guess was 110, actual figure 111.95.
Perhaps your guesses were better!

5.4
(a) 1.27 (b) 12.98 (c) 129.76 (d) 129 763.56

5.5
(a) 137 (b) 0.000786 (c) 3980 (d) 1.00

5.6
£38. It doesn't matter which order the discounts are calculated: $0.95 \times 0.8 \times 50$ is the same as $0.8 \times 0.95 \times 50$. Or work out the price after subtracting first a fifth, second a twentieth, or vice versa if you prefer.

5.7
(a) $\frac{2}{3}$ (b) $\frac{3}{4}$ (c) $\frac{2}{3}$ (d) 2 (e) $\frac{4}{3}$ or $1\frac{1}{3}$ (f) $\frac{3}{4}$ (g) $\frac{1}{2}$

5.8
(a) $\frac{1}{5}$ (b) $\frac{1}{3}$ (c) $\frac{1}{y(1+y)}$ (d) $\frac{1}{4}$ (e) $\frac{1}{x}$ (f) $\frac{(y+1)}{10}$ (g) $\frac{xy}{2}$

5.9
(a) $\frac{1}{8}$ (b) $\frac{1}{9}$

5.10
(a) $\frac{2}{9}$ (b) $\frac{3y}{2x}$ (c) $\frac{3(x+4)}{(x+1)(x+2)}$ (d) $\frac{5(y+1)}{4x(x+1)}$ (e) $\frac{9x}{8y}$

5.11
(a) $\frac{13}{8}$ or $1\frac{5}{8}$ (b) $\frac{(2y+4x)}{xy}$ (c) $\frac{(3x-1)}{y}$ (d) $\frac{(9x+10)}{15}$ (e) $\frac{3}{8}$ (f) $\frac{y(5x+1)^2 + x^2y}{x(5x+1)}$

(g) $\frac{5(x-2) - 3(x-1)}{(x-1)(x-2)}$ or $\frac{(2x-7)}{(x-1)(x-2)}$

5.12
(a) 32% (b) 32:100 or 8:25 (c) 128:272 or 8:17

5.13
(a) 12.5% (b) 198% (c) 33% (d) −4%, i.e. a negative return

5.14
After two years debt will be £1322.50, after three years £1520.87.

5.15
(a) £2260 (b) £2343.75 (c) £20 113.57

5.16
(a) $x = 2y - 5$ (i) −1 (ii) −11 (iii) −5

(b) $x = \frac{(y+3)}{3}$, or $\frac{y}{3} + 1$ (i) $\frac{5}{3}$ (ii) 0 (iii) 1

(c) $x = 4$ (i) 4 (ii) 4 (iii) 4

(d) $x = \dfrac{y}{2} - 6$ (i) -5 (ii) $-7\frac{1}{2}$ (iii) -6

(e) $x = \dfrac{3}{y}$ (i) $\frac{3}{2}$ (ii) -1 (iii) infinity (or undefined)

(f) $x = y^2 + \frac{1}{2}$ (i) 5 (ii) $7\frac{1}{2}$ (iii) 0

(g) $x = \dfrac{y}{4} - 3$ (i) $-2\frac{1}{2}$ (ii) $-3\frac{3}{4}$ (iii) -3

(h) $x = (y + 4)(3y + 1)$ (i) 42 (ii) -8 (iii) 4

5.17

(a) $6ab + 4ac$

(b) $3xy - 2xz$

(c) $3rs + 6rt + 6rs + 3st$, or $9rs + 6rt + 3st$

(d) $2xy + 4x + y^2 + 2y$

(e) $\dfrac{3z + 4y}{4a + 4b}$ Note it was possible to divide top and bottom by $(2y + z)$

6.1

Correct versions are:

1 The father's going to take his children **there**. The mother is away on holiday. (Even better, The father is going . . .)
2 The dog is **completely uninterested** in **its** ball.
3 Studying **English** is very different **from** studying engineering.
4 When I **received** them the data surprised me.
5 The essay **comprised four** separate parts. (OR The essay **consisted** of . . .)
6 He **was unique** in having a choice between a career as a rock singer in a leading band **and** as a brain surgeon. (Well, maybe he wasn't unique, who knows, but you are or you aren't.)
7 A range of statistics was available from **their** search of the literature. (Still not very nice, but technically, I think, correct.)
8 I will probably come to see you and **him** tomorrow.
9 There were many mistakes in your letter, **including your** spelling and **your unskilful** choice of words.
10 One can easily improve **one's** writing by redrafting after an interval has **elapsed**. (Or **You** can easily improve your . . .)

6.2

The main clause (I think) is 'the overall effect of complexity is usually far from satisfactory' – all the other clauses qualify or explain this. I think I counted nine subordinate clauses.

6.3

The number of words is 122. It is a single sentence, therefore this is the 'average' sentence length. The number of words of three or more syllables is 21. This is 17% of the total – not bad. 122+17 is 139. Multiplying by 0.4 gives 55.6. No wonder you had difficulty following it. This is seriously in excess of 12.

8.1

Note there is no 'right' answer to this. Many forms of map and outline could produce a good answer. What follows is merely an example.

Initial notes in form of mind map

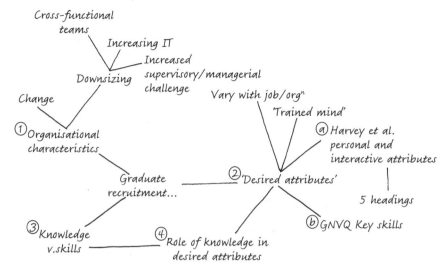

Subsequent plan

1 Introduction
   Brief overview of approach: required attributes depend on job and organisational situation; evidence drawn from employer statements and GNVQ key skills specification; conclusion that true for some jobs, for many more, transferable skills more important.

2 Relevant characteristics of organisations
   Outline: IT revolution, downsizing, restructuring, emphasising continuing change, cross-functional teams, management responsibilities at lower levels, near-universal IT use.
   Draw out implications: need for flexibility, continuous learning, range of relevant skills.

3 Graduate recruiters' perspective
   Note variability depending on job and specialism (and sophistication).
   Outline Harvey *et al.* personal and interactive attributes and derived headings, cross-linking these to GNVQ skills.
   Note that even for specialist jobs these skills also likely to be necessary.

4 Knowledge/skills relationship
   Discuss role of knowledge within skills outlined – more important for some (e.g. IT) than others (e.g. 'fitting in'/working with others). Comment on extent to which this 'knowledge' likely to be gained during degree studies or merely during time as a student.

5 Conclusions
   Suggest (referring back) that while true for a minority of jobs, unlikely to be true for majority of graduate recruitment, reiterating important skills and suggesting even where statement strictly true, these would still be important.

9.1

(a) aggression; (b) avoidance; (c) aggression; (d) assertion; (e) avoidance; (f) assertion; (g) avoidance; (h) assertion; (i) avoidance; (j) avoidance; (k) assertion (probably); (l) aggression; (m) avoidance.

14.1

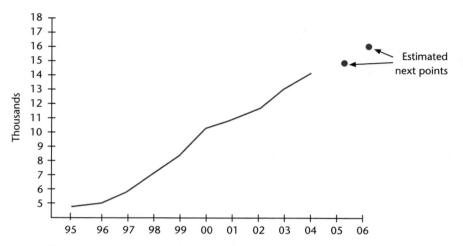

(a) Applicants accepted onto selected business and management degrees (UK)

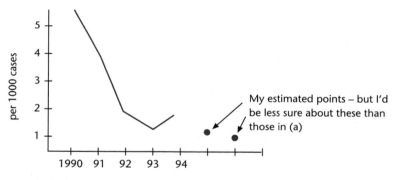

(b) Rabies cases (Germany)

14.2

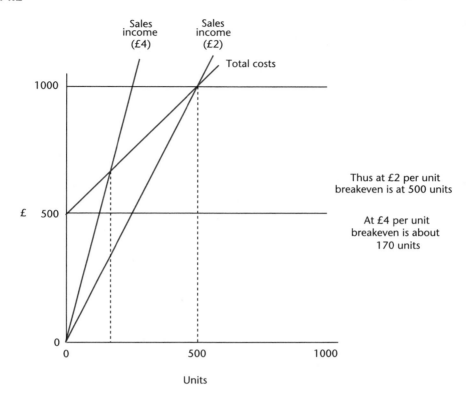

Units

Thus at £2 per unit breakeven is at 500 units

At £4 per unit breakeven is about 170 units

14.3

$C = F + Vx$

$I = Px$

At breakeven $C = I$ so $F + Vx = Px$

Arrange x terms on one side: $F = Px - Vx$

or: $x(P - V) = F$

Divide both sides by $(P - V)$: $x = F/(P-V)$

You can use this to test your answers to Test exercise 14.2, substituting 500 for F, 1 for V and either 2 or 4 for P. In the first case breakeven is 500 divided by 2 – 1, or 500. In the second it is 500 divided by 4 – 1, i.e. by 3, which is approximately 167.

14.4

(a) If $y = x^2$, $dy/dx = 2x$

(b) If $y = 3x + 1$, $dy/dx = 3$

(c) If $y = x^3 + 2x + 2$, $dy/dx = 3x^2 + 2$

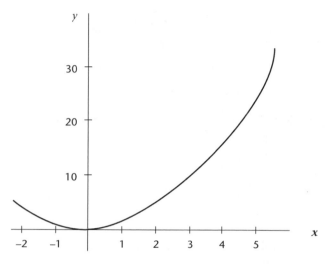

(a) Curve of $y = x^2$
   (Note that additional points are added to give the 'feel' of the curve)

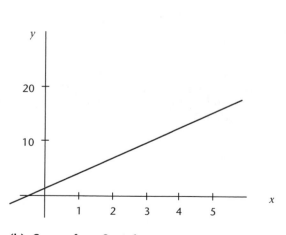

(b) Curve of $y = 3x + 1$

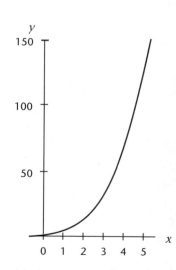

(c) Curve of $y = x^3 + 2x + 2$

14.5

(a) $dt/dd = 6d + 1$
(b) $dy/dx = 8x^3 - 2x + 5$
(c) $dr/dy = 2y + 10$
(d) $dy/dx = 7x^6 - 15x^4 + \frac{1}{2}x^{-\frac{1}{2}}$

or $7x^6 - 15x^4 + \dfrac{1}{2\sqrt{x}}$

14.6

(a) $\int 3x^2\, dx = x^3 + K$
(b) $\int (8x^2 - 12x^2 + 1)\, dx = 2x^4 - 4x^3 + x + K$
(c) $\int (1/x + 3) = \log x + 3x + K$

(Sorry, this was unfair. The only place the rule does not work is for $1/x$. After all, when you differentiate a constant it disappears: it doesn't turn into $1/x$.)

14.7

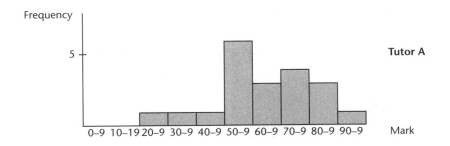

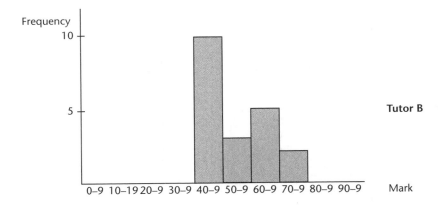

14.8

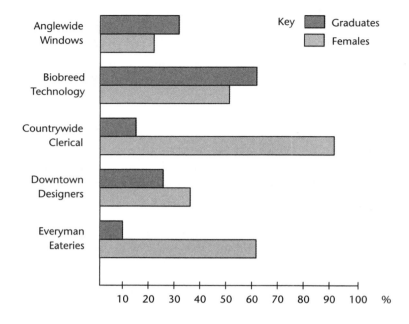

14.9

My estimate of A was upper 60s and of B upper 50s. The calculator gave 61.55 and 52.95. Both were lower than expected. When I looked at the figures for an explanation, I realised that both tutors were marking in 'round tens' quite often, so within each band a lot of figures were right at the bottom.

14.10

	f	mid-point (x)/f	x
Tutor A	1	95	95
	3	85	255
	4	75	300
	3	65	195
	6	55	330
	1	45	45
	1	35	35
	1	25	25
			Total 1280 mean 64
Tutor B	2	75	150
	5	65	325
	3	55	165
	10	45	450
			Total 1090 mean 54.5

(Like my estimates, these are higher than the actual means, for the same reason.)

14.11

$\frac{1}{2}(n + 1)$

14.12

Modal band:	Tutor A	50–59
	Tutor B	40–49

14.13

	Mean	Median	Mode
(a)	5.4	5	5
(b)	4.9	3	3

References

Adair, J. and Allen, M. (2003) *The Concise Time Management and Personal Development*, Thorogood.

Andreas, S. and Faulkner, C. (1996) *NLP: The new technology of achievement*, Nicholas Brealey.

Back, K. and Back, K. (1999) *Assertiveness at Work*, 3rd edn, McGraw-Hill.

Baguley, P. (1992) *Teams and Team-Working*, Teach Yourself Books, Hodder and Stoughton.

Belbin, R.M. (1981) *Management Teams*, Heinemann.

Belbin, R.M. (1993) *Team Roles at Work*, Butterworth-Heinemann.

Bell, J, (1999) *Doing your Research Project*, 3rd edn, The Open University Press.

Bentley, T.J. (1978) *Report Writing in Business*, Kogan Page.

Bird, P. (1998) *Teach Yourself Time Management*, Hodder Arnold Teach Yourself.

Blamires, H. (2000) *The Penguin Guide to Plain English*, Penguin.

Bloch, S. and Bates, T. (1995) *Employability*, Kogan Page.

Bolt, L.C. (1999) *Zen and the Art of making a Living*, Penguin Arkana.

Bowden, J. (1997) *Writing a Report: a step by step guide to effective report writing*, 4th edn, How To Books.

Bradley, A. (2000) *Successful Presentation Skills*, 2nd edn, Kogan Page.

Bryon, M. (2000) *How to pass Graduate Recruitment Tests*, 2nd edn, Kogan Page.

Bryon, M., Cameron, J. and Allen, C. (1998) *An Artist's Way at Work: Twelve weeks to creative freedom*, Pan.

Bryman, A. (2001) *Social Research Methods*, Oxford University Press.

Burchfield, R.W. (ed.) (1996) *The New Fowler's Modern English Usage*, 3rd edn, Oxford University Press.

Burley-Allen, M. (1995) *Managing assertively – a self teaching guide*, 3rd edn, Wiley.

Buzan, T. (2003a) *Use Your Head*, BBC Publications.

Buzan, T. (2003b) *The Speed Reading Book*, BBC Publications.

Buzan, T. and Buzan B. (2003) *The Mind Map Book: Radiant Thinking – Major Evolution in Human Thought*, BBC Publications.

Cameron, J. (1992) *The Artist's Way*, Tarcher.

Cameron, S. and Pearce, S. (1997) *Against the Grain*, Butterworth-Heinemann.

Caunt, J. (2000) *Organise Yourself*, Kogan Page.

Caunt, J. (2001) *Stay Confident*, The Sunday Times/Kogan Page.

Checkland, P. (1981) *Systems Thinking, Systems Practice*, Wiley.

Clegg, B. (1999) *Instant Time Management*, Kogan Page.

Collins, J./Video Arts (1998) *Perfect Presentations*, Marshall Publishing.

Conradi, M. and Hall, R. (2001) *That Presentation Sensation*, Financial Times Prentice Hall.

Crosby, A.W. (1997) *The Measure of Reality*, Cambridge University Press.

de Bono, E. (1971) *Lateral Thinking for Management*, Penguin.

Department for Education and Employment (1997) Survey of those graduating in last six years.

Drucker, P.F. (1999) *Management Challenges for the 21st Century*, HarperCollins.

Easton, G. (1992) *Learning from Case Studies*, 2nd edn, Prentice-Hall.

Eggert, M. (2000) *The Best Job Hunt Book in the World*, Random House Business Books.

Fayol, H. (1916) *Administration Industrielle et Générale*, published in English in 1949 as *General and Industrial Management*, Pitman Publishing.

Fineman, S. and Gabriel, Y. (1996) *Experiencing Organisations*, Sage.

Frost, P.J., Mitchell, V.F. and Nord, W.R. (eds) (1997) *Organisational Reality: Reports from the Firing Line*, 4th edn, Addison Wesley Longman.

Giles, K. and Hedge, N. (1994) *The Manager's Good Study Guide*, The Open University.

Gill, J. and Johnson, P. (1997) *Research Methods for Managers*, 2nd edn, Paul Chapman Publishing.

Golzen, G. and Garner, A. (1992) *Smart Moves*, Penguin.

Gowers, E. (1954) *The Complete Plain Words*, HMSO, now available from Penguin.

Graham, L. and Sargent, D. (1981) *Countdown to Mathematics*, Vol. 1, Addison-Wesley.

Gravett, S. (1998) *The Right Way to Write Reports*, Elliot Right Way Books.

Hackman, J.R. and Lawler, E.E. III (1971) 'Employee reactions to job characteristics', *Journal of Applied Psychology*, **55**, 259–65.

Handy, C. (1989) *The Age of Unreason*, Business Books.

Hardingham, A. (1995) *Working in Teams*, Institute of Personnel Development.

Harris, T.A. (1973) *I'm OK – You're OK*, Pan Books.

Hart, R. (1996) *Effective Networking for Professional Success*, Kogan Page.

Harvey, L., Moon, S. and Geall, V. (1997) *Graduates' Work: Organisational Change and Students' Attributes*, Centre for Research into Quality, University of Central England in Birmingham.

Henry, J. (ed.) (1991) *Creative Management*, Sage, in association with the Open University.

Honey, P. and Mumford, A. (1986) *The Manual of Learning Styles*, Peter Honey.

Hopson, B. and Scally, M. (1999) *Build your own Rainbow: a workbook for career and life management*, 3rd edn, Management Books 2000.

Hornby, M. (2000) *3 Easy Steps to the Job You Want*, Pearson Education.

Hourd, S. (1999) *Creating a successful CV*, Dorling Kindersley.

Howard, K. and Peters, J. (1990) 'Managing management research', *Management Decision*, **28**: 5 (whole issue).

Howard, K. and Sharpe, J.A. (1996) *The Management of a Student Research Project*, 2nd edn, Gower.

Huff, D. (1991) *How to Lie with Statistics*, Penguin.

Jankowicz, A.D. (2000) *Business Research Projects*, 3rd edn, Business Press.

Kepner, C.H. and Tregoe, B.B. (1965) *The Rational Manager*, McGraw-Hill.

Kneeland, S. (1999) *Thinking Straight*, Pathways.

Kolb, D.A., Rubin, I.M. and Mackintyre, J.M. (1984) *Organisational Psychology*, 4th edn, Prentice-Hall.

Krishnamurti, J. (1995) *The Book of Life*, HarperCollins.

Lawler, E.E. III and Porter, L. (1967) 'Antecedent attitudes of effective managerial performance', *Organizational Behavior and Human Performance*, **2**, 122–42.

Leech, T. (2001) *Say it like Shakespeare*, McGraw-Hill.

Lifeskills International (1999) *Staying Healthy at Work*, Gower.

Luthans, F., Hodgetts, R.M. and Rosenkrantz, S. (1988) *Real Managers*, Ballinger.

Manchester Open Learning (1993) *Making Effective Presentations*, Kogan Page.

Maslow, A.H. (1943) 'A theory of human motivation', *Psychological Review*, **50**, 370–96.

McGregor, D.M. (1957) 'The human side of enterprise', reprinted in Vroom, V.H. and Deci, E.L. (1970) *Management and Motivation*, Penguin.

Mintzberg, H. (1976) 'Planning on the left side and managing on the right', *Harvard Business Review*, **54**: July–August, 49–58.

Mitroff, I.I. and Linstone, H.A. (1993) *The Unbounded Mind*, Oxford University Press.

Morgan, G. (1986) *Images of Organization*, Sage.

Moroney, M.J. (1951) *Facts from Figures*, Penguin.

Morris, C. (2000) *Quantitative Approaches in Business Studies*, 5th edn, Financial Times Prentice Hall.

Morris, C. and Thanassoulis, E. (1994) *Essential Mathematics: a Refresher Course for Business and Social Studies*, Macmillan.

Morris, S. and Smith, J. (1998) *Understanding Mind Maps in a Week*, Institute of Management.

Naughton, J. (2003) 'How PowerPoint can fatally weaken your argument', *The Observer*, 21 December.

Pidd, M. (2003) *Tools for Thinking: modeling in management science*, 2nd edn, Wiley.

Powell, J. (1991) *Quantitative Decision Making*, Longman.

Race, P. (1999) *How to get a Good Degree*, Open University Press.

Robinson, J. and McConnell, C. (2003) *careers un-ltd*, Pearson.

Rose, C. and Nicholl, M.J. (1997) *Accelerated Learning for the 21st Century*, Piatkos.

Rowntree, D. (1987) *Statistics without Tears: a Primer for Non-mathematicians*, Penguin.

Russell, L. (1999) *The Accelerated Learning Field Book*, Jossey-Bass Pfeiffer.

Saunders, M., Lewis, P. and Thornhill, A. (2003) *Research Methods for Business Students*, 3rd edn, Financial Times Prentice Hall.

Seeley, J. (2002) *Writing Reports*, Oxford University Press.

Senior, B. (1997) *Organisational Change*, Financial Times Pitman Publishing.

Senge, P.M. (1990) *The Fifth Discipline*, Century Business.

Simon, H. (1960) *The New Science of Management Decision*, Harper & Row.

Stewart, M.A. and O'Toole, F.J. (1998) *30 Days to the GMAT CAT*, Arco.

Stutely, R. (2003) *The Definitive Guide to Managing the Numbers*, Pearson.

Targett, D. (1983) *Coping with Numbers*, Blackwell.

Truss, L. (2003) *Eats, Shoots and Leaves: the zero tolerance approach to punctuation*, Profile Books.

Tuckman, B.W. (1965) 'Developmental sequences in small groups', *Psychological Bulletin*, **63**, 384–99.

Vroom, V.H. (1964) *Work and Motivation*, Wiley.

White, B. (2000) *Dissertation Skills for Businesss Students*, Continuum.

Williams, J.S. (1995) *The Right Way to Make Effective Presentations*, Elliot Right Way Books.

Index